General U. S. Grant's Tour Around the World

Embracing his speeches, receptions, and description of his travels: with a biographical sketch of his life

Editor

L. T. Remlap

Alpha Editions

This edition published in 2020

ISBN : 9789354047428

Design and Setting By
Alpha Editions
www.alphaedis.com
email - alphaedis@gmail.com

As per information held with us this book is in Public Domain.
This book is a reproduction of an important historical work. Alpha Editions uses the best technology to reproduce historical work in the same manner it was first published to preserve its original nature. Any marks or number seen are left intentionally to preserve its true form.

General U. S. Grant's

Tour Around the World,

EMBRACING HIS

SPEECHES, RECEPTIONS, AND DESCRIPTION
OF HIS TRAVELS.

WITH A

BIOGRAPHICAL SKETCH OF HIS LIFE

EDITED BY

L. T. REMLAP.

HARTFORD, CONN.:
JAMES BETTS & CO.
1879.

CONTENTS.

CHAPTER I.

LIFE OF GENERAL U. S. GRANT.

His Birth—His Father—Early Education at West Point—In Mexico—Garrison Life—Marriage—A Farmer—April 12, 1861—A Colonel—Battle of Belmont—Forts Henry and Donaldson—Shiloh—At Vicksburg—With the Army of the Potomac—Surrender of Lee—Farewell Address—Disbandment of the Army—Secretary of War *ad interim*—Nomination for President—Inaugural—A Second Term—His achievements, - - - - - - - - - - 9

CHAPTER II.

OFF FOR EUROPE.

Departure from Philadelphia—Rousing Demonstration—On the Ocean—Arrival at Queenstown—Liverpool—Grand Reception—A Round of Pleasure—At the Docks—Mayor's Reception and Ball, . 17

CHAPTER III.

GENERAL GRANT IN LONDON.

His Arrival—Prince of Wales—Grand Banquet—Duke of Wellington—Waterloo Chamber—At Westminster Abbey—Reception at the American Legation—Grand Ball—Buckingham Palace—Freedom of the City of London—Magnificent Reception—Its Significance—Gold Casket—Distinguished Guests—Marquis of Lorne, - - - - 27

CHAPTER IV.

GRANT IN ENGLAND.

A Letter to D. W. Childs—Dining with the Prince of Wales—At Minister Pierrepont's—Royal Opera House—Banquet by Trinity House—Speech by the Prince of Wales—Address by Earl Carnarvon—General

Grant's Reply—Reception by Queen Victoria—State Dinner—Ladies Toilets—State Concert—Grand Banquet Tendered by the City of Liverpool—Addresses—General Badeau—United Service Club—American Legation, - - - - - - - - - 43

CHAPTER V.

ON THE CONTINENT.

At Brussels — Reception and Dinner by King Leopold — At Cologne — Visiting Churches and the Cathedral — At Frankfort — Great Reception — A Grand Ball — At Hamburg — At Lucerne — Berne — Geneva — Laying a Corner Stone — At Pallanza — At Copenhagen — Ulysses — A Happy Speech, - - - - - - - 56

CHAPTER VI.

RETURN TO GREAT BRITAIN.

Presented with the Freedom of Edinburgh — Enthusiastic Reception — Lord Provost's Speech — Grant's Reply — Tay Bridge — Its Description — City of Wick — At Glasgow — The Finest and Most Enthusiastic Reception — Speech of Mr. Anderson — Grant's Long Speech — Remarkable Reception at Newcastle — At Northumberland — Gateshead — At Sheffield — At Birmingham — Speeches, - - - 61

CHAPTER VII.

GENERAL GRANT IN PARIS.

Adieu to England — Bologne — At Paris — Enthusiastic Reception — Palace d' Elysee — Grand Banquet by Resident Americans — Reception by Minister Noyes — *Menu* — Brilliant Assemblage — Banquet at Marshal McMahon's — Address — Grant's Reply — A Comparison — Mrs. Mackay's Reception — Extravagance of Display — Dinner at Mrs. Sickles' — At Mr. Harjes, - - - - - - - 74

CHAPTER VIII.

THROUGH FRANCE—ITALY.

At Lyons — Marseilles — Genoa — Reception on Board the Vandalia — At Naples — Mt. Vesuvius — " House of Refuge " — Ruins of Pompeii — Special Excavation — Interesting Relics — Royal Palace — At

Palermo — Christmas Dinner — *Menu* — How He Traveled — Land of Many Civilizations — Brigandage — At Malta — Duke of Edinburgh — Palace San Antonio — Adieu,   -   -   -   -   .   -   -   89

CHAPTER IX.

IN EGYPT AND THE LOTUS LAND.

A Severe Storm — At Alexandria — Oriental Etiquette — The Pacha — Reception — Brilliant Entertainment at Vice-Consul Salvage — Henry M. Stanley — The Khedive calls on General Grant — A Host's Thoughtfulness — At Siout — The Donkey Ride — Inspecting the Town — Speech of the Pacha's Son — At Girgel to Ruined City of Abydos — God Osiris — Excavations — At Thebes — City of a Hundred Gates — Its Magnificent Ruins — The Great Temple of Karnak — At Keneh — At Assowan — Phile — The First Cataract — The Return — At Memphis — Sacred Bulls at Kaser-el-Nousa,   -   .   -   -   -   -   -   96

CHAPTER X.

TURKEY AND THE HOLY LAND.

At Jaffa — Ruins of Gezer — David and Goliah — At Jerusalem — Bishops and Patriarchs — Stroll on the Via Dolorosa — Ruins and Relics — Dives — Calvary — Brook Kedron — Valley of Jehoshaphat — Mount of Olives — Bethany — At Damascus — At Athens — Grand Entertainment by the King at Naples — At Rome — His Clerical Visitor — At Turin — Return to the French Capital — At the Exposition — A Game of Polo — Ball at Mr. Healy's — At the Hague — Great Demonstration at Rotterdam — At Amsterdam — Enthusiastic Welcome — The Dutch Excited,   -   -   -   -   -   -   -   -   -   -   110

CHAPTER XI.

GRANT IN GERMANY, NORWAY, SWEDEN, RUSSIA AND AUSTRIA.

General Grant at Berlin — An Evening Stroll — Prince Bismarck — Great Peace Congress — Attempt to Assassinate the Emperor — Bismarck Calls on Mrs. Grant — Reception at Minister Taylor's — Crown Prince — Military Manœuvers — Dining with Bismarck — Bottle of Schnapps — At Gothenburg — **Immense Crowd** — At Christiana — King Oscar II. — Turning out *en masse* at Stockholm — Grand Banquet — At St. Petersburgh — Prince Gortschakoff — With the Czar — At the Versailles of St. Petersburgh — Grand Duke Alexis — At Moscow — At Warsaw — Vienna — Grand Reception — At Zurich, - - - - 119

CHAPTER XII.
GENERAL GRANT IN SPAIN AND PORTUGAL.

Again at Paris — Reception by Minister Noyes — In Spain — Spanish Life and Character — Alfonso XII. — San Sebastian — Grand Annual Military Review at Victoria — Palace of *Ayuntamiento* — At Madrid — Attempt on Alfonzo's Life — The Shot Seen by General Grant — Escape — Congratulations — At Lisbon — Dining with King Luis — A Cordial Reception — At Seville — Duke de Montpensier — At Cadiz — Enthusiastic Reception — At Gibraltar — Old Friends — Lord Napier — Grand Review — At Pau — Return to Paris, - - - - 135

CHAPTER XIII.
GENERAL GRANT IN IRELAND.

Irish Interest — A Citizen of Dublin — Grand Ovation — Long Speech from General Grant — Good Times Coming — Trinity College — Insult from Cork — Grant's Friendship Toward Catholics — Unparalleled Reception at Derry — Denouncing the Insult of Corkonians — Curiosities of Ulster — Old Soldiers — At Belfast — Imposing and Extraordinary Reception — Stopping the Linen Mills — At the Ship Yards — At Kingston — The Irish Welcome Compared to others, - - 146

CHAPTER XIV.
GENERAL GRANT IN INDIA.

Again in London — Paris — Marseilles — Delightful Trip Through the Mediteranean — Description of Trip — At Alexandria — A Railroad Ride in Egypt — At Suez — On the Red Sea — At Aden — Bombay — Enthusiastic Reception — Holy Place of the Hindoos — A Parsee Merchant — The Byculla Club — Flagship Eurydius — Elephanta Caves — Reception at the Government House — Singular Custom — Caste — Hatred of Races — A Farewell — At Tatulpur — At Allahabad — Agra — The Maharajah of Jeypore — At Amber — A Native City Under Native Rule — Gas in India — Elephant Ride — The Temple — A Kid Sacrificed at the Palace — Nautch Dancing Girls — Playing Billiards — A Royal Photograph, - - - - - - - - 161

CONTENTS. 7

CHAPTER XV.

STILL IN INDIA.

At Burtpoor — A Princely Reception — Tuttehpoor Sikva — Akbar — Interesting Ruins — At Benares — Sacred City — At the Ganges " Holy Kasi " — A City of Priests — Fourteen Hundred and Fifty Temples — A Sacred Ruler — Burning the Body — At Delhi — Military Reception — Its Splendor — The Palace of the Grand Mogul — The Kutah Tower — At Calcutta — Lord Lytton's Speech — Continuous Round of Enjoyment — At Rangoon, Burmah — The Philadelphia of Burmah — Commercial Advantages — Opening for American Merchants, - - 186

CHAPTER XVI.

GENERAL GRANT IN SIAM.

At Singapore — Interesting Letter from the King of Siam — Bangkok — Another Letter — Embarking — Reception at the King's Palace — The ex-Regent — An Aged Statesman — Mr. Borie and the King — Royal Proclamation — A Second King — His Income — A Political Influence — First King of Siam — Grand Palace — Elegant Furnishing — An Audience with the King — The King Returns the Visit — An Interesting Conversation — Correspondence Promised — A State Dinner — Who Were There — The Surroundings — King's Speech — General Grant's Reply — A Delightful Week, - - - - - 200

CHAPTER XVII.

GENERAL GRANT IN CHINA.

At Saigon — The Government House — Hong Kong — At Canton — Its Situation — The Viceroy — Special Honors — Bulletin — Chairs of Rank — Two Hundred Thousand People — Members of Court — The Entertainment — Dinner at Consul-General Lincoln's — Greatest Demonstration of Trip — At Macao — The Grotto of Camoens — Reception at Hong Kong — An Address — General Grant's Reply — Parting Salutes — At Swatow — Chinese Governor — Amoy — A Stroll Through the Town — Letters from the King of Siam and King of the Sandwich Islands and the Viceroy of Canton — General Grant's Replies — At Shanghai — Unexpected Greetings — An Address — Reply — At Tientsin — The Viceroy — Extraordinary Conversation at Pekin — Reception by the Prince Imperial — Confidential Proposition — Flattering Reception — Unusual Demonstration by the Prince — Return to Tientsin — The Viceroy's Friendly Visits — Pleasure of General Grant — Farewell to China, - - - - - - - - - - 220

CHAPTER XVIII.

GENERAL GRANT IN JAPAN.

At Nagasaki — Banqueted by Citizens — The *Herald's* Graphic Description — Address of Merchants — Fish and Soup — Arrival at Tokio — Palace of Euriokwan — Its Gardens — The Bazaars — A Native Dance — Reception at the College of Engineering — At Yokohama — Grand Reception — Address of Welcome — Feast of Lanterns — A Brilliant Spectacle — Reception by the Emperor — His Palace — Japanese Etiquette — Address of the Emperor and Empress — In the Mountains — At the Old Capital — Interesting *tete a tete* with the Emperor — Farewell to Japan — Sailing of the Tokio, - - - - - 256

CHAPTER XIX.

GENERAL GRANT'S RETURN.

Embarking From Tokio — Date of Arrival — Review of Tour — Preparation for His Reception — The Great Excursion — Not Flattering to the American People — Out of the Presidential Race — Admiral Ammen — Hon. E. B. Washburn — Murat Halstead — His Positive Acceptance of the Presidency of the Nicaragua Ship Canal Company — Letter to Admiral Ammen — Reception Programme at San Francisco — On the Watch — Magnificent Ovation Expected — The "Sand Lot" Braggart — Threat to Hang Grant in Effigy — Intense Excitement — Probable Result, - - - - - - - - - - 312

CHAPTER XX.

ARRIVAL AT SAN FRANCISCO.

Preparation for His Reception — Arrival — Immense Crowds — Procession — Addresses — California Theatre — Municipal Reception — At Produce Exchange — At Oakland — Veterans' Reception — At San Jose — Santa Clara — In the Yosemite — At Portland, Oregon — At Salem — Return to San Francisco — Munificent Reception at Senator Sharon's — At Sacramento — In Nevada — Receptions En Route to Galena — At Chicago — Unparalleled Enthusiasm — Return to Galena — Finale, - -

GENERAL GRANT'S TOUR AROUND THE WORLD.

CHAPTER I.

LIFE OF ULYSSES S. GRANT.

ULYSSES SIMPSON GRANT was born April 23, 1822, at Point Pleasant, Clermont county, Ohio, a small town on the Ohio river, twenty-five miles above Cincinnati. The Grants are of Scotch descent, and the motto of their clan in Aberdeenshire was, "Stand fast, stand firm, stand sure." Grant inherits from many of his ancestors a love for freedom and a determination to fight for its cause. In 1799, his grandfather, a Pennsylvania farmer, joined the great tide of emigration moving to the Northwest Territory.

His great-grandfather, Captain Noah Grant, of Windsor, Connecticut, and his brother, Lieutenant Solomon Grant, were soldiers in the old French war, and were both killed in battle in 1756.

His grandfather, also Noah Grant, of Windsor, hurried from his fields at the first conflict of the Revolution, and appeared as a lieutenant on Lexington Common on the morning of the memorable 19th of April, when the embattled farmers "fired the shot heard round the world."

His father, Jesse R. Grant, was born in Westmoreland county, Pa., in 1794. Was apprenticed to the tanner's trade at the early age of eleven years. Removed to Mayville, Kentucky, thence to Point Pleasant, Ohio, where he followed the business of a tanner. In 1869 he was appointed postmaster at Covington, Kentucky, by President Grant, and died in 1874.

Like other great men, Grant had an excellent mother —a pious woman, cheerful, unambitious of worldly display, watchful of her children, and "looking well to the ways of her household." Her husband pays her the highest tribute which can be paid to any wife and mother in saying, "Her steadiness, firmness and strength of character have been the stay of the family through life."

Love of their children has ever been a marked trait in the Grant family.

He was originally christened Hiram Ulysses; his grandfather giving the name of Hiram; his grandmother, who was a great student of history, giving the name of Ulysses, whose character had strongly attracted her admiration. The member of congress who appointed Grant to his cadetship at West Point when a boy of seventeen, by accident changed his name, in filling his appointment, to U. S. Grant. Grant repeatedly endeavored to have the mistake corrected at West Point, and at the war department at Washington; but this was one of the few things in which he failed; his applications were never complied with. As if fate foresaw the patriotic duty, the filial love, the transcendant services he was one day to render his country, the government seemed to insist, when adopting him among her military children, on renaming him, and giving to him her own initials, "U. S.," which he has ever since borne.

Grant was neither a precocious nor a stupid child; he was a well-behaved, dutiful boy. He attended the public school in the village; he learned well, but was no prodigy.

He never liked his father's business of tanning. It was disagreeable; and he early determined not to follow it. He wanted an education. He said he would be a farmer, or trade down the river; but a tanner he would not be.

His father, with limited means, did not feel that, in justice to himself and his other children, he could afford the money to send him to college.

He applied, with the boy's assent, for a vacant cadetship at West Point. The appointment was made by Hon. T. L. Hamer, the member of congress from the district.

It is remarkable that, without any preparatory study, he passed the rigid examination which all cadets are obliged to undergo.

But Grant received at West Point the best education a man can receive, namely, that which fits him for his work in life. He was subjected to a course of physical training which invigorated his body. He was taught fencing, drawing, riding, dancing; he was taught science, mathematics, the modern languages, constitutional and international law, and engineering.

Young Grant appreciated and improved all the opportunities which were offered to him. He gave those years diligently to self-improvement in the widest sense. He graduated with a good rank in his class; and, what was better, without vices which enfeebled his body, or mental habits which depraved his mind.

In July, 1843, he entered the United States army as a brevet second lieutenant in the fourth infantry. Ordered to the frontier of Missouri among the Indians, he remained nearly two years, when, in 1845, he was ordered to Corpus Christi, Texas, where United States troops were gathering under command of General Taylor. From the first attack on Fort Brown, opposite Matamoras, Grant was in every battle in the Mexican war except Buena Vista—fourteen in all—and conducted himself with distinguished bravery, which elicited special mention from his superiors in command. In 1847 he was appointed brevet captain, and in 1853 to a full captaincy.

At the close of the war, Captain Grant returned to the United States, and was subsequently stationed on the Canadian frontier, in California and in Oregon. But garrison life, in that lonely region, offered no opportunities of usefulness, and he determined to resign his commission, which he did in July, 1854. He moved to St. Louis, and there married Miss Julia Dent, daughter of a merchant of that city. Taking a small farm in the suburbs of St. Louis, he labored in the life of a farmer. In 1859 he moved to Galena, Illinois, entered in business, and was residing there on the 12th of April, 1861. The "first shot" at Fort Sumter moved Grant to the utmost depths of his being. He said to a friend: " The government has educated me for the army. What I am, I owe to my country. I have served her through one war, and, live or die, will serve her through this." Recruiting a company at Galena, he was at once made adjutant-general of the State; on the 15th of June, 1861, was commissioned colonel of the Twenty-first Illinois Volunteers, stationed at Mexico, Missouri; made brigadier-general May 17, 1861, and on 1st September ordered to Cairo, and at once took possession of Paducah, Kentucky; 7th of November, fighting the battle of Belmont, with 2,850 men, against 7,000 Confederates—Federal loss, 400; Rebel, 875. On the 2d of February he, with the aid of the navy, under Commodore Foote, captured Fort Henry, on the Tennessee river. On February 15th, captured Fort Donaldson, on the Cumberland river, the key to Nashville, Tennessee, with 65 guns, 17,600 small arms, nearly 15,000 soldiers, with horses, mules and army supplies; his loss was about 2,000 men. Grant was immediately nominated and confirmed as a major-general. By this victory the Cumberland and Tennessee rivers were opened, Nashville fell, Columbus was abandoned, Bowling Green evacuated, and the States of Kentucky and Tennessee were rescued from the Rebel armies.

The battles of Shiloh and Pittsburgh Landing were fought April 6 and 7, 1863, resulting in a victory to the

Federal arms, and was one of the most hotly contested fields of the war. General Grant has said, since the close of the war, that it was, with one exception—that of the Wilderness—the most terrific which he saw in the war. On the 3d of June Shiloh was evacuated, and in a few days New Orleans was captured and Memphis fell. April 30, 1863, captured Port Gibson and Grand Gulf; May 14 he captured Jackson, the capital of Mississippi; fought the battle of Champion Hills, defeating the Confederate General Pemberton, losing 2,457 men; the Rebel loss was over 4,000 killed and wounded and 3,000 prisoners; invested Vicksburg May 19, receiving its surrender July 4, 1863. The results of the summer campaign in the investment and capture of Vicksburg were the defeat of the enemy in five battles, the occupation of Jackson, a loss to the enemy of 56,000 prisoners, with 10,000 killed and wounded, arms and munitions of war for 60,000 men, and nearly 200 cannon. Grant had lost 943 killed, 7,095 wounded and 537 missing, and had made the largest capture ever made in war. On November 25 he carried the heights of Missionary Ridge, Ringold a few days after, and relieved the siege of Knoxville, thus virtually closing the war in the southwest. On the 3d of March, 1864, he was confirmed as lieutenant-general and ordered to Washington, and on May 5, 6 and 7 fought the bloody battles of the Wilderness, and June 1 that of Cold Harbor. The whole series of brilliant military operations, by which General Grant had carried an army of 100,000 men, in forty-three days, from the Rapidan to the James, without the loss of a wagon, compelling his able antagonist to race at his side for the safety of the capital, will never cease to be the study and admiration of the military student.

On the 15th of June he invested Petersburg, Virginia, with an army of over 100,000 men, his lines embracing a circuit of thirty miles. During the siege of Petersburg occurred the victorious battles of the Shenandoah under General Philip Sheridan, and the great march of General Sherman "to the sea," when about 65,000 men swept over the country in a track fifty miles wide. Accompanying this army were 3,500 wagons and 35,000 horses; 1,328 prisoners and 167 guns were taken; the Federal loss in killed 63, and 245 wounded; 5,000 horses and 4,000 mules appropriated, 20,000 bales of cotton burned and 25,000 captured at Savannah; 13,000 head of cattle, 10,000,000 pounds of corn, 1,217,527 rations of meat, 919,000 of bread, 483,000 of coffee, 581,534 of sugar, 1,145,500 of soap, 137,000 of salt, and 10,000,000 of fodder were taken. By this severing of the Confederacy, Charleston was evacuated, Columbia, the capital of South Carolina, captured, and April 13 the army had occupied Raleigh, North Carolina. April 2, Grant captured Petersburg, after three days of hard fighting; the capture of Richmond the following day, and the surrender of General Lee and the Army of Virginia at Appomatox Court House April 9, 1865, followed by the surrender of General Joseph E. Johnston to General Sherman on the 26th, and on the 4th of May of General Taylor, with all the Confederate forces east of the Mississippi, and the surrender of General Kirby Smith, with all of his command west of the Mississippi, on May 26th. The war was thus terminated with the surrender of all the Confederate Government, its President, Jefferson Davis, having been captured on the 11th of May, at Irwinsville, Georgia. The number of Rebel soldiers who surrendered was 174,223. The number of prisoners was 98,802. The Union armies under command of General Grant numbered 1,000,516 soldiers. Their commander might well be proud of the great services which with him they had performed for the country. He issued the following farewell address:

"SOLDIERS OF THE ARMIES OF THE UNITED STATES: By your patriotic devotion to your country in the hour of danger and alarm, your magnificent fighting, bravery and endurance, you have maintained the supremacy of the Union and the Constitution, overthrown all armed opposition to the enforcement of the laws and the proclamations forever abolishing slavery—the cause and pretext of the Rebellion—and opened the way to the rightful authorities to restore order, and inaugurate peace on a permanent and enduring basis on every foot of American soil. Your marches, seiges and battles, in distance, duration, resolution and brilliancy of results, dim the lustre of the world's past military achievements, and will be the patriot's precedent in the defence of liberty and right in all time to come. In obedience to your country's call, you left your homes and families, and volunteered in her defence. Victory has crowned your valor and secured the purpose of your patriotic hearts; and with the gratitude of your countrymen, and the highest honors a great and free nation can accord, you will soon be permitted to return to your homes and families, conscious of having discharged the highest duty of American citizens. To achieve these glorious triumphs, and secure to yourselves, fellow-countrymen and posterity, the blessings of free institutions, tens of thousands of your gallant comrades have fallen, and sealed the priceless legacy with their blood. The graves of these a grateful nation bedews with tears, honors their memories, and will ever cherish and support their stricken families."

The war had now closed, and General Grant now addressed himself with great energy to the works of peace. By the 22d of August he had succeeded in mustering out of the army 719,338, and by November 15, 1865, there had been returned to their homes 800,963 men. This was rapidly followed every month until 1,023,021 had been discharged. Horses and mules had been sold to the value of $15,269,000; barracks and hospitals $447,873; damaged clothing yielded $902,770; military railroads, 2,630 miles, with 6,695 cars and 433 locomotives transferred over to proper authorities, and railroad equipments were sold amounting to $10,910,812.

The whole number of men enlisted at different times during the war was 2,688,522. Of these, 56,000 were killed in battle; 219,000 died of wounds and disease in the military hospitals, and 80,000 died after discharge, from disease contracted during service; making a total loss of about 300,000 men. About 200,000 were crippled or permanently disabled. Of colored troops, 180,000 enlisted and 30,000 died. More than $300,000,000 was paid in bounties, and by States, towns and cities for the support of the families of soldiers. The Sanitary Commission disbursed, in money and supplies, $14,600,000. The Christian Commission disbursed $4,500,000.

Congress at once passed a bill to revive the grade, "General of the army of the United States," and General Grant was appointed to the position.

On December 12, 1867, he was appointed by President Johnson Secretary of War *ad interim*, in the place of Hon. E. M. Stanton, suspended, which position he held until December following, when the senate refused to sanction the suspension of Mr. Stanton. On the 21st of May, 1868, General Grant was nominated by the national republican convention, assembled at Chicago, having received every vote cast; elected President the November following, having received two hundred and fourteen electoral votes, against eighty for Horatio Seymour, democrat. Inaugurated March 4, 1869, and was re-elected in 1872, over Horace Greeley, receiving two hundred and eighty-six votes against sixty-three scattering (Mr. Greeley having died). Inaugurated March 4, 1873, he vacated the Presidency only upon the expiration of his time, March 4, 1877.

To one who has read what General Grant has done, little need be said as to what manner of man he is. The outline of his life shows his ability. Such achievements are not the result of luck or accident. They are seldom seen in history. He has not only shown great ability, but wisdom, practical sagacity and independence in the whirl of extraordinary and important events which have occurred at Washington and in the South since the close of the war.

For some months previous to the expiration of General Grant's second term of office, he felt the need of absolute rest, and that he might be entirely relieved from all cares and annoyances that would necessarily reach him, even in retirement, he planned a tour of the world, to occupy at least two years, hoping to find the relief sought for. The history of this tour, with its unprecedented and unlooked-for ovations and triumphal tour will be found of intense interest to every American.

CHAPTER II.

OFF FOR EUROPE.

On May 17th, 1877, ex-President U. S. Grant, his wife, and son Jesse, sailed from Philadelphia for Europe, via American Line steamer Indiana. His departure was made the occasion of a great parting demonstration, in which all classes of the community seemed to take a hearty and enthusiastic share. The courtesies extended to him in every city through which he had passed since his retirement from the Presidency were alike creditable to those who proffered, and to him who received them, and were the outburst of a people who recognized his great military and civil services. Before leaving the steamer that conveyed the General to the Indiana, a very interesting ceremony took place on board. In the ladies' cabin a private table was spread for the distinguished guests, among whom were General Grant, at the head of the table; General Sherman, on his right; Mayor Stokley, of Philadelphia, on his left; Honorable Hamilton Fish, Colonel Fred. Grant, Honorable Zach. Chandler, Honorable Simon Cameron, Honorable Don Cameron, and other prominent military and civil officers. After luncheon, Mayor Stokley arose and toasted the "honored guest of the day" in a few appropriate and eulogistic remarks. General Grant replied:

"MR. MAYOR AND GENTLEMEN: I had not expected to make a speech to-day, and therefore can do nothing more than thank you, as I have had occasion to do so often within the past week. I have been only eight days in Philadelphia, and have been received with such unexpected kindness that it finds me with no words to thank you. What with driving in the park, and dinners afterward, and keeping it up until after midnight, and now to find myself still receiving your kind hospitality, I am afraid you have not left me stomach enough to cross the Atlantic."

This was followed by short and highly complimentary speeches from General Sherman, ex-Secretary Fish, ex-Secretary Chandler, ex-Secretary Robeson, ex-Senator Cameron, General Bailey, Governor Hartranft, and others; and so affected General Grant that he replied:

"My Dear Friends: I was not aware that we would have so much speech-making here, or that it would be necessary for me to say any more to you, but I feel that the compliments you have so showered upon me were not altogether deserved—that they should not all be paid to me, either as a soldier or as a civil officer. As a General your praises do not all belong to me—as the executive of the nation they are not due to me. There is no man who can fill both or either of these positions without the help of good men. I selected my lieutenants when I was in both positions, and they were men, I believe, who could have filled my place often better than I did. I never flattered myself that I was entitled to the place you gave me. My lieutenants could have acted perhaps better than I, had the opportunity presented itself. Sherman could have taken my place, as a soldier or in a civil office, and so could Sheridan, and others I might name. I am sure if the country ever comes to this need again there will be men for the work. There will be men born for every emergency. Again I thank you, and again I bid you good-bye; and once again I say that, if I had failed, Sherman or Sheridan, or some of my other lieutenants, would have succeeded."

Shortly after this, the General was transferred to the Indiana, last good-byes were said, and the steamer proceeded on her way to England, arriving at Queenstown May 27, without mishap, the General and party having passed a delightful voyage, almost entirely free from the disagreeable effects of "seasickness", that renders an "ocean trip" so unpleasant. He was met by a delegation of prominent city officials, and tendered the hospitalities of Queenstown, with the assurance that every village and hamlet of Ireland had resounded with the praises of his name, and would welcome him with all the warmth and candor of the Irish people. He replied that he could not then avail himself of their hospitality, but would return to Ireland within a short time.

Reaching Liverpool at half past two P. M., all the shipping in the Liverpool docks exhibited a profuse display of bunting, the flags of all nations waving along the seven miles of water front. An immense crowd was gathered on the docks to welcome the ex-President, and he landed amid cheers such as must have reminded him of the days directly after the war, when he was received by New York and other American cities. The Mayor of Liverpool read him an address of welcome, saluting him as an illustrious statesman and soldier, and when the ex-President modestly and in a few brief words acknowledged the honor done him, and expressed the very great pleasure he had from his reception, new cheers burst forth and a great crowd followed his carriage to the hotel.

The judgment of strangers resembles somewhat the judgment of posterity. As he is regarded in European countries, so, doubtless, he will stand in history, when the **bitterness and the littleness of partisan strife have passed** away, and his real services to his country and his real character are better understood. But in spite of partisan bitterness and personal opposition, such as a man of his positive character, placed in the most difficult position in the world, and kept there during eight long years, could not fail to arouse, nothing is more certain than that General Grant has to-day a larger share of the gratitude and the affection of the American people than any other of our public men. No matter how widely men may have differed from him, no matter how they may have opposed him, if they are really Americans, and if they are manly and patriotic men, in their hearts they wish well to the man who led our armies to victory; whose firm will saved the Union, and who—no matter what they may think his errors during his Presidency—entered political life against his will, and at the demand of the people gave up the great and permanent position the nation had given him, to serve it in a new and to him untried and unwelcome field; and who, during sixteen long and weary years, stood at his post of duty unrelieved and without rest.

It is a fact not generally remembered, that Grant's great lieutenants in the war—Sherman, Sheridan and Farragut—all enjoyed the "vacation in Europe" which they had so well earned. To General Grant, their honored chief, alone, was rest denied. The country required of him, and him alone, that he should derange all his plans in life, that he should put off the period of rest which he coveted and which he had earned, that he should even surrender the place at the head of the armies, to which he was appointed amid the plaudits of the people, in order continuously to serve them. Few men of such arduous and conspicuous services have had so long and difficult a tour of duty imposed upon them. Republics are said to be ungrateful, but our own is not so entirely cold and devoid of gratitude that men do not feel a keen sense of gratification when they see their faithful and tired servant taking his ease at last, and receiving in foreign lands the honors and the respect to which his remarkable career so eminently entitle him.

To the statesmen and soldiers whom he will meet, even more than to the general mass, he will be an object of great curiosity. Except Field Marshal Von Moltke, no general of our days has commanded and wielded such masses of men; no general whom he will meet can boast of a more brilliantly conceived or a more daringly executed campaign than that of Vicksburg; no one of them has had the control of so vast a field of war as he, and surely none has seen hotter fire than Grant withstood in the desperate days of the Wilderness, Spottsylvania and Cold Harbor. In every country in Europe which he may visit, he will find distinguished military chiefs who have studied his campaigns, who know how to appreciate the dogged courage of Shiloh, the brilliant audacity of Vicksburg, the genius which recovered an imperilled position before Chattanooga, the indomitable perseverance of the Virginia campaigns, and the broad and comprehensive view which enabled him to plan the operations of armies stretched across half a continent.

Nor will distinguished civilians be less eager to hear his voice and to scrutinize his features, for they will remember that he acted a foremost part in many of the most notable events of the century; they will see in him the supporter and right hand of Lincoln in the emancipation of the slaves, the restorer of peace, the general who returned a million of soldiers to peaceful industries, the ruler of the American republic during eight years of extraordinary political turbulence.

All the journals of the city next day appeared with highly complimentary editorials, assuring General Grant of a generous hospitality. The *Daily News* said that

"General Grant was unquestionably the greatest soldier living." The General and Mrs. Grant had a perfect round of festivities at Liverpool. Hurried visits were made to all points of interest, visiting and examining the docks of the city, enlisting great interest from General Grant in the magnificent dock system, and, contrasted with the system of piers in the United States, he admitted the superiority of these supurb and substantial structures over those of the East and North rivers.

The party returned to the city, and were driven to the town hall to lunch with the Mayor and other civic dignitaries. This building is one of the most interesting in the city, and the figure of Britannia, looking abroad from the summit of the great dome, reminds the visitor of the now celebrated Hermann monument in Germany. The ex-President was escorted to the reception saloon, and subsequently examined the portraits of former mayors and wealthy merchants, who have long since passed away; the famous Chantry statues of Canning and Roscoe, and the elegant tapestry with which the various saloons are fitted up.

Lunch was prepared. Covers were laid for fifty, the table being beautifully decorated with choice flowers and ornaments in confection, suggestive of very elaborate preparation. Among those present, were the Mayor, the Mayoress, members of the city council, one member of parliament, the City Solicitor and several prominent merchants. Mrs. Grant sat on the left of the Mayor, and our ex-President on his right. The repast was served immediately the guests assembled, and was a most enjoyable affair.

At the conclusion of lunch, the Mayor arose and proposed the health of the Queen, in accordance with the tradition which places English majesty first on all state and festive occasions. This was drank standing. The host next proposed the health of "General and ex-President Grant, the distinguished soldier and statesman present," remarking that it would be unnecessary for him to repeat the earnestness of their welcome, their desire to draw closer the bonds of friendship between the two greatest commercial nations in the world, and especially to honor the hero of a hundred battles, whose courage and skill challenged their admiration.

Grant responded with unusual gayety of manner, acknowledging the pleasure with which he received their constant manifestations of good will, believing that ultimately the bonds of union must be strengthened between the two countries. He excused himself from an extended reply. During the luncheon, the streets leading to the town hall were packed with spectators.

General Grant afterward visited the exchange and news-rooms, where he was received with great enthusiasm. Leaving Liverpool for Manchester, May 30, immense crowds gathered along the route, and the stations were beautifully decorated, the American flag being everywhere prominent. Arriving at Manchester at eleven o'clock, he was received by the Mayor and Aldermen and a tremendous crowd of citizens, who manifested their enthusiasm by continued cheering. The Mayor's speech was quite lengthy, and referred feelingly to a similar occasion, when, in 1863, the ship Griswold brought a cargo of provisions to the suffering operatives of the city, who had been thrown out of employment, owing to the failure of the cotton crop from the South. This address was followed by a laudatory and congratulatory address by Sir John Heron, recalling the kind expressions which the Queen's birthday had evoked in America. He hoped for a constant increase of the existing good feeling, and trusted that the visit of the ex-President would ultimately lead to free commercial intercourse between England and the United States.

The General, who had listened to the addresses with

that quiet composure of manner peculiar to him — as unmoved, though the target of thousands of eyes, as though alone—rising, acknowledged the presentation. "It is scarcely possible for me," he said, "to give utterance to the feelings evoked by my reception upon your soil from the moment of my arrival in Liverpool, where I have passed a couple of days, until the present moment. After the scene which I have witnessed in your streets, the elements of greatness, as manifested in your public and industrial buildings, I may be allowed to say, that no person could be the recipient of the honor and attention you have bestowed upon me, without the profoundest feelings. Such have been incited in me, and I find myself inadequate to their proper expression. It was my original purpose on my arrival in Liverpool to hasten to London, and from thence proceed to visit the various points of interest in the country. Among these I have regarded Manchester as the most important. As I have been aware for years of the great amount of your manufactures, many of which find their ultimate destination in my own country, so I am aware that the sentiments of the great mass of the people of Manchester went out in sympathy to that country, during the mighty struggle, in which it fell to my lot to take some humble part. The expressions of the people of Manchester at the time of the great trial, incited within the breasts of my countrymen a feeling of friendship toward them, distinct from that felt toward all England; and in that spirit I accept, on the part of my country, the compliments paid me as its representative, and thank you."

After General Grant had concluded his address of thanks, luncheon was served in the large banquet hall. Toasts to the Queen and the Prince of Wales were proposed and drank with all the honors. The Mayor of Manchester responded to each in loyal speeches. The health of **President Hayes was then proposed, and was received with** enthusiasm. Mr. Newton Crane, United States consul to Manchester, responded amid applause. After these formalities, the Mayor of Manchester proposed the health of General Grant, amid the plaudits of the assemblage.

General Grant replied, with a humorous twinkle in his eye, that Englishmen had got more speeches and of greater length out of him than his own countrymen; but they were poorer, because they were longer than he was accustomed to make. He warmly returned thanks for the reception he had received at the hands of the people of Manchester, and concluded his remarks by proposing the health of the Mayoress and the ladies. The Mayor replied in suitable terms.

Mr. Jacob Bright, M. P., being called upon for a speech, said: "No guest so distinguished has ever before visited Manchester. General Grant is a brave soldier, and he has pursued a generous, pacific policy toward the enemies he had conquered. He should be honored and beloved, and deserves the hearty reception he will receive throughout the realm." After the banquet, the General was introduced to the assemblage, and a general hand-shaking followed. In the evening he visted the Theatre Royal, and spent a short time at the Prince's Theatre. His reception at both places was very enthusiastic.

The journey from Manchester to London was marked by hearty greetings and welcomes at the several stations, and imposing demonstrations were made at Leicester and Bedford, as the handsomely decorated cars reached those places. To some of the addresses that were made to him, General Grant replied with an ease and sincerity which, no doubt, made our British cousins wonder how he came by his title of the "silent president." The secret lies, probably, in the fact that the General detests forms and shams and political intrigue, and he had good reasons for his taciturnity when he found himself surrounded by politicians whom his judgment told him it was dangerous to trust. His welcome in England was a genuine outpouring of a nation's respect and admiration, and as such General Grant received it, and responded to it with an unembarrassed and earnest sincerity.

CHAPTER III.

GENERAL GRANT IN LONDON.

General Grant arrived at the terminus of the Midland Railway (St. Pancras Station), London, June 1, where he was met by Minister Pierrepont, in behalf of the United States, and Lord Vernon. Huge crowds thronged the entrance to the station, and cheered loudly, but there were no speeches. General Grant and party at once entered Minister Pierrepont's carriage, and were driven rapidly down Tottenham Court Road into Oxford street, thence to the residence of the American Minister. During the afternoon he was introduced to the Prince of Wales, it being his first visit of importance since reaching the city.

The following day General Grant, Prince of Wales, Duke of Cambridge, Lord Dudley, Lord Eicho, the Duke of Hamilton, the German Ambassador, Count Munster, and a number of Peers, left London by rail to witness the races at Epsom. Returning to London, General Grant was entertained at a grand banquet at Apsley House, given in his honor by the Duke of Wellington. It was a splendid and hearty reception. The guests were Mrs. and General Grant, Count and Countess Gleichen, Lord and Lady Abercromby, Lord and Lady Churchill, Marquises Tweeddale, Sligo and Ailesbury, Earl Roden, Viscount Torrington, Lords George Paget, Calthorpe, Houghton, Strathnairn, the Marchioness of Hertford, Countess of Hardwicke, Countess of Bradford, Lady Wellesley, Lady Emily Peel and Lady Skelmersdale, Miss Wellesley, and a number of others well known to the London world of high social life.

The banquet was served up in the famous Waterloo Chamber, where the old Iron Duke loved to meet the war generals of 1815 on the 18th of June every year, and celebrate the anniversary of the great battle which forever closed the fortunes of Napoleon Bonaparte. Here, overlooking Hyde Park and within view of his own statute at the entrance to the park at Hyde Park corner, the old Duke presided over the annual banquet, reviewing the events of the momentous times when the supremacy of Great Britain was hanging in the balance, with strong probabilities of the scale turning against her. The Waterloo Chamber has been closed a good deal since the death of Arthur Wellesley, for the present Duke and Duchess have spent most of their time when in England at the lovely estate in Winchelsea, which was presented to the eminent soldier by the Crown after the close of the great European wars.

The present owner of the estates and titles of Wellington is a quiet, unassuming gentleman, who loves the fine arts, is a writer of ability, fishes in his lake at Winchelsea, and, during the season in London, patronizes the clubs. He is Lord of the Manor of Surrey, appoints the justices of the peace and attends to the poor. He is a member of the House of Lords, of course, but he has rarely done more than record his vote on such extraordinary occasions as the disestablishment of the Church of Ireland, and matters affecting the autonomy in his party. The Duchess is considered one of the handsomest ladies in Europe, and has always been a great favorite with Queen Victoria. As a lady in waiting, she attends Her Majesty on all state occasions. Hence the tastes and desires of the Duke and Duchess have lead them to neglect Apsley House to some extent.

This Waterloo Chamber still contains some of the fine old paintings which were hung upon the walls by the first Duke. For instance, there is the celebrated painting, "Signing the treaty of Westphalia," where the commander-in-chief is the central figure of a galaxy of generals, such as has seldom been gathered together since. A magnificent life-size portrait of Napoleon, Landseer's "Van Amburgh and the Lions," Correggio's "Christ on the Mount of Olives," on a panel, and full length portraits of foreign sovereigns and notabilities, by Velasquez, Wilkie and Teniers, are in the saloons adjoining. The Duke was looking out of the main window overlooking the park at the time the house was mobbed by the reformers whom he opposed.

It was a dramatic incident, that the conqueror of Lee should meet in this revered chamber the descendant of the conqueror of Napoleon the Great. General Grant was given precedence in the honors of the evening, escorting the Duchess of Wellington to supper, and afterward escorting her to the reception, at which were present the Duke and Duchess of Cleveland, the Duke and Duchess of Sutherland, the Duke and Duchess of Manchester, and many of those already mentioned above.

There were no speeches of note at the supper, which was a quiet though brilliant affair. The grand gaseliers lit up the magnificent hall and the lovely damasks and laces, and revealed the wealth of gold and silver and the flowers and confections of the table.

General Grant attended divine service on the 3d in Westminster Abbey. An eloquent sermon was preached by Dean Stanley, from Genesis xxvii. 38. In the course of his sermon he alluded to ex-President Grant, saying, "that in the midst of the congregation there was one of the chiefest citizens of the United States, who had just laid down his sceptre of the American commonwealth, who, by his military prowess and generous treatment of his comrades and adversaries, had restored unity to his country. We welcome him as a sign and pledge that the two great kindred nations are one in heart, and are equally at home under this fraternal roof. Both regard with reverential affection this ancient cradle of their common life."

Although the Duke of Wellington was the first to exhibit to a circle of admirers the great lion of the season, yet it was only possible for him to make a restricted use of his triumph in favor of the type of humanity that can be invited to a ducal mansion. The real introduction of the ex-President to the world of Londoners was made on the 5th, by the American Minister, in a reception so brilliant that all occasions of the sort which have hitherto shone in the annals of our legations abroad will become a prey to "dumb forgetfulness." In each one of the engagements scored for a month ahead, the ex-President met some one set of English society — men of this or that party or shade of opinion, men of science or of letters, army men or navy men—but at the legation, and presented by the American Minister, he had an opportunity to make the acquaintance of English society, without regard to the lines which divide it into so many coteries, and saw at its best that average quantity of the London world which he could never get at one view save on some such neutral ground as our Minister's parlors. The reception at Minister Pierrepont's was immensely successful. The legation in Cavendish Square was interiorly decorated with the grandest profusion of flowers, with the grand old American flag over all. Since the announcement was made that the Minister would receive the ex-President, Mrs. Pierrepont had been overwhelmed with requests for invitations, and out of her good nature acceded, until the number of cards out guaranteed perhaps a greater throng than would ordinarily be comfortable. But, after all, what is a reception without a crush? Despite the immense crowd, especially of on-lookers, in Cavendish Square, there was not the slightest confusion. Carriages rolled up, occupants moved out and up into the mansion, with that absence of surrounding noise and shouting that characterizes your true reception where the *ton* is *bon* and the servants well drilled.

On entering, the guests were shown into the cloak rooms, on the ground floor, where wraps were left and a last glance in the mirrors taken. Who, even a philosopher, disdains that last reflective glance?

On ascending the drawing-room floor, the guests were announced in the small ante-room where stood Mrs. Pierrepont, General Grant, Colonel Badeau, Mrs. Grant, and Mr. Pierrepont, in the order given.

General Grant was attired in plain evening dress, which was conspicuous in its plainness amid the stars, garters and ribbons worn by many of lesser note; even the Japanese Minister was more gorgeous. As for the Chinese Embassy, no tea chest ever equalled their curious splendor.

Mrs. Grant wore a toilet of claret-colored stamped velvet, and cream satin, high-necked, and with long sleeves.

Mrs. Pierrepont was clad in an elaborate costume of scarlet and black.

Among the English notables present, were the Lord Chancellor, the Dukes of Leeds and Bedford, the Marquises of Salisbury and Hertford, the Earls of Derby, Belmore, Longford, Dunravan, Ducie, Caithness and Shaftesbury, Lord Airey, General Probyn, Mr. and Mrs. Gladstone, with peers and peeresses innumerable.

Every American resident responded to the Minister's invitation. The Morgans and the Peabodys, Mr. James McHenry, Chevalier Wikoff, Mr. G. W. Smalley, Chief Justice Shea, Mr. Moncure D. Conway, Mr. Newton Crane, Consul at Manchester, Mrs. Fairchild, Mrs. Julia Ward

Howe and her daughter Maud, Mr. and Mrs. Ives, Mrs. Hicks and Miss Nannie Schomberg, were among the most prominent.

The immense majority of the dresses of the ladies were in excellent taste, and none were censurable. The American belles carried away the palm for style and beauty, as they usually do on such occasions.

At half-past twelve Mrs. Pierrepont and General Grant came down stairs, and, standing in the lower hall, bade farewell to the parting guests, while Mrs. Grant, Mr. Pierrepont and Colonel Badeau took up position in a separate room, the amiable Secretary of Legation, Mr. William J. Hoppin, hovering over one and all. The children of both nations left the legation with a feeling that the tie between them had been strengthened in the generous hospitality of the American representative and the cordial response of England's best and greatest.

On the 6th, General Grant dined with the Earl Carnarvon, and in the evening attended the royal concert at Buckingham Palace; on the 7th, dined with Lord Houghton; on the 8th, with the Marquis of Hertford, where he met about fifty of the members of the house of lords, and in the evening a grand reception tendered by General Badeau, in Beaufort Gardens. Here his reception was brilliant, and only eclipsed by that of Minister Pierrepont. When General Grant arrived, a distinguished company had already assembled in the drawing-room, by whom he was most warmly greeted. Among the first to welcome him was Mr. Gladstone, who appeared to take great interest in American affairs.

As General Grant moved about the saloon, he encountered Lord Northbrooke, Lord Fitzwilliam, Lord O'Hagan, Sir Charles Dilke, Sir James Colville, Viscount Reidhaven, Sir Patrick and Lady Grant, who claim some kind of kinship with our illustrious countryman; the Lord

Bishop of Bristol and Gloucester, Jacob and Mrs. Bright, Mr. Kinglake, Tom Hughes, who has become almost a hero to Americans; Mr. Macmillan, the publisher of the celebrated magazine bearing his name; Mr. Walter, proprietor of the *Times;* Mr. Bothwick, of the *Morning Post*, and Baron Reuter.

On the 9th, General Grant attended a reception at the Hertford mansion, having lunched with Lord Granville previously. On the 11th, he was at his daughter's, Mrs. Sartoris, remaining until the 15th, when occurred the grand reception by the corporation of London, at which time he was made an honorary citizen, and presented with the freedom of the city.

The presentation of the freedom of the city of London is always an event of importance. It is no common honor. The greatest heroes and the proudest monarchs have been reckoned among the "freemen." George III., who always expressed a supreme contempt for ordinary matters and mortals, had to acknowledge that the city of London could bestow a franchise more valuable than all the knighthoods and baubles of the crown. Since his day hundreds of men, whose works will ever be regarded as the gems of history —statesmen, scientists, lawyers, merchants, princes—have been recorded in the grand old book which is prized by the corporation of London more than all the privileges and immunities granted by the government. George Peabody, the noble and benevolent American merchant, whose name is ever uttered by the poor of the English metropolis with affectionate reverence, was made a freeman. General Garibaldi, the liberator of Italy and the father of Italian unity, received the same privilege. The Shah of Persia, the Sultan of Turkey, the Czar of Russia, Prince Leopold of Belgium, Napoleon III., General Blucher and M. Thiers were also presented with the rights, privileges and immunities of the dwellers within " ye Bishopsgate " and Temple Bar.

It has often been asked, What is the freedom of the city of London? It is simply this—a small slip of parchment, inscribed with the name and titles of the person to whom it is to be presented, guarantees to the holder and his children after him forever the right to live and trade within the city prescribed by St. Clements in the west, Bishopsgate in the east, Pentonville on the north, and the shores of the Thames on the south, without having to pay a tax on the goods as they are brought through the gates. It exempts them from naval and military service, and tolls and duties throughout the United Kingdom. It insures to his children the care of the Chamberlain, who, in case they are left orphans, takes charge of their property and administers it in their interest until they arrive at years of maturity. The parchment bears the seal and signature of the Lord Mayor and Chamberlain, and is generally ornamented with ribbon, and illuminated. It is always enclosed in a long, thin gold box, and is intended, of course, as an heirloom.

When the corporation have decided to confer the parchment upon any distinguished individual, he is notified in the old-fashioned style by the City Chamberlain, whose missive begins, " You are hereby commanded to appear in the common hall," etc., naming the date when the city fathers will be present. He is met in the common hall by the Mayor and Councillors. The City Chamberlain informs him that the city has decided to confer upon him the privileges of a free citizen, and makes an address, usually applaudatory of the special services or merits of the individual. The recipient signs his name in the Clerk's book, and this official and the City Chamberlain then sign their names beneath, guarantors or " compurgators," becoming, according to the rule, responsible for his acts as a citizen. The recipient then steps forward, the oath is administered by the Chamberlain, who demands that he shall be in all and every respect true and loyal to the interests of the city; he shakes hands with the Mayor, Chamberlain, Clerk and Councillors, and the gold box is committed to his care.

The reception was a complete success. It was a historical event in the history of two great nations. The event excited unusual interest, even in cynical London. The day was sunny and clear, being what many of the spectators called "Queen's weather."

General Grant arrived most unostentatiously in the private carriage of the American Minister, accompanied by his wife, Jesse (his son), Mr. and Mrs. Pierrepont and General Badeau. Ten thousand spectators crowded to the edge of the barricades and greeted him with that hearty cheering peculiar to the English when they desire to welcome a stranger of distinction.

Just as much enthusiasm was manifested as on the occasion of the visits of the Shah, four years before, and when Garibaldi took the Emperor of the French by surprise and accepted an ovation such as will never be forgotten by those who witnessed it at the Mansion House.

As Grant alighted, he was met by a deputation of London Aldermen, arrayed in their gorgeous crimson robes and with the gold chains of office glittering in the sunlight. As he passed on into the corridor, a company of the City Guards and Yeomen presented arms and the crowd again gave a long cheer. It was a brilliant scene.

The distinguished party were then escorted into the library. Here the scene became bewildering in its antique splendor. The stately hall, with its stately alcoves lined with books, and its many colored windows which blushed in the golden sunlight, the ladies attired in their variegated spring toilets, the Aldermen in scarlet and the Councilmen in their mazarine robes, all presented an *ensemble* at once charming and inspiring. The band played "Hail Columbia" as the party entered.

General Grant walked in a dignified and self-possessed manner toward the Mayor's chair, and took a seat to the left of the dais, amid the most cordial cheering. The City Chamberlain arose, and read the formal address on behalf of the Mayor, tendering to the General the right hand of fellowship, and referring at length to the fact that he was the first President of the American Republic who had been elevated to the dignity of citizenship of the city of London.

Alluding to the kindness extended by America to the Prince of Wales and Prince Arthur, he said the corporation received General Grant, desiring to compliment the General and the country in his person by conferring on him the honorary freedom of their ancient city, a freedom existing eight centuries before his ancestors landed on Plymouth Rock—nay, even before the time of the Norman Conqueror. London, in conferring the honor, recognized the distinguished mark he has left on American history, his magnanimity, his triumphs and his consideration for his vanquished adversaries. It also recognized the conciliatory policy of his administration.

They, the corporation, fervently hoped he would enjoy his visit to England; that he might live long, and be spared to witness the two great branches of the Anglo-Saxon family go on in their career of increasing amity and mutual respect, in an honest rivalry for the advancement of the peace, the liberty and the morality of mankind.

In conclusion, the speaker said: "Nothing now remains, General, but that I should present to you an illuminated copy of the resolution of this honorable court, for the reception of which an appropriate casket is preparing, and, finally, to offer you, in the name of this honorable court, the right hand of fellowship as a citizen of London." The Chamberlain then shook General Grant's right hand amid loud cheering.

Grant arose, and very briefly and appropriately thanked the court for the distinguished honor, and then signed his name to the roll of honor, with the Clerk and Chamberlain as compurgators.

The gold casket, containing the freedom of the city, is in the cinque cento style, oblong, the corners mounted by American eagles, and beautifully decorated. On the reverse side is a view of the entrance to the Guildhall, and an appropriate inscription. At the ends are two figures, also in gold, finely modeled and chased, representing the city of London and the United States, and bearing their respective shields, the latter executed in rich enamel. At the corners are double columns laurel wreathed with corn and cotton, and on the cover a cornucopia, emblematic of the fertility and prosperity of the United States. The rose, shamrock and thistle are also introduced. The cover is surmounted by the arms of the city of London. The casket is supported by American eagles, modeled and chased in gold, the whole standing on a velvet plinth decorated with stars and stripes.

The company then proceeded to the banqueting hall, where seats had been provided for one thousand guests. The Lord Mayor presided. At his right sat General and Mrs. Grant, Minister and Mrs. Pierrepont, General Badeau and Jesse Grant.

Among the distinguished guests present, were Sir Stafford Northcote, Lord and Lady Tenderden, Mr. Stansfield, Mr. A. E. Foster, several peers prominent in the house of lords, a number of the members of the house of commons, consuls, merchants, and other citizens of London.

The room was decorated with miniature English and

American flags, and the tables presented an interesting and artistic appearance.

After the *dejeuner*, the toastmaster, dressed in a gorgeous silk sash formed of stars and stripes, arose, and the bugle sounded. The first toast was "The Queen," the second was "The Health of General Grant," which was received by the guests standing, and amid great cheering.

The Lord Mayor then said: "I, as chief magistrate of the city of London, and on the part of the corporation, offer you as hearty a welcome as the sincerity of language can convey. Your presence here, as the late President of the United States, is especially gratifying to all classes of the community, and we feel that, although this is your first visit to England, it is not a stranger we greet, but a tried and honored friend. Twice occupying, as you did, the exalted position of President of the United States, and, therefore, one of the foremost representatives of that country, we confer honor upon ourselves by honoring you. Let me express both the hope and the belief that, when you take your departure, you will feel that many true friends of yours personally, and also of your countrymen, have been left behind. I have the distinguished honor to propose to your health. May you long live to enjoy the best of health and unqualified happiness."

General Grant's reply was made with deep emotion, and was simply to return his thanks for the unexpected honor paid him, and his desire to say much more for their brilliant reception than he could express.

"The United States" was coupled with the name of Mr. Pierrepont, who responded in a happy speech, complimenting Grant and England. The final toast was "The city of London," and responded to by the Lord Mayor. The company then dispersed with "three cheers for General Grant and the United States."

After leaving the Guildhall, the company proceeded

to the Mansion House, at the corner of what was once the famous Bucklesbury and Poultry. Here they took coffee with the Mayor.

Then the Mayor's state carriage was ordered, and they drove over to Sydenham to the crystal palace, arriving at the main entrance at half past four o'clock P. M. They were received with the most boisterous enthusiasm. There were at least thirty thousand persons present. A tour of the vast building was rapidly made, the party dining in the west wing. General Grant avoided all demonstrations made by the crowd. When darkness set in, Grant was escorted to the place of honor in the Queen's corridor of the palace, where he remained for some time smoking and chatting with his friends and their ladies.

A grand display of fireworks took place during the evening. The principal pyrotechnic display pieces were the portrait of Grant and the capitol at Washington, which were received with prolonged cheers.

At about eleven o'clock the demonstration finished, and the party returned to town in their carriages. General Grant, on parting with the Mayor, expressed his extreme gratification and pleasure.

On the 16th, General and Mrs. Grant dined with the Marquis of Lorne and the Princess Louise, at Kensington castle; on the 18th, at breakfast with Mr. George W. Smalley, correspondent New York *Tribune*. Everything was *recherche*, and the company of the choicest. Among the guests were Professor Huxley, the scientist; Matthew Arnold, Sir Charles Dilke, Sir Frederick Pollock, Robert Browning, A. W. Kinglake, Anthony Trollope, Tom Hughes, Meredith Townsend, Frank Hill, Right Honorable James Stanfield, and many others.

In the evening General Grant was the guest of the Reform club, Earl Granville presiding. The party numbered forty, and represented the liberal ideas which the club sets itself the task of embodying. The dinner itself was among the finest ever given in London, the *cuisine* of this association of liberal gentlemen being celebrated all over the world, and free from all danger of its *chef* ever being called on to fight for his reputation in the courts, as the Napoleon of the soup tureen who composes banquets for a rival club was obliged to do of late. The table was a picture in itself, not to speak of the good things between the top and bottom of the *menu*.

Earl Granville, as soon as the cloth was removed, proposed the health of Her Majesty the Queen. To this the Right Honorable William E. Forster responded in a singularly eloquent speech. In the course of his remarks he referred to the great services of General Grant in the cause of human freedom. He dwelt with particular emphasis upon the importance to civilization of the cultivation of amicable relations between the two great countries, England and the United States. With great felicity he pictured the results of such a state of friendliness, and elicited continued cheering. Passing on to a more practical branch of his subject, he amplified upon the opportunities for advancement to the human race, which a hearty concord between the two nations would give. He saw in it the acceleration of discoveries in every branch of science, the material progress of the masses and the setting up of loftier standards of private taste and public virtue.

Earl Granville proposed the health of "the Illustrious Statesman and Warrior, General Ulysses S. Grant," alluding in the course of his pithy speech to the beneficent results accruing to both nations from the settlement of the Alabama Claims. "England and America," he said, "nay, civilization throughout the universe, recognize in General Grant one of those extraordinary instruments of Divine Providence bestowed in its beneficence to the human race."

Upon rising to reply, General Grant was greeted with

a perfect storm of applause. "I am overwhelmed," he said, "with the kindness shown by Englishmen to me and expressed to America. I regret that I am unable adequately to express, even with the temptation to do so of the omnipresent enterprise of the New York *Herald* [cheers]—to express my thanks for the manifold fraternal courtesies I have received. Words would fail, especially within the limitations of a public speech, to express my feelings in this regard. I hope, when an opportunity is offered me of calmer and more deliberate moments, to put on record my grateful recognition of the fraternal sentiments of the English people, and the desire of America to render an adequate response." "The speech of Earl Granville," he continued, " has inspired thoughts in my bosom which it is impossible for me adequately to present. Never have I lamented so much as now my poverty in phrases to give due expression to my affection for the mother country."

General Grant spoke under the pressure of unusual feeling, and continued with unusual eloquence to express the hope that his words, so far as they had any value, would be heard in both countries and lead to the union of the English speaking people and the fraternity of the human race. During the delivery of his speech the applause and cheering was almost continuous while he was on his feet. The dinner was the greatest demonstration yet made in the ex-President's honor.

The interest taken by the American public in the movements of General Grant not only concerns itself with the honors showered upon the great soldier, but also partakes of curiosity to observe what effect all this will have upon the man. He has always been individually an object of speculation.

During the war, people studied his cigar stumps, and we all remember what Lincoln, judging by results, thought of his brand of whisky. His silence was symbolical, and eager partisans, and often the nation, grasped at his contentious utterances—if not as the rallying cries of new ideas, at least as old ones put into fighting form. From operating on millions of men he has become a being to be operated on. Princes, dukes, earls, marquises, viscounts, have him within short range, and fire dinners and receptions at him. Princesses, duchesses, marchionesses, open all their batteries and smiles and soft speech upon him. The heavy shot of statesmen, scientists and philanthropists bang into his brain. British brass bands blaze away at him, British crowds let fly volleys of cheers at him, and away ahead are seen the ammunition trains of the nobility, gentry and common people, coming up with more dinners, receptions, civic honors, brass bands and cheers. Almost enough to make us pity him. How will he come out of the ordeal?

CHAPTER IV.

GRANT IN ENGLAND.

The following letter, written by Gen. Grant to George W. Childs, of Philadelphia, will be of general interest:

"LONDON, ENG., June 16, 1877.

"MY DEAR MR. CHILDS:—After an unusually stormy passage for any season of the year, and continuous sea-sickness generally among the passengers after the second day out, we reached Liverpool Monday afternoon, the 28th of May. Jesse and I proved to be among the few good sailors. Neither of us felt a moment's uneasiness during the voyage.

"I had proposed to leave Liverpool immediately on arrival, and proceed to London, where I knew our Minister had made arrangements for a formal reception, and had accepted for me a few invitations of courtesy; but what was my surprise to find nearly all the shipping in port at Liverpool decorated with flags of all nations, and from the mainmast of each the flag of the Union was most conspicuous.

"The docks were lined with as many of the population as could find standing room, and the streets, to the hotel where it was understood my party would stop, were packed. The demonstration was, to all appearances, as hearty and as enthusiastic as at Philadelphia on our departure.

"The Mayor was present with his state carriage, to convey us to the hotel, and after that to his beautiful country residence, some six miles out, where we were entertained at dinner with a small party of gentlemen, and remained over night. The following day a large party was given at the official residence of the Mayor, in the city, at which there were some one hundred and fifty of the distinguished citizens and officers of the corporation present. Pressing invitations were sent from most of the cities of the kingdom to have me visit them. I accepted for a day at Manchester, and stopped a few moments at Leicester, and at one other place. The same hearty welcome was shown at each place, as you have no doubt seen.

"The press of the country has been exceedingly kind and courteous. So far I have not been permitted to travel in a regular train, much less in a common car. The Midland road, which penetrates a great portion of the island, including Wales and Scotland, have extended to me the courtesy of their road, and a Pullman car to take me wherever I wish to go during the whole of my stay in England. We arrived in London on Monday evening, the 30th of May, when I found our Minister had accepted engagements for me up to the 27th of June, having but a few spare days in the interval.

"On Saturday last we dined with the Duke of Wellington, and last night the formal reception at Judge Pierrepont's was held. It was a great success, most brilliant in the numbers, rank and attire of the audience, and was graced by the presence of every American in the city who had called on the minister or left a card for me. I doubt whether London has ever seen a private house so elaborately or tastefully decorated as was our American minister's last night. I am deeply indebted to him for the pains he has taken to make my stay pleasant, and the attentions extended to our country. I appreciate the fact, and am proud of it, that the attentions I am receiving are intended more for our country than for me personally. I love to see our country honored and respected abroad, and I am proud to believe that it is by most all nations, and by some even loved. It has always been my desire to see all jealousy between England and the United States abated, and every sore healed. Together they are more powerful for the spread of commerce and civilization than all others combined, and can do more to remove causes of wars by creating moral interests that would be so much endangered by war.

"I have written very hastily, and a good deal at length, but I trust this will not bore you. Had I written for publication, I should have taken more pains.

"U. S. GRANT."

On the 19th, General and Mrs. Grant, Minister and Mrs. Pierrepont, and Consul-General Badeau, dined at Marlborough House with the Prince of Wales. The dinner was a full dress affair. Earls Beaconsfield, Derby and Granville, and the leading members of the government, were present. The ex-President occupied the seat of honor at the table. The dinner proved one of the most enjoyable since the General's arrival.

On the 20th, a deputation waited on ex-President Grant at General Badeau's house, to present an address and express gratitude for his aid in procuring from the government of the United States recognition of the claims of Mrs. Carroll, whose husband was killed in a naval engagement during the American war. The deputation was presented by Mr. Mullaly. Dr. Brady, M. P., said he had been greatly gratified, as had all Irishmen to whom he had spoken, at the reception of General Grant in this country.

The General said it was very gratifying to him to know that a case, no doubt worthy and deserving, had been righted, and that this act of justice had been performed under his government. As to himself, he was simply the executive, and could claim no credit in the matter further than for having approved what was done. The government of the United States was much like that of England, and was divided into three branches, each distinct and independent. Of course, his own branch had its share in urging the claims of this case, but without legislative action nothing could have been done.

On the 21st, ex-President Grant dined at the residence of Minister Pierrepont. The Prince of Wales was present, attended by Major General Sir Dighton Probyn, controller of his household. General Grant sat on the right of the prince, and Mrs. Pierrepont on the left. Mrs. Grant sat opposite the Prince, having the Duke of Richmond on her right and Mr. Pierrepont on her left. Mesdames Grant and Pierrepont were the only ladies present. The other guests were the Turkish, Austrian, German, French, Italian and Russian ambassadors; the Dukes of Argyle, Wellington and Westminster; the Marquises of Salisbury, Hertford and Lansdowne; the Earls of Beaconsfield, Derby and Carnarvon; Earls Granville and Manvers; Lords Cairne, Manners and Houghton, also Sir Stafford Northcote; Mr. Cross, Home Secretary; Mr. Gawthorne Hardy, Mr. Hoppan, Mr. Beckwith and Jesse Grant.

On the 22d, a special performance at the London Royal Italian Opera was given in honor of General Grant. The house was filled. General and Mrs. Grant and General Badeau arrived at half-past eight. The curtain immediately rose, disclosing Mlle. Albani and the full chorus of the company, behind whom was a group of American flags. Mlle. Albani sang the "Star Spangled Banner," with the full chorus and orchestra. General Grant, for the first time since his arrival in England, was dressed in the full uniform of a major general. The entire audience rose on the General's entrance, and remained standing during the singing, as did also the General and wife. After the song was finished, he was loudly applauded and bowed in response.

General Grant was obliged to leave early to go to the Queen's ball at Buckingham Palace. The General's box was decorated with flowers.

On the 24th, General Grant was present at a banquet given by the corporation of Trinity House. The Prince of Wales presided. Prince Leopold, Prince Christian, the Prince of Leinington, the Prince of Saxe-Weimar, the Duke of Wellington, the Marquis of Hertford, the Earl of Derby, the Earl of Carnarvon, Sir Stafford Northcote, Mr. Cross, and Chief Justice Sir Alexander Cockburn, were among the distinguished company present.

The Prince of Wales, referring to General Grant, in the course of his speech, said: "On the present occasion it is a matter of peculiar gratification to us as Englishmen to receive as our guest General Grant. I can assure him for myself, and for all loyal subjects of the Queen, that it has given us the greatest pleasure to see him as a guest in this country."

Earl Carnarvon proposed the health of the visitors, and coupled with it General Grant's name.

He said "Strangers of all classes, men of letters, arts, science, state, and all that has been most worthy and great, have, as it were, come to this center of old civilization. I venture, without disparagement to any of those illustrious guests, to say that never has there been one to whom we willingly accord a freer, fuller, heartier welcome than we do to General Grant on this occasion—not merely because we believe he has performed the part of a distinguished general, nor because he has twice filled the highest office which the citizens of his great country can fill, but because we look upon him as representing that good will and affection which ought to subsist between us and the United States. It has been my duty to be connected with the great Dominion of Canada, stretching several thousand miles along the frontier of the United States, and during the last three or four years I can truthfully say that nothing impressed me more than the interchange of friendly and good offices which took place between the two countries under the auspices of President Grant."

General Grant replied that he felt more impressed than he had possibly ever felt before on any occasion. He came here under the impression that this was Trinity House, and that trinity consisted of the army, navy, and peace. He thought it was a place of quietude, where there would be no talk or toasts. He had been, therefore, naturally surprised at hearing both. He had heard some remarks from His Royal Highness which compelled him to say a word in response. He begged to thank His Highness for these remarks. There had been other things said during the evening highly gratifying to him. Not the least gratifying was to hear that there were occasionally in this country party fights as well as in America. He had seen before now a war between three departments of the state, the executive, the judicial, and the legislative. He had not seen the political parties of England go so far as that. He would imitate their chaplain, who had set a good example of oratory — that was shortness — and say no more than simply thank His Royal Highness and the company on behalf of the visitors.

This reception at Windsor Castle, on the 26th, may be regarded as the culmination of the remarkable social attentions which were bestowed on General Grant in such profuse abundance during his visit to England. No such honors, nor anything approaching them, have ever before been paid to an American citizen. While their distinguished recipient modestly regards them as a compliment to his country rather than to himself, it is pretty safe to say that there is no other American citizen through whom such honors to our Republic would have been possible. The English people feel, as all mankind in all ages have felt,

GENERAL GRANT ENTERTAINED BY QUEEN VICTORIA AT WINDSOR CASTLE.

the magic of great military names. It is General Grant's resplendent and successful career as a soldier, rather than the fact that he has been twice elected the chief magistrate of a great country, that has broken down so many social barriers in his favor. His quiet and undemonstrative personal manners have contributed to his favorable reception. He is such a contrast to the offensive bumptiousness too often exhibited by Americans, that Englishmen are ready to concede a great deal more than he would ever think of claiming for himself. While his splendid reception is no doubt a compliment to the American people, it is also a great personal compliment to the only man who could have evoked such a series of demonstrations.

General Grant and wife left London by the five P. M. train from Paddington, and arrived at Windsor at thirty-five minutes past five. The Mayor, several members of the corporation, and a number of spectators, were assembled on the platform to witness the arrival. The General and Mrs. Grant, who were accompanied by Minister Pierrepont, were conveyed in one of Her Majesty's carriages to the castle, where they were received by the Queen at the bottom of the staircase at the Queen's entrance, and conducted through the state corridor to the white drawing room. After a short interview, General Grant and wife were conducted to apartments over the Waterloo Gallery, overlooking the Home Park. In the evening a grand dinner party was given in General Grant's honor.

Dinner was served in Oak Room, according to custom, which reserves St. George's Hall for state banquets. The party was small, because etiquette requires that the Queen shall converse with every guest.

The introductions were made as follows: Minister Pierrepont, advancing, introduced General Grant; then Lord Derby stepped forward with Mrs. Grant. The Queen shook hands with them, while the ladies in waiting simply bowed. This formality at an end, the gentlemen led the way to the Oak Room. The Queen sat at the head of the table. On her right were respectively Prince Leopold, Princess Christian and General Grant; on her left Prince Christian, Princess Beatrice and Minister Pierrepont. Then came the Duchess of Wellington, Lord Elphinstone and Mrs. Pierrepont; Lord Derby and Mrs. Grant; the Duchess of Roxburgh and Lord Biddulph; the Countess of Derby and Jesse Grant.

During the dinner, the band of the Grenadier Guards, under Dan Godfrey, played in the quadrangle. The enjoyment of the party was unconstrained, the Queen taking a prominent part in the lively conversation, during which all kinds of topics were discussed, American and English, political and social. The Princess Beatrice is a brilliant conversationalist, and she was particularly interesting on many American social topics, which she thoroughly understood.

Most of the ladies were all dressed in black with white trimmings, owing to the deaths recently of the Queen of Holland and the Duke of Hesse-Darmstadt. The Queen was attired in a similar style, but her toilet comprised a very magnificent array of diamonds.

After dinner, the Queen's party proceeded to the corridor, for the purpose of enabling the visitors to examine it more closely. Here they met another party from the Octagon, and a lively conversation ensued, during which Her Majesty talked with every person present.

At about ten o'clock Her Majesty shook hands with her lady guests, bowed to the gentlemen, and retired, followed by other members of the royal family present.

The guests then entered one of the magnificent drawing-rooms along the east front, where they were entertained by the Queen's private band.

Refreshments having been served, General Grant and

Minister Pierrepont played whist with the Duchesses of Wellington and Roxburgh, during which, of course, the gentlemen were beaten. Mr. Pierrepont played badly; so did the ex-President.

At half-past eleven o'clock, the Americans retired to the rooms, which were in a different part of the palace.

The following morning, General and Mrs. Grant were driven in the great park, in a carriage usually used by the Queen, at half-past ten. He, with Americans, accompanied by Mr. Ward Hunt, first Lord of the Admiralty, and Colonel Gardiner, went to the station and took the train for Bishop's road (Paddington).

A state concert was given at Buckingham Palace at night. General Grant and Mrs. Grant, the Emperor and Empress of Brazil, the Prince and Princess of Wales, the Duke and Duchess of Teck, Prince Christian and the Princess Helena, the Princess Louise and the Marquis of Lorne and the Duke of Cambridge were present.

On the 28th, Liverpool again honors General Grant with a grand banquet. Upwards of two hundred gentlemen, including representatives of all public bodies in the town, attended the banquet, which was held in the large ballroom of the town hall, and was a very grand affair. General Grant, who was in the uniform of a major general, was received with the greatest enthusiasm. He sat on the right of the Mayor. Next to General Grant sat Lieutenant General Sir Henry de Bathe, commander of the forces in the northern district.

The Mayor, proposing General Grant's health, spoke of the sterling qualities he possessed as a soldier, which had enabled him to restore peace and prosperity to his country.

General Grant, responding, said the reception he encountered in Great Britain was far beyond his expectation, and was such as any living person might well be proud of. He believed, however, that it was indicative of the friendly relations which existed between two peoples, who were of one kindred blood and civilization. He hoped that friendship would continue to be cultivated and long endure. Referring to some remarks relative to the British army, he said there were as many soldiers now at Aldershott as in the regular army of the United States, which had a frontier of thousands of miles; but if necessary the United States could raise volunteers, and he and Mr. Fairchild were examples of what those volunteers were.

On the 30th, General Grant attended a dinner given by a personal friend belonging to the American press, at Grosvenor Hotel. The company numbered forty, consisting chiefly of distinguished journalists of the London press, and authors. There were no speeches, the dinner being strictly a social and private one.

On the 3d of July, a deputation of forty men, each representing a different trade, and representing altogether about one million English workingmen, waited upon General Grant at Consul General Badeau's house, and presented him an address, welcoming him to England, and assuring him of their good wishes and deep regard for the welfare and progress of America, where British workmen had always found a welcome. Impromptu speeches were then made by various members of the deputation, all of which were extremely cordial.

General Grant replied as follows: "In the name of my country, I thank you for the address you have presented to me. I feel it a great compliment paid my government and one to me personally. Since my arrival on British soil I have received great attentions, which were intended, I feel sure, in the same way, for my country. I have had ovations, free hand-shakings, presentations from different classes, from the government, from the controlling authorities of cities, and have been received in the cities by the populace, but there has been no reception which I am prouder of than this to-day. I recognize the fact that whatever there is of greatness in the United States, as indeed in any other country, is due to labor. The laborer is the author of all greatness and wealth. Without labor there would be no government, or no leading class, or nothing to preserve. With us, labor is regarded as highly respectable. When it is not so regarded, it is because man dishonors labor. We recognize that labor dishonors no man; and, no matter what a man's occupation is, he is eligible to fill any post in the gift of the people; his occupation is not considered in selecting, whether as a law maker or as an executor of the law. Now, gentlemen, in conclusion, all I can do is to renew my thanks for the address, and repeat what I have said before, that I have received nothing from any class since my arrival which has given me more pleasure."

After the speech there was an informal exchange of courtesies, and the deputation then withdrew.

In the evening, a banquet was given by the United Service Club. The Duke of Cambridge presided, having on his right General Grant and Lord Hampton, and on his left Minister Pierrepont and Lord Strathnairn. Admiral Sir Charles Eden was the vice-president, having on his right Sir George Sartorios, and General Sir William Codington on his left. There was a very full attendance of guests.

The Duke of Cambridge proposed the health of General Grant. The General, in reply, alluded to the visit of the Prince of Wales to the United States. He said he knew from all his friends, as well as of his own personal knowledge, that His Royal Highness was received, as the son of England's Queen, with the sincerest respect. He thanked the company for their hospitality, which was one of the greatest honors he had received.

On the 4th, a reception was given at the American Legation, which was a social event of a very high order, and very enjoyable throughout. It lasted from four until seven o'clock. Nearly all the Americans in London, estimated at over one thousand, called during that time. A large silk American flag hung over the entrance, and the interior was beautifully decorated with flowers. Mr. and Mrs. Pierrepont, General and Mrs. Grant, received all the guests. The reception closed with the singing of the "Star Spangled Banner" by Miss Abel, an American.

On the 5th, General and Mrs. Grant, their son, and General Badeau, left London for the continent. They were accompanied to the station by a number of friends, and the parting was most enthusiastic. With the exception of brief stops at Tunbridge and Ashford, there was nothing worthy of note.

A large crowd had collected at the Folkestone station when the train arrived, and as General Grant alighted he was loudly cheered. The Mayor's carriage was in waiting, and the party were driven to the town hall. Here the Mayor received them in his robes of office, surrounded by the members of the town council and a large number of citizens. As the clerk to the corporation read the address, the whole assemblage remained standing. The address recited the idea of honoring the General for his deeds in the battle-field, and concluded by expressing the wish that he might have a third term as President of the United States, and advancing the opinion that he would. In his reply the ex-President ignored this. He thanked them, as he said he did all their countrymen, for their kindness and courtesy. He believed it would be to the mutual interests of the two great English-speaking nations to maintain the friendly relations which now existed. England and America must lead in commerce and civilization. He also expressed his gratification at the settlement of the Alabama claims, which had been referred to. But he carefully avoided any allusion to politics.

The reception over, the party started at once for the pier, where the steamer Vittoria was waiting to convey them to Ostend, Belgium. The American flag was seen flying among the shipping in the harbor, in honor of the town's guest. A great crowd had gathered again at the pier, and cheered loudly as the Vittoria left and passed out into the straits, the General bowing repeatedly from the bridge of the steamer. General Grant's stay in England had been made pleasant by honors which were extremely gratifying to Americans. His excellent taste in ignoring the toadyism of the Englishman at Folkestone, shows how quickly the General could resent such a piece of impertinence, and that he thought, correctly, that foreigners have no business with our politics.

CHAPTER V.

ON THE CONTINENT.

General Grant arrived at Brussels, Belgium, at six o'clock on the evening of July 6, and proceeded to the Bellevue Hotel. No official reception was given him, as it was understood that he was traveling *incognito*. Within an hour of his arrival, an aide-de-camp of King Leopold visited the General, conveying from his royal master an invitation to dinner, and placing at his disposal his aides and the carriage of state. In the evening General Grant dined with ex-Minister Sanford. Several Belgian functionaries were in attendance at the board.

On the 8th, General Grant dined with the King and royal family; all the high officials of state and foreign ministers were present. King Leopold took Mrs. Grant to dinner, and the ex-President had the honor of escorting the Queen. On Sunday the King paid the General a visit, a step which is considered by the Belgians as being a great honor, as it is entirely out of the usual course. The General and Mrs. Grant visited the King and Queen in the afternoon. On Monday morning all the foreign ministers in Brussels called on the General, previous to his departure. The King's aide-de-camp and members of the American legation accompanied the party to the railway station. During General Grant's stay he was treated with the greatest distinction.

On the 9th, General Grant arrived at Cologne, and was received at the railway station by the American Consul,

President of Police, and the civil and military governors of the city, the Emperor having commanded that every attention should be paid to their honored guest. At Cologne the General visited several churches and the cathedral, and made an excursion over the suspension bridge to Deutz, returning by the bridge of boats. In the evening he was serenaded at the Hotel du Nord, by a military band.

On the 10th, he left Cologne, and proceeded up the river Rhine, stopping at Bingen, Coblentz and Weisbaden, reaching Frankfort on the 12th, where a grand reception was given him at the Palmer-garten; the burgomaster presided, and one hundred and twenty guests were present. This included all the prominent officials of the town, officers of the garrison, and leading citizens. The banquet hall was beautifully illuminated and decorated. After the toasts to the Emperor and President Hayes had been drunk and duly responded to, Henry Seligman, the banker, proposed the health of General Grant. Mr. Seligman, in giving the toast, made a few appropriate remarks, in the course of which he said that the General was universally honored and esteemed. General Grant, in reply, thanked the city of Frankfort for the confidence it placed in the Union during the late civil war. He concluded by drinking to the welfare and prosperity of the city. At the conclusion of this short speech, the General was given a magnificent ovation. The guests rose to their feet and cheered lustily, and the crowd outside, numbering six thousand people, caught up the cheer, and were enthusiastic in their demonstrations of welcome.

After the conclusion of the banquet, a grand ball was given, at which the elite of the city was present. Jesse Grant opened the ball with an American lady.

On the following day, General Grant visited Hamburg, and held a reception, the chief burgomaster presenting the guests. A grand concert was given in the grounds of the zoological garden afterward, which was attended by many thousands of people.

On the 16th, General Grant spent several days in the immediate vicinity of Lucerne and Interlaken, Switzerland, whence he made excursions to the mountains in the vicinity. On the 24th, we find him at Berne, Switzerland, where he was received by the President of the Swiss Confederation. On the 27th, he was at Geneva, where he laid the corner stone of a new American Protestant church in that city. Large crowds were present, and hundreds of American flags were displayed from the windows of citizens' houses. The authorities of the city, and also the English and American clergymen of Geneva, were present. Speeches complimentary to General Grant were made by M. Carteret, President of Geneva, and by several of the principal clergymen. General Grant said, in replying to the toast given to America, that the greatest honor he had received since landing in Europe was to be among Americans, and in a republic, and in a city where so great a service had been rendered to the Americans by a Swiss citizen in the settlement of a question which might have produced war, but which left no rancor on either side. On the 30th, the General left Geneva for the North Italian lakes, thence to Ragatz, where he spent several days for rest and recuperation with his brother-in-law, M. J. Cramer, American Minister to Denmark.

On the 5th of August, General Grant went to Pallanza, on Lake Maggiore; thence to Lake Como, stopping at Bellagio; thence to Varese. At each of these points he was received with great enthusiasm, his stay being one grand round of festivities, each city seeming to vie with the other in the hospitalities offered. At Lake Maggiore, addresses were made by the Mayor and an officer who served under General Garibaldi. General Grant, in his reply, referred to the exceeding hospitality he had received, praised the general conduct of the people so far as he had seen them, expressed his delight at the grand and lovely scenes that had met his eye at every turn since he had crossed the Alps, and concluded by saying, "There is one Italian whose hand I wish especially to shake, and that man is General Garibaldi." This allusion was greeted with a perfect storm of applause.

On the 18th, the General visited Copenhagen, where he was received with distinguished honors, and at Antwerp a like cordial reception was given.

On the 25th, he returned to England, having made a hurried and fatiguing continental tour, where he rested, previous to accepting the urgent and flattering invitation to visit Scotland.

The fact that General Grant is named Ulysses, and that, in making "the grand tour," has suggested a classic comparison to the good-natured jokers of the obvious. It seems, too, as though the General had determined to keep up the character of the wandering king of Ithaca; for the heavy English journals, after slowly lifting their eyebrows to the point of astonishment that Ulysses the Silent could speak at all, have found the word "wise" to apply to what he did utter. Indeed, one of them believed that the term silent was ironical, and as proof quoted from "his remarkable speech" that sentence about fighting it out on a certain line if it took all summer. Perhaps if we use a society phrase, and say that General Grant has been "happy" in his recent after-dinner utterances, we shall come nearer the mark. When there are certain unpleasant topics that might be touched on, it is "happy" to avoid them at such times; and when the speaker who ignores them plunges into platitudes about "common blood and kindred peoples," he may be called felicitous when he is only politely adroit. In England, for instance, the General kept clear of blockade runners and Confederate scrip, and, when the Alabama was forced before him, only touched on that piratical craft as a sort of blessing in disguise to both peoples. On the other hand, he was overwhelmingly unctuous in calling the English our blood relations, making the glasses dance on the festive board with the thunderous applause he evoked from noble lords and lofty commoners.

In Frankfort, however, he had a chance to say a "happy" thing, and he said it. In Frankfort they bought our bonds, when it was vital to the nation that our securities should find purchasers. To be sure, they made a good thing of it, for they bought them cheap; but England and poor generals had cheapened them. Hence it was a "happy" thing for the soldier who brought our "boys" and our bonds "out of the wilderness"—the former to Richmond, and the latter to par and beyond—to tell the Frankforters how well they had stood by the Union in its darkest days. There was much good German blood spilled in the cause of the Union, so that his hearers were aware that the General referred to heart-strings as well as purse-strings in his compliment to them. So, also, at Geneva, his compliment to the representative whose "casting vote" turned the scales in the Geneva award was not forgotten; in fact, the General seemed to be in a "happy" vein, complimenting without stint. This change, or rather drawing out of General Grant's thoughts, will surprise none more than his intimate friends, who have known him only by works, not words.

CHAPTER VI.

RETURN TO GREAT BRITAIN.

The freedom of the city of Edinburgh was presented to General Grant on the 31st of August. He left London in a Pullman car. On the way from London — four hundred miles — the scenery was exceedingly attractive. All through England and in the south of Scotland, the country is a perfect garden, and only when you get among the chilly hills, valleys and crags of northern Scotland, do you feel that you are getting into the open country. What a pity that there are no forests to cover these beautiful and historic mountains, where in centuries gone by the horns of the leaders summoned the clans to bloody work!

The reception given to General Grant as each station was reached, was whole-souled and fully meant hospitality. At Carlisle—the dinner stopping-place—at Galashiels, Melrose, Harwick, and a number of smaller towns in Scotland, there were expressions of joy and enthusiasm that reminded one of the railroad receptions that General Grant gets at the towns of Illinois and Ohio. It seemed as though they knew him perfectly well — his face, his history, etc. — for they recognized him everywhere, and demanded as much handshaking as could be done in the limited time the train was to stay. Then the cheers and hurrahs always sounded in the distance above the whistle of the locomotive. Mrs. Grant was quite cheerful and talkative. She looked very much better than when she left Washington, though she said she was always in good health there. Washington has a slightly malarial atmosphere, and the complexion of a Washingtonian changes for the better after a trip to Europe. She enjoyed her European trip. She said her lines of association there had always fallen in pleasant places, and that she had been greatly pleased with every acquaintance she made in Europe. Mrs. Grant is a quiet, rather reserved lady, but one who impresses her associates by her kind nature, her broad views upon the subject under discussion, be it commonplace or important, and her sensible ideas of life. She sprang from one of the best families of the Mississippi Valley, well known and highly respected since a hundred years and more ago, and her early training was not lost. All the ladies who met her and became her acquaintances at the White House, loved her, from first to last.

The freedom of the city of Edinburgh was presented to ex-President Grant by Lord Provost Sir James Falshaw, in Free Assembly Hall, two thousand persons being present. In reply to the Lord Provost's speech, General Grant said:

"I am so filled with emotion that I scarcely know how to thank you for the honor conferred upon me by making me a burgess of this ancient city of Edinburgh. I feel that it is a great compliment to me and to my country. Had I the proper eloquence, I might dwell somewhat on the history of the great men you have produced, on the numerous citizens of this city and of Scotland who have gone to America, and the record they have made. We are proud of Scotchmen as citizens of America. They make good citizens of our country, and they find it profitable to themselves. I again thank you for the honor conferred upon me."

On September 1st, General Grant and party visited Tay Bridge. One of the most striking features of the view obtained from the deck of the little steamer is that of the bridge itself, which, as seen from some little distance, combines massiveness with airiness of structure, impressing one even more than the almost fairy-like span of the Menai tubular bridge, or the larger and equally reputed, though perhaps less elegant, viaduct across the Hollandsche Diep.

A few minutes' sailing brought the party to Wormi Pier, on the south side of the river, and immediately under the first span of Mr. Bouch's grand structure. At this place Admiral Maitland Dougal, Mr. Matthew McDougal, United States Consul at Dundee, and ex-Provost Ewan, Dundee, were in waiting to do honor to the General, not to speak of a numerous concourse of the public, comprising seemingly most of the workmen connected with the bridge, as well as many persons from the neighboring villages. After landing General Grant, Mrs. Grant and some others were conducted to one of the rooms in the contractor's offices, where Mr. Grothe, the resident engineer, explained, with the aid of models and diagrams, the manner in which the large piers of the bridge were constructed, mentioning first that the bridge was designed on what is known as the lattice girder principle, and then stating that the piers were built on shore, floated out between two barges to the desired position in the river, sunk to a suitable foundation, and then brought up to high water mark. By means of another working model, the manner in which the girders were transported from the shore was illustrated, it being shown that the tide was the motive power by which masses of iron work weighing as much as two hundred tons were moved. The method by which these girders were raised from the river to the required height of eighty-eight feet above high water mark, through the agency of hydraulic apparatus, was also explained.

Describing the work generally, Mr. Grothe said there were in all eighty-five spans, thirteen of which, over the navigable part of the river, were each two hundred and forty-five feet in length, and carried nearly two hundred tons weight, while the smaller ones on either side of the channel were from sixty-seven to one hundred and forty-five feet long. It was further stated that considerable progress had been made with the works during the present season, and especially during the last month, nine spans of an aggregate weight of more than nine hundred tons having been lifted and fixed in their places within the latter period — a feat which has been accomplished by almost incessant work. In concluding his remarks, Mr. Grothe stated that in the winter the shortness of the day had of course been found very much against the progress of the work, and that to get over this difficulty there were used powerful electric lights, the currents for which were generated by magneto-electric machines driven by a four-horse-power engine. It was added that the bridge was nearly completed, all the spans up forming a continuous line, and the fixing of timber and laying of rails on the top at present actively carried on.

On the 7th September, General Grant was presented with the freedom of the city of Wick, and, in accepting, said: "During the eight years of my Presidency it was my only hope, which I am glad to say was realized, that all differences between the two nations should be healed in a manner honorable to both. In my desire for that result it was my aim to do what was right, irrespective of any other consideration whatever. During all the negotiations, I felt the importance of maintaining friendly relations between the great English speaking peoples, which I believe to be essential to the maintenance of peace and principle throughout the world."

On the 8th, at Inverness, General Grant was presented with the freedom of the city, and a great reception given him.

Ex-President Grant received the freedom of the city of

Glasgow on the 13th. Replying to the address of the Lord Provost, he said that he would ever remember the day, and when back in America would refer with pride to his visit to Glasgow. He was so much a citizen of Scotland that it would be a serious question where he would vote. He thanked the Lord Provost for his kind words and the audience for its welcome. The parchment was contained in a gold casket. The ceremony was witnessed by a large crowd, and the General was enthusiastically cheered. A banquet in his honor was given in the evening, but was of a private character.

The reception of General Grant in Scotland was hearty and continuously enthusiastic. There was not a day since the General came to Scotland that he was not overwhelmed with kindnesses.

The enthusiasm of the Scotch people and the great attention shown to General Grant have a double significance. The people of Scotland sympathized with the North during the civil war, and always rejoiced when Grant or his generals won a victory. They have been curious to see the great man they have talked so much about, and take great pride in the fact that he is of Scotch descent. Hence the magnificent ovations at Edinburgh, Dundee, Melrose, Ayr, Glasgow, the Trossachs, and all the places at which he stopped.

The finest and most enthusiastic reception was given at Glasgow. An immense hall, accommodating several thousand persons, was, all but places for four hundred specially invited guests, thrown open to the public. The cheering was so general and continuous that the ceremonies could only with difficulty be heard. At night the grand banquet at corporation hall was a splendid affair, embracing in the *menu* the viands and wines that make the best dinner Scotland could furnish. Even tropical delicacies were in profusion, and the wines were exceptionally fine and in great variety. Several toasts were given, and speeches followed up to eleven o'clock.

At this banquet the Lord Provost announced that there were no reporters present, and the editors there were expected to let the speeches pass without comment, in order that everybody could feel perfectly free in speaking. General Grant, on this account, probably, made the longest speech of his life, and the Lord Provost was finally, at the end of the feast, persuaded to yield his position against newspaper enterprise.

The speech of General Grant was brought about by a speech of Mr. Anderson, M. P., of Glasgow, wherein he charged, turning to General Grant, that the United States had gained a victory over Great Britain in the creation of the Geneva arbitration. However, he said, Great Britain had agreed to the Washington treaty, and while disappointed with the result at Geneva, had stood manfully by it. In view of this, and the fact that the United States had completed the distribution of the award, and had some $8,000,000 left after all claims had been satisfied, he would be pleased to see the government return that amount in the interests of concord and thorough amity. This was said in a half earnest, half joking way, but was met with "hear, hear," all along the tables.

General Grant in reply said that he had a great deal to do with the negotiations concerning the Washington treaty, and that he had always felt that our government had yielded too much to Great Britain in the matter. He was determined, however, from the first, that, if possible, the experiment of peaceful arbitration should prevail. It was his ambition to live to see all national disputes settled in this way. "I am called a man of war," said he, "but I never was a man of war. Though I entered the army at an early age, I got out of it whenever I found a chance to do so creditably. I was always a man of peace, and I shall always continue of that mind. Though I may not live to see the general settlement of national disputes by arbitration, it will not be very many years before that system of settlement will be adopted, and the immense standing armies that are depressing Europe by their great expense will be disbanded, and the arts of war almost forgotten in the general devotion of the people to the development of peaceful industries. I want to see, and I believe I will, Great Britain, the United States and Canada joined with common purpose in the advance of civilization, an invincible community of English-speaking nations that all the world beside could not conquer." The General went on in this vein for some time, and finally again touched the Alabama-claims question. He said: "There was one point in connection with that matter that I was glad we yielded — that was the indirect damage claim. I was always opposed to it, because I feared the future consequences of such a demand. In any future arbitration we would have been placed at a great disadvantage by its allowance. After that was settled we made our other demands, you made yours. It was a long time before the Joint High Commission came together, but each side yielded here a bit and there a bit, until about as good a treaty as we could expect to get was completed. Mr. Anderson says many of the people of Great Britain believe we got the best of the bargain. I can assure you that we did not come out of the discussion as much benefited as we should have been. Many of our people were quite incensed, and fought the confirmation of the treaty, claiming that its terms were not broad enough to cover the losses of local interests, but a very large majority determined to stand by it in the interests of peace and manly dealing with friends. We yielded more than we intended to yield, but had gone so far into the business of doing what we advocated that nine-tenths of our people had no desire to recede. We did not want war, or even a new arbitration. We had been satisfied with the former, and the latter meant delay. We wanted the question settled peacefully, at once and forever. As to the $8,000,000 surplus Mr. Anderson mentions, I will explain that briefly. After the $15,500,000 awarded at Geneva was paid by Great Britain, the matter of its distribution was presented to Congress. It became necessary to distribute it under the terms of the treaty, and it was found that if the insurance companies which had received war premiums were admitted to participation in the sum, it would not be large enough to go around. So they and other parties were excluded. Congress will legislate further in the matter, and the money will be distributed to rightful claimants, so that it will not be necessary to discuss the question of returning it to Great Britain." The General explained the workings of the system of distributing the money, details of fact that are familiar to all Americans. We cannot reproduce his speech in full, because lead pencils and note books were prohibited. But the above, with expressive remarks touching his magnificent receptions in Scotland, and the renewed expressions of good feeling between Great Britain and the United States, is his speech in carefully prepared substance. At the end of it, the entire party, of perhaps two hundred persons, applauded to the echo, and in this applause Mr. Anderson was one of the most ardent participants.

General Grant's visit to Newcastle-on-Tyne, on the 21st, was the occasion of a most enthusiastic and remarkable demonstration. During the day the visitors visited the Exchange and other places of interest in Newcastle. There were numerous banners along the route, and large crowds of spectators. In the Exchange, General Grant received an address from the Chamber of Commerce, and, replying, thanked the large and enthusiastic audience for its kind reception, which was highly gratifying to him and the American people, who would accept it as a token of friendship between the two nations — he could not say two peoples, for they were really one, having a common destiny, which would be brilliant in proportion to their friendship. He referred to the honorable settlement of all differences between England and America, and said they ought not only keep peace with each other, but with all the world, and by their example stop the wars which are now devastating Europe. The speech was loudly cheered. General Grant and the corporation then proceeded down the Tyne in a steamer, which was saluted with guns from almost every factory on the banks, every available spot on which was crowded with people. General Grant stood on the bridge of the steamer during the greater part of the voyage, bowing in response to repeated cheers. The steamer stopped at Jarrow and Tynemouth, at both of which places the municipal authorities presented most cordial addresses. The ceremony was witnessed by large and enthusiastic crowds. General Grant made suitable replies, of similar tenor to his Newcastle speech. At Tynemouth he said he had that day seen one hundred and fifty thousand people leave their homes and occupations to manifest friendship to America. The ex-President held a reception at Newcastle in the evening.

A great demonstration of the workmen of Northumberland and Durham was held on the town moor of Newcastle in honor of General Grant. Twenty-two trade societies participated in a procession, which occupied twenty minutes in passing a given point. The number of persons present on the moor was estimated at from forty to fifty thousand. The demonstration had no precedent since the great political meetings at the time of the Reform Agitation. Mr. Thomas Burt, member of Parliament for Morpeth, presented an eulogistic address to General Grant, who said he thanked the workingmen for their very welcome address, and thought this reception was the most honorable he could meet with. Alluding to what Mr. Burt had said concerning the late civil war, General Grant declared he had always been an advocate of peace, but when war was declared he went to the war for the cause which he believed to be right, and fought to the best of his ability to secure peace and safety to the nation. In regard to the relations between America and England, the General said that friendship now existed between the two countries, which he fully believed was increasing, and which would, in common with industry and civilization, increase in the future.

On the same day the Mayor and Town Council of Gateshead presented the ex-President with a congratulatory address. General Grant expressed pleasure at his enthusiastic reception in all the towns in the North of England, and said he was glad the good feeling between England and America was warmer to-day than it had ever been. A banquet was given in honor of General Grant in the evening, by the Mayor of Newcastle. In response to a toast to his health, the General said his reception in Newcastle exceeded anything he had expected, and had been the warmest and best he had had or could have had.

General Grant was met at Sunderland railway station by the Mayor and Messrs. Gourley and Burt, members of Parliament. The day was observed as almost a general holiday. Nearly ten thousand members of trade and friendly societies marched in procession. General Grant was present at the laying of the foundation stone of the library and museum. Replying to an address of the friendly and trade societies, General Grant said he would simply renew what he had said relative to the way in which labor was regarded in the United States, and the way in which he personally regarded it.

At Leamington, Warwick, a grand reception was given General Grant, and participated in by the Mayor and leading citizens.

On arriving at Sheffield, on the 26th, General Grant was received at the railway station by the Mayor and corporation. A procession then formed to the Cutlers' Hall, where congratulatory addresses were presented by the Corporated Cutlers' Company and the Chamber of Commerce, to which General Grant briefly replied, referred to the American tariff, and reminded his hearers that the United States had to raise money to pay off the great debt incurred by the war. The revenue from imports was regarded solely as the means of attaining that end. If the United States were to abolish the revenue from imports, foreign bondholders would very soon cry out when their interest was not forthcoming. He added: "We get along well enough with the payment of our debt, and will compete with you in your manufactures in the markets of the world. The more of your merchants and mechanics that go to America, the better. Nothing pleases us more than the immigration of the industry and intelligence of this community. We have room for all, and will try to treat you as you have treated me to-day." The General was loudly cheered.

The following evening a grand banquet was given in his honor by the Mayor and corporation of Sheffield. The proceedings were most enthusiastic and cordial.

General Grant arrived at Stratford-on-Avon on the 28th, and met with a brilliant reception. His visit was made the occasion of a festival, in which the whole town took part. The houses were decorated with flags, among which the American colors were conspicuous. The stars and stripes were displayed from the Town Hall and the Mayor's residence. The Mayor and members of the corporation received the General and Mrs. Grant, who were accompanied by General Badeau, at the railway station, and escorted them to Shakespeare's birthplace. Thence the party proceeded to the Museum, the church, Anne Hathaway's cottage, and other places of interest.

The distinguished visitors were subsequently entertained at a public lunch in the Town Hall. A toast to the health of General Grant was proposed and drank with cheers, and he was presented with a very cordial address, enclosed in a casket made from the wood of the mulberry tree planted by Shakespeare. The General, replying to the toast, spoke most heartily of the welcome given him. He declared it would have been impossible for him to leave England without visiting the birthplace and home of Shakespeare. He pointed to the numerous American Shakespearian societies as proof of the honor paid the poet in the United States.

General Grant and wife spent several days visiting their daughter, Mrs. Sartoris, at Southampton.

On the 6th October, the corporation of the city received him, presenting a complimentary address. At Torquay, Mr. Alfred D. Jessup, of Philadelphia, gave a brilliant reception, the leading residents and noblemen of Torquay and vicinity being present.

On the 16th, General Grant and party visited Birmingham. On their arrival, they were received by the Mayor, and driven to the Town Hall, where the Town Council, a deputation of workingmen, and the Peace Society, presented the General with addresses, which he briefly acknowledged. He was the guest of Mr. Chamberlain, M. P. The following evening General Grant was entertained at a banquet, the Mayor presiding. After the health of the Queen was drank, the Mayor proposed that of the **President of the United States, as a potentate all should honor. This was received with due honor by the company.**

Mr. Chamberlain, M. P., then proposed the health of ex-President Grant in a happy speech, complimentary to the distinguished guest and his countrymen.

General Grant, in response, referring to the last speaker's allusion to the prompt disbandment of the army after the civil war, said: "We Americans claim so much personal independence and general intelligence that I do not believe it possible for one man to assume any more authority than the constitution and laws give him." As to the remarks that had been made as to the benefits which would accrue to America by the establishment of free trade, the General said he had a kind of recollection that England herself had a protective tariff until her manufactures were established. American manufactures were rapidly progressing, and America was thus becoming a great free trade nation. [Laughter.] The General then warmly thanked the company for the reception they had given him.

General Grant found the labor of accepting the hospitality of his English friends more arduous than the cares of State. It had, in fact, become so great a tax upon his health that from the first of October he had determined to retire to private life, and that the first thing he would do would be to avail himself of the courtesy extended by the Secretary of the Navy, to visit the Mediterranean in one of the vessels of the European squadron, and spend some time in the waters of Italy.

CHAPTER VII.

GRANT IN PARIS.

Ex-President Grant, accompanied by his wife and son, left London for Paris on the morning of October 24, 1877. On the arrival of the General and party at the railway station in Charing Cross, to take the train for Folkestone, he was greeted by a large crowd of Americans and Englishmen, who gave him a hearty cheer as he stepped out of his carriage. A special train was in waiting to convey the distinguished party. The large space in front of the hotel and station, extending through to Trafalgar square, was filled with vehicles and pedestrians. After considerable hand-shaking in the waiting-room, and lively greetings on the platform, Sir Edward Watkin, the chairman of the Southeastern Railway Company, being in attendance, he and his guests boarded the train, which moved off precisely at ten o'clock. After a pleasant run of about two hours the train arrived at Folkestone, where General Grant was met at the wharf by the Mayor and members of the Common Council; and fully two thousand of the inhabitants of this old Kentish town welcomed the ex-President with loud cheers. The General at once went on board the special yacht Victoria, accompanied by the Herald correspondent, Sergeant Gazelee, and one or two other officials, these being the only guests. As the trim-looking yacht, with the American flag flying at its fore, left the chalk cliffs of old England, the General stood upon the bridge and waved his hat, responsive to the cheers and adieus from the shore.

The sea was calm, with only a gentle swell, and a fine summer yachting breeze prevailed. The General paced the deck, enjoying his cigar and studying the interesting points and scenery along the majestic cliffs on the southeastern coast, where William the Conquerer landed and fought the battle of Hastings. On nearing the French coast he beheld the sunny hills and shores of the memorable site of Napoleon's Boulogne camp, where the Austerlitz army so long prepared for the invasion of England.

The Victoria arrived at the Boulogne wharf at a quarter to two o'clock. A large crowd of Frenchmen, who had been advised of the arrival of the *grand guerrier Americain*, was in attendance, and received the guests with a hearty greeting. On entering the special train, the sub-Prefect of the Department met and was introduced to the General. In the name of the Marshal-President and of the French people, he welcomed him to the shores of France.

The General expressed his warm acknowledgments, saying he had long cherished the wish to visit France, and he was delighted with the present opportunity. M. Hoguet-Grandsire, the Senator representing the Department of the Pas de Calais, also bade him welcome in a brief address, full of sympathy and kindly feeling.

After a long delay, somewhat in contrast to the promptness of the English railroads, the train started for Paris. On the way the General studied closely the scenery of the lovely country along the route, noted the principal industrial sections, and especially observed the wonderful agricultural resources of the country.

General Grant spoke a great deal about his reception in England; that it had been unvarying in warmth, and, as to the hospitality of the people there, nothing could be more kind, considerate and gracious. Everywhere he had experienced, both in official and private circles, courtesy and respect. At Amiens General Grant quietly partook of a dish of *cousomme*.

As the train neared Paris the moon rose, and the General curiously studied the prominent features of the great French capital. They reached the station at a quarter to eight o'clock. Generals Noyes and Torbert entered the car, accompanied by the Marquis d'Abzac, first Aide-de-Camp of the Marshal-President, the official whose duty it was to introduce ambassadors.

In the name of the President of the French Republic, the Aide-de-Camp tendered General Grant a cordial welcome. In reply, the General thanked the Marshal, saying he anticipated great pleasure and interest from his visit to France. Generals Noyes and Torbert greeted him warmly. The party had borne the journey splendidly, none of them showing the least fatigue.

Among the Americans awaiting the arrival of General Grant at the station, in the company of the Minister, were General Meredith Read, from Greece; ex-Minister Partridge, Admiral Worden, the bankers Seligman, Winthrop and Munroe; Dr. Johnson, Dr. Warren, and the representatives of the leading New York journals.

A richly carpeted *salon* was prepared at the station for the reception of the distinguished party. The ladies of the party, conducted by General Torbert, passed through this salon on their way to the carriages. A splendid bouquet was presented to Mrs. Grant by a French journalist on the way. General Grant followed, leaning on the arm of Minister Noyes. As soon as he appeared in the crowded *salon*, several rounds of hearty cheers were given, and a number of people were presented to him.

The party then entered carriages, in company with General Noyes and the Marshal's Aide-de-Camp and introducer of ambassadors. They drove to the Hotel Bristol, where a handsome suite of rooms had been engaged for them. After a quiet dinner, General Grant smoked a cigar and retired early.

The following morning opened dismally. Rain fell in torrents, and there seemed no prospect of its cessation. During the morning General Grant called upon his bankers, Messrs. Drexel, Harjes & Co. Upon his return, a multitude of visitors, including diplomatists, ambassadors and Americans, began to arrive, and continued to come until noon. The most eminent men of France were among the callers. At two o'clock, General Grant, wife and son, with Minister Noyes, drove to the Elysee, through a pouring rain. President MacMahon, the Duchess of Magenta, and the Duke Decazes, received the General most cordially. The Duchess did everything in her power to render the occasion agreeable.

General Grant wore plain evening dress, calling upon the official head of the French people simply as any American citizen, properly introduced, might.

President MacMahon said that he was truly glad to welcome so eminent a soldier and citizen to France.

In brief, the ex-President of the United States replied that the opportunity of expressing to the chief magistrate of France the friendly sentiments entertained throughout the length and breadth of America toward the French people was equally pleasing to him.

The interview was entirely informal and exceedingly cordial. President MacMahon extended and General Grant accepted an invitation to dine at the Elysee on the Thursday following.

At four o'clock the committee of resident Americans called to invite General Grant and family to a grand banquet to be given in his honor by the American residents of Paris, upon any date the General might see fit to appoint. General Grant named November 6, thanking the committee for the honor conferred upon him by his own countrymen in a foreign land. Much agreeable conversation followed.

In the evening General Grant, accompanied by a personal friend, took a long walk around the Tuilleries, Palais Royal, Place de la Concord and the Boulevards, for two hours, seeing Paris by gaslight.

This unanimity of the American residents in Paris, in assisting to make his stay a pleasant one, was one of the most pleasing incidents of the General's tour, and the courteous reception accorded by President MacMahon was not so much formality as it was an expression of the kindly feelings that exist between the French nation and our own, and will be regarded as an evidence that the century-old ties that bind the two nations together are not weakened by time or any alterations of the political conditions that have arisen, or are likely to arise, in either country.

On the 27th, General Grant visited the *Herald* Bureau, remaining an hour or more. He then went to the studio of Mr. Healy, the American artist, and gave a sitting for a portrait; afterwards strolled about Montmartre and climbed the hill, which affords a fine view of Paris. In the evening he was honored by visits from several distinguished people, including the Comte de Paris, head of the Orleans family, and the Duchess of Magenta, wife of the Marshal-President.

If being much *feted* brings much pleasure, General Grant must have been in a happy frame of mind. After the stately round of London festivities, which were led off by the magnificent reception at Minister Pierrepont's; after becoming a citizen of some twenty-five Scotch burghs; after going through Belgium, and dining with kings and such; after the return to England, which led to the eating of dinners with some twenty-five fine old English corporations, the imperturbable ex-President took his way to

Paris. He who would fight anything out on a certain line, if it took him all the four seasons, is not the man you can frighten with a string of long dinners. He has the confidence in himself that says, I can eat my way through all the marshals and marquises, from Finistere to the Alps. His Scotch campaign, no less than his English, proved what broadsides of hospitality he can safely withstand.

On the 29th, Minister Noyes gave a grand banquet and reception to General Grant. The banquet was a superb effort of culinary skill, which can work such gastronomic wonders when given *carte blanche* and where there is a cellar of monte christo to draw upon. President MacMahon had been invited, but declined on the ground of having recently refused to be present at several diplomatic dinners. He promised to be present at the reception in the evening. Twenty-two guests were present at the table: General and Mrs. Grant; Minister and Mrs. Noyes; Mme. Berthaut; M. Caillaux, Minister of Finance; M. Brunet, Minister of Public Instruction; M. Voisin, Prefect of Police; General Berthaut, Minister of War; M. Paris, Minister of Public Works; General Marquis d' Abzac, Aid-de-Camp to the President; Duc de Broglie, President of the Council, Keeper of the Seals, Minister of Justice; Miss Lincoln; Jesse R. Grant; M. Duval, Prefect of the Seine; M. De Fourtou, Minister of the Interior; Viscounte de Meaux, Minister of Commerce; Miss Stevens; Duchess Decazes; M. Mollard, Introducer of Ambassadors; Lieutenant de la Panouse, Staff Officer of the Marshal; and M. Vignaux, Assistant Secretary of Legation. The following was the *menu*:

MENU.
POTAGES.
Tortue a l'Anglaise.
Consomme a la Sevigne.
HORS D'ŒUVRES.
Bouchees Agnes Sorel.
RELEVE.
Turbot, sauce creme, et crevettes.

PUNCH.
Rose.
ROTIS.
Faisans truffes.
Cailles sur croustades.
ENTREMETS.
Pate de foie gras de Strasbourg.
Salade Parisienne.
Crepes a la Bordelaise.
Timbales d'ananas, Pompadour.
Gateaux noisettes.
DESSERT.
VINS.
Vieux Madere.
Chateau d'Yquem, creme 1864.
Chateau Lafitte, 1864.
Chateau Margaux, 1869.
Johannisberg, Metternich's, 1857.
Clos Vougeot, 1858.
Romanee Conti, 1865.
Champagne Dry Monopole, 1870.
Amontillado.
Vieux Port, vintage 1858.
Cognac, 1844.

Kirschwasser.   Anisette.   **Chartreuse.**
Curacoa.

The banquet passed off without any special incident worthy of note, that charming flow of polite and witty, or, at least, pleasantly pointed conversation which characterizes French dinners, kept time to the melody of the repast itself. There was no English reserve to thaw — the French and the American *entendent* without difficulty, and hence they make the best of neighbors around the snowy damask.

At about nine o'clock the general reception began. A heavy rain had been falling all the afternoon and evening. It, of course, had no deterrent effect on the invited. It was not long before the *salons* were filled with guests. The guests were received by General Grant, Mrs. Grant and their son, General and Mrs. Noyes, Consul-General Torbert, and Secretary Vignaux making the introductions. Mrs. Grant was dressed in a costume of heavy white satin, Mrs. Noyes appeared in a similar dress, General Grant and Minister Noyes wore plain evening dress, and General Torbert appearing in the full uniform of a major-general.

The rooms, as the guests arrived, became perfect gardens of lovely colors. Brilliant uniforms, diplomatic orders and decorations, mingling with the sheen of silks and satins, made up a wonderful picture. Marshal MacMahon arrived early. He wore a plain evening dress, with the ribbon of the Legion, and a breast covered with orders. The Marshal stood for nearly an hour beside General Grant, joining in the conversation and receiving congratulations. As the two renowned soldiers stood side by side, one could not help contrasting them. Marshal MacMahon's ruddy, honest, Celtic face, white moustache and white hair, recalled the poet's figure of "a rose in snow"; Grant, calm, massive and reserved, wore the same imperturbable face so well known at home. MacMahon seemed all nerve and restlessness; Grant looked all patience and repose. The contrast in person was indeed remarkable. Although each had come to the Presidency of a powerful republic over the same red road, the passion of arms commanding two great nations had led each to choose its foremost soldier as executive head. One had laid down his power at the feet of the people who conferred it. The other, a few months later, after a long and severe struggle with the hot and ungovernable radicals, was forced to give way to one more in sympathy with the dominant party. Meantime two great warlike careers touched in friendship in the parlors of Minister Noyes.

The reception drew together the largest assembly of the American colony known in years, and they compared favorably with the many European nations represented there.

The refreshment tables were exquisitely arranged and well patronized, which is just how such a host as General Noyes would desire to have his sumptuous hospitality appreciated.

On the 31st, General Grant visited the Palais d'Industrie, and the works where the statue of "Liberty" for New York harbor is being constructed. The sculptor, M. Bartholdi, presented him with a miniature model of the statue. In the evening the General attended the opera, where he was enthusiastically received by the audience, and treated with great ceremony by the officials.

On November 1, Marshal MacMahon gave a dinner at the Elysee, in honor of General Grant. Cabinet and Marshal's military household and prominent French and American residents were present. The banquet was a very brilliant and animated affair. After dinner, General Grant and President MacMahon had a long conversation in the smoking-room. The Marshal invited General Grant to breakfast with him, as a friend, and also to witness some of the sittings of the Senate and Chamber of Deputies, which the General accepted, and was much pleased with his cordial reception.

If Paris is the place where good Americans go after death, it is, all the same, a good place for great Americans to go during life. The magnificent banquet tendered November 6, in the gay capital, to General Grant, by the resident Americans, is a proof of the latter. The three hundred and fifty Americans who greeted our great soldier so handsomely, one and all, thought so. As for the General, himself, he has had so many courtesies from occasional kings and nobles, that he must have felt a thrill of pleasure pass through him, as he found himself face to face with a company in which every man was a sovereign. As for the ladies, God bless them! they are queens everywhere. Among those beside the General at the banquet, were men who carried the names, dear to all patriotic Americans, of Rochambeau and Lafayette. Thus did old France look kindly through the eyes of her descendants upon the children of the Republic of the West, which her blood and treasure did so much to found.

The banqeting hall was splendidly decorated and illuminated. The Franco-American Union contributed a portrait of General Grant, which, adorned with flags, was hung over the principal table. A band stationed in the gallery played at intervals, and vocal music was given by a chorus furnished by the director of the Italian opera.

General Grant, Minister Noyes and General Torbert were in full military uniform.

Mr. Noyes, as chairman, proposed the following toasts:—

"The President of the United States," which was responded to by music only.

"The President of the French Republic," to which a similar response was made.

These were followed by the toast of the evening, "Our Guest, General Grant," which was proposed by the Chairman in the following speech:—

"LADIES AND GENTLEMEN: It has generally happened, according to the world's history, that when a great public crisis has occurred, such as a revolution for independence or a struggle for national existence, some man has been found specially fitted for and equal to the emergency. He appears suddenly from unexpected quarters, and is not always selected from the arena of politics or from among the most prominent of his countrymen. He assumes at the proper time leadership and control, simply because he was born for it and seems to have waited for the opportunity and the necessity.

"When the war of secession was inaugurated in America, in 1861, a quiet and silent man, who had received a military education, was pursuing an avocation in civil life in a small town in Illinois. As soon as the first hostile guns opened upon Fort Sumter, he offered his services to his country and was appointed colonel of a regiment of volunteers. It was then believed that the war would be of short duration and limited in extent, but the North had underrated the spirit and perhaps the courage and endurance of the rebellious section. Early reverses and doubtful contests that were either defeats or drawn battles soon made it apparent that all the energies and resources of the government would be taxed to the uttermost. The theater of war rapidly extended until it stretched westward a thousand miles from the sea, across great rivers and mountain ranges. Immense armies were assembled in the South, composed of brave and chivalric soldiers and commanded by able and accomplished leaders. There were serious political troubles and divided sympathies among the people of the North, but both sides nerved themselves for the bloody and terrible struggle, which lasted four years and resulted in the success of the national forces.

"Meantime our Illinois Colonel had risen in rank until there was no grade sufficient for his recognition and reward, and two new ones were successively created. This silent man had shaken the continent with the thunder of his artillery and the tramp of his victorious columns. At the close of the war he was general-in-chief, commanding all the armies of the Republic, which carried upon their muster rolls 1,100,000 men. The Union was preserved, and its flag everywhere respected. After the close of the war he was twice called by a grateful nation to the highest office in the gift of forty-five million people.

"He administered the government with moderation, generosity, wisdom and success. The civil power was confronted by many complicated and difficult questions. He solved them with rare patriotism and intelligence, and his place in history as a civil magistrate will be among the foremost. After sixteen years of such labor as few men could endure, after such success in war and peace as few men ever attain, he seeks recreation in many lands, and an opportunity to compare the institutions of his own country with the civilization and forms of government of the Old World. It is our happy privilege to-night to welcome the great soldier and statesman to this, the Queen City of the world, and to wish for him and his family health and happiness. Without detaining you longer, I propose the health of the distinguished guest of the evening, General Grant, ex-President of the United States."

The delivery of General Noyes' speech was frequently interrupted by enthusiastic applause.

General Grant, on rising to reply, was received with prolonged cheering. He said:

"LADIES AND GENTLEMEN: After your flattering reception, and the compliments of Governor Noyes, I am embarrassed to thank you as I should wish. During the five and a half months I have been in Europe, my reception has been very gratifying, not only to me, but also, above all, to my country and countrymen, who were honored by it. I thank the American colony of Paris. I hope its members will enjoy their visit here as I am doing and hope to do for some weeks yet. I hope when you return home you will find you realized the benefits predicted by our Minister."

Loud and enthusiastic applause followed the General's speech.

M. de Lafayette replied to the toast of "France." He said France duly appreciated the great leader and great citizen who honored her by his visit. M. de Lafayette remarked that General Grant quitted power solely to bow before the laws of his country. He thanked him for visiting France, because he was a great example for her, and because France gained from close inspection. In conclusion, he alluded to the Revolutionary war, and expressed an ardent wish that the French and American republics should never be separated, but form an indissoluble union for the welfare, liberty and independence of peoples.

The Marquis of Rochambeau also spoke in eulogy of General Grant.

The toast, " The Army and Navy," was responded to by the singing of the " Star Spangled Banner " by the Italian chorus.

Mr. Noyes finally proposed " The Ladies," and General Torbert offered " The Health of the United States Minister." Mr. Noyes replied briefly, and the company then adjourned to the drawing-room.

After nearly a month's stay in Paris, having been dined and *feted* by nearly all the prominent and distinguished civilians and officials in this gay city, the great sensational event was the *fete*, consisting of a dinner and ball, given in honor of ex-President Grant by Mrs. Mackay, wife of " Bonanza " Mackay, on November 21, at her splendid mansion in the Rue Tilsit. The affair overshadowed in importance, as far as the American colony and fashionable society are concerned, anything that had preceded it in brilliant extravagance of display. Even the reporters were at a loss for hyperboles of descriptive style that could do justice to the pomp, splendor and sparkle of the occasion.

The house where the affair took place cost one million five hundred thousand francs, and the furniture five hundred thousand francs. It looks out upon the Place d'Etoile, and is a splendid residence. The garden was brilliantly illuminated and decorated with national flags, and with emblems set in thousands of gas jets. The orchestra, consisting of thirty-six musicians, was stationed on a pavilion built out from the house in front of the Rue Tilsit. A dozen footmen, in liveries of crimson and gold, lined the entrance and stairway.

The carriages occupied the causeway in front. The vestibule, staircase and passage-ways were profusely decorated with flags and beautiful flowers. The rooms were magnificent. Everything that money could supply and elegant taste select was there to add to the beauty and impressiveness of the scene.

There were covers for twenty-four, and the guests were General Grant and family, and the members of the American Legation and Consulate and their families. There were no unofficial Americans present at the dinner. The *menu* was inscribed on small silver *tablettes*, as in the case of the famous dinner to Senator Sharon at San Francisco.

After the dinner, a grand reception and ball took place, at which three hundred guests were present. Among the guests were the Marquis de Lafayette, MM. de Rochambeau and de Bois-Thierry, the Duc de Rivoli, the Duc and Duchesse de Bojano, the Duc and Mlle. Ribon de Trohen, Comtes de Beon, Serrurrier, de Montferrant, de Divonns and Excelmans, the Baronne Delort de Gleon, Barons Houbeyran and de Reinach, and Vicomtes de Villestrux and Marchand, the Duc Decazes, Senator Laboulaye, MM. Henri Martin and Leon Say, Mme. Guizot, Mr. and Mrs. Seligman and M. Cernuschi.

The American colony was largely represented, and the number of beautiful women was very remarkable. The ladies' costumes displayed extraordinary taste, elegance and richness. The dancing commenced early and continued till four o'clock in the morning.

During the latter part of November, General Grant was *feted* and dined by Mrs. General Sickles, at her residence in the Rue Presbourg, which was a brilliant affair; by the Marquis de Talleyrand-Perigord; by the Comte de Paris; Emile Girardin, editor of *La France;* M. Gambetta; Mr. Healy, the American artist; M. Laugel, a prominent Orleanist, and at the house of Mr. Harjes, the banker, was toasted for the last time in Paris. The gentlemen in the party were all Americans, and the affair was one of the most elegant which has taken place in Paris this season.

As a guest of many distinguished persons in the gay capital, and a man honored in all circles, he had enjoyed an uncommonly brilliant round of festivities, and had been the subject of wide and various criticism, and had stood the fire of festivities and criticism alike with that imperturbable tranquility which is an inseparable element of his identity.

CHAPTER VIII.

THROUGH FRANCE.—ITALY.

General Grant and party reached Lyons on the 2d of December, and were received by the Prefect, the President of the Municipal Council, American residents and several of the leading silk merchants of Lyons. After a tour of inspection of the quays and places of interest, he left for Marseilles on the 3d, where he was received with great enthusiasm. On the 15th we find him at Genoa, he having previously visited Villa Franca and Leghorn. After visiting the town of Genoa, the General gave a reception to the authorities on board the United States steamer Vandalia, Commander Robeson.

Reaching Naples, early on the evening of the 17th, on the following day, in company with Mrs. Grant and son, he made the ascent of Mount Vesuvius, but, the day being cold, the party did not reach the crater. Luncheon was served at the "House of Refuge," near the Observatory, and a pleasant hour spent in enjoying the remarkable view of Capri and Ischia. The plain is studded with twenty villages and lined with snow clad hills, and the snow looked beautifully clear and white in the gorgeous sunlight of an Italian sky. They returned in the evening to the Vandalia, after having spent a delightfully pleasant day.

On Wednesday the General and family, accompanied by Consul Duncan, Commander Robeson, Lieutenants Strong, Rush and Miller, and Engineer Baird, visited the ruins of

Pompeii. The government had made arrangements for a special excavation in honor of General Grant, so that he might see how the work was done, and see some of the curiosities recovered just as they were placed when the city was suddenly destroyed. The day was a little cold, but clear, and in every way favorable for the work. The director of the excavations received General Grant and party, and conducted them to the principal points of interest. Two hours were spent wandering among the ruins of this ancient and memorable city, and at every step something of interest was seen. The workingmen then proceeded to dig out the chamber of a buried house, and discovered some fragments of a table made of wood and bronze. The workmanship was very curious and elaborate, and was examined with great interest by the whole party. The next object of interest discovered was a loaf of bread, wrapped neatly in cloth and perfectly distinguishable. Many other curious and interesting articles were found and inspected by the party of visitors, and all expressed themselves as highly gratified with their visit to the ruins of the ancient city. They returned in the evening.

On Thursday ex-President Grant returned the official visits of the civil and military authorities of the city. As he left the Vandalia the yards were manned and a salute fired, the salute being returned by the Italian Admiral. General Grant then landed, and was met by the General commanding the district, who had a regiment of Bersaglieri drawn up in front of the Royal Palace, and reviewed by General Grant. Accompanied by the Italian officials, he then visited the naval and military schools and the palace, after which he attended a reception at the house of Consul Duncan.

During these visits General Grant was accompanied by his son, Commander Robeson, Lieutenants Rush and

Miller, and a splendid retinue of Italian officials. The whole tone of the reception accorded him was cordial and stately. The General expressed himself with the greatest admiration of the Italian troops.

Christmas we find General Grant and party on board the **Vandalia, at Palermo**. The General remained on board until noon to receive the visit of the Prefect, who came in state, and was honored with a salute of fifteen guns. His Honor remained only a few minutes, during which he tendered the General all the hospitalities and courtesies of the town, but General Grant declined them, with thanks.

After the departure of the city authorities, the General and Captain Robeson went on shore, and sauntered about for two or three hours, looking on the holiday groups, who made the day a merry one in their Sicilian fashion. A Christmas dinner was furnished from the ship's larder. The hosts were Chief Engineer J. Trilley, Surgeon George Cooke, Lieutenant-Commander A. G. Caldwell, Lieutenant E. T. Strong, Past-Assistant-Engineers G. W. Baird and D. M. Fulmer, Lieutenant Jacob W. Miller, Paymaster J. P. Loomis, Lieutenant Richard Rush, Captain L. E. Fagan, commanding the marines, Lieutenant H. O. Handy, Lieutenant W. A. Hadden and Master J. W. Daunehower. These comprised the names of the ward-room officers of the Vandalia — a gallant, manly, chivalrous company they were. The guests of the evening were General Grant and wife, Commander H. B. Robeson, and Jesse R. Grant. This was the company; the *menu* will give an idea of what a ship's kitchen can do for a Christmas dinner:

MENU.
Potage.
Tomate puree.
Bouchees a la reine.
Cabellon a la Hollandaise.
Puree de pommes.
Dindonneau aux huitres.
Haricots verts.

> Filets aux champignons.
> Petits pois.
> Punch a la Romaine.
> Salade.
> Plum pudding.
> Mince pies.
> Dessert.

It was nearly six when the soup made its appearance, and it was half-past eight before the waiters brought in the coffee. There was no hurry — no long pauses. The chat went round the table, the General doing his share of talk. It was a genial, home-like feast. Thus, Christmas, 1877, closed merry and pleasant.

The next morning there were calls to make — official calls; this is one of the duties of the General's trip. The incognito of General Grant is one that no one will respect. He declines all honors and attentions, so far as he can do so without rudeness, and is especially indifferent to the parade and etiquette by which his journey is surrounded. It is amusing, knowing General Grant's feelings on the subject, to read the articles in English and American papers about his craving for precedence, and his fear lest he may not have the proper seat at the table and the highest number of guns for a salute. He had declined every attention of an official character thus far, except those whose non-acceptance would have been misconstrued. When he arrived at a port, his habit was to go ashore with his wife and son, see what was to be seen, and drift about from palace to picture gallery, like any other wandering, studious American, "doing Europe." Sometimes the officials were too prompt for him, but generally, unless they called by appointment, they found the General absent.

In this country a large class of our citizens have been misled by the false reports of the press and enemies of ex-President Grant, and believe that the General traveled like a prince, with a large retinue; that he was enabled to do so, because the men who fattened on the corruptions of his administration gave him a share of their plunder. The truth is, General Grant traveled as a private citizen. He had one servant and a courier. His courier arranged for his hotel accommodations, and the one who did office for the General took pains to get as good bargains for his master as possible. So far as General Grant being a rich man, it is known by his friends that, when he left this country, the duration of his trip would depend entirely upon his income, and this income depends altogether upon the proceeds of his investment of the money presented to him at the close of the war. The Presidency yielded him nothing in the way of capital, and he has not now a dollar that came to him as an official. By this is meant, that the money paid to General Grant as a soldier and as a President was spent by him in supporting the dignity of his office. Everybody knows how much money was given him at the close of the war; as this was all well invested and has grown, one may estimate the fortune of the General, and about how long that fortune would enable him to travel like a prince over Europe.

At Palermo General Grant and family remained several days, enjoying the delightful climate and picturesque attractions. This Sicily is the land of many civilizations. Here Greek, the Carthagenian, the Roman and the Saracen, have made their mark. This is the land of the poetry of Homer, the genius of Archimedes, the philosophy and piety of Paul. These hills and bays and valleys have seen mighty armies striving for the mastery of the world. Certainly if example or precept, or the opportunity for great deeds, could ennoble a nation, Sicily should be the land of heroes. But its heroism has fallen into rags, and the descendants of the men who destroyed the Athenian fleet in Syracuse, and who confronted the power of Carthage at Agrigentum, now spend their time sleeping in the sun, swarming around chapel doors to beg, and hiding in the hills to waylay travelers and rob them or keep them for a ransom. Brigandage has for generations been the dominant industry in the Sicilies, but it is due to the present Italian government to say that they are doing all in their power to suppress it.

On the 28th, General Grant and party arrived at La Valetta, Malta. At this place the General was visited by the Duke of Edinburgh, who was at Malta in command of the Sultan, an English ironclad. His Royal Highness was received at the gangway by Captain Robeson. He was dressed in his uniform as Captain, wearing on his breast the star of the Garter.

General Grant advanced and greeted the Duke, and presented the gentlemen with him, and they retired to the cabin. They remained in conversation for the best part of an hour, talking about Malta, its antiquities, its history, England, education and the Eastern question. The Duke spoke of the visit of his brother-in-law, the Grand Duke Alexis, to America, and of the gratification of the family at the reception tendered him in America. His Royal Highness is a pattern of a sailor, and has all the ease and off-hand grace of the family. On taking his leave, he invited the General and family to visit him at his palace of San Antonio and take luncheon, which was accepted.

The palace of San Antonio is about four miles from town; it is surrounded by orange groves and walls, and is noted as the only large garden on the island. The drive was through an interesting country, and greatly enjoyed by the visitors. At the palace, the Duke and Duchess received the General and Mrs. Grant and their son in the most gracious manner. After luncheon His Royal Highness escorted them through the orange groves. At noon General Grant visited the Governor-General of Malta.

On leaving, the General was saluted with twenty-one guns. A regiment was drawn up in front of the palace as a guard of honor. The Governor, a famous old English

General, Van Straubeuzee, wore the Order of the Grand Cross of the Bath. He received the General and party at the door of the palace, surrounded by his council and a group of Maltese noblemen. After presentation to Lady Van Straubeuzee, the same ceremonies were repeated. In the evening there was a state dinner to the General and party at the palace, including, among the guests, Commander Robeson and Lieutenant-Commander Caldwell, of the Vandalia, as well as the Captain and executive officers of the Gettysburg. At the dinner General Grant's health was proposed, which was responded to in the heartiest manner.

There were many temptations to remain in Malta. Hospitalities were showered upon General Grant. All the great ones vied with one another in making his visit a pleasant one. Yet on the last day of the year the General bid good-bye, and sailed for the land of the Lotus.

CHAPTER IX.

IN EGYPT AND THE LOTUS LAND.

The voyage from Malta to Egypt was exceedingly unpleasant. A severe storm prevailed most of the time, rendering life anything but comfortable. Unlike the majority of military heroes, General Grant seems to take kindly to the waves, and to be as much at home on them as if he had been educated at Annapolis instead of West Point.

No storm, however severe, could deprive him of his cigar, or, to use a sea phrase, keep him below. In this respect he is very unlike Napoleon, who detested the sea, and whom the smell of tar invariably sickened. The English humorists never tired of twitting him on the fact, and the patriotic prints and cartoons at the time he was planning his celebrated invasion depict the conqueror of the continent in some exceedingly ludicrous positions.

The General and party stopped at Alexandria because they wanted a safe anchorage, though they had intended going direct to Cairo. He remained there three days. The Vandalia had hardly anchored when the Governor of the district, the Admiral and the General, Pachas and Beys, Consul-General Farman, Judges Barringer and Morgan, and resident missionaries, came on board, and were received by General Grant. The Governor, in the name of the Khedive, welcomed General Grant to Egypt, and offered him a palace in Cairo, and a special steamer up the Nile. It is Oriental etiquette to return calls as soon as possible, and accordingly in the afternoon the General, accompanied

A STREET IN ALEXANDRIA.

by his son, Commander Robeson, Chief Engineer Trilley, and Lieutenant Handy of the navy, landed in the official barge. As this was an official visit, the Vandalia manned the yards and fired twenty-one guns. These salutes were responded to by the Egyptian vessels; a guard of honor received the General at the palace, and the reception was after the manner of the Orientals.

We enter a spacious chamber and are seated on a cushioned seat or divan, according to rank. The Pacha offers the company cigarettes. Then compliments are exchanged, the Pacha saying how proud Egypt is to see the illustrious stranger, and the General answering that he anticipates great pleasure in visiting Egypt. The Pacha gives a signal, and servants enter bearing little porcelain cups about as large as an egg, in filigree cases. This is the beverage — coffee — or, as was the case with this special Pacha, a hot drink spiced with cinnamon. Then the conversation continues with judicious pauses, the Orientals being slow in speech and our General not apt to diffuse his opinions. In about five minutes we arise and file down-stairs in slow, solemn fashion, servants and guards saluting, and the visit is over.

General and Mrs. Grant dined with Vice-Consul Salvage, and in the evening attended a ball given in their honor. This was an exceedingly brilliant entertainment, and interesting in one respect especially, because it was here that the General met Henry M. Stanley, just fresh from the African wilderness. Stanley sat on the right of the General, and they had a long conversation upon African matters and the practical results of the work done by the intrepid explorer. The Consul-General proposed the health of General Grant, and Judge Barringer proposed that of Mrs. Grant, who was prevented by fatigue from attending. Then a toast was proposed in honor of Stanley, who made a grateful response, saying that it was one of the proudest moments of his life to find himself seated by the guest of the evening. The entertainment at Mr. Salvage's at an end, the visitors returned on board the Vandalia. Sunday was spent quietly in a stroll about the town. Here the General and party left the Vandalia to visit Cairo and the Nile. Going by rail, they reached Cairo after a run of four hours. Here he was met by General Stone, the representative of the Khedive, and also General Loring, both Americans, and late of the Confederate States army. General Grant and General Stone were together at West Point, and old friends. Their meeting was quite enthusiastic. The General asks General Loring to ride with him, while General Stone accompanies Mrs. Grant, and so they drive off to the Palace of Kassr-el-Doussa — the palace placed at General Grant's disposal by the Khedive. Commander Robeson and Lieutenant Rush accept the General's invitation to reside in the palace while they are in Cairo, and the remainder of the party find homes in the hotel.

The General dined quietly with his family, and next day called on the Khedive. The hour fixed for the reception was eleven, and a few minutes before that hour the state carriages called at the palace. The General wore plain evening dress, and was accompanied by the following officers: Commander H. B. Robeson, commanding the Vandalia; Joseph Trilley, chief engineer; George H. Cooke, surgeon; Lieutenant E. T. Strong, Lieutenant J. W. Miller, Paymaster J. P. Loomis; G. W. Baird, engineer; H. L. Hoskinson, ensign; B. F. Walling and E. S. Hotchkin, midshipmen; E. R. Freeman, engineer. Jesse R. Grant and Consul-General Farman accompanied the General. They reached the palace shortly after eleven. There was a guard of honor, and the officers of the household were ranged on the stairs. The General entered, and was met by His Highness the Khedive at the foot of the stairs. The General, his son, and Mr. Farman, went into an inner room, where the ceremonies of the formal presentation took place. The officers then entered, and were received by His Highness, who expressed his gratification at seeing so many representatives of the navy. This reception lasted about half an hour. They then returned to the palace, and had scarcely entered when the carriage of the Khedive was announced. The General received the Khedive, who was accompanied by his Secretary for Foreign Affairs, and welcomed him in the grand saloon. The officers of the Vandalia were present, and their striking uniforms, the picturesque costumes of the Khedive and his attendants, and the splendid, stately decorations of the room in which they assembled, made the group imposing. At the close of the interview, General Grant escorted the Khedive to his carriage. Official calls were then made upon the two sons of the Khedive, who at once returned the calls, and so ended official duties.

Judge Batcheller and Consul-General Farman each gave a grand dinner and ball in honor of the General, which were attended by the notables of all nations residing at Cairo.

The thoughtful Khedive gave our distinguished traveler a steamer specially adapted to the intricate and difficult navigation of the Nile, also guides, interpreters, and professors learned in the mysterious language of the monuments and ruins which tell of a civilization that was old a thousand years before the dawn of the Western Roman empire. The party consisted of General and Mrs. Grant, their son, Sami Bey, Emile Brugsch, Consul-General Farman, Chief Surgeon Cooke, Lieutenant Hadden, Ensign F. A. Wilner, and a correspondent of the New York *Herald* — ten in all.

On the morning of the 19th of January, General Grant and party reached Siout, the capital of Upper Egypt, and containing twenty-five thousand inhabitants, where we have a Vice-Consul, the city being at some distance from the river. After having received a call from Vice-Consul Wasif-el-Hayat, a Syrian, they all drove to the town. It was over parched fields, through a country parched with the drought, but in more favorable years blooming like a garden. All the town seemed to know of their coming, for wherever they went great crowds swarmed around, and they had to force their donkeys through masses of Arabs and Egyptians, of all ages and conditions. The stores are little holes of rooms, in front of which the trader sits and calls upon you to buy. As these avenues are less than six feet, one can imagine the trouble had in making progress. The town has some fine mosques and houses, but in the main is like all the towns of Upper Egypt, a collection of mud hovels. A grand reception was given by the Vice-Consul. The dinner was regal in its profusion and splendor, and consisted of fully twenty courses, all well served. When it was concluded, the son of the host arose, and, in remarkably clear and correct English, proposed the General's health. We give a fragment of this speech:

"Long have we heard and wondered," said the speaker, "at the strange progress which America has made during this past century by which she has taken the first position among the most widely civilized nations. She has so quickly improved in sciences, morals and arts that the world stands amazed at this extraordinary progress, which surpasses the swiftness of lightning. It is to the hard work of her great and wise men that all this advance is imputed, those who have shown to the world what wise, courageous, patriotic men can do. Let all the world look to America and follow her example — that nation which has taken as the basis of her laws and the object of her undertakings to maintain freedom and equality among her own people, and secure them for others, avoiding all ambitious schemes which would draw her into bloody and disastrous wars, and trying by all means to maintain peace internally and externally. The only two great wars upon which she has engaged were entered upon for pure and just purposes— the first for releasing herself from the English yoke and erecting her independence, and the other for stopping slavery and strengthening the union of the States; and well we know that it was mainly, under God, due to the talent, courage and wisdom of his excellency, General Grant, that the latter of the two enterprises was brought to a successful issue." The speech closed by a tribute to the General and the Khedive. General Grant said in response that nothing in his whole trip had so impressed him as this unexpected, this generous welcome in the heart of Egypt. He had anticipated great pleasure in his visit to Egypt, and the anticipation had been more than realized. He thanked his host, and especially the young man who had spoken of him with so high praise, for their reception. The dinner dissolved into coffee, conversation and cigars.

On the 21st, at the town of Girgel, the General and party take to the donkeys and make a trip under the broiling hot sun, to the ruined city of Abydos. This was the oldest city in Egypt. It went back to Menes, the first of the Egyptian Kings, who reigned, according to Egyptian history, four thousand five hundred years before Christ. The ruins are on a grand scale. Abydos is a temple which the Khedive is rescuing from the sand. Here, according to tradition, was buried the god Osiris. To the ancient Egyptian, the burial place of that god was as sacred as Mecca to the Moslems, or the Holy Sepulchre was to the Mediæval Christians. The government is trying to reclaim this temple, and has been digging in all directions. One excavation over fifty feet deep was visited. Remnants of an old house or tomb could be seen. Millions of fragments of broken pottery around. The strata, that age after age had heaped upon the buried city, were plainly visible. The city was really a city of tombs. In the ancient days the devout Egyptian craved burial near the tomb of Osiris, and so for centuries their remains were brought to Abydos from all parts of Egypt. Lunch was taken with Salib, an Arabian, who had for twenty years been working at the excavations, working with so much diligence that he had become entirely blind, and it is now his only comfort to wander through the ruins, direct the workmen, and trace with his finger many a loved inscription that his zeal has brought to light. Salib lives near the ruin, on a pension allowed by the Khedive. After an hour's rest, having ridden fifteen miles on donkeys and walked two or three in the sand, the visitors returned to the shelter and repose of the cabin of the Vandalia.

We next find our visitors at Thebes, once a city that covered both banks of the Nile, was known to Homer as the city of the hundred gates. It had a population of three hundred thousand inhabitants, and sent out twenty thousand armed chariots. It was famed for its riches and its splendor until it was besieged. Here was the temple of Memnon and its colossal statues, and the palace temple of the great Rameses, the only ruin in Egypt known to be the home of a King; the columns of the Luxor, and the stupendous ruins of Kanark, and the tombs of the kings. Visiting the town of Luxor, a collection of houses built upon the ruins of the old temple, erected over three thousand years ago; there is a fine obelisk here, the companion to the one now standing in the Place Concordia, Paris; also a statue of Rameses, of colossal size, now broken and partly buried in the sand. Next morning the party crossed the river, and prepared for a ride to visit Memnon statues; arrived at their destination, they found all that is left of Memnonism are the two colossal statues. A good part of the base is buried in the earth, but they loom up over the plain, and can be seen miles and miles away. Some idea of their size can be formed, when it is known that the statue measures eighteen feet three inches across the shoulders, sixteen feet six inches from the top of the shoulder to the elbow, and the portions of the body in due proportion. After examining these statues and resting a half hour, they visited the temple of Medesnet Habro, one of the great temples of Thebes, and the palace temple of the great Rameses, who lived thirteen hundred years before Christ, and is supposed by some to be the Pharaoh that brought the plagues upon Egypt. The walls of the palace are covered with inscriptions. After carefully exploring these interesting ruins, and luncheon being served in one of the old King's apartments, our party returned by the route of the early morning. Next morning, after a ride of forty minutes from Luxor, our party were at the ruined temple of Karnark, built in the days of Abraham. It is hard to realize that in the infinite and awful past, in the days when the Lord came down to the earth and communed with men and gave His commandments, these columns and statues, these plinths and entablatures, these mighty, bending walls, upon which chaos has put its seal, were the shrines of a nation's faith and sovereignty; yet this is all told in stone.

Karnark, which was not only a temple, but one in the series of temples which constituted Thebes, is about half a mile from the river, a mile or two from the temple of Luxor. The front wall or propylon is 370 feet broad, 50 feet deep, and the standing tower 140 feet high. Leading up to this main entrance is an avenue, lined with statues and sphinxes, 200 feet long. When you enter this gate, you enter an open court-yard 275 feet by 329. There is a corrider or cloister on either side; in the middle a double line of columns, of which only one remains. We now come to another wall or propylon, as large as the entrance, and enter the great hall — the most magnificent ruin in Egypt. The steps of the door are 40 feet by 10. The room is a 170 feet by 329, and the roof was supported by 134 columns. These columns are all or nearly all standing, but the roof has gone. Twelve are 62 feet high without the plinth, and 11 feet 6 inches in diameter. One hundred and twenty-two are 42 feet 5 inches in height, and 28 feet in circumference. They were all brilliantly colored, and some of them retain their colors still; and you can well imagine what must have been the blaze of light and color, when the kings and priests passed through in solemn procession. We pass through another gate into an open court. Here is an obelisk in granite 75 feet high, and the fragments of another, its companion. The inscriptions on them are as clear as though they had been cut yesterday, so gentle is this climate in its dealings with time. They celebrate the victories and virtues of the kings who reigned 1700 years before Christ, and promise the kings in the name of the immortal gods that their glory shall live for ages. We pass into another chamber very much in ruins, and see another obelisk, 92 feet high and 8 feet square — the largest in the world. This monument commemorates the virtues of the king's daughter — womanly and queenly virtues, which met their reward, let us hope, thirty-five centuries ago. One may form some idea of what the Egyptians could do in the way of mechanics and engineering, when it is known that this obelisk is a single block of granite, that it was brought from the quarry, miles and miles away, erected and inscribed, in seven months. The next room was the sanctury, the holy of holies, and is now a mass of rubbish requiring nimble feet to climb. We scramble over stones and sand, until we come to what was the room where King Amenophis III., who lived sixteen centuries before Christ, was represented as giving offerings to fifty-six of his royal predecessors. The hall is a ruin, and some French Vandals carried off the tablet — one of the most valuable in Egypt — to Paris. Altogether the

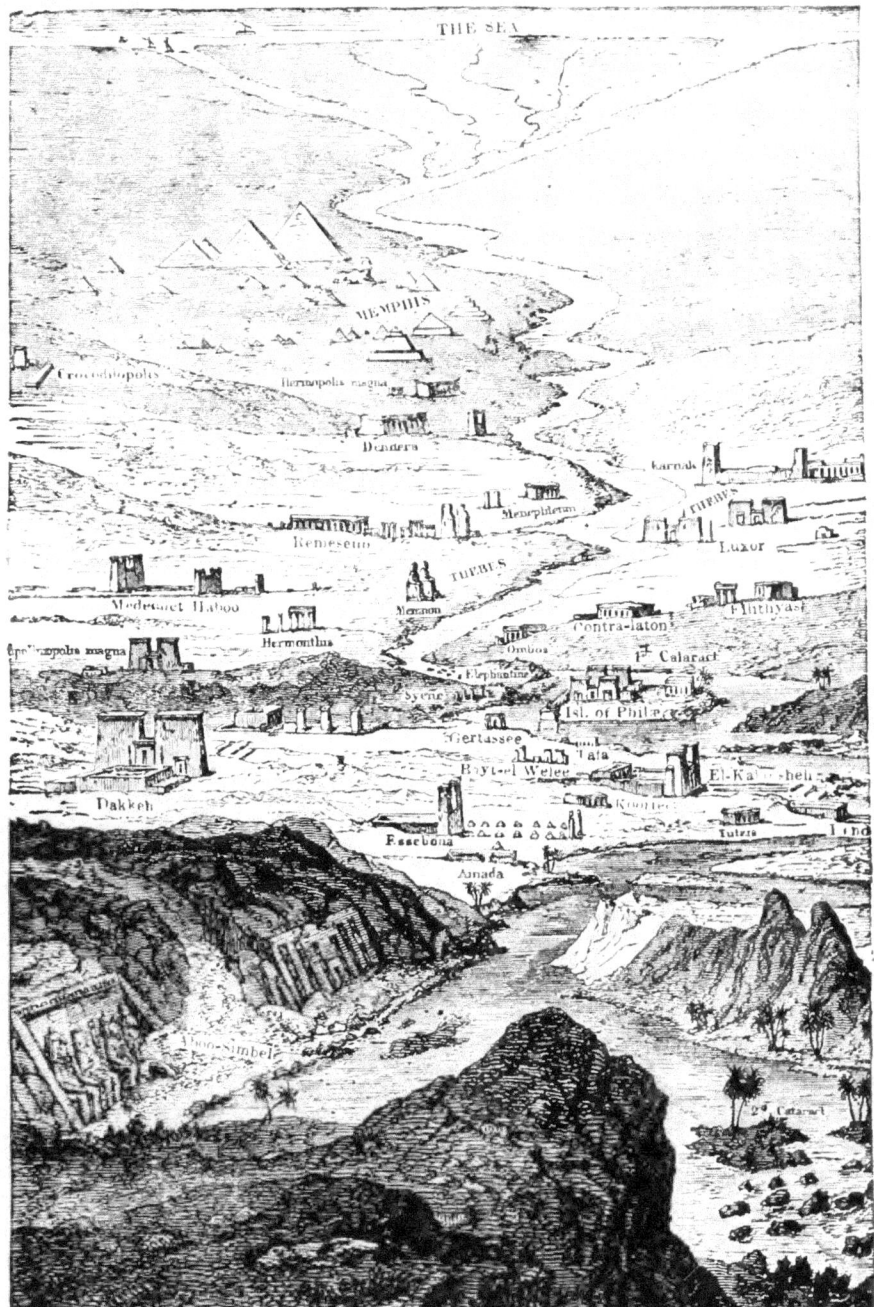

DOWN THE NILE.

building alone was 1,108 feet long, and about 300 feet wide, the circuit around the outside, according to a Roman historian who saw it in its glory, being about a mile and a half.

This was the temple, but the temple was only a part. There were three avenues leading from it to the other temples; these avenues were lined with statues, large and small, generally of the Sphinx. Some distance from the temple is a pool of water, known as the Sacred Lake. When an Egyptian died and was embalmed, his body was brought to the lake, where, if the deceased had lived worthily, the body was sprinkled with water from the lake by the priests, and was carried across to the other shore, and removed from there to the catacombs.

Wherever we find walls we have inscriptions. The inscriptions are in hieroglyphic language — a language as clear to scholars now as the Latin or Sanscrit. They tell of battles and the glory of the King Rameses, who is supposed to be the Sesostris of the Greeks. We see him leading his men to attack a fortified place. Again we see him leading foot soldiers and putting an enemy to the sword. We see him leading his captives as an offering to the gods, and offering not only prisoners, but booty of great value. The group of prisoners are rudely done, but you see the type of the race clearly outlined. We trace these types, and thus learn of the warlike achievements of this monarch whose fame is carved all over Egypt, and about whose name there is an interesting debate. Again and again these war themes are repeated, one king after another reciting his conquests and his virtues, wars and treaties of peace. It seemed in the building of these temples that the intention was to make the walls monumental records of the achievements of various reigns. When the walls were covered, or a king wished to be especially gracious to the priests, or, as is more probable, desired to employ his soldiers, he would build a new wing or addition to the temple already existing, striving, if possible, to make his own addition more magnificent than those of his predecessors. In this way came the great temple of Karnak. As a consequence, these stupendous, inconceivable ruins were not the work of one prince or one generation, but of many; and as there was always something to add, and always a new ambition coming into play, we find these temples, tombs, pyramids and obelisks, all piled one upon another, all inspired by the one sentiment, and all telling the same story. Here are the records, and here are the ruins. If the records read like a tale of enchantment, these ruins look the work of gods. The world does not show, except where we have evidences of the convulsions of nature, a ruin as vast as that of Karnak. Let the reader imagine a city covering two banks of the Hudson, running as far as the Battery to Yonkers and back, seven miles, all densely built, and you have an idea of the extent of Thebes. But this will only give you an idea of size. The buildings were not Broadways and Fifth Avenues, but temples and colossal monuments and tombs, the greatness of which, and the skill and the patience necessary to build them, exciting our wonder to-day. Thebes in its day must have been a wonder of the world — even of the ancient world, which knew Nineveh and Babylon. To-day all that remains are a few villages of mud huts, a few houses in stone, flying consular flags, a plain here and there strewed with ruins, and under the sand ruins even more stupendous than those we now see.

At Keneh the General and his party landed and inspected the town, making several purchases. The Pacha of the province, learning that so illustrious a visitor was in his domain, sent couriers at once to invite the General to his palace, which was accepted. This palace was a low brick building, like a barracks. The visitors were shown into the reception chamber, and ranged on the divan. There was a long waiting, when the Governor appeared, a stout, pleasant looking, gray mustached soldier, in his full uniform of a general. He received the General with courtesy, and there was the usual exchange of compliments; then came the coffee and the pipes, and the adieu. The Governor accompanied General Grant in his return walk, calling upon the German Consul, who had waylaid him and begged that he would honor his house. This officer lived in style approaching splendor, and when his visitors were served with coffee and pipes they noticed that the pipestems were amber garnished with diamonds, and the coffeecups were of the finest porcelain in cases of silver and gold. These ceremonies over, the General and party returned to the boat, through a gust of sand.

At Assouan, a town of four thousand inhabitants, five hundred and eighty miles south of Cairo and seven hundred and thirty from the Mediteranean, General Grant and party intended to end their journey. Assouan is the frontier station of Old Egypt, on the boundary of Nubia, and supposed to lay directly under the equator. In the ancient days the town was a quarry, and here were found the stones which became obelisks, temples and tombs. When Islam was marching to conquer the world, the Saracens made a town here and an outpost, and for years was the battlefield in the constant strifes and schisms between Nubian and Egyptian. At Assouan the aspect of the tour changes; we see the Nubian type, the predominance of the Negro. The people seem happy enough. They are sparing of clothes, live on sugar cane, and lie in the sun — a happy, laughing, idle, dirty, good humored race.

Next day General Grant visited Philæ, situated on an island at the foot of the first cataract of the Nile. It was by far the most interesting and picturesque ruin that our party had seen. The island is green, and the date palms of luxuriant growth, and, unlike other portions of Egypt, we miss the sand, and can step trippingly over stones and turf. The river here spreads in various channels, and runs over rocks. One channel is used for vessels ascending the river; the other for vessels descending the stream. The river is narrow, the banks are steep, and the stream rolls and dashes like a sea, the waves roaring and lashing the banks. The danger is from the rocks and being dashed against its banks.

In the morning the boat's prow is turned, and the General is moving back toward the Vandalia. On his return trip the General stopped over night at Keneh, saw his old friend the Governor, stopped an hour at Siout, and on the 3d of February reached Memphis. Here are the tombs of the sacred bull.

It was believed in the Egyptian mythology that the god Osiris came to earth and allowed himself to be put to death in order that the souls of the people might be saved. After his death there was a resurrection, and the immortal part of him passed into a bull, called Apis.

The ride to the tombs of Memphis was a pleasant one. The ruins of Memphis are two or three tombs and the serapeum or mausoleum of the sacred bulls. One of the tombs being open, the visitors examined it, the walls having the same profuse decoration as had been noted at other points, entering a long, arched passage, with parallel passages, candles having been placed at various points. On each side of this passage were the tombs. Each tomb was in its alcove; the bull was placed in a huge sarcophagus, the surface finely polished and covered with inscriptions. These coffins were stupendous. The tombs have all been violated by the early conquerors, to find gold and silver. In most cases the cover has been shoved aside. The inside was so large that eight or ten men could enter.

After finishing this study of the tombs, the party of visitors rode back to their boat, and in the morning steamed down to Cairo.

General Grant had seen the Nile much more rapidly than is the custom.

The General sent for the captain, and thanked him, and made him a handsome present, and gave presents to all on the boat, including the crew.

At 12 o'clock the boat passed the bridge and moored at the wharf. The General and party returned to the palace of Kaser-el-Nousa, where he remained three days, and then resumed his journey.

CHAPTER X.

TURKEY AND THE HOLY LAND.

General Grant and party arrived at Jaffa on the morning of Sunday, February 10, having spent just one month on the Nile and vicinity. Upon landing, the visitors at once went to Vice-Consul Hardegg, and there found welcome and entertainment. There was a little archway of flowers and branches over the road, surmounted by the inscription, "Welcome, General Grant," and all the town was out to do him honor. After visiting all the places of interest, General and Mrs. Grant, with four of the officers of the Vandalia, prepared to visit the Holy City. Having obtained three clumsy open wagons, each drawn by three horses, they drove out of the town into the plain of Sharon. It was too early in the season to see Palestine in its glory, but the plain was rich and fertile. The party reached Ramleh at about sundown, and remained over night, resuming their journey at six in the morning. Passing from the plain of Sharon into the country of Joshua and Sampson, the road becomes rough and stony, and the carts go bumping, thumping over the worst road in the world. The fertility of Palestine lies in the plain below. Around and ahead, the beauty of Palestine, the beauty of Nature in her desolation; no houses, no farms, no trace of civilization but the telegraph poles. The first biblical view is the ruins of Gezer, once a royal city of Canaan. Passing through the Kirjath Jearim, the valley of Ajalon and the scene of the great battle between David and Goliath, the valley is deep and the brook still runs a swift course. This was the last ravine this side of the heights of Jerusalem, and one of the strongest natural defenses of the city. At this point General Grant was met by a troop of cavalry, representatives from all of the Consulates, delegations from the Americans, Jews, Armenians and Greeks, resident in Jerusalem — in all quite a small army—and, instead of quietly entering the city as he had expected, he was commanded to enter as a conqueror, in a triumphal manner.

Arrived at the city, General Grant was at once called upon by the Pacha and the Consuls. The Bishops and the Patriarchs all came and blessed the General and his house. The Pacha sent his band of fifty pieces in the evening to serenade the ex-President. The Pacha also gave a state dinner, which was largely attended. Early the following morning General Grant stole away, before the reception ceremonies, and walked over the street Via Dolorosa, consecrated to Christianity as the street over which Jesus carried His cross. The General lived while in Jerusalem within five minutes' walk of Calvary, and within sight from his chamber. The first place of interest on this street is the Coptic monastery. Here Christ sank under the weight of the cross. At the ruins of the Hospice of the Knights of St. John; here is where Jesus addressed the women who followed him. A few steps further and we are at the house and tomb of Veronica, who wiped the blood from Jesus' holy brows, and left His image on her napkin. Descending a slippery path, and at the corner is the house against which Christ leaned, overcome by agony. You see a dent in the stone. This dent was made by the hand of our Lord, as He stretched it out to support His burden. It is smooth and dark with the kisses of millions of believing lips.

The next house is that of Dives, the rich man. At this corner Simon of Cyrene took the cross and carried it a part of the way. In front of the house of Dives is a stone, and over it a hovel. The hovel was the house of the beggar; the stone is where he sat in quest of alms, and under this archway Jesus stood and pronounced the parable which is found in the sixteenth chapter of Luke. Here the road makes another bend, and we pass a broken column, that must at one time have been a stately ornament. The column broke where Jesus sank upon it, and the fissure is clear and deep. We keep on until we come to a church, a bright, new church, with an arch overhanging the street. This is the church of Ecce Homo. It was here or hereabouts that the road to the cross began. There is a barracks on the site of Pilate's judgment hall. We go into the church. Behind the altar is an arch, and under this arch Pilate stood when he delivered over Jesus to the Jews and washed his hands of innocent blood. Here, in an enclosure, was the whipping, the crowning with thorns, the decoration with the purple robes, and here also Jesus took up the cross, which He carried to Calvary.

We can readily see, as we retrace our way up the Via Dolorosa, that it must have been a rough and weary road to one rent and torn and bleeding and crushed under the cruel burden of the cross. Even to the wayfarer, in full possession of his faculties, it is a tedious task to climb the hill of Calvary.

After finishing the Via Dolorosa, the visitors kept on outside of the gates and over the valley of Jehoshaphat. Crossing the brook Kedron, the very brook hallowed by our Lord's holy and sorrowful footsteps, and ascending the hill a short distance, they come to a walled garden. Here Jesus knelt and prayed, and made holy forever the Garden of Gethsemane. The good monk gathered some flowers for Mrs Grant, and for the others twigs and leaves from the "Tree of Agony."

The party climbed the Mount of Olives to the summit,

and entered the chapel, said to be the site of the Ascension, now a Moslem mosque. From its minerets one can look far beyond to the land of Moab, the valley of the Jordan and the Dead Sea. Here a French princess has erected a tomb, and around the walls of which is the Lord's Prayer in thirty-two languages.

Resuming the walk over a hill, they came to the village of Bethany, where Jesus lived when He preached in Jerusalem. Here was Lazarus, His friend, whom He raised from the tomb. Here lived Mary and Martha, whom Jesus loved. Riding under the overhanging ruins of the dwelling in which Jesus found home, shelter, friendship, love, they walk around Bethany, which is only a collection of ruins and hovels.

Passing over the graveyard where Lazarus was buried, they continue along the road that leads to Jerusalem again, by the road sloping at the base of the mountain. It was over this road that Jesus rode when He entered Jerusalem on an ass. At the head of the hill, Jesus wept over the city and prophesied its destruction.

Entering the city by the Damascus gate, it was but a few minutes before General Grant and party reached their hotel. The walk had been a long and weary one, yet full of interest, every moment awakening a memory of the noblest moment of life, and every step taken had been over hallowed ground.

Leaving Jerusalem, they visited Damascus, where their stay was made enjoyable by the attention of the Turkish officials.

On March 10th General Grant and party arrived at Athens, and were escorted by three Greek ironclads, a large crowd witnessing the landing. On the 9th they were presented to the King and Queen of Greece, and a grand banquet given in their honor on the 10th. The ruins of the ancient temples and the Parthenon were brilliantly illuminated. On the 13th General Grant entertained the King of Greece at luncheon on board the United States Steamer Vandalia, and also lunched with the King on the 14th at the American Legation. The General's reception had been enthusiastic and hospitable.

General Grant reached Naples on Monday evening, and proceeded at once to Rome. Here he was visited by Cardinal McCloskey, Lieutenant-General Count Sounaz, King Humbert's Aid-de-Camp, and all the dignitaries of the government, diplomatic agents, and prominent citizens. On the 25th, Minister Marsh gave a grand banquet and *soiree* in honor of General Grant. The foreign ministers, members of the cabinet, and most of the American residents were present. Several days were spent in visiting places of interest.

On May 5th, General Grant arrived at Turin, where he met with a hearty and enthusiastic reception, and on the 7th returned to the gay French capital. On Thursday the Ex-President paid visits to President McMahon, the Prince of Wales, Duc 'd Aosta, the Duc Saxe-Coburg, the Prefect of the Seine, and the Prefect of Police. On Friday he called upon the English, Turkish, Swedish and Japanese Ministers; in the afternoon he drove to the Bois de Boulogne and witnessed a game of polo, in which he took a lively interest. On Saturday the General and Mrs. Grant and their son visited the Exposition. He was received by Chief Commissioner McCormick and staff, and by the Commissioners from the various States of the Union, Minister Noyes, Consul-General Torbert and wife, and the leading ladies and gentlemen of the American colony in Paris.

The American marines were drawn up in military array, and gave the party a military salute on their arrival at the American section.

The General and his party then examined the whole American department in detail. They spent a good deal of time among Tiffany's exhibit, where Bonanza Mackay's gorgeous service of silver plate, which cost one hundred and fifty thousand dollars, is exhibited.

Then they proceeded to the machinery department, where the General was placed upon a square American platform — that of the Howe scale. General Grant, in fact, was weighed, and for the first time in his life "found wanting," having lost seventeen pounds by his Egyptian trip.

Mr. Cunliffe Owen did the honors, in the Prince of Wales' pavilion, to the General and his party.

A handsome collation was served in the Alimentation group, No. 17, of the American department, after which the party proceeded to visit the other sections.

The following week, General Grant was the object of further attention, and enjoyed the amenities of Paris life to the full, receiving a visit from President McMahon and his wife, Prince Hassan of Egypt, Prince Albert and Prince Frederick of Austria, Prince and Princess of Denmark. The Comte de Paris sent his boxes at the Italian for Thursday, and at the grand opera on Friday. He dined with Mr. Ridgeway on Saturday.

One of the pleasant things of the week was General Grant's visit to the polo grounds in the Bois de Boulogne. The Prince of Wales also went the same day. They witnessed a very interesting game. General Grant was accompanied by his family and ex-Minister Beale. They remained an hour.

The General said he thought the game might be introduced with great effect into the cavalry regiments and at West Point, as a good school of horsemanship for young soldiers.

The third week of General Grant's stay in Paris was equally as pleasant, and every attention shown him. Mr. Morton, the banker, gave a "stag" dinner on Monday, and the same night Mr. Waddington, the minister of foreign affairs, gave the grandest ball of the season. Five thousand invitations were issued, and there was a perfect crush, but the costumes of the ladies were something even for a man to rave about.

On Tuesday the American artist, Healy, gave a ball. On Wednesday there was a reception and ball at the Ministry of Agriculture. On Friday Mrs. Hooper's private theatricals attracted a distinguished party. On Saturday there was a *soiree dansante* at Mrs. Wagner's, and on Sunday Prince Orloff, the Russian minister, gave a grand dinner to General Grant, which proved to be one of the most enjoyable entertainments given in his honor. These festivities were kept up, with little abatement, until the middle of June, when General Grant turned his eyes toward the northern lands of Europe, and paid his respects to his friends in Paris, and bowed himself out of that dazzling sphere of dissipation, to recuperate in a series of mild Dutch festivities — mild compared to the mad whirl of festive Paris.

General Grant arrived at the Hague in safety, and was met by Minister Birney, and, with Mrs. Grant, took up his residence, by special invitation, in the latter gentleman's house.

Immediately upon the ex-President's arrival — almost before he had time to repose himself after his journey — invitations began to pour in upon him, and the routine of dinners, receptions, balls and visits began anew. On Monday evening Minister Birney entertained his distinquished guest at a splendid dinner, which proved to be one of the great events of the season. Preparations on a large scale had been made for this occasion, which was a gratifying success in every respect.

All the members of the diplomatic corps in the city were present at this dinner, which was rendered still more brilliant by the presence of the wives and lady friends of the diplomats. After the dinner, which went off joyously, a splendid reception was given, in which the court circle, with its picturesque retinue of noble ladies and gentlemen, most of the members of Parliament, and other distinguished guests, participated. General Grant was, of course, the centre of attraction, and was treated with marked deference and honors. His manly, soldier-like bearing was admired on all sides, and every one was desirous of making his acquaintance. The reception continued until the small hours of morning, and was thoroughly enjoyable from beginning to end.

On Tuesday evening a similar dinner was given in honor of the General at the residence of the Minister of Foreign Affairs, Baron de Heckeven de Kell. This was also followed by a reception no less brilliant than its predecessor.

On the same day General Grant accepted an invitation to visit His Royal Highness Prince Frederic, uncle of the King. He chose the forenoon for the purpose of paying his respects to the Prince, who entertained him generously at a private *dejeuner*. After this friendly repast, the Prince ordered his carriage and had his guest driven through the spacious and beautiful grounds of the estate. A call was also made on Prince Alexander, son of the King.

Each day was destined to bring its separate enjoyment. Wednesday was set apart for a parade of a portion of the troops of Holland, and the General was invited to review these sturdy Dutch soldiers, whose martial bearing impressed him very favorably. A large number of distinguished ladies and gentlemen were present at the review, and the scene was exceedingly picturesque and attractive. The troops looked their best, and marched with fine precision and dignity.

The General limited his stay at The Hague, although he expressed a hope that he might return there before his departure. He then took the train for Rotterdam, where he arrived in a short time. He was received by the Burgomaster of that city, and was escorted around and shown various objects of interest by this dignitary. The Burgomaster gave a dinner in his honor, to which a great many of the principal citizens were invited. The affair was very social and cordial.

On Thursday the General made his way into the famous city of Amsterdam, where he was greeted by throngs of people, who welcomed him in a truly enthusiastic manner. Several prominent citizens escorted him about, and extended to him an invitation for dinner on Saturday evening. His residence in Amsterdam, although necessarily short, was as pleasant as could have been desired.

General Grant's flying tour on Dutch territory was marked by attentions as gracious and as flattering as any he had yet received. In the steady, plodding cities of Holland, the phlegmatic citizens had been excited to enthusiasm by the presence of the ex-President, and signified their admiration of his character and achievements by crowding the streets which he passed.

CHAPTER XI.

GRANT IN GERMANY, NORWAY, SWEDEN, RUSSIA AND AUSTRIA.

On Wednesday, June 26, General Grant and party arrived at Berlin, Minister Taylor having met them at Stendahl, sixty miles below Berlin.

On the evening of his coming, he strolled along the Unter den Linden, and his Berlin visit may be summed up in this sentence, that he walked the greater part of each day, and there was not a quarter of Berlin that he did not explore on foot with an energy as sightseer which no amount of exertion seemed to diminish. The General had an early interview with the members of the Congress of great diplomats assembled in Berlin to settle the Eastern question.

At an interview with Prince Gortschakoff, the General, in company with Mr. Taylor, calling at the Prince's request (as the gout prevented the Prince calling on the General), Gortschakoff said that Russia would be glad to see and welcome the General, and he seemed delighted with the visit. Of the members of the Congress, Lord Beaconsfield, Lord Salisbury, M. Waddington and Count Corti were known to the General. Mehemet Ali he had met in Turkey. Visits were exchanged with these gentlemen and with the other members of the Congress.

Among the first calls left on the General was that of Prince Bismarck, and as it did not find him at home it was left again. As the General was anxious to see the Prince, for whose character and services he had so high an admiration, he returned these calls at once, and sent His Highness a message saying that he would make his visit at any time that would suit the Prince, whom he knew to be a busy and an ill man.

The afternoon at four was the hour named for the visit, and, as the General lives within a few moments' walk of the Bismarck Palace, at five minutes to four he slowly sauntered through the Frederick Place. The Frederick Place is a small square, with roads and flowers and some famous old trees, laid out in memory of the great Frederick. It is decorated with statues of his leading generals. Everything runs to war in Germany, and the prevailing religion is swordsmanship. In this park are bronze statues of Ziethen, Seidlitz, Winterfeldt, Keith, Schwerin, and the Prince of Dessau. Passing out of the park, on the right, is the palace and home of the famous Prince Bismarck. An iron railing separates it from the street, and from the roof the flag of the German empire floats in the breeze.

The General saunters into the courtyard, and the sentinels eye him a moment curiously, and then present arms. His visit had been expected, but certainly an ex-President of the United States would come in a carriage and six, and not quietly on foot. Throwing away a half-smoked cigar as he raises his hat in honor of the salute, he advances to the door, but before he has time to ring, two servants throw them open, and he passes into an open marble hall. Of all princes now living, this is, perhaps, the most renowned — this of Bismarck-Schinhausen — who comes with a swinging, bending gait through the opened and opening doors, with both hands extended, to meet the General. You note that time has borne heavily on the Prince these past few years. The iron-grey hair and mustache are nearly white; there is weariness in the gait, a tired look in the face. But all the lines are there that are associated with Bismarck; for

WADDINGTON, *France.*
GORTCHAKOFF, *Russia.*
BISMARCK, *Germany.*
BEACONSFIELD, *England.*
ANDRASSY, *Austria.*

EUROPEAN PRIME MINISTERS.

if ever manhood, courage, intellect are written on a man's face by his Creator, they are written on this face of the German Chancellor. There is the lofty station, which seems to belong to the Bismarck stamp of men, the bold outlines of the brain, under which empires have found their fate, the frank, intrepid, penetrating eye, and in that firmly knit mouth the courage of the Saxon race. The Prince wore an officer's uniform, and, on taking the General's hand, said, "Glad to welcome General Grant to Germany."

The General answered that there was no incident in his German visit that more interested him than this opportunity of meeting the Prince. Bismarck expressed surprise at seeing the General so young a man, but on a comparison of ages it was found that Bismarck was only seven years the General's senior.

"That," said the Prince, "shows the value of a military life; for here you have the frame of a young man, while I feel like an old man."

The General, smiling, announced that he was at that period of life when he could have no higher compliment than being called a young man. By this time the Prince had escorted the General to a chair.

It was his library or study, and an open window looked out upon a beautiful park, upon which the warm June sun was shining. This is the private park of the Radziwill Palace, which is now Bismarck's Berlin home. The library is a large, spacious room, the walls a gray marble, and the furniture plain. In one corner is a large and high writing-desk, where the Chancellor works, and on the varnished floors a few rugs are thrown. The Prince speaks English with precision, but slowly, as though lacking in practice, now and then taking refuge in a French word, but showing a thorough command of the language.

After inquiring after the health of General Sheridan, who was a fellow-campaigner in France, and became a great friend of Bismarck's, they discussed the Eastern question, military armament and strength, and the late atrocious attempt to assassinate the Emperor, giving the two great men an opportunity to discuss this phase of socialism. In speaking of this attempt on the life of the Emperor, the Prince paid this glowing tribute to the Emperor:

"It is so strange, so strange and so sad. Here is an old man — one of the kindest old gentlemen in the world — and yet they must try and shoot him! There never was a more simple, more genuine, more — what shall I say? — more humane character than the Emperor's. He is totally unlike men born in his station, or many of them, at least. You know that men who come into the world in his rank, born princes, are apt to think themselves of another race and another world. They are apt to take small account of the wishes and feelings of others. All their education tends to deaden the human side. But this Emperor is so much of a man in all things! He never did any one a wrong in his life. He never wounded any one's feelings; never imposed a hardship! He is the most genial and winning of men — thinking always, anxious always for the comfort and wellfare of his people, of those around him. You cannot conceive a finer type of the noble, courteous, charitable old gentleman, with every high quality of a prince, as well as every virtue of a man. I should have supposed that the Emperor could have walked alone all over the Empire without harm, and yet they must try and shoot him."

The Prince asked the General when he might have the pleasure of seeing Mrs. Grant. The General answered that she would receive him at any convenient hour.

"Then," said the Prince, "I will come to-morrow before the Congress meets."

Both gentlemen arose, and the General renewed the expression of his pleasure at having seen a man who was so well known and so highly esteemed in America.

"General," answered the Prince, "the pleasure and the honor are mine. Germany and America have always been in so friendly a relation that nothing delights us more than to meet Americans, and especially an American who has done so much for his country, and whose name is so much honored in Germany as your own."

The Prince and the General walked side by side to the door, and after shaking hands the General passed into the square. The guard presented arms, and the General lit a fresh cigar and slowly strolled home.

"I am glad I have seen Bismarck," he remarked. "He is a man whose manner and bearing fully justify the opinions one forms of him. What he says about the Emperor was beautifully said, and should be known to all the Germans and those who esteem Germany."

Notable, also, among incidents of the Berlin stay, was a quiet, informal reception given to the General by Mr. Taylor, American Minister. Mr. Taylor was not aware of the General's coming until a day or two before his arrival, and the news found him an ill man. Then he had had no personal acquaintance with the General, and if his home political sympathies ran in one direction more than another it was not in the direction of the General. Mr. Taylor regretted that the state of mourning in which the attempt on the Emperor's life had thrown Berlin, and the presence of the Congress, prevented his entertaining the General in a more ostentatious manner. But he made all the arrangements with the Court, and gave the General an evening party, which all the Americans in Berlin attended. The evening was enjoyable and interesting. The next day there was a small dinner party at the Embassy, and, in addition, there was a great deal of going around and seeing Berlin in a quiet way, which form of foreign life the General enjoys beyond any other.

The Crown Prince sent word to General Grant asking him to name an hour when he would review some troops in all arms. The General answered that any hour most convenient for the troops would be pleasant to him. So it was arranged at half-past seven in the morning. The General asked Mr. Coleman, of the Legation, to be one of his company. It had rained all night, a heavy, pitching, blowing rain, and when the morning came the prayers which Mr. Coleman had been offering up all night for better weather were found to have availed not. The General himself had a severe cold and a chill, which had been hanging over him for two days, and when he arose he could scarcely speak. There was a suggestion that the review be postponed. But the troops were under way, and the General would not hear of the suggestion. The place selected was the Tempelhof, a large open field outside of Berlin. When General Grant drove on the ground in a palace carriage he was met by the General commanding the Berlin troops and a large staff. A horse from the royal stables was in waiting, but the General was suffering so much that he would not mount. The rain kept its wild way, and the wind swept it in gusts across the open field, so much so that in a few moments, even with the protection of a carriage, the occupants were all thoroughly drenched.

The manœuvres went on all the same. There was a sham fight with infantry, all the incidents of a real battle — moving on the flank, in skirmish line, firing and retreating, firing and advancing. Then came the order to fix bayonets and charge at double quick, the soldiers shouting and cheering as they advanced with that ringing cheer which, somehow, no one hears but in Saxon lands, and which stirs the blood like a trumpet. General Grant was attended by Major Igel, an intelligent officer. The General complimented the movements of the troops highly.

After the manœuvres and the sham fight, there was a march past, the General reviewing the line with bared head, to which the pitiless rain showed no mercy.

"These are fine soldiers," he said, and thanked the commander for his courtesy.

Then came artillery practice, the guns firing and sweeping over the field in a whirling, mad pace. This was followed by an artillery march past, which the General reviewed on foot, the rain still beating down.

Then came cavalry. This was the most interesting phase of the display, especially one movement, where the battalion broke into disorder and rallied again.

"This," said the Major, "we do to accustom our men to the contingency of disorder on the field, and enable every man to know how to take care of himself."

The movement was effective and beautiful, and showed, said the General, the highest state of discipline. It was followed by a charge and a march past, the General, on foot, reviewing, and the rain whirling like a gust.

After this they all drove to a military hospital and inspected it. Then to the quarters of a cavalry regiment, under the command of the Prince of Hohenzollern. The General was received by the officers, and went carefully through the quarters. After inspection there was a quiet mess-room lunch and a good deal of military talk, which showed that the General had not forgotten his trade.

The General, at the close of the lunch, asked permission to propose the prosperity of the regiment and the health of the Colonel. It was a regiment of which any army would be proud, and he hoped a day of trial would never come; but, if it did, he was sure it would do its part to maintain the ancient success of the Prussian army. He also desired to express his thanks to the Crown Prince for the pains that had been taken to show him this sample of his magnificent army.

The Prince answered in German, which Major Igel translated, that he was much complimented by the General's toast, and that the annals of his regiment would always record the pride they felt in having had at their mess and as their guest so illustrious a leader. This closed the military services of the day.

About midday a coupe stopped at the door of Minister Taylor's residence, and Prince Bismarck descended and touched his hat to the crowd. He wore a full military uniform, a gilded helmet covering his brows, and was conducted to the apartments of the General, who presented the Prince to his wife and Mrs. Taylor, the wife of the Minister. The Prince expressed again his satisfaction at seeing General Grant and his wife in Germany, and hoped Mrs. Grant would carry home the best impressions of the country. It had been raining, and the skies were heavy with clouds, and the General himself, suffering from a cold, had been sitting in a carriage for two hours, the rain beating in his face, watching horsemen, artillery and infantry march and countermarch over the Tempelhof grounds. Altogether it had been a trying day, and everybody felt cheerless and damp. But Mrs. Grant has a nature that would see as much sunshine in Alaska as in Italy, on whose temper rain or snow never makes an impression, and she told His Highness how delighted she was with Germany, with Potsdam and the Crown Prince, and more especially the Crown Princess, whose motherly, womanly ways had won quite a place in her womanly, motherly heart. They had had pleasant talks about children and households and wedding anniversaries, and domestic manners in Germany, and had no doubt exchanged a world of that sweet and sacred information which ladies like to bestow on one another in the confidence of friendly conversation. Moreover, she was pleased to see Prince Bismarck, and expressed that pleasure, and there was a half hour of the pleasantest talk, not about politics or wars or statesmanship, but on very human themes.

The gentler side of the Prince came into play, and one who was present formed the opinion that there was a very sunny side to the man of blood and iron. As two o'clock drew near, the Prince arose and said: "I must go to my Congress, for, you see, although the business does not concern us greatly, it is business that must be attended to." The General escorted the Prince, and as he descended the crowd had become dense, for Bismarck rarely appears in public, and all Berlin honors him as foremost among German men.

On July 11, the General dined with the Prince. The invitation card was in German, not French — a large, plain card, as follows:

>FUERST VON BISMARCK
>beehrt sich General U. S. GRANT zum Diner am Montag, den 1, Juli, um 6 Unr, ganz ergebenst einzuladen.
>U. A. w. g

The *menu* was in French.

>MENU.
>Lundi, le 1er juillet.
>Potage Mulligatawny.
>Pates a la financiere.
>Turbot d'Ostende a l'Anglaise.
>Quartier de bœuf a la Holsteinaise.
>Canetons aux olives.
>Ris de veau a la Milanaise.
>Punch romain.
>Poulardes de Bruxelles.
>Salade. Compotes.
>Fonds d'artichauts a la Hollandaise.
>Pain de Fraises a la Chantilly.
>Glaces.
>Dessert.

The General, with his military habits of promptness, entered the palace at six precisely, accompanied by his wife,

Mr. Bayard Taylor, the Minister, and Mrs. Taylor, and H. Sidney Everett, the Secretary of Legation. The Prince and Princess Bismarck, and the Countess Marie Grafin Von Bismarck, accompanied by the Prince's two sons, met the General at the door of the *salon* and presented him to the various guests. There was a hearty greeting for the Minister and his party, and the Princess and Mrs. Grant were soon on the waves of an animated conversation. The company numbered about thirty, and a few moments after the General's arrival dinner was announced. The Prince led the way, escorting Mrs. Grant, who sat on his right, with Mrs. Taylor on his left, the General and the Princess *vis-a-vis*, with Mr. Von Schlozer, the German Minister at Washington, between. The remainder of the company were members of the Cabinet and high persons in Berlin.

About half-past seven, or later, the dinner was over, and the company adjourned to another room.

General Grant had several interviews with Bismarck, and the interchange of opinion and criticism took a wide range, and seemed to strengthen the high opinion each had for the other. The contrast between the two faces was a study; no two faces, of this generation, at least, have been more widely drawn. In expression Bismarck has what might be an intense face, a moving, restless eye, that might flame in an instant. His conversation is irregular, rapid, audacious, with gleams of humor, saying the oddest and frankest things, and enjoying anything that amuses him so much that, frequently, he will not, cannot finish the sentence, for laughing. Grant, whose enjoyment of humor is keen, never passes beyond a smile. In conversation he talks his theme directly out with care, avoiding no detail, correcting himself if he slips in any, exceedingly accurate in statement, and who always talks well, because he never talks about what he does not know.

One notes in comparing the two faces how much more

INTERVIEW BETWEEN PRINCE BISMARCK AND GENERAL GRANT.

youth there is in that of Grant than of Bismarck. Grant's face was tired enough two years ago, when fresh from that witches' dame of an Electoral Commission — it had that weary look which you see in Bismarck's, but it has gone, and of the two men one would certainly deem Grant the junior by twenty years.

Mr. Taylor, the American Minister, was evidently impressed with the historical value of the meeting of Grant and Bismarck. He remembered a German custom that you can never cement a friendship without a glass of old-fashioned schnapps. There was a bottle of a famous schnapps cordial, among other bottles — no matter how old it was — and the Minister said, "General, no patriotic German will believe that there can ever be lasting friendship between Germany and the United States unless yourself and the Prince pledge eternal amity between all Germans and Americans over a glass of this schnapps." The Prince laughed, and thanked the Minister for the suggestion. The schnapps was poured out, the General and Prince touched glasses, and the vows were exchanged in hearty fashion.

General Grant arrived at Gothenburg on the 12th of July. He was met by a crowd of over five thousand people, who cheered loudly for him of whom they had heard so much. The Swedes, who have emigrated in such large numbers to the United States, have spread his fame among their countrymen at home. The ships in the harbor were all decorated in his honor. He passed the day in Gothenburg, and then continued his journey to Christiana. All the villages along the route were decorated, and his coming was made the occasion of a gala day.

He landed at Christiana on the 13th, and was received with great ceremony. Ten thousand people flocked to greet him. King Oscar II. came to Christiana from Stockholm to meet the General, and gave him a dinner and a reception.

The General set out sightseeing, and was conducted to the old castle of Aggershuus, with its citadel and church on the brow of a point jutting out into the fiord, over whose winding shore-line and smooth waters, broken by wooded islands, it gives a fine view.

The reception of the ex-President throughout Scandinavia was enthusiastic and remarkable, everywhere the citizens turning out *en masse* to welcome and honor him. At Stockholm, on the 24th, he was tendered a grand state banquet and dinner at the Embassy, and was serenaded, and a large crowd assembled and cheered him as he embarked for Russia.

General Grant arrived at St. Petersburg July 30. On arriving in the Russian capital, he was met by Minister Stoughton, whose wonderful coronal of snowy locks never shone more magnificently over his rosy cheeks.

The Emperor's Aid-de-Camp, Prince Gortschakoff, and other high officials of the imperial court, called immediately, welcoming the ex-President in the name of the Czar.

On the following day General Grant had an audience with the Emperor Alexander, which was of a pleasant nature.

The imperial yacht conveyed the General to Peterhof, the Verseilles of St. Petersburg. It is fifteen miles from the capital, but it has one advantage over the old French royal extra-mural residence in that, from the imperial palace, one has almost urivaled views over Cronstadt and the Gulf of Finland, and of the capital itself. The fountains were played in honor of the visit.

He afterward visited the great Russian man-of-war, Peter the Great. The band played American airs, and a royal salute of twenty-one guns was fired. The imperial yacht then steamed slowly among the Russian fleet lying off Cronstadt, the ships running out American colors, and the sailors cheering.

Subsequently the General had an interview with the Czar at St. Petersburg. The Emperor manifested great cordiality. The General was presented by Prince Gortschakoff. His Majesty talked of his health and the General's travels. He seemed greatly interested in our national wards, the Indians, and made several inquiries as to their mode of warfare.

At the close of the interview, the Emperor accompanied General Grant to the door, saying:—

"Since the foundation of your government, the relations between Russia and America have been of the friendliest character; and as long as I live nothing shall be spared to continue that friendship."

The General answered that, although the two governments were directly opposite in character, the great majority of the American people were in sympathy with Russia, and would, he hoped, so continue.

At the station, General Grant met the Grand Duke Alexis, who was very cordial, recalling with pleasure his visits to America.

A visit was also made to the great Chancellor, Prince Gortschakoff, with whom the General spent some hours, smoking and discussing American and European affairs.

The Czarowitch also received General Grant at special audience.

The French Ambassador gave a dinner to the General, and there was a special review of the fire brigade in his honor. The attentions of the Emperor and the authorities were so marked that he prolonged his stay several days.

On the 9th instant he was in Moscow, the ancient capital of Russia. He dined with Prince Dogoroff on the 10th, was at Warsaw the 13th. At all of these cities he was received with the same marked cordiality, and his visit recalled with feelings of pleasure.

On the 18th our ex-President arrived at Vienna. At the railroad station he was met by Minister Kasson, the secretaries and members of the American Legation, and a large number of the American residents. He was loudly cheered as he stepped out of the railway carriage.

On the 19th the General was visited at the Legation of the United States by Count Andrassy, the First Minister of the Council, and several colleagues. In the evening he dined with the Countess and Mrs. Grant at Post's. On the 20th he had an audience of His Imperial Majesty Francis Joseph, at the lovely palace of Schoenbrunn, spending the remainder of the day driving about the imperial grounds and forests, and visiting points of interest in that romantic and historic neighborhood.

On the 21st General and Mrs. Grant were entertained by the imperial family, and dined with the Emperor in the evening. During the morning Baron Steinberg accompanied the Emperor's American guests to the Arsenal.

On the 22d Minister Kasson gave a diplomatic dinner in honor of our ex-President, at which nearly all the foreign Ambassadors were present. The members of the Austro-Hungarian Cabinet attended the reception in the evening, and added to the attractiveness and brilliancy of the occasion. The General expressed himself greatly pleased with Vienna, and thought it a charming city. He was gratified also at the marked attentions of the Emperor's household, and the earnest endeavor shown to honor him as a citizen of the United States.

On September 23 General Grant was at Zurich, and dined with the American Consul, S. H. Byers, at the Hotel Bauer. Among the distinguished guests were Burgomaster Roemer, of Zurich; Feer-Herzog, a National Councillor; the German poet, Kinkel; General Vogelli, of the Swiss army; Mr. Nicholas Fish, the American Charge d'Affaires at Berne, and many prominent Swiss citizens.

When the cloth was removed, Consul Byers, after a few appropriate remarks, asked his guests to drink the health of his renowned countryman, "who, having led half a million of men to victory, and having governed a great nation for eight years, needs no praise from me." General Grant's health was then drank with all the honors. The Burgomaster expressed, in a brief and happy speech, the interest with which the Swiss people followed General Grant's career as a soldier and as President of the great Republic, and said that the honor done and the pleasure given to the citizens of Zurich by ex-President Grant's visit was very great.

In response, General Grant expressed a deep sense of pleasure and honor at meeting such distinguished Swiss gentlemen. He thanked the citizens of Zurich, through their Mayor, for their cordial reception, which he regarded as a symbol of the good feeling existing between the two countries. The General concluded by proposing the health of the President of the Federal Council and nation, and the prosperity of the city of Zurich.

Feer-Herzog replied in an eloquent allusion to the amity existing between the two countries, and ended by proposing the health of President Hayes. Mr. Nicholas Fish responded, testifying to "the memory cherished by all true United States citizens of the Switzers who fought and died during the American war — giving their lives and services from the pure, unselfish sympathy of their hearts and their inborn love of freedom. The acts of those heroes are to Americans the guarantee of Switzerland's sympathy in the hour of need and of despair."

Other speeches were made, and the dinner was, altogether, a thoroughly enjoyable occasion. In every respect General Grant's reception in the land of William Tell has been as hearty as in any place in Europe. The General left for Paris the following morning.

CHAPTER XII.

GENERAL GRANT IN SPAIN AND PORTUGAL.

General Grant arrived at the French capital on September 25, from Belfort. He was met at the station by Minister Noyes, ex-Governor Fairchild, ex-Governor McCormick, and other American officials. The General was in excellent health and spirits, and had experienced so little fatigue during his journey that, after dining *en famille*, he strolled along the boulevards for more than two hours.

A grand dinner was given to the ex-President October 3 by Mr. Edward F. Noyes, the United States Minister, at the Legation. Among the invited guests were the following distinguished Americans: General and Mrs. Grant, John Welsh, Minister to England; John A. Kasson, Minister to Austria; J. Meredith Read, Charge d'Affaires to Greece; General Hazen, United States Army; General Lucius Fairchild, Consul-General at Paris; ex-Governor McCormick, Commissioner-General to the Paris Exposition; ex-Governor Smith, of New Hampshire, and Miss Waite, daughter of the Chief Justice of the Supreme Court of the United States.

General Grant, having abandoned his contemplated trip to India for the present, concluded to remain in Paris and vicinity for the winter, and planned a month's tour through Spain, Portugal and Algiers.

The ex-President and party arrived in Vittoria, having entered Spain from France by the Bayonne route. The little town of Irun, which is just over the frontier, afforded the first glimpse of Spanish life and character. Its neat railway station was draped with flags and bunting, and on the platform was a group of officers of the royal guard, standing apart from those privileged citizens who had been admitted within the barriers. Beyond, clearly seen through the gates and station windows, struggling for a glimpse of the distinguished visitor, were the villagers and the country people, who, denied admission to the yard, were none the less active in their demonstrations of curiosity.

As the train drew up at the platform, General Grant alighted from his carriage. The ranking officer of the delegation, a general on the staff of Alfonzo XII., advanced, and, saluting the visitor, welcomed him, in the King's name, to the Iberian Peninsula. He stated that he was directed by His Majesty to place at the General's disposal the special railway carriage of the King, and to beg an acceptance of the same. General Grant expressed his thanks in a few words, and accepted the proffered courtesy. The train moved out of the little village toward the war-begrimed city of San Sebastian — the last stronghold of the Carlists.

At San Sebastian, General Grant was received by Emilio Castelar, ex-President of the Spanish Republic. To the well known statesman and journalist, General Grant was exceedingly cordial. He concluded his remarks by saying: "Believe me, sir, the name of Castelar is especially honored in America." Here, as at Irun, were gathered many people to see General Grant, and he was presented to the town officials and the distinguished citizens. The contracted harbor reflected the green of the tree-covered hills that encircle it so nearly, and beyond the cone-like isle at its mouth was the sheen of the noonday sun on the Bay of Biscay.

Leaving this place, the road leads southward toward Tolosa and Vergara. At both of these stations a squad of soldiers was stationed. The usual military guard had been doubled in honor of the American General. After winding about the hills beyond the station of Tolosa, the train suddenly leaves the defiles behind and smoothly skirts the side of a great hill, giving the occupants of the carriages a grand view to the southward. Near at hand are seen the peaks of the Pyrenees — only the extreme western spur of the range, to be sure, but very formidable looking barriers to railway engineering. Altogether, the journey is a charming, Swiss-like ride, creeping, as the traveler does, through what were once dangerous mountain paths, and where, even yet, the railway coaches are alternately in the wildest forests of scraggy pine and the long-leaved chestnut.

Passing the summit, the descent southward is soon marked by a radical change in the aspect of the country. Villages are met more frequently, until, winding toward the west through the Welsh-looking hills, the train dashes into Vittoria. Here the General was received on alighting by the civil and military authorities attached to the King's military and civil staff. He repaired at once to his hotel. The annual manœuvres of the Spanish army were being held here, and the King and his entire staff were in Vittoria. At night the General strolled out through the tangled streets of the old part of the town. He inspected the bazaars in the Plaza Nueva, and the pretty streets in the new portion of the city. The Alameda was crowded with people, and the General seemed to enjoy the life *al fresco* almost as much as the citizens of the capital of Alava.

The following morning General Grant was received by King Alfonzo at the *Ayuntamiento*, or residence of the Alcade, quite a palace in its exterior and interior adornments. The King, who speaks English fluently, said that he had long had a curiosity to meet the General, whose civil and military career was so familiar to him. He said there was no man living whom Spain would more gladly honor. The interview was long and cordial, and much good feeling was shown on both sides.

At eleven o'clock, General Grant, King Alfonzo and a splendid retinue of generals, left the King's official residence to witness the manœuvres that were to take place on the historic field of Vittoria, where the French, under Joseph Bonaparte and Jourdan, were finally crushed in Spain by the allies, under Wellington (June 21, 1813).

King Alfonzo and General Grant rode at the head of the column side by side, His Majesty pointing out the objects of interest to the right and the left, and, when the vicinity of the famous field was reached, halting for a few minutes to indicate to his guest the locations of the different armies on that famous June morning. As they proceeded thence, General Concha was called to the side of the King and introduced to General Grant. Several other distinguished officers were then presented. The weather was very fine, and the scene was one of great interest to the American visitor. General Grant spent all day on horseback, witnessing the manœuvres.

The King and his guest, returned to the city late in the afternoon. At night he dined with the King, and the next day General Grant reviewed the troops, and at night he left for Madrid. Altogether, both at the palace and on the field, General Grant's reception was royal in pomp and attention, and will be likely to impress the reader with the opinion that in no country has the reception of our great soldier been more free, manly and royal than in Spain. Met at the frontier by representatives of His Majesty, escorted to the presence of the monarch, shown a review on the battlefield of Vittoria, and treated in all ways as the especial guest of the sovereign, the ex-President certainly received in this case every mark of consideration and honor that a king could bestow upon a visitor. General Grant, it is true, has expressed in Europe the sense of his satiety with the military shows of life, and they might have hit his individual taste more accurately in some other way; yet a review on a famous battlefield is a piece of historic pageantry aside from ordinary reviews; and an honor in which history itself is called upon to pay tribute to a visitor is not to be had every day.

The General was especially favored in the conditions under which he has visited the various nations of Europe, meeting all its great statesmen on friendly terms. Beaconsfield, Bismarck, Gortschakoff, Gambetta and others have chatted with him familiarly, and he has heard much from them about the socialists and their crazy theories. In Berlin he heard from Bismarck's lips his hot indignation over the recent wounding of the Emperor, and now in Spain he actually witnesses an attempt on the life of a king. With all the horror of the crime and contempt of the criminals which must have entered his mind, he has, doubtless, pondered over the state of society in Europe which makes these atrocious attempts seem epidemic. He must have recognized a social disease, to diagnose which the statesmen he met did not bring unbiassed minds. It would be curious to know his impressions on the subject of misgovernment in Europe.

The excitement occasioned by the attempt on King Alfonso's life was intense. The criminal fired from the sidewalk in front of house No. 93 Calle Mayor, not far from the arched entrance to the Plaza Mayor. He aimed too low, however, and the ball passed through the hand of a soldier standing guard on the opposite side of the street. The King saw the flash, and, with an involuntary movement of his hand, checked his horse momentarily. He then rode tranquilly onward toward the palace. Several women who were standing near the man who fired pointed him out with loud cries, and he was at once secured. He did not make the slightest attempt to escape. Terrible indignation was manifested among the people forming the crowd that almost immediately gathered from the bazaars and the markets in the Plaza Mayor — that doleful old enclosed square, where the *autos da fe* and the *fiestas reales* took place during and even since the days of the Inquisition, but now given over to the venders of dates, pomegranates and base metal jewelry. Attempts were made to wreak summary vengeance upon the assassin when he was on his way to the Gobierno Civil. Thence he was soon removed to the Captain-Generalcy.

The prisoner displayed great coolness during his commitment. He insolently drew a cigar from his pocket, which, after having struck a match, he coolly lit and began to smoke. He is a very thin man, of medium height, wears a light mustache, and has his hair closely cropped. He admitted the crime, and triumphantly declared himself a socialist and internationalist; but, when interrogated as to who his accomplices were, denied that he had acted in concert with any one. He said that he came alone from Taragona purposely to kill a king. This was his first serious disappointment in life.

General Grant was standing, when the shot was fired, at a window of the Hotel de Paris (situated at the junction of the Carrera San Geronimo and the Calle de Alcala), overlooking the Puerta del Sol. This hotel is a long distance from the scene of the attack, but looks across the great central plaza of Madrid, directly down the Calle Mayor. General Grant, who was following with his eyes the progress of the royal cavalcade which had just passed across the Puerta del Sol before him, said that he clearly saw the flash of the assassin's pistol. The General had already "booked" for Lisbon by the night train leaving at seven o'clock, and therefore could not in person present his congratulations to King Alfonso; but to Senor Silvera, the Minister of State, who called soon after and accompanied him to the railway station, General Grant expressed his sympathies, and regrets that he was unable to postpone his journey in order that he might personally call upon His Majesty. He begged Senor Silvera to convey to the King his sincere congratulations on his escape from the assassin's bullet. There was a great gathering of diplomats, nobles and men of all parties at the palace to offer congratulations on Friday night and Saturday morning. Marshal Serrano (Duke de la Torre) was one of the first callers. Minister James Russell Lowell and Mr. Ried, Secretary of Legation, called at the palace Saturday, and expressed their gratification at the King's escape. The King made light of the whole affair, but the popular indignation was intense.

General Grant dined with King Luis at Lisbon, November 1. All the members of the ministry were present, including the Marquis of Avilae Bolama, Minister of State and of Foreign Affairs; Conseilhero J. de Mello e Gauvea, Finance Minister; Conseilhero J. de Sande Magalhaes Mexia Salema, Minister of Justice; Conseilhero A. F. de Sousa Pinto, Minister of War; the Count De Castro, and other members of the judiciary and military departments of the kingdom. The palace was gayly trimmed with flags, and the day was a festival throughout the city.

King Luis' reception of the ex-President of the United States was very cordial. His Majesty offered the General the highest decoration of knighthood known to the kingdom. General Grant thanked the King, but said he was compelled to decline the honors, as the laws of the United States made it impossible for an officer to wear decorations, and, although he was not now in office, he preferred to respect the law. He thanked His Majesty heartily for the honor intended. King Luis then offered him a copy of his translation of "Hamlet" into Portuguese, which General Grant accepted with many thanks.

Amoug the pleasantest experiences of his **European**

tour General Grant will certainly rank his cordial reception by King Luis at Lisbon. Overshadowed as Portugal is politically by the greater power on the Iberian Peninsula, it has a sturdy life of its own, which, until thrones are abolished, it promises to retain. The house of Braganza, which, through the stress of circumstances, sent its scions to this side of the Atlantic, builded better than it knew. In Brazil it found a scope for its usefulness that it could not have hoped for in the narrower limits of the parent kingdom. The coming of General Grant was, doubtless, quite an important event in the somewhat dull routine of court life at Lisbon, and everything appears to have been done to make it pleasant and memorable for the guest. General Grant's polite but firm refusal to accept the highest order of knighthood in the kingdom may have come with a certain shock to the monarch, for kings are seldom refused in such matters.

The ex-President arrived at Seville on the 8th, and was received with great honor by the civil and military authorities of the city. The populace showed every mark of respect to the distinguished American, and the bearing of the officials was most cordial. On Friday he breakfasted with the Duke de Montpensier, father of the late Queen Mercedes.

On Tuesday he reached Cadiz. He was received at the landing place by the Mayor of the city and the civil and military officials. A guard of honor was in attendance, and a large crowd cheered the ex-President as he passed out. The reception was most enthusiastic on the part of the people, and very cordial on that of the authorities.

On the 17th General Grant and party left Cadiz for Gibraltar. The sea was very calm, and the delightful voyage was greatly enjoyed by all. The first welcome sight to the visitors was the American flag flying from one of our men-of-war. There was some trouble in distinguishing the vessel until a near approach, when old friends were recognized in the persons of Captain Robeson and shipmates of the Vandalia.

The General directed his vessel to steam around the Vandalia, and cordial greetings were exchanged between the two ships. As they headed into port, the Vandalia mounted her yards, and Captain Robeson came in his barge to take the General on shore. The American Consul, Mr. Sprague, and two officers of Lord Napier's staff, met the General and welcomed him to Gibraltar in the name of the General commanding. Amid a high sea, which threw its spray over most of the party, they pulled ashore. On landing, a guard of honor presented arms, and the General drove at once to the house of Mr. Sprague, on the hill.

Mr. Sprague has lived many years at Gibraltar, and is the oldest consular officer in the service of the United States. General Grant was the third ex-President he has entertained at his house. Lord Napier, of Magdala, the commander at Gibraltar, had telegraphed to Cadiz, asking the General to dinner on the evening of his arrival. At seven o'clock, the General and Mrs. Grant, accompanied by the Consul, went to the palace of the Governor, called The Convent, and were received in the most hospitable manner by Lord Napier. His Lordship had expressed a great desire to meet General Grant, and relations of courtesy had passed between them before — Lord Napier, who commanded the expeditionary force in Abyssinia, having sent General Grant King Theodore's bible. The visit to Gibraltar may be summed up in a series of dinners — first, at the Governor's palace; second, with the mess of the Royal Artillery; again, at the Consul's. Then there were one or two private and informal dinners at Lord Napier's; and, in fact, most of General Grant's time at Gibraltar was spent in the company of this distinguished commander — a stroll around the batteries, a ride over the hills, a gallop along the beach, a review of troops, and taking part in a sham battle. Lord Napier was anxious to show General Grant his troops, and although, as those who know the General can testify, he has a special aversion to military display, he spent an afternoon in witnessing a march past of the British garrison, and afterward a sham battle. It was a beautiful day for the manœuvres. General Grant rode to the field, accompanied by Lord Napier, Gen. Conolly, and others of the staff. Mrs. Grant, accompanied by the Consul and the ladies of the Consul's family, followed, and took up her station by the reviewing post. The English bands all played American airs out of compliment to the General, and the review was given in his honor. Lord Napier was exceedingly pleased with the troops, and said to General Grant he supposed they were on their best behavior, as he had never seen them do so well. The General examined them very closely, and said that he did not see how their discipline could be improved. "I have seen," said the General, "most of the troops of Europe; they all seemed good; I liked the Germans very much, and the Spaniards only wanted good officers, so far as I could see, to bring them up to the highest standard; but these have something about them — I suppose it is their Saxon blood — which none of the rest possess; they have the swing of conquest."

The General would have liked to have remained at Gibraltar longer, but there is nothing in the town beyond the garrison. We suppose his real attraction to the place was the pleasure he found in Lord Napier's society, and again coming in contact with English ways and customs, after having been so long with the stranger.

General Grant spent several days at Pau, where he was engaged in hunting, and making short journeys into the Pyrenees. He returned to Paris on the 11th of December, having accepted the offer of President Hayes to go to India on the United States corvette Richmond. The President's offer was made in the most flattering terms. After visiting Ireland, his plan was to embark at Marseilles and proceed direct to India via the Suez Canal. In no country had the great American soldier been more royally received, or favored with more noteworthy associations, than in Spain and Portugal.

CHAPTER XIII.

GENERAL GRANT IN IRELAND.

If anything was a moral certainty, it was that when General Grant visited Ireland he would meet with a popular reception of the most enthusiastic description. That he was a great and successful soldier was a high claim upon a people with such admiration of the chivalrous; that he had led to victory so many thousands of Irishmen and sons of Irishmen in the war for the Union, brought him still closer to them, for there is scarcely a household in all Ireland that has not some family link with the Irish beyond the Atlantic. To him Fame justly ascribes the salvation of that government and that flag under which the famine-stricken, the oppressed and the evicted of Ireland had found homes, prosperity and freedom. During the war for the Union the people of Ireland prayed, like Lincoln at Gettysburg, that this "government of the people, for the people and by the people, should not perish from the earth." They could not fit out ships to fight the Alabamas that England was letting go, but they sent out many a sturdy son to do battle for the Union. To an immense proportion of the Irish people General Grant typifies the republican form of government which they hope for. By the officials of the British government General Grant was, of course, received as a foremost citizen of a friendly power; but it was in its popular feature that his visit was the most interesting.

General Grant and family, accompanied by Minister Noyes, arrived in Dublin, by boat, on the morning of

January 3, 1879. The ex-President was met by representatives of the corporation. He was driven to the Shelbourne Hotel, and at once prepared to visit the City Hall to meet the Lord Mayor. The city was full of strangers, and much enthusiasm was manifested when the General and his party left their hotel to drive to the Mansion House. On arriving at the Mayor's official residence, they were cheered by a large crowd that had gathered to greet the illustrious ex-President. The Lord Mayor, in presenting the freedom of the city, referred to the cordiality always existing between America and Ireland, and hoped that in America General Grant would do everything he could to help a people who sympathize with every American movement. The parchment, on which was engrossed the freedom of the city, was inclosed in an ancient, carved bog-oak casket.

General Grant appeared to be highly impressed by the generous language of the Lord Mayor. He replied: "I feel very proud of being made a citizen of the principal city of Ireland, and no honor that I have received has given me greater satisfaction. I am by birth the citizen of a country where there are more Irishmen, native born or by descent, than in all Ireland. When in office I had the honor — and it was a great one, indeed — of representing more Irishmen and descendants of Irishmen than does Her Majesty the Queen of England. I am not an eloquent speaker, and can simply thank you for the great courtesy you have shown me." Three cheers were given for General Grant at the close of his remarks, and then three more were added for the people of the United States.

Mr. Isaac Butt, the well known home-rule member of Parliament, speaking as the first honorary freeman of this city, congratulated General Grant on having consolidated into peace and harmony the turbulent political and sectional elements over which he triumphed as a soldier.

His speech throughout was highly complimentary of the ex-President.

In the evening a grand banquet was given in honor of the ex-President, over two hundred guests being present.

The Lord Mayor presided. General Noyes returned thanks for a toast to President Hayes' health. When General Grant's name was proposed, the company arose and gave the Irish welcome.

The ex-President made in response the longest speech of his life, speaking in a clear voice, and being listened to with rapt attention. He referred to himself and fellow citizens of Dublin, and intimated, amid much laughter and cheering, that he might return to Dublin one day and run against Barrington for Mayor, and Butt for Parliament. He warned those gentlemen that he was generally a troublesome candidate.

Then passing to serious matters, the General said:—
"We have heard some words spoken about our country — my country, before I was naturalized in another. We have a very great country, a prosperous country, with room for a great many people. We have been suffering for some years from very great oppression. The world has felt it. There is no question about the fact that, when you have forty-five millions of consumers such as we are, and when they are made to feel poverty, then the whole world must feel it.

"You have had here great prosperity because of our great extravagance and our great misfortunes. We had a war which drew into it almost every man who could bear arms, and my friend who spoke so eloquently to you a few moments ago lost a leg in it. You did not observe that, perhaps, as he has a wooden one in place of it.

"When that great conflict was going on, we were spending one thousand million dollars a year more than we were producing, and Europe got every dollar of it. It made for you a false prosperity. You were getting our bonds and our promises to pay. You were cashing them yourselves. That made great prosperity, and made producers beyond the real necessities of the world at peace. But we finally got through that great conflict, and with an inflated currency which was far below the specie you use here. It made our people still more extravagant. Our speculations were going on, and we still continued to spend three or four hundred millions of money per year more than we were producing.

"We paid it back to you for your labor and manufactures, and it made you apparently and really prosperous. We, on the other hand, were getting really poor, but being honest, however, we came to the day of solid, honest payment. We came down to the necessity of selling more than we bought. Now we have turned the corner. We have had our days of depression; yours is just coming on. I hope it is nearly over. Our prosperity is commencing, and as we become prosperous you will, too, because we become increased consumers of your products as well as our own. I think it safe to say that the United States, with a few years' more such prosperity, will consume as much more as they did. Two distinguished men have alluded to this subject—one was the President of the United States, and he said that the prosperity of the United States would be felt to the bounds of the civilized world. The other was Lord Beaconsfield, the most far-seeing man, the one who seems to me to see as far into the future as any man I know, and he says the same as President Hayes."

General Grant's speech created a profound sensation, and was loudly cheered during its delivery.

The following morning ex-President Grant, Mr. Noyes and Mr. Badeau visited the Royal Irish Academy, in Kildare Street, in company with Lord Mayor Barrington.

Here, after some time spent in inspecting the treasures of ancient Irish art in gold, silver and bronze, Saint Patrick's bell and sacred cross, and O'Donneil's casque, the party went to the building that was the old Parliament house. It is now the bank of Ireland, and the walls which formerly echoed with the eloquence of Grattan, Curran and Plunkett, now resound with the chaffering of the money changers. Trinity College was then visited. The party was received by the Provost and Fellows and escorted through the library, chapel and halls of this venerable and majestic pile.

General Grant drove to the vice-regal lodge of the Duke of Marlborough, Phœnix Park, early in the afternoon, where he had *déjeuner* with the Viceroy. He afterward visited the Zoological Gardens, then returned to his hotel, where he rested a couple of hours.

It may be interesting to notice the contrast between the generous welcome extended to General Grant by the people of Dublin, and the uncalled-for and spiteful slight aimed at him by a clique of the Cork City Council, as showing to what lengths sectional and religious agitation are sometimes carried. The United States Consul at Cork addressed a letter to the Council, announcing that Grant would probably arrive in Cork within a few days. Mr. Tracy, a nationalist, proposed at the Council meeting that the letter should simply be marked "read," and that no action should be taken. Mr. Harris, a conservative, said: " It will be to the interest of our fellow-countrymen in the United States if a proper reception is accorded to General Grant, who represents the governing party in that country. There can be no personal antipathy to the gentleman himself; neither was there anything in the government of the ex-President objectionable to the Irish people nor unpleasant to the Irish in America. Probably General Grant would again be at the head of the United States, in which event it would be to the interest of our fellow-countrymen in America if proper recognition was given to General Grant on his arrival at Cork."

Mr. Barry, an extreme nationalist, said the ex-President had insulted the Irish people in America. He got up the "No Popery" cry there.

Mr. Tracy said it would be unbecoming for the Catholic constituency of Cork to welcome such a man. It would be ungenerous to refuse him hospitality if he deserved it, but he saw nothing in General Grant's career that called for sympathy from the Irish nation. He never thought of the Irish race as he thought of others, and he went out of his way to insult their religion.

Mr. Dwyer, an advanced nationalist, would not couple General Grant's name with America. The Irish who sought a refuge and a home in the United States had received kindness and attention from the American people. President Grant had never given them the same recognition as the other inhabitants. It would be an impropriety to pay any mark of respect personally to General Grant.

Messrs. McSweeny and Creedon, nationalists, spoke to the same effect, and with a great shout of "Aye," there being no dissenting voices, Cork refused to receive General Grant.

The New York *Herald*, commenting on this action of the City Council of Cork, said:

"The Town Council of Cork has done more to advertise itself in connection with General Grant than the municipal authority of any other city in Europe. The respectful hospitalities of which the American ex-President has been the object since he left his native shores nearly two years ago have been so constant, so uniform, so unbroken, that the recital of them was beginning to pall upon public attention. Monotony at last grows tiresome, even if it be a monotony of highly seasoned compliments. A break of continuity in the long round of festive receptions given to General Grant heightens their effect by a little dash of contrast. It is like one of those rough lines which poets sometimes introduce into their compositions to recall attention to the harmony which pervades the general structure of their verse."

"The Town Council of Cork has made a discovery which had escaped the rest of Catholic Europe and of Catholic Ireland. It proclaims, as a justification of its discourtesy, that President Grant went out of his way to insult its religion. The deeds of General Grant have not been done in a corner, and it seems odd enough that it was reserved for the Town Council of Cork to detect and proclaim a fact which has escaped the knowledge of Europe and America. Our traveling ex-President has been as warmly received in Catholic Italy and Spain as in Protestant England and Germany; he has been as much honored by the Catholic President MacMahon, as by the Protestant, Queen Victoria; and even Catholic Dublin has not fallen behind the sister cities of the United Kingdom. The Town Council of Cork would seem to be better Catholics than the Pope himself.

"General Grant had decided, before learning of the singular action at Cork, that it would not suit his convenience to pay a visit to that city. He thinks that its authorities have convicted themselves of a strange inattention to American history. It is, indeed, well enough known that General Grant is not a Catholic; but it is equally well known that he is superior to all narrow and illiberal prejudices against members of that communion. His two most intimate friends in the army are General Sherman and Lieutenant-General Sheridan, both Catholics. He did all in his power to advance the interests of these distinguished soldiers before he became President, and after his accession he promoted them to the two highest positions in the

American army. His zealous friendship was not founded on their religion, but their personal qualities; but their Catholic connection never abated in the least his generous care of their interests. In civil affairs his freedom from religious bigotry has been equally genuine, though less conspicuous. He appointed Mr. Thomas Murphy Collector of the Port of New York, one of the most important and responsible positions in the civil service, and both in office and out of office Mr. Murphy was treated by him as an intimate personal friend and favorite.

"We suppose the Cork orators must have heard of President Grant's Des Moines speech, in which he declared himself in favor of anti-sectarian free schools. But many American Catholics are supporters of our common school system. The ablest and most distinguished Catholic now in public life in this country, Senator Kernan, has always been a steady friend of our common schools. He was for many years the most efficient member of the School Board of Utica, the city of his residence. The Town Council of Cork has acted on a misconception, and its members have reason to be heartily ashamed of their ignorance, as well as of their illiberality and discourtesy."

This action of the city of Cork produced a profound sensation throughout Ireland, the people looking at it as a violation of the rites of hospitality. General Grant smiled when told of the action of the Cork Councilmen, and said he was sorry the Cork people knew so little of American history.

The respectable liberals and conservatives of the city and county of Cork were indignant at the action of the clique in the Council who insulted ex-President Grant. An ex-Mayor of the city said: "The obstructionists who opposed a *cead mille failthe* to General Grant are not worth a decent man rubbing up against. It is a pity that the General has determined to return to Paris instead of visiting Cork, where he would have received such an ovation from the self-respecting populace as would prove that the Irish heart beats in sympathy with America."

General Grant quietly left Dublin on Monday morning, January 6, Lord Mayor Barrington taking leave of him at the railway station. The morning was cold, and, as the train progressed northward, ice, snow, cold winds and finally rain were encountered. At Dundalk, Omagh, Strabane and other stations, large crowds were assembled and the people cheered the ex-President, putting their hands into the cars and shaking hands with him whenever possible. The expressions of ill-feeling toward General Grant in Cork had aroused the Protestant sentiments of the Irish people of Ulster in his favor.

At two o'clock the train reached Derry. A heavy rain had covered the ground with ice, rendering the view of the city and surroundings most charming, as seen through the mists and gossamer of falling snow. At the station an immense crowd, apparently the whole town and neighborhood, had assembled. The multitude was held in check by the police. The Mayor welcomed General Grant cordially, and he left the station amid great cheering, mingled with groans from the nationalist members of the crowd, who called out, "Why didn't ye receive O'Connor Power?" The great majority of the crowd cheered madly, and followed General Grant's carriage to the hotel. The ships in the harbor were decorated with flags and streamers, and the town was *en fête*. A remarkably cold, driving rain set in at three o'clock, just as General Grant and his party drove in state to the ancient town hall. The crowd was so dense near the hall that progress through it was made with great difficulty. At the entrance of the building the Mayor and Council, in their robes of office, received the ex-President. Amid many expressions of enthusiasm from the people of Londonderry, an address was read extolling the military and civil career of General Grant, which was pronounced second in honor only to that of Washington.

General Grant signed the roll, thus making himself an Ulster Irishman. He then made a brief address. He said that no incident of his trip was more pleasant than accepting citizenship at the hands of the representatives of this ancient and honored city, with whose history the people of America were so familiar. He regretted that his stay in Ireland would be so brief. He had originally intended embarking from Queenstown direct for the United States, in which case he would have remained a much longer time on the snug little island; but, having resolved to visit India, he was compelled to make his stay short. He could not, however, he said in conclusion, return home without seeing Ireland and a people in whose welfare the people of the United States took so deep an interest. The ex-President returned to his hotel, making a short visit at the house of Consul Livermore *en route*.

A banquet was tendered to the General, at which he was present. The leading citizens of the province of Ulster attended, and the dinner was remarkably good. The reception of the ex-President was enthusiastic and cordial in the extreme. General Grant, in response to a toast, made a brief speech, saying that he should have felt that his tour in Europe was incomplete had he not seen the ancient and illustrious city of Londonderry, whose history was so well known throughout America. Indeed, the people of Derry, and all about there, had had a remarkable influence upon the development of American character. He cordially welcomed to the United States all the Irishmen who chose to make their homes there, and this was a welcome shared by the American people. Minister Noyes made a speech of the same general tenor, and at eleven o'clock the company separated.

The following morning General Grant strolled about,

looking at the historic walls, visiting Walker's Pillar, Roaring Meg, and the other curiosities of the town. The General's treatment by the people of Londonderry during his stay was unusually cordial.

General Grant's tour in Ulster was, in some respects, the most remarkable of his European experiences. People resented the action of the city of Cork as a slander upon Irish hospitality.

General Grant left Derry on the 7th, accompanied by Sir Hervey Bruce, Lieutenant of the county, Mr. Taylor, M. P. for Coleraine, and other local magnates. A cold rain and mists, coming from the Northern Ocean, obscured the wonderful view of the Northern Irish coast. The General studied the country closely, remarking on the sparseness of the population, and saying he could see no evidence of the presence of seven millions of people in Ireland.

At every station there were crowds assembled, and, when the cars stopped, the people rushed forward to shake hands with the General. Some were old soldiers who had been in the American army. One remarked that Grant had captured him at Paducah. Another asked General Grant to give him a shilling in remembrance of old times. The people were all kindly, cheering for Grant and America. At Coleraine there was an immense crowd. General Grant, accompanied by the Member of Parliament, Mr. Taylor, left the cars, entered the waiting-room at the depot, and received an address. In reply, General Grant repeated the hope and belief, expressed in his Dublin speech, that the period of depression was ended, and that American prosperity was aiding Irish prosperity. At Ballymoney there was another crowd. As the train neared Belfast, a heavy rain began to fall.

The train reached Belfast station at half-past two o'clock. The reception accorded General Grant was imposing and extraordinary. The linen and other mills had stopped work, and the workmen stood out in the rain in thousands. The platform of the station was covered with scarlet carpet. The Mayor and Members of the City Council welcomed the General, who descended from the car amid tremendous cheers. Crowds ran after the carriages containing the city authorities and their illustrious guest, and afterward surrounded the hotel where the General was entertained. Belfast was *en fete*. The public buildings were draped with American and English colors, and in a few instances with orange flags. Luncheon was served at four o'clock, and the crowd, with undaunted valor, remained outside amid a heavy snow storm, and cheered at intervals. The feature of the luncheon was the presence of the Roman Catholic Bishop of the diocese, who was given the post of honor. The luncheon party numbered one hundred and seventy — the Mayor said he could have had five thousand.

The Belfast speakers made cordial allusions to many people in America, and were anxious to have Grant declare himself in favor of free trade, but the General in his reply made no allusions to the subject, to the disappointment of many of those present. Minister Noyes made a hit in his speech when he said that General Grant showed his appreciation of Belfast men by appointing A. T. Stewart, of Belfast, Secretary of the Treasury, and offering George H. Stuart, a Belfast boy, the portfolio of Secretary of the Navy.

After the luncheon was over, General Grant remained quietly in his apartments, receiving many calls, some from old soldiers who served under him during the war.

At ten o'clock on the morning of January 9, General Grant and his party, accompanied by Mayor Brown, visited several of the large mills and industrial establishments of the city. Before he left the hotel he was waited on by a number of the leading citizens and several clergymen. Bishop Ryan, the Catholic Bishop of Buffalo, and Mr. Cronin, editor of the *Catholic Union*, were among the callers, and had a pleasant interview. The General then drove to the warehouses of several merchants in the linen trade, to the factories and shipyards. At the immense shipyard where the White Star steamers were built, the workmen, numbering two thousand, gathered around Grant's carriage and cheered as they ran alongside. The public buildings and many of the shops were decorated. The weather was clear and cold.

At three o'clock in the afternoon the General left for Dublin. Immense crowds had gathered at the hotel and at the railway station. The Mayor, with Sir John Preston and the American Consul, James M. Donnan, accompanied the General to the depot. As the train moved off the crowd gave tremendous cheers, the Mayor taking the initiative. One Irishman in an advanced stage of enthusiasm called out: "Three cheers for Oliver Cromwell Grant!" To this there was only a faint response.

At Portadown, Dundalk, Drogheda and other stations, there were immense crowds, the populations apparently turning out *en masse*. Grant was loudly cheered, and thousands surrounded the car with the hope of being able to shake the General by the hand, all wishing him a safe journey. One little girl created considerable merriment by asking the General to give her love to her aunt in America. All the Belfast journals, in more or less acrimonious terms, denounced the action of the Council of Cork. At Dundalk, the brother of Robert Nugent, who was Lieutenant-Colonel of the Sixty-ninth New York Regiment in 1861, and afterward commander of a brigade in the Second Corps, Army of the Potomac, said he was glad to welcome his brother's old commander.

The Belfast limited mail train, conveying General

Grant, arrived at Dublin fourteen minutes behind time on the 8th. Lord Mayor Barrington and a considerable number of persons were on the platform at the railway station, and cordially welcomed the General. As soon as all the party had descended, the Lord Mayor invited the General into his carriage and drove him to Westward Row, where the Irish mail train was ready to depart, having been detained eight minutes for the ex-President.

There was a most cordial farewell and a great shaking of hands. The Mayor and his friends begged General Grant to return soon and make a longer stay. Soon Kingston was reached, and in a few minutes the party were in the special cabin which had been provided for them on board the mail steamer. Special attention was paid to the General by the officers of the vessel. General Grant left the Irish shores at twenty minutes past seven o'clock.

When the steamer was about to start, the Inspector of Detectives inquired minutely concerning each member of the General's party then on board, apparently to satisfy himself that they were exactly the same gentlemen who landed here five days before, and that none who came were disguised Fenian emissaries masquerading as American generals, and who had remained behind while allowing some of their accomplices to get away under the same disguise.

In his reception at Belfast was shown, down to the very moment of his departure, an exuberant enthusiasm of welcome, that is, perhaps, justly understood as owing some part of its warmth to a desire to protest against the Corkonian blunder. His welcome at Dublin by the Lord Mayor was another pleasant tribute of good will; while the uneasiness of the police inspector, eager to know whether this descent of a foreign soldier on Irish soil was not, after all, some Fenian project in disguise, was characteristic, laughable, and perhaps the best a policeman could do in the way of a compliment. General Grant's visit to Ireland was ended; and it may be fairly said of it that a public man, from a far distant country, without official character, known to the world for his military glory and for services that saved a great republic from anarchy, was never more genially, warmly, earnestly and enthusiastically made to feel that heroism, and, above all, heroism in the cause of liberty, has no country, but is equally at home in any part of the world, where there is a people with a soul to appreciate great services and the aspiration to be free. An event like General Grant's welcome in Ireland does not happen in the lives of many men. Our own welcome to Lafayette on his revisiting this country might be compared to it, but that we were under the obligation of a people in whose own cause that soldier fought; and the Irish welcome to General Grant was, therefore, even more generous, for there was not even the obligation of gratitude in it. As for the little fly spot put on this fine picture by the Corkonians, why, it may be admitted that even an Irish city can produce some pitiful fellows, who want to become distinguished for their very meanness, if they have no worthier qualities. Some sharp-sighted democrats have seen in this visit to Ireland a strategic move on the Irish vote, should the General ever enter public life again. It is one of the misfortunes that dog public men in a country like ours, that every act of their lives has to be judged from the standpoint of those who contemplate it in the light of the ignoble hunt for votes. Some ground is given by what opponents of General Grant say to the opinion that they have stirred up this Corkonian trouble to head off this hunt. If this be true, they must have been inspired under the influence of Grant's lucky star, for they have done him a service for which he could not have counted upon them, except under the general principle that a great part of every distinguished man's good fortune is due to blunders of his adversaries.

CHAPTER XIV.

GRANT IN INDIA.

General Grant again visited London, where a grand dinner and reception was given him by our Minister to England, Mr. Welsh, which was largely attended by the *elite* of London, and American residents. At every station en route the greatest enthusiasm was manifested. The General left the next day for Paris, where he was the recipient of a grand dinner at the United States Legation on January 14, and a grand state dinner and reception at the Palais d' Elysee, the residence of President Mac-Mahon.

Among the invited guests were General Grant and family, M. Waddington and wife, General Noyes and wife, Miss King, Miss Stevens, the members of the Chinese Embassy, the representatives of San Salvador, Buenos Ayres, Chili, Guatemala, Peru, Colombia and Uruguay, and many French generals and admirals.

The General left Paris for Marseilles on the evening of January 21. The party accompanying him consisted of Mrs. Grant, Colonel Fred. Grant, ex-Secretary of the Navy A. E. Borie, Dr. Keating, and the *Herald* correspondent, who made the whole trip to India. General Badeau went as far as Marseilles. Generals Noyes and Fairchild, Secretaries Hill, Itgneau, and a large number of Americans, went to the station to see the party off. The train left at a quarter past seven o'clock, and arrived at Marseilles the following morning at eleven o'clock. Consul John B. Gould received them at the railway station. An afternoon reception was held at the Consulate, where General Grant met the leading citizens of Marseilles. At noon the party embarked on the French steamship Labourdonais for India, via Suez. The party embraced General and Mrs. Grant, ex-Secretary Borie, Lieutenant-Colonel Frederick D. Grant, Dr. Keating, of Philadelphia, and the *Herald* correspondent.

General Badeau, Consul Gould, J. B. Lippincott, of Philadelphia, John Munroe, the banker, and many other citizens, took leave of General and Mrs. Grant. The day was cold and the sky was filled with masses of gray cloud. The people of Marseilles evinced great interest in the General's departure. The ships in the harbor were dressed with flags and streamers. General Grant and his party were in the best of health and spirits.

The steamer moved out of the harbor shortly after twelve o'clock, and the land journey of General Grant in Europe closed amid the kindest manifestations of his countrymen at Marseilles and the French citizens of that great Mediterranean port. Marshal MacMahon had sent orders to the French admirals on foreign stations and to the governors of French colonies to treat ex-President Grant with all the honors due to the head of an independent State.

The first hours on the Mediterranean were on a high sea, but on second the day the sea went down and charming yachting weather was enjoyed. On Friday, January 24, the steamer passed between Corsica and Sardina, having a a fine view of the dusky coasts of the former island. On the 25th, about noon, Ischia was sighted, and through the hazy atmosphere faint outlines of Vesuvius could be traced. Ischia is a beautiful island, dotted with smiling villages, and presenting an inviting appearance. Passing the island, Capri was left to the right, and the vessel sailed into the beautiful Bay of Naples. The King's palace, the convent, the range of hills and the towering landscape remained unchanged, and at once recognized, though a year had nearly passed since the General's first visit. As soon as the anchor was dropped, Mr. Maynard, our Minister to Turkey, and Mr. Duncan, our Consul at Naples, came on board, and a delightful hour was passed. In the afternoon the Labourdonais steamed out to sea. On the morning of the 26th Stromboli was in sight. The General and party, owing to the stormy weather, were unable to see this famed island upon the previous voyage over this same route, but they were now sailing under the shadow of this ancient island. The volcano was throwing out ashes and smoke in a feeble, fretful manner. At the base of this volcano is a cluster of houses or a village. What reason any human being can give for remaining in Stromboli is beyond the knowledge of man. They are at the absolute mercy of the sea and the furnace, and far away from neighbors and refuge and rescue. It must be to gratify some poetic instinct, for Stromboli is poetic enough. With every turn of the screw our visitors were coming into the land of classic and religious fame; these islands through which they were sailing are the islands visited by the wandering Ulysses.

Reggio was passed, which in ancient days was called Rhegium. It was here that St. Paul landed, after Syracuse and Malta adventures, carrying with him the message of Christ, going from this spot to preach the gospel to all mankind.

Leaving Etna to the left, they sailed through Messina Straits, the sea scarcely rippling, and were soon again in the open sea, the land fading from view.

On the second morning Crete was passed, the snow upon her mountain ranges being plainly visible from the decks of the steamer. At noon Crete faded from their sight, and a last farewell to Europe was uttered — farewell to many a bright and happy hour spent on its shores, of which all that remains is the memory.

On the evening of the 29th of January — it being the evening of the seventh day of their journey from Marseilles — they came to anchor outside of the harbor of Alexandria. There was some disappointment that the steamer did not enter that evening, but they were an hour or so late, and so they swung at anchor and found what consolation they could in the enrapturing glory of an Egyptian night. In the morning when the sun arose, the steamer picked her way into the harbor, and when our visitors came on deck they found themselves at anchor, with Alexandria before them, her minarets looking almost gay in the fresh light of the morning sun. A boat came out about eight, bringing General C. P. Stone, Mr. Farman, our Consul-General, Mr. Salvago, our Consul in Alexandria, and Judge Morgan of the International Tribunal. General Stone came with kind messages from the Khedive, and the hope that General Grant might be able to come to Cairo. But this was not possible, as he had to connect with the English steamer at Suez, and Suez was a long day's journey. So all that was left was that they should pull ashore as rapidly as possible and drive to the train. The Consul-General, with prudent foresight, had arranged that the train should wait for the General, and thus it came that the General's ride through Egypt, from Alexandria to Suez, was during the day, and not, as otherwise would have happened, during the long and weary night.

It must have been pleasant to General Grant to land in a quiet, unostentatious fashion, without pomp and ceremony and pachas in waiting and troops in line, the blaze of trumpets and the thunder of guns. The escape from a salute and a reception was a great comfort to the General, who seemed to enjoy having no one's hands to shake, to enjoy a snug corner in an ordinary railway car, talking with General Stone and Mr. Borie and the Consul-General. The train waited half an hour for the General and party, and would have been detained longer but for the energy and genius shown by Hassan — the General's old friend Hassan — who accompanied him on the Nile. Hassan, as the official guard of the Legation, wearing a sword, was an authority in Egypt, and he used his authority to the utmost in having the traps and parcels carried from the wharf to the train. The ride to Suez was without incident, and Egypt, as seen from the car windows, was the same Egypt about which so much has been written. The fields were green, the air was clear and generous, the train people were civil. When Arabs gathered at the doors to call for backsheesh in the name of the prophet Hassan made himself, not without noise and effect, a beneficent influence. The General chatted with Stone about school times at West Point, about friends. Mr. Borie made various attempts to see the Pyramids from the cars, and talked over excursions that some of the party had made, and so much interested was he that the party offered to remain over one steamer to enable him to visit the Pyramids, and the Sphinx, and the Serapeum at Memphis. But General Grant was too late for India, and Mr. Borie would not consent to the sacrifice of valuable time on the General's part, and so they kept on to Suez. The hotel at Suez was formerly a harem of the Egyptian princes. From the balcony one can look out on the Red Sea, on the narrow line of water which has changed the commerce of the world — the Suez canal Suez is a small, clean town — clean from an Oriental standpoint. As the steamer that was to convey General Grant and party to India had not arrived, but was blocked in the canal, the visitors had a fine opportunity to visit the bazaars and town.

About five in the afternoon the boat was sighted, and, as the sun went down, General Grant went on board the steamer, Mr. Farman and General Stone remaining until the last moment, to say farewell. At eight o'clock on the evening of January 30, the steamer Venetia, of the Peninsular and Oriental Steamship Company's line, moved out into the Red Sea, and the last words of farewell were spoken. Owing to heavy head winds, the Venetia did not make much headway, losing nearly two days. At the mouth of the Red Sea is Aden, a town with a population of over twenty thousand inhabitants. It juts into the mouth of the Red Sea, commanding the entrance. It was taken by the British in 1838, as a part of the English policy of dotting the world with guns and garrisons. There is a garrison, and the forts are manned with heavy guns. The government is martial law, tempered with bribery. The British pay the native chiefs annual tribute money to behave themselves. Aden is a sort of gateway to the Red Sea and the Indian Ocean, and the regulations of the British government in reference to commerce are stringent, and would scarcely be tolerated on the coasts of a stronger power than Arabia. Every vessel carrying more than a certain number of passengers must stop at Aden. The nominal reason is to obtain a clean bill of health. The real reason is, that it enables the government to keep a close scrutiny upon all that is doing in the Indian waters. It also adds to the revenues of Aden, for every vessel that stops sends money on shore, and thus the fort, while securing a most important position, while commanding the Red Sea and making it almost a British lake, supports itself. It is observed in studying the growth of the British Empire, that the self-supporting principle is always encouraged. The British give good government and make the governed ones pay the bills, with a little over for home revenues when possible. Remaining at Aden only long enough to coal, on the morning of February 6 the steamer headed for Bombay. The trip was a delightful one, the steamer scarcely rolling. On the morning of February 13 Bombay was reached.

The departure from Europe had been so sudden that General Grant had no idea that even our Consul at Bombay knew of his coming. All arrangements were made to go to a hotel, and from thence make their journey; but the Venetia had scarcely entered the harbor before evidences were seen that the General was expected. Ships in the harbor were dressed with flags, and at the wharf was a large crowd — soldiers, natives, Europeans. As the English flag-ship was passed, a boat came alongside with an officer representing Admiral Corbett, welcoming the General to India. In a few minutes came another boat bearing Captain Frith, the military aid to Sir Richard Temple, Governor of the Presidency of Bombay. Captain Frith bore a letter from the Governor welcoming the General to Bombay, and offering him the use of the Government House at Malabar Point. Captain Frith expressed the regret of Sir Richard that he could not be in Bombay to meet General Grant, but duties connected with the Afghan war kept him in Sind. The Consul, Mr. Farnham, also came with a delegation of American residents, and welcomed the General and party.

At nine o'clock in the morning the last farewells were spoken. They took leave of the many kind and pleasant friends they had made on the Venetia, and went on board the government yacht. The landing was at the Apollo Bunder — the spot where the Prince of Wales landed. As they drew near the shore there was an immense crowd lining the wharf, and a company of Bombay volunteers in line. As the General ascended the steps he was met by Brigadier-General Aitcheson, commanding the forces; Sir Francis Souter, Commissioner of Police; Mr. Grant, the Municipal Commissioner, and Colonel Sexton, commanding the Bombay Volunteers, all of whom gave him a hearty welcome to India. The volunteers presented arms, the band played our national air, and the General, amid loud cheers from the Europeans present, walked slowly with uncovered head to the state carriage. Accompanied by Captain Frith, who represented the Governor, and attended by an escort of native cavalry, the General and party made off to Malabar Point.

The General's home in Bombay was at the Government House, on Malabar Point, in the suburbs of the city. Malabar Point was in other days a holy place of the Hindoos. Here was a temple, and it was also believed that if those who sinned made a pilgrimage to the rocks there would be expiation or regeneration of the soul. The Portuguese who came to India were breakers of images, who believed that the religion of Christ was best served by the destruction of the Pagan temples. Among the temples which were subjected to their pious zeal was one on Malabar Point. There are only the ruins remaining, and masses of rock, bearing curious inscriptions, lie on the hillside. Malabar Point is an edge of the island of Bombay jutting out into the Indian Ocean. Where the bluff overlooks the waters it is one hundred feet high. This remnant of the rock has been rescued from the sea and storm and decorated with trees and shrubbery, the mango and the palm. Overlooking the sea is a battery with five large guns, shining and black, looking out upon the ocean and keeping watch over the Empire of England. It is difficult to describe a residence like Government House on Malabar Point. Architecture is simply a battle with the sun. The house is a group of houses. As you drive in the grounds through stone gates that remind you of the porter's lodges at some stately English mansions, you pass through an avenue of mango trees, past beds of flowers throwing out their delicate fragrance on the warm morning air. You come to a one-storied house surrounded with spacious verandas.

There is a wide state entrance covered with red cloth. A guard is at the foot, a native guard wearing the English scarlet, on his shoulders the number indicating the regiment. You pass up the stairs, a line of servants on either side. The servants are all Mohammedans; they wear long scarlet gowns, with white turbans; on the breast is a belt with an imperial crown for an escutcheon. They salute you with the grave, submissive grace of the East, touching the forehead and bending low the head, in token of welcome and duty. You enter a hall and pass between two rooms — large, high, decorated in blue and white, and look out upon the gardens below, the sea beyond and the towers of Bombay. One of these rooms is the state dining-room, large enough to dine fifty people. The other is the state drawing-room. This house is only used for ceremonies, for meals and receptions.

General Grant was the guest of the Governor, and the honors of his house were done by Captains Frith and Radcliff of the army. Meals were taken in the state dining-room. Mrs. Grant enjoyed every moment of her visit.

The attentions paid to the General and his party by the people of Bombay were so marked and continuous that most of their time was taken up in receiving and acknowling them. What most interested them, coming fresh from Europe, was the entire novelty of the scene, the way of living, the strange manners and customs. All impressions of India, gathered from the scattered reading of busy days at home, are vague. Somehow one associates India with ideas of pageanty. The history of the country has been written in such glowing colors — one who has read Oriental poems, and fallen under the captivating rhetoric of Macaulay, looks for nature in a luxuriant form, for splendor and ornament, for bazaars laden with gems and gold, for crowded highways, with elephants slowly plodding their way along.

Therefore, when India is seen — India as seen in this her greatest city — one is surprised to find it all so hard and baked and brown. The greenness of field and hillside is missed. A people who have nothing in common with any race known. There are so many types, curious and varying, that impressions are bewildering and indefinite. In time, as the country is known and understood, it will be seen that this civilization has lines of harmony like that left behind; that there are reasons for all the odd things, just as there are reasons for many odd things in America; and that Indian civilization even now — when its glory has departed, its mightiest States are mere appendages of the British Empire, when day after day it bends and crumbles under the stern hand and cold brain of the Saxon — is rich in the lessons and qualities which have for ages excited the ambition and wonder of the world.

On Friday night, General Grant visited the ball of the Volunteer Corps, and was received by Colonel Sexton. The ballroom was profusely decorated with flags — the American flag predominating. On Saturday, at two o'clock, he visited Dossabhoy Merwanjee, a Parsee merchant. The reception was most cordial, the ladies of the family decorating the General and party with wreaths of jasmine flowers. In the afternoon he drove to the Byculla Club, lunched, and looked at the races. In the evening there was a state dinner at the Government House, with forty-eight guests. The government band played during dinner. The member of council, Hon. James Gibbs, who represents the Governor, was in the chair. At the close of the dinner, he proposed the health of the General, who arose, amid loud cheering, and said that he was now carrying out a wish he had long entertained, of visiting India and the countries of the ancient world. His reception in Bombay had been most gratifying. The cordiality of the people, the princely hospitality of the Governor, the kindness of the members of the household, all combined to make him feel the sincerity of the welcome. It was only a continuance of the friendliness he had met in Europe, and which was especially grateful to him because it indicated a friendly feeling toward his own country. In this spirit he accepted it, for he knew of nothing that would go further toward insuring peace to all nations, and with peace the blessings of civilization, than a perfect understanding between Englishmen and Americans, the great English-speaking nations of the world. The General said he hoped he might see his hosts in America. He would be most happy to meet them, and return the hospitality he had received. He was sorry he could not see Sir Richard Temple, the Governor of Bombay, of whom he had heard a great deal and whom he was anxious to meet. But he would ask them to join with him in drinking the health of the Governor. This sentiment was drank with all the honors. The dinner was finely served, and after dinner the General and guests strolled about on the veranda, smoking or chatting, looking out on the calm and murmuring ocean that rolled at their feet, and the lights of the city beyond. There was a luncheon with Sir Michael R. Westropp, Chief Justice of Bombay.

Subsequently General Grant visited the English man-of-war Euryolus, the flagship of the English squadron in India. Admiral Corbett received the General, and on his leaving the vessel fired twenty-one guns. There was a visit to the Elephanta caves, one of the sights in India. The visitors left the wharf, and steamed across the bay in a small launch belonging to the government. The afternoon was beautiful, the islands in the bay breaking up the horizon into various forms of beauty, that resembled the islands of the Mediterranean. Elephanta caves belong to Hindoo theology. Here in the rocks the Brahmins built their temples, and now on the holy days the people come and worship their gods according to the ritual of their ancestors. What the temple might have been in its best days cannot be imagined from the ruins.

Having reached the temples, they strolled about, studying the figures, noting the columns and the curious architecture, full, rude, massive, unlike any forms of architectural art familiar to Americans. The main temple is one hundred and twenty-five feet long, and the same in width. The idols are hewn out of the rock. The faces of some are comely, and there is a European expression in the features that startles you. The type is a higher one than those seen in Egypt. One of the idols, supposed to be the Hindoo Trinity — Brahmin, Vishnu and Siva. There is a figure of a woman — the wife of Siva — and it is seen in these pagan faiths that woman, who holds so sad a place in their domestic economy, was worshiped as fervently as some of us worship the Virgin. It is the tribute which even the heathen pays, as if by instinct, to the supreme blessing of maternity. But when the Portuguese came, with the sword and the cross, little mercy was shown to the homes of the pagan gods. It is believed that these temples were cut out of the rocks in the tenth century, and that for eight hundred years these stony emblems were worshiped.

On Monday the General was entertained in state at the Government House at Malabar Point. Hon. James Gibbs, the member of the council who acted as Governor in the absence of Sir Richard Temple, presided, and at the close of the dinner the company drank the health of the General. In response the General referred to the kindness he had received in India, which was only renewing the kindness shown him all over Europe, and which he accepted as an evidence of the good will which really existed between Englishmen and Americans, and which was to his mind the best assurance of peace for all nations. After the dinner the General received a large number of the native merchants and gentlemen of Bombay. It may seem odd to American eyes that merchants and gentlemen should be asked to come in at the end of a feast, and not to take part. But this exclusion is their own wish. Many of these merchants and gentlemen belong to castes who look on the food of the Europeans as unclean, who believe in the sacredness of life and will not eat animal food, and who could not sit at the table with the General without losing caste. These men will meet you in business, will serve you in various ways, but their religion prevents their sharing your table. So the invitation to the natives to meet the General was fixed at an hour when dinner was over.

They came in groups — Hindoos, Arabs, Parsees, native officers — in uniforms, in quaint flowing costumes. The General stood at the head of the hallway, with Mr. Gibbs and Major Rivet-Carnac, the Governor's military secretary. As each native advanced, he was presented to the General with some word of history or compliment from Mr. Gibbs. "This is So-and-So, an eminent Brahmin scholar, who stands high among our barristers;" or, "this is So-and-So, a Parsee merchant, who has done a great deal of good to Bombay, and has been knighted for his services by the Queen;" or, "this is the oldest Arab merchant;" or, "this is a gallant officer of our native cavalry;" or, "this is the leading diamond merchant in Bombay, a Hindoo gentleman, one of the richest in India." As each of them advanced, it was with folded hands, as in prayer, or saluting by touching the breast and brow in the submissive, graceful, bending way. Here were men of many races — the Parsee, from Persia, the Arab, from Cairo, whose ancestors may have ridden with Omar; the Brahmin of a holy caste, in whose veins runs the stainless blood of Indian nobility, descendant of men who were priests and rulers ages before England had risen from her clouds of barbarism. Between these races there is no love. If they do not like England, they hate one another. Religious differences, tradition, memories of war and conquest, the unaccountable antipathies of race which have not been eliminated from their civilization — all generate a fierce animosity which would break into flames once the restraining hand were lifted. What welds them together is the power of England; and as you look at this picturesque group — their heads, full eyes, their fine Asiatic type of face, clear and well cut — here assembled peacefully, you see the extent of the empire to which they all owe allegiance, and admire the genius and courage which has brought them to submit to a rule which, whatever it may have been in the past, grows more and more beneficent.

The General left Bombay on Tuesday, February 18, having driven into town and made some farewell calls. At five he left Government House in a state carriage, accompanied by Major Carnac, who represented Governor Temple, and escorted by a squadron of cavalry. On arriving at the station there was a guard of honor of native infantry drawn up, which presented arms and lowered colors. All the leading men of the Bombay Government — Parsee and native merchants; our Consul, Mr. Farnham, whose kindness was untiring; Mr. Gibbs, and all the members of the government household, were present. In a few minutes the signal for leaving was made, and, the General thanking his good friends of Malabar Point, the train pushed off amid cheers and the salutes of the military.

On the 20th of February the party arrived at Tatulpur, and visited the Marble Rocks, on the Norbudda River, riding there on elephants provided by the government.

The General arrived at Allahabad on the 22d of February, where he was received by Sir George Cowper, Lieutenant-Governor of the Northwest Provinces, and was escorted to the Government House.

The General arrived at Agra on the 23d, and on the following day he visited Jeypore, where he was received by the Maharajah with his ministers, and the English Resident, Dr. Hendley. As the General descended, the Maharajah, who wore the ribbon and star of the Order of India, advanced and shook hands, welcoming him to his dominions. The Maharajah is a small, rather fragile person, with a serious, almost a painful, expression of countenance, but an intelligent, keen face. He looked like a man of sixty. His movements were slow, impassive — the movements of old age. This may be a mannerism, however, for on studying his face you could see that there is some youth in it. On his brow were the crimson emblems of his caste — the warrior caste of Rajpootana. His Highness does not speak English, although he understands it, and our talk was through an interpreter. After the exchange of courtesies and a few moments' conversation. the General drove off to the English Residency, accompanied by a company of Jeypore cavalry. The Residency is some distance from the station. It is a fine, large mansion, surrounded by a park and garden.

It was arranged that the General should visit Amber, the ancient capital of Jeypore, one of the most curious sights in India. Amber was the capital until the close of the seventeenth century. It was one of the freaks of the princes who once reigned in India, that when they tired of a capital or a palace, they wandered off and built a new one, leaving the other to run to waste. The ruins of India are as a general thing the abandoned palaces and temples of kings who grew weary of their toy and craved another. This is why Amber is now an abandoned town and Jeypore the capital. If the Maharajah were to tire of Jeypore and return to Amber, the town would accompany him, for without the Court the town would die. Traveling in India must be done very early in the morning, and, although the visitors had had a severe day's journey, they left for Amber at seven in the morning. A squadron of the Maharajah's cavalry accompanied them. They are fine horsemen, and wear quilted uniforms of printed cotton. The drive through Jeypore was interesting, from the fact that they were now in a native city, under native rule. Heretofore the India they had seen was India under Englishmen; but Jeypore is sovereign, with power of life and death over its own subjects. The city is purely Oriental, and is most picturesque and striking. There are two or three broad streets, and one or two squares, that would do no discredit to Paris. The architecture is Oriental, and, as all the houses are painted after the same pattern, in rose color, it gives you the impression that it is all the same building. The streets had been swept for the coming of the visitors, and men, carrying goatskins of water, were sprinkling them. Soldiers were stationed at various points to salute, and sometimes the salute was accompanied with a musical banging on various instruments of the national air. The best that India can do for a distinguished American, is "God Save the Queen."

There are gas lamps in Jeypore; this is a tremendous advance in civilization. One of the first things General Grant heard in India, was that in Jeypore lived a great prince, a most enlightened prince, quite English in his ideas, who had gas lamps in his streets. He had a theatre almost ready for occupancy; there was a troupe of Parsee players in town, who had come all the way from Bombay, and were waiting to open it. The Maharajah was sorry he could not show the General a play.

To go to Amber, General Grant and party must ride

elephants, for after a few miles the hills come, and the roads are broken, and carriages are of no value. Camels or horses could be used, but the Maharajah had sent elephants, and they were waiting for them under a grove of mango trees, drawn up by the side of the road, as if to salute. The principal elephant wore a scarlet cloth, as a special honor to the General. The elephant means authority in India, and, when you wish to do your guest the highest honor, you mount him on an elephant. The Maharajah also sent sedan chairs for those who preferred an easier and swifter conveyance.

Mrs. Grant chose the sedan chair, and was switched off at a rapid pace up the ascending road by four Hindoo bearers. The pace at which these chairs is carried is a short, measured quickstep, so that there is no uneasiness to the rider. The rest mounted the elephants. Elephant-riding is a curious and not an unpleasant experience. The animal is under perfect control, and very often, especially in the case of such a man as the ruler of Jeypore, has been for generations in the same family. The elephant is under the care of a driver, called a mahout. The mahout sits on the neck, or more properly the head, of the elephant, and guides him with a stick or sharp iron prong, with which he strikes the animal on the top of the head. Between the elephant and mahout there are relations of affection. The mahout lives with the elephant, gives him his food, and each animal has its own keeper. The huge creature becomes in time as docile as a kitten, and will obey any order of the mahout. The elephant reaches a great age. It is not long since there died at Calcutta the elephant which carried Warren Hastings when Governor General of India, a century ago. There are two methods of riding elephants. One is in a box like the four seats of a carriage, the other on a square quilted seat, your feet hanging over the sides, something like an Irish jaunting car. The first plan is good for hunting, but for comfort the second is the better. At a signal from the mahout the elephant slowly kneels. When the elephant rises, which he does two legs at a time, deliberately, the rider must hold on to the rail of the seat. Once on his feet, he swings along at a slow, wabbling pace. The motion is an easy one, like that of a boat in a light sea. In time, if going long distances, it becomes very tiresome.

Arrived at Amber, the General found Mrs. Grant with her couriers, having arrived some time before, and had mounted to a window high up in the palace, and was waving her handkerchief. The visitors had reached the temple while worship was in progress. Dr. Hendley informed the General that he was in time to take part in the services and to see the priest offer up a kid. Every day in the year in this temple a kid is offered up as a propitiation for the sins of the Maharajah.

The temple was little more than a room in the palace — a private chapel. At one end was a platform raised a few inches from the ground and covered over. On this platform were the images of the gods — of the special God. Whatever the god, the worship was in full progress, and there was the kid ready for sacrifice. Entering the enclosure, the visitors stood with uncovered heads; only some half a dozen worshipers were crouching on the ground. One of the attendants held the kid, while the priest was crouching over it, reading from the sacred books, and in a half humming, half whining chant blessing the sacrifice, and as he said each prayer putting some grain or spice or oil on its head. The poor animal licked the crumbs as they fell about it, quite unconscious of its holy fate. Another attendant took a sword and held it before the priest. He read some prayers over the sword and consecrated it. Then the kid was carried to the corner, where there was a small heap of sand or ashes and a gutter to carry away the blood. The priest continued his prayers, the kid's head was suddenly drawn down and with one blow severed from the body. The virtue of the sacrifice consists in the head falling at the first blow, and so expert do the priests become that at some of the great sacrifices, where buffalo are offered up in expiation of the princely sins, they will take off the buffalo's head with one stroke of the sword. The kid, having performed the office of expiation, becomes useful for the priestly dinner.

Of the palace of Amber the most one can say is that it is curious and interesting as the home of an Indian King in the days when India was ruled by her Kings, and a Hastings and a Clive had not come to rend and destroy. The Maharajah has not quite abandoned it. He comes sometimes to the great feasts of the faith, and a few apartments are kept for him. His rooms were ornamented with looking-glass decorations, with carved marble which the artisan had fashioned into tracery so delicate that it looked like lacework. What strikes one in this Oriental decoration is its tendency to light, bright, lacelike gossamer work, showing infinite pains and patience in the doing, but without any special value as a real work of art. The general effect of these decorations is agreeable, but all is done for effect. There is no such honest, serious work as you see in the Gothic cathedrals, or even in the Alhambra. One is the expression of a facile, sprightly race, fond of the sunshine, delighting to repeat the caprice of nature in the curious and quaint; the other has a deep, earnest purpose. This is an imagination which sees its gods in every form — in stones and trees and beasts and creeping things, in the stars above, in the snake wriggling through the hedges — the other sees only one God, even the Lord God Jehovah, who made the heavens and the earth and will come to judge the world at the last day. As you wander through the courtyards and chambers of Amber, the fancy is amused by the character of all that surrounds you. There is no luxury. All these Kings wanted was air and sunshine. They slept on the floor. The chambers of their wives were little more than cells built in stone. Here are the walls that surrounded their section of the palace. There are no windows looking into the outer world, only a thick stone wall pierced with holes slanting upward, so that if a curious spouse looked out she would see nothing lower than the stars. Amber is an immense palace, and could quite accommodate a rajah with a court of a thousand attendants.

There were some beautiful views from the terrace. The General would like to have remained, but the elephants had been down to the water to lap themselves about, and were now returning refreshed to bear us back to Jeypore. The visitors had only given themselves a day for the town, and had to return the call of the Prince, which is a serious task in Eastern etiquette.

Mr. Borie was much exhausted by his ride and the heat of the sun, and was prevailed upon to make the descent in a chair, as Mrs. Grant had done. Returning to Jeypore the same day, our party were very tired, and early sought rest.

The following day, at Jeypore, the General visited the school of arts and industry, in which he was greatly interested, one of his special subjects of inquiry being the industrial customs and resources of the country. This school is one of the Prince's favorite schemes, and the scholars showed aptness in their work. Jeypore excels in the manufacture of enameled jewelry; some of the specimens seen were exceedingly beautiful and costly. The Mint was visited, and here the workmen were seen beating the coin and stamping it.

At the collection of tigers, a half dozen brutes were caged, each of whom had a history. There were man-eaters; one enormous creature had killed twenty-five men before he was captured. Having passed the day in seeing the sights, the party returned to the Residency, and found a group of servants, from the palace, on the veranda, each carrying a tray laden with sweetmeats and nuts, oranges and fruit. This was an offering from the Prince, and it was necessary that the General should touch some of the fruit and taste it, and say how much he was indebted to His Highness for the remembrance; then the servants returned to the palace.

The Maharajah sent word that he would receive General Grant at five. The Maharajah is a pious prince, a devotee, and almost an ascetic. He gives seven hours a day to devotions. He partakes only of one meal. When he is through with his prayers he plays billiards. He is the husband of ten wives. His tenth wife was married to him a few weeks ago. The court gossip is that he did not want another wife, that nine were enough; but in polygamous countries marriages are made to please families, to consolidate alliances, to win friendships, very often to give a home to the widows or sisters of friends. The Maharajah was under some duress of this kind, and his bride was brought home, and is now with her sister brides behind the stone walls, killing time as she best can, while her lord prays and plays billiards. These wives live in cloistered seclusion. They are guarded by eunuchs, and even when ill are not allowed to look into the face of a physician, but put their hands through a screen. It was said in Jeypore that no face of a Rajput Princess was ever seen by a European.

These prejudices are respected and protected by the Imperial Government, which respects and protects every custom in India so long as the States behave themselves and pay tribute. In their seclusion the princesses adorn themselves, see the Nautch girls dance, and read romances. They are not much troubled by the Maharajah. That great prince, I hear, is tired of everything but his devotions and his billiards. He has no children, and is not supposed to have hopes of an heir. He will, as is the custom in these high families, adopt some prince of an auxiliary branch.

The government of the kingdom is in the hands of a council, among whom are the Prime Minister and the principal brahmin.

General Grant drove to the palace at four o'clock, and at once inspected the stables. There were some fine horses, and exhibitions of horsemanship which astonished even the General. He was shown the astronomical buildings of Jai Singh II., which were on a large scale and accurately graded. He climbed to the top of the palace, and had a fine view of Jeypore. The palace itself embraces one-sixth of the city, and there are ten thousand people within its walls — beggars, soldiers, priests, politicians, all manner of human beings — who live on the royal bounty. The town looked picturesque and cool in the shadows of the descending sun.

At five precisely we entered the courtyard leading to the reception hall. The Maharajah came slowly down the steps, with a serious, preoccupied air, not as an old man, but as one who was too weary with a day's labors to make any effort, and shook hands with the General and Mrs. Grant. He accompanied the General to a seat of honor and sat down at his side. They all arranged themselves in the chairs. On the side of the General sat the members of his party; on the side of the Maharajah the members of his Cabinet. Dr. Hendley acted as interpreter. The Prince said Jeypore was honored in seeing the face of the great American ruler, whose fame had reached Hindostan. The General said he had enjoyed his visit, that he was pleased and surprised with the prosperity of the people, and he should have felt he had lost a great deal if he had come to India and not seen Jeypore. The Maharajah expressed regret that the General made so short a stay. The General answered that he came to

India late, and was rather pressed for time from the fact that he wished to see the Viceroy before he left Calcutta, and to that end had promised to be in Calcutta on March 10.

His Highness then made a gesture, and a troop of dancing girls came into the court-yard. One of the features of a visit to Jeypore is what is called the Nautch. The Nautch is a sacred affair, danced by Hindoo girls of a low caste in the presence of the idols in the palace temple. A group of girls came trooping in, under the leadership of an old fellow with a long beard and a hard expression of face, who might have been the original of Dickens' Fagin. The girls wore heavy garments embroidered, the skirts composed of many folds, covered with gold braid. They had ornaments on their heads and jewels in the side of the nose. They had plain faces, and carried out the theory of caste, if there be anything in such a theory, in the contrast between their features and the delicate, sharply-cut lines of the higher class Brahmins and the other castes who surrounded the Prince. The girls formed in two lines, a third line was composed of four musicians, who performed a low, growling kind of music on unearthly instruments. The dance had no value in it, either as an expression of harmony, grace or motion.

The Nautch dance is meaningless. It is not even improper. It is attended by no excitement, no manifestations of religious feeling. A group of course, ill-formed women stood in the lines, walked and twisted about, breaking now and then into a chorus, which added to the din of the instruments. This was the famous Nautch dance, which they were to see in Jeypore with amazement, and to remember as one of the sights of India. Either as an amusement or a religious ceremony it had no value.

The General did not appreciate the dance, though he remained during its performance. Dr. Hendley, evidently thinking that the dance had served every useful purpose, said a word to the Prince, who made a sign, the dance stopped, the girls vanished, and the whole party retired to the billiard room.

The Maharajah plays billiards when he is not at prayers. He was anxious to have a game with the General. The General played in an indiscriminate, promiscuous manner, and made some wonderful shots in the way of missing balls he intended to strike. Mr. Borie, whose interest in the General's fortunes extends to billiards, began to deplore those eccentric experiments, when the General said he had not played billiards for thirty years. The Maharajah tried to lose the game, and said to one of his attendants that he was anxious to show the General that delicate mark of hospitality. The game ended, His Highness winning.

Then they strolled into the gardens, and looked at the palace towers, which the Prince took pleasure in showing to the General, and which looked airy and beautiful in the rosy shadows of the descending sun. There were beds of flowers and trees, and the coming night, which comes so swiftly in these latitudes, brought a cooling breeze. Then His Highness gave each a photograph of his royal person, consecrated with his royal autograph, which he wrote on the top of a marble railing. Then they strolled toward the grand hall of ceremony to take leave. Taking leave is a solemn act in India. The party entered the spacious hall, where the Prince received the Prince of Wales. Night had come so rapidly, that servants came in all directions carrying candles and torches that lit up the gaudy and glittering hall. An attendant carried a tray bearing wreaths of the rose and jasmine. The Maharajah, taking two of these wreaths, put them on the neck of the General. He did the same to Mrs. Grant, and all the members of the party. Then, taking a string of gold and silken cord, he placed that on Mrs. Grant as a special honor. The Gen-

NAUTCH GIRLS DANCING BEFORE THE RAJAH AND GENERAL GRANT.

eral, who was instructed by the English Resident, took four wreaths and put them on the neck of the Maharajah, who pressed his hands and bowed his thanks. Another servant came, bearing a small cup of gold and gems containing ottar of roses. The Maharajah, putting some of the perfume on his fingers, transferred it to Mrs. Grant's handkerchief. With another portion he passed his hands along the General's breast and shoulders. This was done to each of the party. The General then taking the perfume, passed his hands over the Maharajah's shoulders, and so concluding the ceremony, which, in all royal interviews in the East, is supposed to mean a lasting friendship. Then the Prince, taking General Grant's hand in his own, led him from the hall, across the garden and to the gateway of his palace, holding his hand all the time. The carriages were waiting, and the Prince took his leave saying how much he was honored by the General's visit. The cavalry escort formed in line, the guard presented arms, and the visitors drove at full gallop to their home. And so ended one of the most interesting and eventful days in the General's visit to India.

CHAPTER XV.

STILL IN INDIA.

General Grant and party visited the Maharajah of Burtpoor, a young prince about thirty years of age. His state is small — its area 1,974 miles, with a population of 743,710, and a revenue of $15,000,000. The day was hot, and the ride had been through a low country, the scenery not very attractive at the best, but now brown and arid under a steaming sun. Arrived at the station, all Burtpoor seemed to be awaiting the General's appearance, with the Maharajah at the head. The prince was accompanied by the British officers attached to his court, and, advancing, shook hands with the General and welcomed him to his capital. He wore a blazing uniform, covered with jewels. He had a firm, stern face, with strong features, a good frame, and unlike his brother of Jeypore, who gives his days to prayers and his evenings to billiards; and, although he has the Star of India, has long since seen the vanity of human glory, and hates power, is a soldier and a sportsman, and is called a firm and energetic ruler. From the station the party drove to the palace, through a town whose dismantled walls speak of English valor and English shame, past bazaars, where people seemed to sell nothing, only to broil in the sunshine, and under a high archway into a courtyard, and thence to the palace. There was nothing special about the palace, except that it was very large and very uncomfortable. The prince does not live in this palace, but in one more suited to Oriental tastes. It was here where he received the Prince of Wales on the occasion of his visit in 1876. There was a breakfast prepared, which the prince left his guests to enjoy in company with their English friends. In this country the hospitality of the highest princes never goes so far as to ask you to eat. The rules of caste are so marked that the partaking of food with one of another caste, and especially of another race, would be defilement. The host at the close of the breakfast returned in state, and there was the ceremony of altar and pan, and cordial interchanges of good feeling between the Maharajah and the General.

The General and party visited the famous ruins of Futtehpoor Sikra. In the days of the great Mohammedan rulers there was none so great as Akbar. He founded the city and built the palace. The night had fallen before the visitors arrived at their destination, so that they were compelled to remain over night in the ruins. Mr. Lawrence, the British Collector at Agra, had sent forward bed and bedding, and all that was necessary to make the guests comfortable. After a night's rest, the following morning an early start was made to view the ruins. To see all of this stupendous ruin would include a ride around a circumference of seven miles. The ruins were well worth a study. The General examined first a courtyard, or quadrangle, four hundred and thirty-three feet by three hundred and sixty-six feet. On one side of this is the mosque, which is a noble building, suffering, however, from the overshadowing grandeur of the principal gateway, the finest, it is said, in India, looming up out of the ruins with stately and graceful splendor, but dwarfing the other monuments and ruins. This was meant as an arch of triumph to the glory of the Emperor, "King of Kings," "Heaven of the Court," and "Shadow of God." There are many of these inscriptions in Arabic, a translation of which is found in Mr. Keene's handbook. The most suggestive is this:

"Know that the world is a glass, where the favor has come and gone. Take as thine own nothing more than what thou lookest upon." The prevailing aspect of the architecture was Moslem, with traces of Hindoo taste and decoration. The mosque, the tombs and the gateway are all well preserved. At one of the mosques were a number of natives in prayer, who interrupted their devotions long enough to show General Grant the delicate tracing on the walls and beg a rupee. One of the pleasures of wandering among these stupendous ruins is to wander alone and take in the full meaning of the work and the genius of the men who did it. The guides have nothing to tell you. The ruins to them are partly dwelling-places, pretexts for begging rupees.

General Grant and party visited Benares — the sacred city of the Hindoos — a city of temples, idols, priests, and worship. The General found so much to interest him in India that it was a source of regret to him that he did not come earlier in the season. Every hour in the country had been full of interest, and the hospitality of the officials and the people so generous and profuse, that his way had been especially pleasant. Travel during the day in India is very severe. Mrs. Grant stood the journey, especially the severer phases of it, marvellously, and justifies the reputation for endurance and energy which she won on the Nile. The General is a severe and merciless traveler, who never tires, always ready for an excursion or an experience, as indifferent to the comforts or necessities of the way as if he had been on the tented field. Upon arriving at the station of Benares, Mr. Daniels, the representative of the Viceroy, met the General and party. A large guard of honor was in attendance, accompanied by the leading military and civic English representatives and native rajahs, who walked down the line with uncovered heads.

In honor of the General's coming, the road from the

station to the Government House had been illuminated. Poles had been stuck in the ground on either side of the road, and from these poles lanterns and small glass vessels filled with oil were swinging. So as they drove, before and behind was an avenue of light that recalled the Paris boulevards as seen from Montmartre. It was a long drive to the house of the Commissioner. A part of his house Mr. Daniels gave to General and Mrs. Grant and Mr. Borie. For the others there were tents in the garden.

Benares, the sacred city of the Hindoos, sacred also to the Buddhists, is one of the oldest in the world. Macaulay's description, so familiar to all, is worth reprinting, from the vividness with which it represents it, as to-day. "Benares," says Macaulay, in his essay on Warren Hastings, "was a city which, in wealth, population, dignity and sanctity, was among the foremost in Asia. It was commonly believed that half a million human beings were crowded into that labyrinth of lofty alleys, rich with shrines and minarets, and balconies and carved oriels, to which the sacred apes clung by hundreds. The traveler could scarcely make his way through the press of holy mendicants and not less holy bulls. The broad and stately flights of steps which descended from these swarming haunts to the bathing places along the Ganges were worn every day by the footsteps of an innumerable multitude of worshipers. The schools and temples drew crowds of pious Hindoos from every province where the Brahminical faith was known. Hundreds of devotees came thither every month to die, for it was believed that a peculiarly happy fate awaited the man who should pass from the sacred city into the sacred river. Nor was superstition the only motive which allured strangers to that great metropolis. Commerce had as many pilgrims as religion. All along the shores of the venerable stream lay great fleets of vessels laden with rich merchandise. From the looms of Benares

went forth the most delicate silks that adorned the halls of
St. James and Versailles; and in the bazaars the muslins
of Bengal and the sabres of Oude were mingled with the
jewels of Golconda and the shawls of Cashmere." Benares to one-half the human race — to the millions in China
who profess Buddhism and the millions in India who worship Brahma — is as sacred as Jerusalem to the Christian
or Mecca to the Mohammedan. Its greatness was known
in the days of Nineveh and Babylon, when, as another
writer says, " Tyre was planting her colonies, when Athens
was gaining in strength, before Rome became known, or
Greece had contended with Persia, or Cyrus had added to
the Persian monarchy, or Nebuchadnezzar had captured
Jerusalem." The name of Benares excites deep emotions
in the breast of every pious Hindoo, and his constant prayer
is, " Holy Kasi! Would that I could see the eternal city
favored of the gods! Would that I might die on its sacred
soil!"

Benares is a city of priests. Its population is over two
hundred thousand; of this number twenty-five thousand
are Brahmins. They govern the city, and hold its temples,
wells, shrines and streams. Pilgrims are constantly arriving; as many as two hundred thousand come in the course
of the year. Not long since, one authority counted fourteen
hundred and fifty-four Hindoo temples, and two hundred
and seventy-two mosques. In addition to the temples,
there are shrines — cavities built in walls, containing the
image of some god — as sacred as the temples. Pious
rahjas are always adding to the temples and shrines. The
streets are so narrow that only in the widest can even an
elephant make his way. They are alleys — narrow alleys,
not streets — and, as you thread your way through them,
you feel as if the town were one house, the chambers only
separated by narrow passages. Benares, the holy city —
holy even now in the eyes of more than half the human

race — whose glories, religious and civic, have been forgotten in the noise and glitter of our recent civilization.

The priest is a sacred ruler. He is the first in caste; the world was made for him, and other men depend upon him. If he is angry and curses, his curses can overturn thrones, scatter troops, even destroy this world and summon other worlds into existence. He is above the King in dignity. His life is sacred, and, no matter the enormity of the crime, he cannot be condemned to death. The Brahmins are the strongest social and religious force in Hindostan. Benares is their city. The policy which founded the order of Jesuits has often been cited as a masterpiece of government, of combining the strongest intellectual force toward missionary enterprise. But the order of Jesuits is a society under rules and discipline only binding its members. The Brahmins not only govern themselves as rigidly as the Jesuits, and hold themselves ready to go as far in the service of their faith, but they have imposed their will upon every other class. Men of the world, men in other callings, use the name of Jesuit as a term of reproach, and even Catholic kings have been known to banish them and put them outside of civil law. There is not a prince in Hindostan who would dare to put a straw in the path of a Brahmin. Brahminism is one of the oldest institutions in the world, one of the most extraordinary developments of human intellect and discipline, and there is no reason to suppose that its power over India will ever pass away.

Here is the sacred river Ganges. No office is so sacred to the dead as to burn his body on the banks of the Ganges. Several slabs were observed near the burning Ghat; these were in memory of widows who had burned themselves on that spot in honor of their husbands, according to the old rite of suttee. Benares sits on the sacred river, an emblem of the strange religion which has made it a holy city, and there is solemnity in the thought that for ages she has kept her place on the Ganges; that for ages her shrines have been holy to millions of men; that for ages the wisest and purest and best of the Indian race have wandered as pilgrims through her narrow streets and plunged themselves as penitents into the waters to wash away their sins. It is all a dark superstition, but let us honor Benares for the comfort she has given to so many millions of sinful, sorrowing souls. And as the white towers and steps of Benares, glistening in the sunshine, are left behind, the tourists look back upon it with something of the respect and affection that belong to antiquity, and which are certainly not unworthily bestowed upon so renowned, so sacred and so venerable a city.

General Grant visited Delhi. Upon his arrival there was a grand reception by troops, and the General and his wife drove to Ludlow Castle, the home of the chief officer Delhi is a beautiful city, as the houses are built for air, and not, as in American cities, several stories high. This will account for the great size of Indian cities — that they are so many miles long and so many broad.

There are few cities in the world which have had a more varied and more splendid career than Delhi. It is the Rome of India, and the history of India centres around Delhi. It has no such place as Benares in the religion of the people, but to the Indians it is what Rome in the ancient days was to the Roman Empire. One of its authentic monuments goes back to the fourth century before Christ. Its splendor began with the rise of the Mogul empire, and the splendor of the Moguls is seen in what they built, and the severity of their creed in what they destroyed. Outside of the English section, nothing but the ruins and desolation of many wars and dynasties.

From the Cashmere gate to the Rutab, a ride of eleven miles, your road is through monumental ruins — tombs, temples, mausoleums, mosques, in all directions. The horizon is studded with minarets and domes, all abandoned, and many in ruins.

The General and party visited the palace of the Grand Mogul; saw the throne of Aurungzebe — the peacock throne. This was simply a mass of jewels and gold, valued at thirty millions of dollars. Mr. Beresford, in his book on Delhi, says it was called the peacock throne from its having the figures of two peacocks standing behind it, their tails expanded, and the whole so inlaid with sapphires, rubies, emeralds, pearls and other precious stones of appropriate colors, as to represent life. The throne itself was six feet long by four feet broad. It stood on six massive feet, which, with the body, were of solid gold, inlaid with rubies, emeralds and diamonds. It was supported by a canopy of gold, upheld by twelve pillars, all richly emblazoned with costly gems, and a fringe of pearls ornamented the borders of the canopy.

A visit to the Kutab tower was worthy of remembrance. This tower ranks among the wonders of India. It is two hundred and thirty-eight feet high, sloping from the base, which is forty-seven feet in diameter, to the summit, which is nine feet. It is composed of five sections or stories, and with every story there is a change in the design. The lower section has twenty-four sides, in the form of convex flutings, alternately semi-circular and rectangular. In the second section they are circular, the third angular, the fourth a plain cylinder, and the fifth partly fluted and partly plain. At each basement is a balcony. On the lower sections are inscriptions in scroll work, reciting, in Arabic characters, the glory of God, verses from the Koran, and the name and achievements of the conqueror who built the tower. It is believed that, when really complete, with the cupola, it must have been twenty feet higher.

Attended by an officer who took part in the siege, the General visited the lines held by the English and the Se poys during the mutiny, when the English Empire in India depended for months upon the valor and endurance of the small army which invested Delhi.

On February 28, General Grant arrived at Calcutta. The railroad authorities, not having any intimation of the General's visit, made no arrangements for his reception at the railway station. Only a few gentlemen were present. A company of the Madras Fourteenth Regiment, with band and colors, were drawn up in line on the platform, and at the bridge was posted the European constabulary of the Calcutta police, under the superintendence of Mr. Percy. The gentlemen on the platform were Captain Muir, Aide-de-Camp to His Excellency the Viceroy; Mr. Lambert, the Deputy Commissioner of Police; General Litchfield, the American Consul; Mr. R. Macallister, Mr. Frederick Coke, Mr. Manockjee Rustomjee and son, and some masters of American ships in the river. When the train arrived, some difficulty was experienced in finding the carriage the General was in, as it was far down the platform, where the company of soldiers was drawn up. The General, Mrs. Grant and Colonel Grant, and two gentlemen belonging to his staff, then stepped out of a first-class carriage and were received by the gentlemen, one of whom handed to the General a letter from Nawab Abdul Gunny Meah, of Dacca, inviting the General over to his place. The party then drove to Government House, in two carriages of the Viceroy, which were in waiting outside the platform. As the party neared Government House, there was a salute of twenty-one guns. In the evening the Viceroy entertained the General and his party at a dinner-party at Government House. About fifty ladies and gentlemen were honored with invitations to meet them. After the toast of the Queen-Empress was drank, Lord Lytton rose, and spoke as follows:

"LADIES AND GENTLEMEN—I sincerely believe that

there is no toast unconnected with our own country and its institutions which is honored with greater cordiality by Englishmen of all classes, and in all parts of the world, than the toast I am now about to propose to you — because, ladies and gentlemen, we English cannot look, and never do look, upon America as a foreign country, or upon the American people as a foreign people. They are flesh of our flesh and bone of our bone. It is true, no doubt, that our fathers and their fathers have had their family quarrels, over which they have shaken hands — for quarrels will occasionally occur in the best regulated families; but these are quarrels which I trust that neither their children nor our children will ever have occasion to renew, for they have been practically settled by a separation of political partnership, prolific in substantial benefits to the best interests of mankind. Meanwhile, we Englishmen of the present day all regard our American kinsfolk as, if I may say so, the rising generation, and the most go-ahead representative of that good old sturdy family stock which, while lovingly, loyally and, I hope, lastingly honoring and keeping honored its ancestral roof-tree, still sends forth from its little island home in the northern seas the hardy offspring of a race that has planted and is spreading in every quarter of the habitable globe the language in which Shakspeare wrote, the liberty for which Washington so nobly labored, the social principles of the Code of Blackstone, and the ethical principles of the creed of Christianity.

"Ladies and Gentlemen, the toast I am going to propose to you is that of the President of the United States of America. This is a toast to which I am sure you would, in any circumstances, respond with cordiality. But I am confident that in the circumstances which have brought us together this evening your cordiality will be quickened by the presence of an eminent guest who has twice filled with renown the high office we are about to honor in the person of its present incumbent. That office, ladies and gentlemen, is, I think, the highest that can possibly be held — the highest that ever has been filled by the citizen of a free country, and never has that high office been more worthily won or more worthily filled than by the distinguished soldier to whose sword America is indebted for the re-established Union and permanent peace of those great sovereign States, over whose united destinies he has twice successfully presided. It was said by the great poet of our own commonwealth that 'peace hath her victories no less renowned than war,' and with the victories of peace, as well as those of war, I am persuaded that the name of General Grant will long be honorably associated by a double renown.

"Ladies and Gentlemen, it is neither customary nor proper to couple the name of any private individual, however eminent he may be, with toasts proposed in honor of the ruling power of a sovereign state. I am not going to infringe that rule; and, as regards the rules of hospitality, I think you must all feel that of hospitality and of sympathy the best expression is in deeds, not words. I think, therefore, that it would be on my part an inhospitable deed if to this toast I added any words which would possibly require from our honored guest the conventional formality of a reply. But, ladies and gentlemen, this at least let me say before I sit down: General Ulysses Grant, like his classic namesake, has seen men and cities in almost every part of the world, enlarging the genius of the statesman and the soldier by the experience of the traveler. Let us hope that when he returns to that great empire of the West, which he has once rescued and twice ruled, he will at least take with him a kindly recollection of his brief sojourn in this empire of the East, where his visit will long be remembered with gratification by many sincere friends and well wishers. Ladies and gentlemen, I have now to

LORD LYTTON AND PROMINENT ENGLISH OFFICIALS IN INDIA.

request that you will fill your glasses and drink with all honor to our last toast this evening. 'The President of the United States of America.' "

General Grant replied, briefly returning thanks for the honor tendered him.

After a continuous round of enjoyment and thorough inspection of all points of interest, the General left Calcutta by steamer for a visit to British Burmah. Arriving at the city of Rangoon, General Grant and party were saluted by two British men-of-war. They had their yards manned in honor of the General. All the vessels in the river were gaily dressed. The landing was covered with scarlet cloth, and the American and British standards were blended. All the town seemed to be out, and the river bank was lined with the muititude, who looked on in their passive Oriental fashion at the pageant. As soon as the boat came to the wharf, Mr. Aitcheson, the Commissioner, came on board, accompanied by Mr. Leishmann, the American Vice-Consul, and bade the General welcome to Burmah.

On landing, the General was presented to the leading citizens and officials, and officers of the men-of-war. The guard of honor presented arms, and they all drove away to the Government House, a pretty, commodious bungalow in the suburbs, buried among trees. Mr. Aticheson is one of the most distinguished officers in the Indian service. He was for some time Foreign Secretary to Calcutta. Burmah, however, is already one of the most important of the British colonies in Asia, and this importance is not diminished by the critical relations between British Burmah and the court of the King. Consequently, England requires the best service possible in Burmah, and, as a result of her policy of sending her wisest men to the most useful places, Mr. Aitcheson finds himself in Rangoon.

The days spent in Rangoon were pleasant; the town is interesting. The streets are wide and rectangular, like those of Philadelphia, and the shade trees are grateful. Over the city, on a height, which you can see from afar, is a pagoda, one of the most famous in Asia. It is covered with gilt, and in the evening, when we first saw it, the sun's rays made it dazzling. This is the land of Buddha and that remarkable religion called Buddhism.

Unlike Brahminism, there is no institution of caste, no priestly caste. The priests are taken from any rank in life, never marry, and they deny themselves all the pleasures of the sense, live a monastic life, dress in yellow gowns, shave their heads and beards, and walk barefooted. The priests go in procession. They chant hymns and prayers, and burn incense. They carry strings of beads like the rosary, which they count and fumble as the say their prayers. There is no single, solemn ceremony like the sacrifice of the mass. Priests and people kneel before the images surrounded by blazing wax lights, the air heavy with incense. They pray together, the priests only known by the yellow gowns. They pray kneeling with clasped, uplifted hands. Sometimes they hold in their hands a rose, or a morsel of rice, or a fragment of bread, as an offering. During their prayers, they frequently bend their bodies so that the face touches the ground. There are convents for women. The temples are places of rest and refuge. Hither come the unfortunate, the poor, the needy, the halt and blind, the belated traveler. All are received, and all are given food and alms.

Rangoon is not only interesting from a religious sense, but it one of the largest commercial centers of the British colonies, and General Grant found no part of his visit more interesting, or more worthy of his attention, than the development of the commerce of Rangoon with the United States. American merchandise now goes to Burmah in English ships, and has to pay an English tax before it can enter this market. With a little effort on the part of the merchants of the United States, a large market would be found for "Yankee notions," petroleum and ice; for, if proper houses were built for storing ice, it could be made a steady and profitable trade. Ice is now made by machinery, but it is poor, costly and unsatisfactory, and the machinery constantly out of order.

A trade based on those articles, established in Rangoon, would supply Burmah, permeate Upper Burmah, Siam and China, and make its way into the islands and settlements.

No country in the East is more worthy of the attention of our merchants than Burmah; the harvest is ripe, and whoever comes in will reap a hundred fold.

CHAPTER XVI.

GENERAL GRANT IN SIAM.

General Grant, on landing at Singapore, was handed an autograph letter by Major Struder—a letter enclosed in an envelope of blue satin, from the King of Siam; the letter read as follows:

THE GRAND PALACE, BANGKOK,
4th February, 1879.

My Dear Sir: Having heard from my Minister for Foreign Affairs, on the authority of the United States Consul, that you are expected in Singapore on your way to Bangkok, I beg to express the pleasure I shall have in making your acquaintance. Possibly you may arrive in Bangkok during my absence at my country residence, Bang Pa In; in which case a steamer will be placed at your disposal to bring you to me. On arrival I beg you to communicate with His Excellency, my Minister for Foreign Affairs, who will arrange for your reception and entertainment.

Yours very truly,
CHULAHLONGKORN, R. S.

To General Grant, late President of the United States.

The letter that the King had taken the trouble to send all the way to Singapore, and the desire of General Grant to see all that was to be seen, decided him in accepting this flattering invitation, and visit Siam. So the General and party prepared at once for Siam. A heavy rain swept over Singapore as they embarked on the small steamer Kang See, on the morning of the 9th of April.

The run to Bangkok is set down at four days, and sometimes there are severe storms in the Gulf of Siam; but fortune was with them in this, as it had, indeed, been with them, so far as weather at sea is concerned, ever since they left Marseilles. The evening of their sailing some one happened to remember was the anniversary of the surrender of Lee — fourteen years ago to-day — and the hero of the surrender was sitting on the deck of a small steamer smoking and looking at the clouds, and gravely arguing Mr. Borie out of a purpose which some one has wickedly charged him with entertaining — the purpose of visiting Australia and New Zealand and New Guinea, and spending the summer and winter in the Pacific Ocean.

On the morning of the 14th of April, the little steamer in putting into Bangkok lost her reckoning and could not pass the inner bar. About ten o'clock the royal yacht anchored within a cable's length — a long, stately craft, with the American colors flying at the fore, and the royal colors at the main. A boat put off at once, conveying Mr. Sickles, our Consul, the son of the Foreign Minister, representing the Siamese government, and an aid of the King. Mr. Sickles presented the Siamese officials to the General, and the King's aid handed him the following letter, enclosed in an envelope of yellow satin:—

THE GRAND PALACE, BANGKOK,
April 11, 1879.

Sir: I have very great pleasure in welcoming you to Siam. It is, I am informed, your pleasure that your reception should be a private one; but you must permit me to show, as far as I can, the high esteem in which I hold the most eminent citizen of that great nation which has been so friendly to Siam, and so kind and just in all its intercourse with the nations of the far East.

That you may be near me during your stay, I have commanded my brother, His Royal Highness the Celestial Prince Bhanurangsi Swangwongse, to prepare rooms for you and your party in the Saranrom Palace, close to my palace, and I most cordially invite you, Mrs. Grant and your party at once to take up your residence there, and my brother will represent me as your host.

Your friend,
CHULAHLONGKORN, R. S.

His Excellency General Grant, late President of the United States.

At four o'clock the General embarked on a royal gondola, and was slowly pulled to the shore. The guard presented arms, the cavalry escort wheeled into line, the band played "Hail Columbia." On ascending the stairs, Mr. Alabaster, the royal interpreter, Captain Bush, an English officer commanding the Siamese navy, and a brilliant retinue, were in waiting. The Foreign Minister advanced and welcomed the General to Siam, and presented him to the other members of the suite. Then entering carriages, the General and party were driven to the palace of Hwang Saranrom, the home of His Royal Highness the Celestial Prince Bhanurangsi Swangwongse. As they drove past the barracks the artillery were drawn up in battery, and the cannon rolled out a salute of twenty-one guns. On reaching the palace a guard was drawn up, and another band played the American national air. At the gate of the palace, Phra Sri Dhammason, of the foreign office, met the General and escorted him to the door of the palace. Here he was met by his Excellency Phya Bashakarawangse, the King's private secretary, and a nobleman of rank corresponding to that of an English earl. At the head of the marble steps was His Royal Highness the Celestial Prince, wearing the decorations of the Siamese orders of nobility, surrounded by other princes of a lesser rank and the members of his household. Advancing, he shook hands with the General, and, offering his arm to Mrs. Grant, led the party to the grand audience chamber. Here all the party were presented to the Prince, and there was a short conversation. The Celestial Prince is a young man about twenty, with a clear, expressive face, who speaks English fairly well, but, during the interview, spoke Siamese, through Mr. Alabaster, who acted as interpreter. The Prince lamented the weather, which was untimely and severe. However, it would be a blessing to the country and the people, and His Royal Highness added a compliment that was Oriental in its delicacy when he said that the blessing of the rain was a blessing which General Grant had brought with him to Siam. The Prince then said that his palace was the General's home, and that he had been commanded by the King, his brother, to say that anything in the Kingdom that would contribute to the happiness, comfort or honor of General Grant, was at his disposal. The Prince entered into conversation with Mrs. Grant and the members of the General's party. The General expressed himself delighted with the cordiality of his welcome, and said he had been anxious to see Siam, and would have regretted his inability to do so. The Prince offered his arm to Mrs. Grant, and escorted her and the General to their apartments, while the members of his suite assigned the remainder of the party to the quarters they were to occupy while they lived in the capital of Siam.

The evening was passed quietly, the General and party dining quietly with the Celestial Prince. The programme arranged by the King for the entertainment of his guests was submitted to General Grant, who regretted his inability to follow the whole of it. Not being on his own ship (the Richmond), which would have awaited his convenience, the General was compelled to return to Singapore on the ordinary mail steamer, which, leaving on Friday, only left him five days for Bangkok. So one or two dinners were eliminated, the visits to the temples and elephants massed into one day, and the run up the river to Ayuthia, the old capital of Siam, added.

On the morning after the General's arrival, a visit was

made to the ex-Regent. This aged statesman is one of the leading men in Siam, the first nobleman in the realm in influence and authority. He was the intimate friend and counsellor of the late King. He governed the Kingdom during the minority of the present sovereign. It was through his influence that the accession of His Majesty was secured without question or mutiny. He is now the chief of the Council of State, and governs several provinces of Siam with the power of life and death. His voice in council is potent, partly because of his rank and experience, and partly because of his old age, which is always respected in Siam. Their journey to the Regent's was in boats in Venetian fashion, and, after a half-hour's pulling down one canal and up another, and across the river to a third canal, and up that to a fourth, they came to a large and roomy palace shaded with trees. Orders had been given by the King that the canals and river should be kept free from trading craft and other vessels at the hours set down in the programme for the official visits. As a consequence, whenever they took to their boats they pulled along at a rapid pace with no chance of collision.

As the boat pulled up to the foot of the palace, the ex-Regent, his breast bearing many orders, was waiting to receive the General. He was accompanied by Mr. Chandler, an American gentleman who has spent many years in Siam, and knows the language perfectly. The ex-Regent is a small, spare man, with a clean-cut, well shaped head, and a face reminding you, in its outlines and the general set of the countenance, of the late M. Thiers. It lacked the vivacity which was the characteristic of M. Thiers, and was a grave and serious face. He advanced, shook hands with the General, and, taking his hand, led him up stairs to the audience room of the palace. A guard of honor presented arms, the band played. The Regent led us into his audience hall, and, placing General Grant on his right, we all ranged ourselves about him on chairs. An audience with an Eastern Prince is a serious and a solemn matter. The Siamese is a grave person. He shows you honor by speaking slowly, saying little, and making pauses between his speeches. After you take your seat, servants begin to float around. They bring you tea in small china cups — tea of a delicate and pure flavor, and unlike our own attempts in that direction. They bring you cigars, and in the tobacco way we noted a cigarette with a leaf made out of the banana plant, which felt like velvet between the lips, and is an improvement in the tobacco way which even the ripe culture of America on the tobacco question could with advantage accept. In Siam you can smoke in every place, and before every presence, except in the presence of the King.

The Regent, after some meditation, spoke of the great pleasure it had given him to meet with General Grant in Siam. He had long known and valued the friendship of the United States, and he was sensible of the good that had been done to Siam by the counsel and the enterprise of the Americans who had lived there.

The General thanked the Regent, and was glad to know that his country was so much esteemed in the East. There was a pause and a cup of the enticing tea and some remarks on the weather. The General expressed a desire to know whether the unusual rain would affect the crops throughout the country. The Regent said there was no such apprehension, and there was another pause, while the velvet-coated cigarettes and cigars passed into general circulation. The General spoke of the value to Siam and to all countries in the East of the widest commercial intercourse with nations of the outer world, and that, from all he could learn from the Siamese and the character of their resources, any extension of relations with other nations would be a gain to them. His Highness listened to this speech, as Mr. Chandler translated it in a slow and deliberate way, standing in front of the Regent, and intoning it almost as though it were a lesson from the morning service. Then there was another pause; then the Regent responded: Siam, he said, was a peculiar country. It was away from sympathy and communion with the greater nations. It was not in one of the great highways of commerce. Its people were not warlike nor aggressive. It had no desire to share in the strifes and wars of other nations. It existed by the friendship of the great powers. His policy had always been to cultivate that friendship, to do nothing to offend any foreign power, to avoid controversy or pretexts for intervention by making every concession.

All this was spoken slowly, deliberately, as if every sentence was weighed, the old Minister speaking slowly, like one in meditation. His deliberate speech seemed to have unusual significance, and made a deep impression upon his visitors — the impression that he who spoke was one in authority and a statesman. After further talk, the Regent addressed himself to Mr. Borie, and asked him his age. Mr. Borie answered that he was sixty-nine. "I am seventy-two," said the Regent: "but you look much older." It is a custom in Siamese, when you wish pay a compliment to an elderly person, to tell him how old he looks, to compliment him on his gray hairs and the lines in his brow. In speaking with Mr. Borie, the Regent became almost playful. "You must not have the trouble of a navy in another war." Mr. Borie expressed his horror of war, and added that America had had enough of it. "At our time of life," said the Regent, putting his hand on Mr. Borie's shoulder in a half playful, half affectionate manner, "we need repose, and that our lives should be made smooth and free from care, and we should not be burdened with authority or grave responsibilities. That belongs to the others. I hope you will be spared any cares." This practically closed the interview, and the Regent, taking the hand of the General in his own, in Oriental fashion, led him down-stairs and across the entrance-way to the boat, the troops saluting and the band playing. Then he took a cordial farewell of Mr. Borie, telling him he was a brave man to venture around the world with the burden of so many years upon him.

The King of Siam issued the following order for the reception and entertainment of General Grant, which was faithfully carried out:

"PROGRAMME for the reception and entertainment of General U. S. Grant, ex-President of the United States of America, subject to such modifications as he may deem expedient:

"FIRST DAY.— On the arrival of the mail steamer Kong See, conveying General Grant and party, at Paknam, a deputation, consisting of Phra Bairaybakya Bhakdi, Phra Sri Sombat and Luang Salayut Witikan, Captain of the Royal Body Guard, will proceed on board the steam yacht Rising Sun to the steamer Kong See. On going on board, they will welcome General Grant in the name of His Majesty, and, on presenting His Majesty's best wishes to General Grant and party, will invite them on board the Rising Sun and convey them up to Bangkok. On their arrival at Bangkok the steam yacht will anchor off the International Court House. Officers of the Foreign Department will then proceed to the steam yacht in house boats, with paddles, one of eight and one of seven fathoms in length, to invite and convey General Grant, Mrs. Grant and party to the landing at the International Court House. There will be a company, consisting of one hundred soldiers, with a military band, at the landing, as a guard of honor. Phya Pihasbarawongree, Private Secretary to His Majesty, Phra Bpaksa Nanaprates Kich, Judge of the International Court, with officers of the Royal Horse Guard and officers of the Foreign Department, will be in waiting at the landing to invite General Grant, Mrs. Grant and party to take carriages and proceed to the Grand Saronrom Palace. A guard of honor will be drawn up in front of the palace, consisting of twenty soldiers and a military band for the occasion. Phra Sudham Maitre and Phra Sri Dhamasan will be in waiting at the door of the palace to receive General Grant and party. His Royal Highness Somdech Chowfa Bhanurangse Sawangwongo, and His Excellency Chow Phya Bhann Wongse Maha Cosa Dhipoti, Minister for Foreign Affairs, will be in waiting in the upper porch to welcome them to the palace. General Grant and party having gone into the palace, a salute of twenty-one guns will be fired. In case the arrival occurs in the night, the salute will be deferred until the morning.

"SECOND DAY.—At ten o'clock A. M. the officers will invite General Grant to visit His Highness Somdech Chow Phya Boom Maha Suramngse, the ex-Regent, and members of the Senabodi, and will be conveyed in carriages to the landing of the International Court, then in boats. They will return by the same route. At four o'clock P. M. the officers will invite General Grant, Mrs. Grant and party to an audience with His Majesty the King of Siam, in the royal palace. The audience will be held in the grand audience hall, Boromraj Satet Maholan. After the royal audience they will be conveyed in carriages to an audience with His Majesty Krow Phrarajawany Pawara Sthan Mongal, second King. At nine o'clock P. M. His Royal Highness Somdech Chowfa Bhanurangse Sawangwongo will hold a reception in honor of General Grant at the Palace Saronrom.

"THIRD DAY.—On the morning of this day His Majesty the King of Siam will return the visit of General Grant at the Palace Saronrom. At four P. M. the officers will invite General Grant and party to pay a visit to His Royal Highness Somdech Phra Chow Boronwongee Ter

Chowfa Maha Mala Krom Phra Bamrap Parapax, and will be conveyed in carriages. At eleven o'clock P. M. General Grant, Mrs. Grant and party will be entertained at a royal banquet in the royal palace, Boromraj Satet Maholan, and will be conveyed in carriages.

"FOURTH DAY.— At four o'clock P. M. the officers will invite General Grant and party to pay a visit to His Royal Highness Somdech Chowfa Chaturomasami Kromduang Chakrapatdipong. After which they will take a look at the Monastery Arunrayweram-Wat-Chung. At seven o'clock General Grant and party will be entertained at dinner at the official residence of His Excellency the Minister for Foreign Affairs, and will be conveyed in carriages and in boats.

"FIFTH DAY.— At three o'clock P. M. the officers will invite General Grant and party to the Monastery Phra Budhoatnesatan and the Monastery Phrasee Ratnesasadahram, also the museum at the royal palace. They will then be invited to a private audience with His Majesty the King, in the royal palace. At seven o'clock P. M. General Grant and party will be entertained at a dinner party at the official residence of His Highness Somdech Chow Phya Borom Maha Sri Suramngse, the ex-Regent.

"SIXTH DAY.— At three o'clock P. M. officers will invite General Grant and party to visit the temple Satatteph Taram and the temple Phra Chattupun Vevnon Niankahram, and from thence will go into the Royal Palace to see the royal white elephants. After that he will proceed to the palace of His Royal Highness Somdech Chowfa Maha Mala Krom Phra Bamap Parapax to see the state elephants and the elephants of war. At eight o'clock P. M. His Royal Highness Somdech Chowfa Chaturong Rasami Krom Luang Chakrapatdipon will entertain General Grant and party with a ball at the old royal palace.

"SEVENTH DAY.— At nine o'clock A. M. the officers

will invite General Grant and party to embark on board the royal yacht Vesatri, to take an excursion, to view the scenery on the River Chow Phya. General Grant and party will be conveyed in carriages to the landing, and thence embark on board the Vesatri, and will return in the same manner. At four o'clock in the afternoon the officers will invite General Grant, Mrs. Grant and party to a royal audience with His Majesty at the royal palace."

In Siam there is a second King, or as occupying a position similar to that of the Vice-President of the United States.

In Siam the second King is a person and an authority, entitled to royal honors, living in a palace, with troops, a court, a harem and a Foreign Minister. He has an income from the State of $300,000 a year. Of authority he has none beyond the management of his household and the command of troops in certain of the provinces.

The second King, therefore, is a political influence in Siam — great, because behind him is the supposed power of England. Take that power away, and His Majesty would be ranked among the nobles, allowed the position of a duke, given his place after the royal family, and the present office would be eliminated altogether from the government of Siam. It certainly seems to be an expensive and an almost useless function, one that might readily be absorbed into the royal office with a gain to the treasury and no loss to the state. The prince who holds the position is in his fortieth year and is a gentleman of intelligence.

His Majesty the first King of Siam, and absolute sovereign, is named Chulahlongkorn. This, at least, is the name which he attaches to the royal signet. His name as given in the books is Phrabat Somdetch Phra Paramendo Mahah Chulah-long-korn Klow.

On the afternoon of April 14, at three o'clock, General Grant and party had their audience with the King of Siam.

Our Palace of Saronrom, in which we are living, is next to the Grand Palace; but so vast are these royal homes that it was quite a drive to the house of our next-door neighbor. The General and party went in state carriages, and at the door of the palace were met by an officer. Troops were drawn up all the way from the gate to the door of the audience hall, and it was quite a walk before, having passed temples, shrines, outhouses, pavilions and statelier mansions, we came to the door of a modest building and were met by aids of the King. A wide pair of marble steps led to the audience room, and on each side of the steps were pots with blooming flowers and rare shrubs. The band in the courtyard played the national air, and as the General came to the head of the stairs the King, who was waiting, and wore a magnificent jeweled decoration, advanced and shook the hands of the General in the warmest manner. Then, shaking hands with Mrs. Grant, he offered her his arm, and walked into the audience hall. The audience hall is composed of two large, gorgeously decorated saloons, that would not be out of place in any palace. The decorations were French, and reminded you of the Louvre. In the first hall were a series of busts of contemporary sovereigns and rulers of states. The place of honor was given to the bust of General Grant, a work of art in dark bronze which did not look much like the General, and seems to have been made by a French or English artist from photographs. From here the King passed on to a smaller room, beautifully furnished in yellow satin. Here the King took a seat on a sofa, with Mrs. Grant and the General on either side, the members of the party on chairs near him, officers of the court in the background standing, and servants at the doors, kneeling in attitudes of submission. The King is a spare young man, active and nervous in his movements, with a full, clear, almost glittering black eye, which moved about restlessly from one to the other, and while he talked his fingers seemed to be keeping unconscious time to the musical measures. When any of his court approached him, or were addressed by him, they responded by a gesture or salute of adoration. Everything about the King betokened a high and quick intelligence, and, although the audience was a formal one, and the conversation did not go beyond words of courtesy and welcome from the King to the General and his party, he gave you the impression of a resolute and able man, full of resources and quite equal to the cares of his station. This impression was confirmed by all that we heard or saw in Siam. The audience at an end, the King led Mrs. Grant and the General to the head of the stairs, and we took our leave.

At three o'clock, on the 15th of April, the King returned the General's visit, by coming in state to see him at our palace of Saronrom. This, we were told, was a most unusual honor, and was intended as the highest compliment it was in His Majesty's power to bestow. A state call from a King is an event in Bangkok, and long before the hour the space in front of the palace was filled with curious Siamese and Chinese, heedless of the rain, waiting to gaze upon the celestial countenance. As the hour came, there was the bustle of preparation. First came a guard, which formed in front of the palace; then a smaller guard, which formed in the palace yard, from the gate to the porch; then a band of music, which stood at the rear of the inner guard; then came attendants, carrying staves in their hands to clear the streets, and give warning that the King was coming, that the streets should be abandoned by all, so that His Majesty should have unquestioned way. Then came a squadron of the royal body guard in scarlet uniform, under the command of a royal Prince. The King sat in a carriage alone on the back seat, with two princes with him, who sat on the front seats. His Royal Highness and the members of the household arrayed themselves in state garments, the Prince wearing a coat of purple silk. The General and his party wore evening dress, as worn at home on occasions of ceremony. When the trumpets announced the coming of the King, the General, accompanied by the Prince, the members of his household and party, came to the foot of the stairs. Colonel Grant, wearing the uniform of a lieutenant-colonel, waited at the gate to receive the King in his father's name.

The General waited at the foot of the marble steps, and, as the King advanced, shook hands with him cordially and led him to the reception room. The King was dressed in simple Siamese costume, wearing the decoration of Siam, but not in uniform. Mr. Alabaster, the interpreter, stood behind the King and the General. The King, who spoke Siamese, said he hoped that the General had found everything comfortable for himself and party at the Saranrom Palace.

The General said that nothing could be more agreeable than the hospitality of the Prince.

The King said he hoped that the General, if he wanted anything, to see any part of Siam, go anywhere or do anything, would express the wish, as he would feel it a great privilege to give him anything in this kingdom.

General Grant said he appreciated the King's kindness, and thanked him.

The King, after a pause, said that General Grant's visit was especially agreeable to him, because, not only in his own reign, but before, Siam had been under obligations to the United States. Siam saw in the United States not only a great but a friendly power, which did not look upon the East with any idea of aggrandizement, and to whom it was always pleasant to turn for counsel and advice. More than that, the influence of most of the Americans who had come to Siam had been good, and those who had been in the government's service had been of value to the State. The efforts of the missionaries to spread a knowledge of the arts and sciences, of machinery and of medicine, among the Siamese, had been commendable. The King was glad to have the opportunity of saying this to one who had been the chief magistrate of the American people.

General Grant responded that the policy of the United States was a policy of non-intervention in everything that concerned the internal affairs of other nations. It had become almost a traditional policy, and experience confirmed its wisdom. The country needed all the energies of its own people for its development, and its only interest in the East was to do what it could to benefit the people, especially in opening markets for American manufactures. The General, in his travels through India and Burmah, had been much gratified with the commendations bestowed upon American products; and although the market was as yet a small one, he felt certain that our trade with the East would become a great one. There was the field at least, and our people had the opportunity. Nothing would please him more than to see Siam sharing in this trade. Beyond this there was no desire on the part of the American government to seek an influence in the East.

The King said nothing would please him more than the widest possible development of the commerce between Siam and America. The resources of Siam were great, but their development limited. Siam was like the United States in one respect, that it had a large territory and a small population, and the development of many sources of wealth that were known to exist had been retarded from this cause.

General Grant thought this difficulty might be met by the introduction of skilled labor, such, for instance, as mining experts from Nevada and California, who could prospect and locate mines, and labor-saving machinery, in which the Americans especially excelled.

The King assented to this, with the remark that the Siamese were a conservative people and studied anything new very carefully before adopting it. Their policy in foreign relations had been a simple one — peace with foreign powers and steady development of the country. Siam was a small country with limited resources, and she knew that she could not contend with the great foreign powers. Consequently she always depended upon the justice and good will of foreign powers. This sometimes led to their appearing to consent or to submit to some things which under other circumstances and by other and greater nations would not be endured. In the end, however, it worked right, and Siam, looking back over her relations with the great powers, found, on the whole, no reason for regret. In the main these relations had been for the good of the Siamese people. From the foreign powers Siam had always received encouragement.

The King led the way to the upper audience chamber, the saloon of the statues. Here ensued a long conversation between the King and the General and the various members of the party. Mrs. Grant, in the inner room, had a conversation with the Queen, who had not been at the table. In conversing with the General, the King became warm and almost affectionate. He was proud of having made the acquaintance of the General, and he wanted to know more of the American people. He wished Americans to know that he was a friend of the country. As to the General himself, the King hoped when the General returned to the United States that he would write the King and allow the King to write to him, and always be his friend and correspondent. The General said he would always remember his visit to Siam; that it would afford him pleasure to know that he was the friend of the King; that he would write to the King and always be glad to hear from him; and if he could ever be of service to the King it would be a pleasure. With Mr. Borie the King also had a long conversation, and his manner toward the venerable ex-Secretary was especially kind and genial. It was midnight before the party came to an end.

On the next morning there was a state dinner at the royal palace. The party consisted of the King, His Royal Highness the Celestial Prince, several princes, members of the royal family of lower rank, General Grant and party, the American Consul, Mr. Sickles, and Miss Struder, daughter of the Consul at Singapore; Mr. Torrey, the American Vice-Consul, and Mrs. Torrey; the Foreign Minister, his son, the King's private secretary, Mr. Alabaster, the members of the Foreign Office, and the aids of the King who had been attending the General. The Siamese all wore state dresses — coats of gold cloth, richly embroidered — and the King wore the family decoration, a star of nine points, the centre a diamond, and the other points with a rich jewel of different character, embracing the precious stones found in Siam. The General was received in the audience hall, and the dinner was served in the lower hall or dining-room. There were forty guests present, and the service of the table was silver, the prevailing design being the three-headed elephant, which belongs to the arms of Siam. This service alone cost ten thousand pounds in England. There were two bands in attendance, one playing Siamese, and the other European music, alternately. The Celestial Prince escorted Mrs. Grant to dinner, and sat opposite the King at the centre of the table. General Grant sat next the King. The dinner was long, elaborate, and in the European style, with the exception of some dishes of curry dressed in Siamese fashion, which we were not brave enough to do more than taste. The night was warm, but the room was kept moderately cool by a system of penekahs or large fans swinging from the ceiling, which kept the air in circulation.

After they had been at the table about three hours there was a pause and a signal. The fans stopped, the music paused, and Mr. Alabaster, as interpreter, took his place behind the King. His Majesty then arose, and the company with him, and, in a clear accent heard all over the saloon, made the following speech in Siamese:

"YOUR ROYAL HIGHNESS, LADIES AND GENTLEMEN, NOW ASSEMBLED: I beg you to hear the expression of the pleasure which I have felt in receiving as my guest a President of the United States of America. Siam has for many years past derived great advantages from America, whose citizens have introduced into my kingdom many arts and sciences, much medical knowledge and many valuable books, to the great advantage of the country. Even before our countries were joined in treaty alliance, citizens of America came here and benefited us. Since then our relations have greatly improved, and to the great advantage of Siam, and recently the improvement has been still more marked. Therefore it is natural that we should be exceedingly gratified by the visit paid to us by a President of the United States. General Grant has a grand fame, that has reached even to Siam, that has been known here for several years. We are well aware that as a true soldier he first saw glory as a leader in war, and, thereafter accepting the office of President, earned the admiration of all men as being a statesman of the highest rank. It is a great gratification to all of us to meet one thus eminent both in the government of war and of peace. We see him and are charmed by his gracious manner, and feel sure that his visit will inaugurate friendly relations with the United States of a still closer nature than before, and of the most enduring character. Therefore I ask you all to join with me in drinking the health of General Grant and wishing him every blessing."

When the King finished, Mr. Alabaster translated the speech into English, the company all the time remaining on their feet. Then the toast was drank with cheers, the band playing the American national air.

General Grant then arose, and, in a low but clear and perfectly distinct voice, said:

"YOUR MAJESTY, LADIES AND GENTLEMEN: I am very much obliged to Your Majesty for the kind and complimentary manner in which you have welcomed me to Siam. I am glad that it has been my good fortune to visit this country and to thank Your Majesty in person for your letters inviting me to Siam, and to see with my own eyes your country and your people. I feel that it would have been a misfortune if the programme of my journey had not included Siam. I have now been absent from home nearly two years, and during that time I have seen every capital and nearly every large city in Europe, as well as the principal cities in India, Burmah and the Malay Peninsula. I have seen nothing that has interested me more than Siam, and every hour of my visit here has been agreeable and instructive. For the welcome I have received from Your Majesty, the princes and members of the Siamese government, and the people generally, I am very grateful. I accept it, not as personal to myself alone, but as a mark of the friendship felt for my country by Your Majesty and the people of Siam. I am glad to see that feeling, because I believe that the best interests of the two countries can be benefited by nothing so much as the establishment of the most cordial relations between them. On my return to America I shall do what I can to cement those relations. I hope that in America we shall see more of the Siamese, that we shall have embassies and diplomatic relations, that our commerce and manufactures will increase with Siam, and that your young men will visit our country and attend our colleges as they now go to colleges in Germany and England. I can assure them all a kind reception, and I feel that the visits would be interesting and advantageous. I again thank Your Majesty for the splendid hospitality which has been shown to myself and my party, and I trust that your reign will be happy and prosperous, and that Siam will continue to advance in the arts of civilization."

General Grant, after a pause, then said:

"I hope you will allow me to ask you to drink the health of His Majesty the King of Siam. I am honored by the opportunity of proposing that toast in his own capital and his own palace, and of saying how much I have been impressed with his enlightened rule. I now ask you to drink the health of His Majesty the King, and prosperity and peace to the people of Siam."

After a round of receptions, entertainments and excursions, the General bade adieu to Siam, having passed a delightful week.

CHAPTER XVII.

GENERAL GRANT IN CHINA.

On April 25, General Grant arrived at Saigon in the French mail steamship Irawaddy. He and his party were invited by Rear-Admiral La Fond, Governor of French Cochin China, to sojourn at the Government House. They passed the night there, and next day visited public buildings and places of interest. A public levee was given on the evening of the 26th. The guests returned to the ship about midnight, and the voyage was resumed on the 27th. They reached Hong Kong on the evening of April 30. The ship was immediately boarded by United States Consuls Mosby, of Hong Kong; Lincoln, of Canton; Charge d'Affaires Holcombe, and deputations of citizens of various countries, including Japan. The same evening the visitors proceeded to the United States ship Ashuelot, where they were received with a salute of twenty-one guns.

After partaking of refreshments, they went ashore in the Colonial government launch. Salutes were fired by batteries all along the river.

General Grant arrived at Canton on the evening of May 6, and was received by the Consular officials, and conducted to the Viceroy's yaman, three miles from the point of debarkation. Canton is situated on the Pearl River, thirty miles from the coast. The Viceroy sent a gunboat out as escort up the river. This vessel, bearing the American flag at the fore out of compliment to the General, followed all the way.

At various points in the river — wherever, indeed, there were forts — salutes were fired and troops paraded. These lines of troops, with their flags — and nearly every other man in a Chinese army carries a flag — looked picturesque and theatrical as seen from our deck.

It was nine o'clock in the evening before the lights of Canton were seen. The Chinese gunboats, as the General and party came to anchorage, burned blue lights and fired rockets. The landing was decorated with Chinese lanterns, and many of the junks in the river burned lights and displayed the American flag. The whole city had been waiting all the afternoon, and had now gone home to dinner. Next morning salutes were exchanged between the Ashuelot and the Chinese gunboats. The General remained at home during the morning to receive calls. The coming of General Grant had created a flutter in the Chinese mind. No foreign barbarian of so high a rank had ever visited the Celestial Kingdom. As soon as the Viceroy learned of the visit, he sent word to the American Consul that he would receive General Grant with special honors. The Viceroy ordered all the houses closed, streets cleared and the troops paraded. A placard issued, that a foreigner was coming to do the Viceroy honor, and that the people must do him honor. We give a translation of one of these extra bulletins:

"We have just heard that the King of America, being on friendly terms with China, will leave America early in the third month, bringing with him a suite of officers, etc., all complete on board the ship. It is said that he is bringing a large number of rare presents with him, and that he will be here in Canton about the 6th or 9th of May. He will land at the Tintsy ferry, and will proceed to the Viceroy's palace by way of the South gate, the Fantai's Ngamun and the Waning Street. Viceroy Lau has arranged that all the mandarins shall be there to meet him, and a full Court will be held After a little friendly conversation he will leave the Viceroy's palace, and visit the various objects of interest within and without the walls. He will then proceed to the Roman Catholic Cathedral, to converse and pass the night. It is not stated what will then take place, but notice will be given."

As the hour approached for the General to enter Canton, the crowd on the street grew larger and larger. A Tartar officer arrived with a detachment of soldiers, who formed, and kept the crowd back. Then came the chairs and the chair bearers, for in Canton you must ride in chairs and be borne on the shoulders of men. Rank is shown by the color of the chair and the number of attendants. The General's chair was a stately affair. On the top was a silver globe. The color was green, a color highly esteemed in China, and next in rank to yellow, which is sacred and consecrated to the Emperor, who alone can ride in a yellow chair. The chair is borne by eight men, and swings on long bamboo poles. In addition to the chair bearers, there was a small guard of unarmed soldiers, some ahead and others behind the chair, whose presence gave dignity to the chair and its occupant. The principal business of this guard seemed to be to shout and to make all the noise possible.

At last they were under way for their visit to the Viceroy. First rode the single Tartar officer, then came the shouting guard, then General Grant in his chair of state. The General wore evening dress. The crowd and enthusiasm manifested all along the route was an extraordinary sight wherever the street was intersected with other streets. The crowd became so dense that additional troops were required to hold them in place, and at various points the Chinese salute of three guns was fired.

The road to the viceregal palace was three miles, and as the pace of the coolie who carries the chair is a slow one, and especially on days of multitudes and pageantry, they were over an hour on their journey, and for this hour they journeyed through a sea of faces, a hushed and silent sea, that swept around them, covering windows, doors, streets, roof tops, wherever there was room for a pair of feet or hands.

Some of the party estimated that there were two hundred thousand people to witness General Grant's progress through Canton. Two hundred thousand men, women and children may be taken, therefore, as an estimate by one who saw and took part in the ceremony. But no massing together of figures, although you ascend into the hundreds of thousands, will give an idea of the multitude. The march was a slow one. There were frequent pauses. Arrived at the palace of the Viceroy, the visitors descend from their chairs, and enter the open reception room or audience chamber. But the booming guns, which boom in a quick, angry fashion; the increasing crowds, the renewed lines of soldiery, now standing in double line, their guns at a present; the sons of mandarins, the Viceroy's guard, under trees, and the open, shaded enclosure into which we are borne by our staggering, panting chair-bearers, tell us that we are at our journey's end, and at the palace of the Viceroy. We descend from our chairs, and enter the open reception room or audience chamber. The Viceroy himself, surrounded by all the great officers of his court, is waiting at the door. As General Grant advances, accompanied by the Consul, the Viceroy steps forward and meets him with a gesture of welcome, which to our barbarian eyes looks like a gesture of adoration. He wears the mandarin's hat, and the pink button and flowing robes of silk, the breast and back embroidered a good deal like the sacrificial robes of an archbishop at high mass. The Viceroy is a Chinaman, and not of the governing Tartar race. He has a thin, somewhat worn face, and is over fifty years of age. His manner was the perfection of courtesy and cordiality. He said he knew how unworthy he was of a visit from one so great as General Grant, but that this unworthiness only increased the honor. Then he presented the General to the members of his Court — Chang Tsein, the Tartar General; Jen Chi, the Imperial Commissioner of Customs; San Chang Mow, the Deputy Tartar General, and Chi Hwo, the Assistant Tartar General. After General Grant had been presented, each of his party in turn were welcomed by the Viceroy, and presented to his suite.

During this interchange of compliments the reception room was filled with members and retainers of the Court. Mandarins, aids, soldiers — all ranks were present. The whole scene was one of curiosity and excitement. The Chinamen seemed anxious to do all they could to show General Grant how welcome was his coming, but such a visit was a new thing, and they had no precedent for the reception of strangers who held so high a position as General Grant.

After the civilities were exchanged, the Viceroy led the General and party into another room, where there were chairs and tables around the room in a semi-circle. Between each couple of chairs was a small table, on which were cups of tea. The General was led to the place of honor in the centre, and the Chinese clustered together in one corner. After some persuasion the Viceroy was induced to sit beside the General, and the conversation proceeded. Nothing was said beyond the usual compliments, which were only repeated in various forms.

After sitting fifteen minutes they drank tea in Chinese fashion. The tea is served in two cups, one of which is placed over the other in such a manner that when you take up the cups you have a globe in your hands. The tea is plain, and as each particular cup has been brewed by itself — is, in fact, brewing while you are waiting — you have the leaves of the tea, avoiding the leaves by pushing the upper bowl down into the lower one so as to leave a minute opening and draw out the tea. Some drank the tea in orthodox home fashion, but others, being sensitive to the reputation of barbarism, perhaps, managed the two bowls very much as though it were an experiment in jugglery, and drank the tea like a mandarin. This ceremony over, they were led into another room that opened on a garden. Here were guards, aids and mandarins and lines of soldiers. They found a large table spread covered with dishes — eighty dishes in all. A part of a Chinese reception is entertainment, and the General's was to be regal. They sat around the table and a cloud of attendants appeared, who with silver and ivory chopsticks heaped their plates. Beside each plate were two chopsticks and a knife and fork, so that they might eat their food as they pleased, in Chinese or European fashion.

The food was all sweetmeats, candied fruits, walnuts, almonds, ginger, cocoanuts, with cups of tea and wine. The Viceroy with his chopsticks helped the General. This is true Chinese courtesy, for the host to make himself the servant of his guest. Then came a service of wine — sweet champagne and sauterne — in which the Viceroy pledged us all, bowing to each guest as he drank. Then, again, came tea, which in China is the signal for departure, an intimation that your visit is over. The Viceroy and party arose and led them to their chairs. Each one was severally and especially saluted as they entered their chairs; and as they filed off under the trees, their coolies dangling them on their shoulders, they left the Viceroy and his whole court, with rows of mandarins and far-extending lines of soldiers in an attitude of devotion, hands held together toward the forehead and heads bent, the soldiers with arms presented. The music, real, banging, gong-thumping Chinese music, broke out, twenty-one guns were fired, so close that the smoke obscured the view, and they plunged into the sea of life through which they had floated, and back again, through one of the most wonderful sights ever seen, back to their shady home in the American Consulate.

Consul-General Lincoln gave a grand State dinner on the 11th. In addition to the members of the General's party there were Captain Perkins, Mr. McEwen, Mr. Deering, Mr. Case and Mr. Strickland, of the Ashuelot, and the leading members of the foreign settlement to the number of forty. The whole house was dressed with wreaths and evergreens and American flags, and in front of the house was a platform for fireworks. The day had been fitful as far as rain was concerned, and heavy black clouds banked themselves in the skies. But the fireworks were fairly successful, and the dinner was good, and Mr. Lincoln made an excellent speech, to which the General replied by thanking the Consul for his courtesy. He had, he said, visited every capital and nearly every large city in Europe, and looked forward with interest to his continued progress through Asia. The honors he received were paid, not to him, but to his country, and in that spirit he accepted them. He believed that peace could have no better assurance than in the harmony and cordial good feeling of the civilized nations of the world, and in presence of so many representatives of these nations he felt he could propose no better sentiment than the health of the rulers and governments they represented. Mr. Rowe then proposed the health in flattering terms of Mr. and Mrs. Lincoln. Mr. Lincoln thanked Mr. Rowe in a few well turned remarks, and the party left the dining-room to witness a grand display of fireworks. A bamboo erection, sixty feet high, had been placed in front of the Consulate, and after a number of rockets, Catherine wheels and colored lights of all kinds had been let off, a set piece displaying a pagoda was fired and a magnificent spectacle was produced, winding up with a volley of rockets of all colors. At ten o'clock a reception was held at the Consulate, when the whole of the American and European community were presented to General Grant by Mr. Lincoln.

The welcome given General Grant at Canton was even more enthusiastic, and, in point of numbers participating, the most demonstrative, of any that had preceded it. There was so much ceremony during the General's visit that he had scarcely any opportunity to see the city, he having given himself but four days to see Canton, and had promised to return to Hong Kong to be present at a garden party to be given on Monday.

General Grant and party sailed down the river from Canton over to Macao, within five hours' sail of Hong Kong. Macao is a colony of Portugal, and has been for more than three centuries. Owing to the serious illness of the Governor, there was no public reception. The Governor sent the most cordial greeting and welcome to Macao. The General landed and drove to a hotel. In the evening he strolled about, and in the morning visited the one site that gives Macao world-wide fame — the home and grotto of Camoens. Camoens was a soldier-poet, lost his sight in a conflict with the Moors, and, dissatisfied with the condition of affairs in Portugal, sailed for the East, and came in banishment to Macao. Here he wrote the "Lusiad." Senor Marques, a Portuguese resident, is now the owner of the Grotto. The General was shown over the grounds by the Senor, who, in honor of his coming, had built an arch over the entrance with the inscription, "Welcome to General Grant." The grounds surrounding the Grotto are beautiful and extensive, and for some time the party walked past the bamboo, the pimento, the coffee, and other tropical trees and plants. Then they ascended to a bluff overlooking the town and sea, and from that point they had a commanding view of the town, the ocean, and the rocky coasts of China. The Grotto of Camoens is enclosed with an iron railing, and a bust of the poet surmounts the spot where, according to tradition, he was wont to sit and muse and compose his immortal poems. General Grant inscribed his name in the visitors' book, and, accompanied by Senor Marques, returned to the Ashuelot, which at once steamed for Hong Kong. Salutes were fired from the Portuguese battery as they left, and at two o'clock they landed in Hong Kong harbor, where Governor Hennessy met the General and took him to the Government House.

General Grant's reception at Hong Kong was as brilliant and enthusiastic as that at Canton. Disembarking amid salutes from the Ashuelot and the Japanese corvette Nishin, they were received at a decorated landing-pier by Governor Hennessy and staff, members of the Legislative Council, heads of the military and naval services, a guard of honor, and a multitude of American, European and Chinese spectators. After introductions, they were escorted to the Government House. Many streets were adorned with flags, etc., and houses were illuminated. On May 1 General Grant called upon Consul Mosby and informally inspected localities of importance. On May 2 he held a public reception at the United States Consulate, and dined with Chief Justice Sir John Smale. May 3 he attended a state dinner at Government House. The felicitous address of Governor Hennessy was warmly commended by the Americans. General Grant responded briefly and effectively, giving the sentiment of "Good will and alliance between Britons and Americans."

The citizens of Hong Kong had arranged a garden party to be given General Grant on Monday, but the weather interfered, and the General was compelled to leave on Monday, to keep engagements made for him in the North. He spent Sunday quietly with the Governor, and on Monday morning took leave of his brilliant and hospitable host. Before leaving, the General, accompanied by the Governor and our Consul, Colonel John S. Mosby, received a deputation of Chinese, who wished to present him with an address. The presentation took place in the parlors of the Government House, when the following address was read: —

"To General ULYSSES S. GRANT, late President of the United States of America, and Commander-in-Chief of the United States Army

"SIR: On the occasion of your honoring Hong Kong with your presence, we, the undersigned, on behalf of the Chinese community, approach you to give you a hearty welcome, and beg to present you an address expressive of our high esteem and respect for you. During your Presidency your geat name and noble deeds were known far and wide, and by the carrying out of a just policy you commanded admiration and respect from all classes of people under your rule. We have been delighted to find that in international questions you have shown a spirit of impartiality and fairness, treating Americans and foreigners alike, and the Chinese who have been trading in the United States have sung, and continue to sing, praises of the many good actions done by you while in office.

"We had longed to see you, but, being far away, we were hitherto not permitted to realize our wish. Now that you have favored us with a visit we avail ourselves of the opportunity to present you with a scroll inscribed with these four words, "Benefit to Chinese People," which we hope may serve as a souvenir of your interview with the Chinese community of Hong Kong.

"Signed by Lee Ting, Ho Amei, Lee Tuck Cheong, and ninety others."

General Grant said:—"Gentlemen, I am very happy to

meet so many representatives of the Chinese community in Hong Kong, and for the kind words of your address accept my thanks. I have looked forward for a long time to my visit to China, and am pleased to see, as I have seen in Hong Kong, that the Chinese are a thrifty, industrious and intelligent people. I have no other wish than that between the two peoples there shall be harmony and the best relations, and in this spirit I accept your address and the beautiful memento which accompanies it, and thank you for your good wishes."

After giving the address the General and party, accompanied by Governor Hennessy and wife and Colonel Mosby, took chairs and proceeded to the landing, to embark for the north. There was a guard of honor at the wharf, and all the foreign residents were present. As the General went on board the launch, hearty cheers were given, which were again and again repeated as he steamed into the bay. The Governor took his leave of General Grant on board the Ashuelot, and, as he left, the vessel fired a salute of seventeen guns in his honor, with the British flag at the fore.

General Grant's trip along the coast of China was exceptionally pleasant, so far as winds and waves were concerned. There was a monsoon blowing, but it was just enough to help along without disturbing the sea. Then it was a pleasure to come once more into cooler latitudes. Ever since they left Naples they had been under the sun, and nearly four months' battle with it had told upon them all. It was a luxury to tread the deck, and feel a cool breeze blowing from the north; to roll yourself in a blanket as you slept on deck; to look out warmer clothing, and feel that life was something more than living in a Turkish bath. On the morning of the 13th they came to Swatow.

Swatow is one of the treaty ports thrown open to foreigners under the treaty of Lord Elgin. It is at the mouth of the river Hau. The entrance to the river is striking in point of scenery, and as they came in sight of the town all the Chinese forts saluted, and the shipping in the harbor dressed. C. C. Williams, Consular Agent, came on board to welcome the General, and in his company he landed, and spent an hour in threading the old Chinese town. The streets were narrow. While in Swatow the Chinese Governor called in state, and said that he had orders from the government to pay all possible attentions to General Grant. It was the custom of the country in making these calls to bring an offering, and, as nothing is more useful than food, he had brought a live sheep, six live chickens, six ducks and four hams. While the Governor was in conference with the General, the animals were outside. There was nothing for the General to do but to accept the homely offering, and present it to the servants.

General Grant visited Amoy, another of the treaty ports open to foreign trade. It is on the Island of Heamun, at the mouth of the Dragon River. The scenery, as seen in approaching the island, is picturesque. All the batteries fired a salute, and there was a welcome from one of the United States men-of-war, the Ranger, commanded by Commander Boyd. Vice-Consul Stevens came on board, and welcomed the General to Amoy. He landed, and strolled through the Chinese town, which was very old and dirty. At noon there was a large luncheon party, at which we met all the Consuls, the leading citizens, and the commanders of the Ashuelot and the Ranger. Among the guests was Sir Thomas Wade, the British Minister to Pekin. Mr. Stevens proposed the health of the General in a complimentary speech, and at five they went on board the Ranger to attend a reception. The Ranger, under the inspiration of the officers, was transformed into a fairy scene, and nothing could have been more kind and hospitable than the captain and officers. Mrs. Boyd assisted her husband in entertaining his guests. At seven o'clock, as the sun was going down, they took their leave of the brilliant gathering in the Ranger, and steamed to Shanghai.

The following letters were exchanged between General Grant and the King of Siam, the King of Hawaii and the Viceroy of Canton:

GRAND PALACE, BANGKOK, April 20, 1879.
MY DEAR GENERAL GRANT:

I received your kind telegram on leaving Siam, and was very much pleased to hear that you were satisfied with your reception.

Your reception was not all I could have wished, for I had not sufficient notice to enable me to prepare much that I desired to prepare, but the good nature of Your Excellency and Mrs. Grant has made you excuse the deficiencies.

You will now pass on to wealthier cities and more powerful nations, but I depend on your not forgetting Siam, and from time to time I shall write to you, and hope to receive a few words in reply.

I shall certainly never forget the pleasure your visit has given me, and shall highly prize the friendships thus inaugurated with Your Excellency and Mrs. Grant.

I send my kind regards to Mr. Borie, wishing him long life, health and happiness, and with the same wish to yourself and Mrs. Grant and your family,

I am your faithful friend,

CHULALONKORN, King of Siam.

To General Grant.

UNITED STATES STEAMER ASHUELOT,
NEAR SHANGHAI, May 16, 1879.

TO HIS MAJESTY THE KING OF SIAM.

Dear Sir: Just before leaving Hong Kong for Shanghai, I received your very welcome letter of the 20th of April, and avail myself of the first opportunity of replying. I can assure you that nothing more could have been done by Your Majesty and all those about you, to make the visit of myself and party pleasant and agreeable. Every one of us will retain the most pleasant recollections of our visit to Siam, and of the cordial reception we received from yourself and all with whom we were thrown in contact.

I shall always be glad to hear from you, and to hear of

ARRIVAL AND RECEPTION OF EX-PRESIDENT GRANT AT SHANGHAI.

the prosperity and progress of the beautiful country over which you rule with so much justice and thought for the ruled.

My party are all well, and join me in expression of highest regards for yourself and Cabinet, and wishes for long life, health and happiness to all of you, and peace and prosperity to Siam. Your friend,
U. S. GRANT.

TOLANI HALL, HONOLULU, HAWAIIAN ISLANDS, Feb. 18, 1879

Dear Sir: The public newspapers give me the information that you are at present on your passage to the East, and are intending to return to the Unitd States across the Pacific Ocean. When I was in the United States during your Presidency, you manifested such interest in the prosperity of my kingdom, that I am proud to think it will not be uninteresting to you to observe the progress we have made, and the general state of the country.

I will not remind you that other travelers have found the natural features of the islands, and more especially their volcanic phenomena, interesting, and I entertain a hope that if you accept the invitation which I now tender to you to visit us, as a guest of myself and this nation, on your return to your native country, such a visit will be a pleasant rememberance to you.

For myself, it will afford me a great gratification to receive and entertain you, and my people will be proud to do everything in their power to make your visit agreeable.

I am your friend, KALAKUA.
To General U. S. Grant.

UNITED STATES STEAMER ASHUELOT,
NEAR SHANGHAI, May 16, 1879.

HIS MAJESTY, KING KALAKAUA.

Dear Sir: On the eve of my departure from Hong Kong for Shanghai, China, I was put in possession of your very polite invitation of the 18th of February for me to visit your kingdom, and to be the guest of Your Majesty. I can assure you that it would afford me the greatest pleasure to accept your invitation if I could do so. I have always felt the greatest desire to visit the Hawaiian Islands, and cannot say positively yet that I may not be able to do so. But it will be impossible for me to give a positive answer until I get to Japan and learn of the running of the vessels between Yokohama and Honolulu, and between the latter place and San Francisco.

I shall visit Pekin before going to Japan, and remain in the latter country a month or six weeks. As soon as it is determined whether I am to have the pleasure of visiting your most interesting country or not, I will inform you. Hoping that I may be able to go, Your friend,

U. S. GRANT.

To His Excellency, the Late President:

It has been a high honor and a source of the deepest satisfaction to myself, the high provincial authorities and the gentry and people of Canton, that Your Excellency, whom we have so long desired to see, has been so good as to come among us.

Upon learning from you of your early departure, while I dared not interfere to delay you, I had hoped, in company with my associates, to present my humble respects at the moment of your leaving. I refrained from doing so in obedience to your command.

I have ventured to send a few trifles to your honored wife, which I hope she will be so kind as to accept.

I trust that you both will have a prosperous journey throughout all your way, and that you both may be granted many years and abundant good. Should I ever be honored by my sovereign with a mission abroad, it will be my most devout prayer and earnest desire that I may meet you again.

I respectfully wish you the fulness of peace.

LIU KUN.

UNITED STATES STEAMER ASHUELOT,
NEAR SHANGHAI, China, May 16, 1879.

His Excellency, the Viceroy of Kwangtung and Kwanghai.

Dear Sir: Before leaving Hong Kong for more extended visits through the Celestial Empire, I was placed in possession of your very welcome letter giving expression to the best wishes of Your Excellency and of all the high officials in Canton for myself and mine. Since then it has been my good fortune to visit Swatow and Amoy, both, I understand, under Your Excellency's government, and have received at each the same distinguished reception accorded at Canton. Myself and party will carry with us from China the most pleasant recollections of our visit to the country over which you preside, and of the hospitalities received at your hands.

Mrs. Grant desires to thank you especially for the beautiful specimens of Chinese work which you presented to her. With the best wishes of myself and party for your health, long life and prosperity, and in hopes that we may meet again, I am your friend,

U. S. Grant.

General Grant's welcome at Shanghai was a fitting climax to the extraordinary reception he had received in China. The story of his two-days' residence here is a story of festivals and pageantry, culminating in the celebration and reception by the Governor and Council. As the General and party came to the spot selected for landing, the banks of the river were thronged with Chinamen, and at least one hundred thousand lined the bank.

At three o'clock precisely the barge of the Ashuelot was manned, the American flag was hoisted at the bow, and General Grant, accompanied by Mrs. Grant, Mr. Borie, Colonel Grant, Mr. Holcombe, Acting Minister at Pekin; Mrs. Holcombe, Consul-General Bailey, and Dr. Keating, embarked. As the boat slowly pulled toward the shore the guns of the Ashuelot thundered out a national salute, while the other men-of-war manned the yards. In a few minutes the boat came to the landing, which was covered with scarlet cloth. Mr. Little, Chairman of the Municipal Council, and the committee, shook hands with the General, and the procession marched into the building. As General Grant entered, the audience rose and cheered heartily. On reaching the seat prepared for him he was presented to the Chinese Governor, who had come to do his part in the reception. The Governor was accompanied by a delegation of mandarins of high rank. The band played "Hail, Columbia," and after the music and cheering ceased, Mr. Little advanced and read the following address:

SHANGHAI, May 17, 1879.

To General U. S. GRANT.

Sir: On behalf of this community I have the honor of welcoming you to Shanghai. In this the easternmost commercial settlement of the continent the lines that unite the old and new worlds meet, and here we on the eastern edge of the oldest empire in the world appropriately greet an illustrious representative of the great Republic of the New World.

Devoted as we are to trade, we have little to show that is of interest to the ordinary traveler. But as the head for two periods of a great cosmopolitan, commercial state, we trust that you will find something to interest you in this small commercial republic, itself as cosmopolitan as the great country from which you come.

We thank you for coming to visit us. We trust that you will find that we have done all in our power to make your visit pleasant. We wish for you a future as happy and distinguished as your past, and that after you leave us you will remember with pleasure this little band of self-governed representatives of all States, united in peaceful pursuits, and furthering, we believe, not without success, the cause of progress in this country.

I have the honor to be, sir, on behalf of the foreign community of Shanghai, your obedient servant,

R. W. LITTLE,
Chairman of the Committee.

After a moment's pause, General Grant, speaking in a low, conversational tone of voice, said:

"LADIES AND GENTLEMEN:—I am very much obliged to you for the hearty welcome which you have paid me, and I must say that I have been a little surprised, and agreeably surprised. I have now been a short time in the country of which Shanghai forms so important a part in a commercial way, and I have seen much to interest me and much to instruct me. I wish I had known ten years ago what I have lately learned. I hope to carry back to my country a report of all I have seen in this part of the world, for it will be of interest and possibly of great use. I thank you again for the hearty welcome you have given me."

The speech over, there were other presentations, and General Grant was escorted to his carriage. There was a guard of honor composed of sailors and marines from the American and French men-of-war, and the Volunteer Rifles of Shanghai.

On Monday night General Grant went to the house of Mr. Cameron to witness a torchlight procession and illumination in his honor. The town had been agog all day preparing for the illumination.

The two occasions on which Shanghai had exerted herself to welcome and honor a guest, were on the visits of the Duke of Edinburgh and the Grand Duke Alexis. The display in honor of General Grant far surpassed these, and what made it so agreeable was the heartiness with which English, Americans, French, Germans and Chinese all united. The scene as the General drove out into the open street was bewildering in its beauty. Wherever you looked was a blaze of light and fire, of rockets careering in the air, of Roman lights and every variety of fire. The ships in the harbor were a blaze of color, and looked as if they were pieces of fireworks. The lines of the masts, the rigging and the hulls were traced in flames. The Monocacy was very beautiful, every line from the bow to the topmast and anchor chain hung with Japanese lanterns. This graceful, blending mass of color thrown upon the black evening sky was majestic, and gave an idea of a beauty in fire hitherto unknown to the visitors. "Never before," said the morning journal — " has there been such a blaze of gas and candles seen in Shanghai."

At ten the General returned to the house of Mr. Cameron, and from there reviewed the firemen's procession. Each engine was preceded by a band, which played American airs. After the procession passed and repassed, there was a reception in Mr. Cameron's house, and at midnight the General drove home to the Consulate. So came to an and a wonderful day — one of the most wonderful in the history of General Grant's tour around the world.

As the Ashuelot came into the Peiho River, the forts fired twenty-one guns, and all the troops were paraded. A Chinese gunboat was awaiting, bearing Judge Denny, our Consul, and Mr. Dillon, French Consul and Dean of the Consular corps. As General Grant and party came near Tientsin the scene was imposing. Wherever they passed a fort twenty-one guns were fired. All the junks and vessels were dressed in bunting. A fleet of Chinese gunboats formed in line, and each vessel manned yards. The booming of the cannon, the waving of the flags, the manned yards, the multitude that lined the banks, the fleet of junks massed together and covered with curious lookers-on, the stately Ashuelot, carrying the American flag at the fore, towering high above the slender Chinese vessels and answering salutes gun for gun; the noise, the smoke, the glitter of arms, the blending and waving of banners and flags which lined the forts and the rigging like a fringe — all combined to form one of the most vivid and imposing pageants of their journey. The General stood on the quarter-deck, with Commander Johnson, Mr. Holcombe, Judge Denny and Mr. Dillon, making acknowledgments by raising his hat as he passed each ship. As they came near the landing, the yacht of the Viceroy, carrying his flag, steamed toward them, and as soon as their anchor found its place hauled alongside. First came two mandarins carrying the Viceroy's card. General Grant stood at the gangway, accompanied by the officers of the ship, and as the Viceroy stepped over the side of the Ashuelot the yards were manned and a salute was fired. Judge Denny, advancing, met the Viceroy and presented him to General Grant as the great soldier and statesman of China. The Viceroy presented the members of his suite, and the General, taking his arm, led him to the upper deck, where the two Generals sat in conversation for some time, while tea and cigars and wine were passed around in approved Chinese fashion.

The great Viceroy, perhaps to-day the most powerful subject in China, had taken the deepest interest in the coming of General Grant. He was of the same age as the General. They won their victories at the same time, the Southern rebellion ending in April, the Taeping rebellion in July, 1865. While General Grant was making his progress in India, the Viceroy followed his movements, and had all the particulars of the journey translated. As soon as the General reached Hong Kong, our Consul, Judge Denny, conveyed a welcome from the Viceroy. When questions were raised as to the reception of the General in Tientsin, the Viceroy ended the matter by declaring that no honor should be wanting to the General, and that he himself would be the first Chinaman to greet him in Tientsin and welcome him to the chief province of the empire. Between General Grant and the Viceroy friendly relations grew up, and while in Tientsin they saw a great deal of each other. The Viceroy had said that he did not care merely to look at, or even to make his acquaintance, but to know him well and talk with him. The Viceroy is known among the most advanced school of Chinese statesmen, anxious to introduce all the improvements of the Western world, to strengthen and develop China. This subject so dear to him was one that the General has, whenever he has met Chinese statesmen, tried to impress upon their minds—the necessity of developing their country, and of doing it themselves.

The General formed a high opinion of the Viceroy as a statesman of resolute and far-seeing character. This opinion was formed after many conversations—official, ceremonial and personal. The visit of the Viceroy to the General was returned next day in great pomp. There was a marine guard from the Ashuelot. They went to the viceregal palace in the Viceroy's yacht, and as they steamed up the river every foot of ground, every spot on the junks, was covered with people. At the landing, troops were drawn up. A chair lined with yellow silk, such a chair as is only used by the Emperor, was awaiting the General. As far as the eye could reach, the multitude stood expectant and gazing, and they went to the palace through a line of troops, who stood with arms at a present. Amid the firing of guns, the beating of gongs, the procession slowly marched to the palace door. The Viceroy, surrounded by his mandarins and attendants, welcomed the General. At the close of the interview General Grant and the Viceroy sat for a photograph. This picture Li-Hung Chang wished to preserve as a memento of the General's visit, and it was taken in one of the palace rooms. A day or two later there was a ceremonial dinner given in a temple. The hour was noon, and the Viceroy invited several guests to meet the General. The dinner was a stupendous, princely affair, containing all the best points of Chinese and European cookery, and, although the hour was noon, the afternoon had far gone when it came to an end.

Before it ended, Mr. Detring, on behalf of the Viceroy, arose and read this speech:

"GENTLEMEN: It has given me great pleasure to welcome you as my guests to-day, more especially as you aid me in showing honor to the distinguished man who is now with us. General Grant's eminent talents as a soldier and a statesman, and his popularity while chief ruler of a great country, are known to us all. I think it may be said of him now, as it was said of Washington a century ago, that he is "first in war, first in peace, and first in the hearts of his countrymen." His fame, and the admiration and respect it excites, are not confined to his own country, as the events of his present tour around the world will prove, and China should not be thought unwilling to welcome such a visitor. I thank the General for the honor he has conferred upon me. I thank you all, gentlemen, for the pleasure you have given me to-day, and I now ask you to join me in drinking the health of General Grant, and wishing him increasing fame and prosperity."

The Viceroy and all his guests arose and remained standing while Mr. Detring read this speech. At the close, the Viceroy lifted a glass of wine, and, bowing to the General, drank the toast. General Grant then arose and said:

"YOUR EXCELLENCY AND GENTLEMEN OF THE CONSULAR CORPS: I am very much obliged to you for the welcome I have received in Tientsin, which is only a repetition of the kindness shown to me by the representatives of all nations since I came within the coasts of China. I am grateful to the Viceroy for the especial consideration which I have received at his hands. His history as a soldier and statesman of the Chinese Empire has been known to me, as it has been known to all at home who have followed Chinese affairs, for a quarter of a century. I am glad to meet one who has done such great service to his country. My visit to China has been full of interest. I have learned a great deal of the civilization, the manners, the achievements, and the industry of the Chinese people, and I shall leave the country with feelings of friendship toward them, and a desire that they may be brought into relations of the closest commercial alliance and intercourse with the other nations. I trust that the Viceroy will some time find it in his power to visit my country, when I shall be proud to return, as far as I can, the hospitality I have received from him. Again thanking your Excellency for your reception, and you, gentlemen of the Consular corps, for your kindness, I ask you to join with me in a toast to the prosperity of China and the health of the Viceroy."

When this speech was ended there was tea, and then

came cigars. The Viceroy had arranged for a photograph of the whole dinner party. So their portraits were taken in the room where they had dined, the Viceroy and the General sitting in the middle, beside a small tea table. On the side of the General were the European, on that of the Viceroy the Chinese, members of the party. This function over, they returned to their yacht amid the same ceremonies as those which attended their coming, and steamed back to the Consulate, the river still lined with thousands of Chinamen.

There was a *fete* at the French Consulate — it was made brilliant by a display of fireworks and also of jugglery; the Viceroy, the General and the ladies of the party sitting on the balcony and watching the performers; at midnight the *fete* ended, and, considering the small colony and the resources possible to so limited a company, was a complete success. After enjoying a delightful series of receptions, dinners and *fetes*, the General and party bid farewell to Tientsin, and embarked in a large, clumsy boat, called a mandarin's boat, for Pekin, one hundred and fifty miles from Tientsin. After a tiresome journey, on the third day their boats tied up to the bank at the village of **Tung Chow**. At this point the party were carried in chairs to Pekin, arriving at midday. After a severe and uncomfortable ride of five hours they entered the Legation, and met a grateful and gracious welcome.

On the evening of their arrival the American residents in Pekin called in a body on the General to welcome him and read an address. Dinner over, the General and party entered the Legation parlors and were presented to the small colony of the favored people who have pitched their tents in Pekin. The members of this colony are missionaries, members of the customs staff, diplomatists and one or two who have claims or schemes for the consideration of the Chinese government. After being introduced to the General and party, Dr. Martin, the President of the Chinese English University, stepped forward and read the following address:

"SIR: Twenty years ago the American flag for the first time entered the gates of this ancient capital. For the greater part of that time your countrymen have been residing here under its protecting folds, and it is with feelings of no ordinary type that we gather ourselves beneath its shadow this day to welcome your arrival; because to you, sir, under God, it is due that its azure field had not been rent in fragments and its golden stars scattered to the winds of heaven. Having borne that banner through a career of victory which finds few parallels in the page of history, it was your high privilege to gather around it in a new cemented union the long discordant members of our national family. Occupying the most exalted position to which it was possible for you to be elevated by the voice of a grateful people, your strength was in the justice and moderation of your administration, a force more potent than that of armed cohorts. After conferring on our country these inestimable benefits, as its leader in war and its guide in the paths of peace, we reflect with pride that you have shown the world how a great man can descend from a lofty station and yet carry with him the homage of his people and the admiration of mankind. As you travel from land to land, everywhere welcomed as the citizen of a wider commonwealth than that of our native country, we cannot forget that your visits to their shores possess an international character of which it is impossible to divest them. You are honored as the highest representative of our country who has ever gone beyond her borders, and America is the more respected for having given birth to such a son. Your presence here to-day directs the attention of this venerable empire to the great republic from which you come. It will also have the effect of turning the eyes of our countrymen toward the teeming millions of Eastern Asia; and fervently do we trust that it will help to impress them with the obligations of justice and humanity in their dealings with the people of China. Your antecedents, sir, leave us in no doubt as to the policy that would meet your approval. Hoping that your influence may contribute to the adjustment of difficulties which threaten to react so disastrously on American interests in China, and that thereby you will add another to the many laurels that crown your brow, we hail your visit as both opportune and auspicious, and again with one heart we bid you welcome to the capital of China.

"W. A. P. Martin, H. Blodget, D. C. McCoy, H. B. Morse, C. C. Moreno, J. H. Pyke, W. F. Walker, H. H. Lowry, J. H. Roberts, W. C. Noble, Chester Holcombe.

"*Pekin, June 3, 1879.*"

The General, in a quiet, conversational tone, said he was always glad to meet his fellow countrymen, and the kind words in which he had been welcomed added to the pleasure which such a meeting afforded in Pekin. The Americans were a wonderful people, he said, smiling, for you found them everywhere, even here in this distant and inaccessible capital. He was especially pleased with the allusion in the address to the fact that in America a career was possible to the humblest station in life. His own career was one of the best examples of the possibilities open to any man and every man at home. That feature in America he was proud to recognize, for it was one of the golden principles of our government. The General again thanked the delegation for their kindness, wished them all prosperity in their labors in China, and a happy return to their homes, where he hoped some day to meet them.

Within an hour after the General's arrival, he was waited upon by the members of the Cabinet, who came in a body, accompanied by the military and civil Governors of

Pekin. These are the highest officials in China, men of grace and stately demeanor. They were received in Chinese fashion, seated around a table covered with sweetmeats, and served with tea. The first Secretary brought with him the card of Prince Kung, the Prince Regent of the Empire, and said that His Imperial Highness had charged him to present all kind wishes to General Grant, and to express the hope that the trip in China had been pleasant. The Secretary also said that, as soon as the Prince Regent heard from the Chinese Minister in Paris that General Grant was coming to China, he sent orders to the officials to receive him with due honor. The General said that he had received nothing but honor and courtesy from China, and this answer pleased the Secretary, who said he would be happy to carry it to the Prince Regent.

General Grant did not ask an audience of the Emperor. The Emperor is a child seven years of age, at his books, not in good health, and under the care of two old ladies, called the Empresses. When the Chinese Minister in Paris spoke to General Grant about audience, and his regret that the sovereign of China was not of age that he might personally entertain the ex-President, the General said he hoped no question of audience would be raised. He had no personal curiosity to see the Emperor, and there could be no useful object in conversing with a child.

As soon as General Grant arrived at Pekin, he was met by the Secretary of State, who brought the card of Prince Kung, and said His Imperial Highness would be glad to see General Grant at any time. The General named the succeeding day, at three. The General and party left the Legation at half past two.

The way to the Yamen was over dirty roads, and through a disagreeable part of the town, the day being warm. When they came to the court-yard of the Yamen, the Secretaries and a group of mandarins received the General and his party, and escorted them into the inner court. Prince Kung, who was standing at the door, with a group of high officers, advanced and saluted the General, and said a few words of welcome, which were translated by Mr. Holcombe, the acting Minister.

The Prince saluted General Grant in Tartar fashion, looking at him for a moment with an earnest, curious gaze, like one who had formed an idea of some kind and was anxious to see how far his ideal had been realized. The sun was beating down, and the party passed into a large, plainly furnished room, where was a table laden with Chinese food. The Prince, sitting down at the centre, gave General Grant the seat at his left, the post of honor in China. He then took up the cards, one by one, which had been written in Chinese characters on red paper, and asked Mr. Holcombe for the name and station of each member of General Grant's suite.

As princes go, few are more celebrated than Prince Kung. He is a Prince of the imperial house of China, brother of the late Emperor and uncle of the present. In appearance the Prince is of middle stature, with a sharp, narrow face, a high forehead — made more prominent by the Chinese custom of shaving the forehead — and a changing, evanescent expression of countenance. He has been at the head of the Chinese government since the English invasion and the burning of the Summer Palace. He was the only Prince who remained at his post at that time, and consequently when the peace came it devolved upon him to make it. This negotiation gave him a European celebrity, and a knowledge of Europeans that was of advantage. European powers have preferred to keep in power a prince with whom they have made treaties before. In the politics of China, Prince Kung has shown courage and ability. When the Emperor, his brother, died, in 1861, a council was formed composed of princes and noblemen of high rank. This council claimed to sit by the will of the deceased Emperor. The inspiring element was hostility to foreigners. Between this Regency and the Prince there was war. The Emperor was a child — his own nephew — just as the present Emperor is a child. Suddenly a decree coming from the child-Emperor was read, dismissing the Regency, making the Dowager Empress Regent, and giving the power to Prince Kung. This decree Prince Kung enforced with vigor, decision and success. He arrested the leading members of the Regency, charged them with having forged the will under which they claimed the Regency, and sentenced three of them to death. Two of the regents were permitted to commit suicide, but the other was beheaded. From that day, under the Empresses, Prince Kung has been the ruler of China.

General Grant could not remain long enough in the Yamen to finish the dinner, as he had an engagement to visit the college for the teaching of an English education to young Chinese. This institution is under the direction of Dr. Martin, an American, and the buildings adjoin the Yamen. Consequently, on taking leave of the Prince, who said he would call and see the General at the Legation, they walked a few steps, and were escorted into the class-room of the College. Doctor Martin presented General Grant to the students and professors, and one of the students read the following address:

"GENERAL U. S. GRANT, EX PRESIDENT OF THE UNITED STATES:

"SIR: We have long heard your name, but never dreamed that we would have an opportunity to look on your face. Formerly the people of your Southern States rebelled against your government and nearly obtained possession of the land, but, through your ability in leading the national forces, the rebel chief was captured and the country tranquilized. Having commanded a million of men and survived a hundred battles, your merit was recognized as the highest in your own land, and your name became known in every quarter of the globe. Raised to the Presidency by the voice of a grateful people, you laid aside the arts of war and sought only to achieve the victories of peace. The people enjoyed tranquility, commerce flourished, manufactures revived, and the whole nation daily became more wealthy and powerful. Your achievements as a civil ruler are equally great with your military triumphs. Now that you have resigned the Presidency, you employ your leisure in visiting different parts of the world, and the people of all nations and all ranks welcome your arrival. It requires a fame like yours to produce effects like these. We, the students of this college, are very limited in our attainments, but all men love the wise and respect the virtuous. We, therefore, feel honored by this opportunity of standing in your presence. It is our sincere hope that another term of the Presidency may come to you, not only that your own nation may be benefited, but that our countrymen resident in America may enjoy the blessings of your protection.

"WANG FENGTSAR, tutor in Mathematics.
"WEN HSII, tutor in English.
"NA SAN, tutor in English.
"On behalf of the students of Tunguon College.
"*Kwang Sii, 5 y. 4 m. 16 d.—June 5, 1879.*"

The General, in response, said:

"GENTLEMEN: I am much obliged to you for your welcome and for the compliments you pay me. I am glad to meet you and see in the capital of this vast and ancient empire an institution of learning based upon English principles, and in which you can learn the English language. I have been struck with nothing so much in my tour around the world as with the fact that the progress of civilization — of our modern civilization — is marked by the progress of the English tongue. I rejoice in this fact, and I rejoice in your efforts to attain a knowledge of English speech and all that such a knowledge must convey. You have my warmest wishes for your success in this and in all your undertakings, and my renewed thanks for the honor you have shown me."

Prince Kung was punctual in his return of the call of General Grant. He came to the Legation in his chair, and was received by General Grant in the parlors of the Legation. Several officers from the Richmond happened to be in Pekin on a holiday, and the General invited them, as well as the officers of the Ashuelot, who were at the Legation, to receive the Prince. As all the officers were in full uniform, the reception of the Prince became almost an imposing affair. The Prince was accompanied by the Grand Secretaries, and, as soon as he was presented to the members of the General's party, he was led into the dining-room, and they all sat around a table, and were given tea and sweetmeats and champagne. During this visit there occurred a remarkable conversation, which may not be without its effect upon the politics of the East. The general features of this conversation were no less than a proposition to utilize the services of General Grant as a peacemaker.

In the form of asking General Grant's "advice," and under cover of an anxiety to confer with him, and with a graceful apology for talking business to a visitor out of the harness, this adroit diplomatist engaged in conversation on the subject of the seizure of the Loochoo Islands by Japan, and the consequent disturbance of friendly relations between Japan and China. "I feel that I should apologize even for the reference," said the Prince, "which I would not have ventured upon, but for our conviction that one who has had so high a place in determining the affairs of the world can have no higher interest than that of furthering peace and justice." There can be no handsomer way than this to compel attention and demand assistance; and, when one is thus pressed by a man of Prince Kung's dignity — by the ruler of the greatest aggregation of human creatures of which history has any record — the generous mind perceives that a grand condescension thus presented as a request cannot be put aside. General Grant's own succinct statement of the spirit of the foreign policy of the American government was also such as to exhibit his sympathy with this fine conception, that a desire to aid the progress of justice in the world should be the first interest of a gentleman in whatever circumstances he might be called upon — a sentiment of knight errantry in statesmanship. Our foreign policy, the General said, is made up of "fair play, consideration for the rights of others, respect for international law," which is a handy adaptation to national circumstances of the three points laid down by Justinian's lawyers as sufficient to properly regulate every human life — "*honeste vivere, alterum non lædere, suum cuique tribuere.*" Between two men of great experience, accustomed to deal in the great concerns of human life, and whose minds have taken color from their great functions, it is not strange to find this ready sympathy on such a topic, and the world will not be astonished to hear that General Grant straightforwardly said: "I told the Viceroy at Tientsin that everything I could do in the interest of peace was my duty and my pleasure. I can conceive of no higher office for any man."

The Prince, when he had finished his conversation, drew toward him a glass of champagne, and, addressing Mr. Holcombe, said he wished to again express to General Grant the honor felt by the Chinese government at having received this visit. He made special inquiries as to when the General would leave, the hour of his departure, the ways and periods of his journey. He asked whether there was anything wanting to complete the happiness of

the General, or show the honor in which he had been held
by China. In taking his leave, he wished to drink especially the health of General Grant, to wish him a prosperous voyage, and long and honorable years on his return
home. This sentiment the General returned, and, rising,
led the way to the door, where the chair of the Prince and
the bearers were in waiting. The other Ministers accompanied the Prince, and, on taking leave, saluted the General in the ceremonious Chinese style. The Prince entered
his chair, and was snatched up and carried away by his
bearers, the guard hurriedly mounting and riding after.

General Grant and party returned to Tientsin by boat,
and immediately upon his landing received a message from
the Viceroy that he was on his way to call. The General
received the Viceroy at the house of Consul Denny. After
a warm welcome, together they passed into an inner room
and received tea and sweetmeats in Chinese fashion. The
Viceroy had received instructions from the Prince Regent
to continue the conversation with General Grant on the
matter of the issue with Japan. After a long and intensely
interesting conversation, and a thorough analysis of the
matters at issue, the Viceroy pressed every point to influence
the General to act as mediator, laying special stress upon
the name and influence of General Grant. The General
thought it was a diplomatic question, and could be settled
through the good offices of ministers of other nations.
The Viceroy claimed that it was not a diplomatic question,
as Japan had refused to notice any communication from
China; consequently there was no chance of reaching a
solution by the ordinary methods of diplomacy. How can
you talk to ministers and governments about matters which
they will not discuss? But when a man like General Grant
comes to China and Japan, he comes with an authority
which gives him power to make peace. In the interest of
peace, China asks the General to interest himself. China

cannot consent to the position Japan has taken. On that point there is no indecision in the councils of the government. The Viceroy had no fear of Japan or of the consequences of any conflict which Japan would force upon China.

General Grant said his hope and belief were that the difficulty would end peacefully and honorably. He appreciated the compliment paid him by the Chinese government. The Viceroy and Prince Kung overrated his power, but not his wish, to preserve peace, and especially to prevent such a deplorable thing as a war between China and Japan. When he reached Japan he would confer with Mr. Bingham and see how the matter stood. He would study the Japanese case as carefully as he proposed studying the Chinese case. He would, if possible, confer with the Japanese authorities. What his opinion would be when he heard both sides he could not anticipate. If the question took such a shape that, with advantage to the cause of peace and without interfering with the wishes of his own government, he could advise or aid in a solution, he would be happy, and, as he remarked to Prince Kung, this happiness would not be diminished if in doing so his action did not disappoint the Chinese government. So came to an end an interesting and extraordinary conversation.

Pleasant, notably, were General Grant and party's relations with the great Viceroy, whose kindness seemed to grow with every hour, and to tax itself for new forms in which to form expression. Li-Hung Chang's reception of General Grant was as notable an event in the utter setting aside of precedents and traditions as can be found in the recent history of China. It required a great man, who could afford to be progressive and independent, to do it.

There was probably nothing more notable than the entertainment given to Mrs. Grant by the wife of the Viceroy, on the last night of the General's stay in Tientsin.

The principal European ladies in the colony were invited. Some of these ladies had lived in Tientsin for years, and had never seen the wife of the Viceroy — had never seen him except through the blinds of the window of his chair. The announcement that the Viceroy had really invited Mrs. Grant to meet his wife, and European ladies to be in the company, was even a more transcendent event than the presence of General Grant. Society rang with a discussion of the question which, since Mother Eve introduced it to the attention of her husband, has been the absorbing theme of civilization — what shall we wear? The question was finally decided in favor of the resources of civilization. The ladies went in all the glory of French fashion and taste. They came back from the viceregal dinner at about eleven at night, and General Grant and party went immediately on board the Ashuelot. Here the farewells to kind friends were spoken, and it was with sincere regret that they said farewell. The Viceroy had sent word that he would not take his leave of General Grant until he was on the border of his dominions and out at sea. He had gone on ahead in his yacht, and, with a fleet of gunboats, would await the General at the mouth of the river, and accompany him on board the Richmond. Orders had been given that the forts should fire salutes, and that the troops should parade, and the vessels dress with flags. About eleven o'clock in the morning the Ashuelot came up with the viceregal fleet, at anchor under the guns of the Waku forts. As they passed, every vessel manned yards, and all their guns and the guns of the fort thundered a farewell. Three miles out the Richmond was sighted, and the Ashuelot steamed direct toward her, and in a short time the Ashuelot swung around amid the thunder of the guns of the Richmond. At noon the General passed over the sides of the Richmond, and was received by another salute. After the General had been received, the ship's barge was sent to the Viceroy's boat, and in a few minutes returned with Li-Hung Chang. General Grant received the Viceroy, and again the yards were manned, and a salute of nineteen guns was fired.

The Viceroy and his suite were shown into the cabin. Tea was served, and, Li-Hung Chang having expressed a desire to see the vessel, he was taken into every part, gave its whole arrangement, and especially the guns, a minute inspection. This lasted for an hour, and the Viceroy returned to the cabin to take his leave. He seemed loath to go, and remained in conversation for some time. General Grant expressed his deep sense of the honor which had been done him, his pleasure at having met the Viceroy. He urged the Viceroy to make a visit to the United States, and in a few earnest phrases repeated his hope that the statesmen of China would persevere in a policy which brought them nearer to our civilization. The Viceroy was friendly, almost affectionate. He hoped that General Grant would not forget him; that he would like to meet the General now and then, and if China needed the General's counsel he would send it. He feared he could not visit foreign lands, and regretted that he had not done so in earlier years. He spoke of the friendship of the United States as dear to China, and again commended to the General and the American people the Chinese who had gone to America. It made his heart sore to hear of their ill usage, and he depended upon the justice and honor of our government for their protection. He again alluded to the Loochoo question with Japan, and begged General Grant would speak to the Japanese Emperor, and in securing justice remove a cloud from Asia which threw an ominous shadow over the East. The General bade the Viceroy farewell, and said he would not forget what had been said, and that he would always think of the Viceroy with friendship and esteem. So they parted, Li-Hung Chang departing amid the roar of our cannon and the manning of the yards, while the Richmond slowly pushed her prow into the rippling waves and steamed along to Japan.

CHAPTER XVIII.

GENERAL GRANT IN JAPAN.

General Grant and party arrived at Nagasaki on June 21, on the United States steamer Richmond, accompanied by the Ashuelot, the latter bringing Judge Denny, Consul at Tientsin, and other friends from China. There was no formal demonstration by foreign residents, further than an address of welcome by the committee of thirteen, chosen to represent all alien nationalities. Frequent entertainments were given by the Japanese.

The Governor of the province gave a state dinner on the evening of the 23d of June, served in French fashion; one that in its details would have done no discredit to the restaurants in Paris. To this dinner the Governor asked Captain Benham, of the Richmond; Commander Johnson, of the Ashuelot, and Lieutenant-Commander Clarke. At the close, His Excellency Utsumi Tadakatsu arose and said:

"GENERAL GRANT AND GENTLEMEN: After a two-years' tour through many lands, Nagasaki has been honored by a visit from the ex-President of the United States. Nagasaki is situated on the western shore of this Empire, and how fortunate it is that I, in my official capacity as Governor of Nagasaki, can greet and welcome you, sir, as you land for the first time on the soil of Japan. Many years ago, honored sir, I learned to appreciate your great services, and during a visit to the United States I was filled with an ardent desire to learn more of your illustrious deeds.

You were then the President of the United States, and little then did I anticipate that I should be the first Governor to receive you in Japan. Words cannot express my feelings. Nagasaki is so far from the seat of government that I fear you cannot have matters arranged to your satisfaction. It is my earnest wish that you and Mrs. Grant may safely travel through Japan and enjoy the visit."

This address was spoken in Japanese. At its close an interpreter, who stood behind His Excellency during its delivery, advanced and read the above translation. When the Governor finished, General Grant arose and said:

"YOUR EXCELLENCY, LADIES AND GENTLEMEN: You have here to-night several Americans who have the talent of speech, and who could make an eloquent response to the address in which my health is proposed. I have no such gift, and I never lamented its absence more than now, when there is so much that I want to say about your country, your people and your progress. I have not been an inattentive observer of that progress, and in America we have been favored with accounts of it from my distinguished friend, whom you all know as the friend of Japan, and whom it was my privilege to send as Minister — I mean Judge Bingham. The spirit which has actuated the mission of Judge Bingham — the spirit of sympathy, support and conciliation — not only expressed my own sentiments, but those of America. America has much to gain in the East — no nation has greater interests — but America has nothing to gain except what comes from the cheerful acquiescence of the Eastern people, and insures them as much benefit as it does us. I should be ashamed of my country if its relations with other nations, and especially with these ancient and most interesting empires in the East, were based upon any other idea. We have rejoiced over your progress. We have watched you step by step. We have followed the unfolding of your old civilization, and its absorbing the new. You have had our profound sympathy in that work, our sympathy in the troubles which came with it, and our friendship. I hope that it may continue — that it may long continue. As I have said, America has great interests in the East. She is your next neighbor. She is more affected by the Eastern populations than any other power. She can never be insensible to what is doing here. Whatever her influence may be, I am proud to think that it has always been exerted in behalf of justice and kindness. No nation needs from the outside powers justice and kindness more than Japan, because the work that has made such marvelous progress in the past few years is a work in which we are deeply concerned, in the success of which we see a new era in civilization, and which we should encourage. I do not know, gentlemen, that I can say anything more than this in response to the kind words of the Governor. Judge Bingham can speak with much more eloquence and much more authority as our Minister. But I could not allow the occasion to pass without saying how deeply I sympathized with Japan in her efforts to advance, and how much those efforts were appreciated in America. In that spirit I ask you to unite with me in a sentiment: ' The prosperity and the independence of Japan.' "

General Grant, a few minutes later, arose and said that he wished to propose another toast — a personal one — the drinking of which would be a great pleasure to him. This was the health of Judge Bingham, the American Minister to Japan. He had appointed the Judge Minister, and he was glad to know that the confidence expressed in that appointment had been confirmed by the admiration and respect of the Japanese people. When a Minister serves his own country as well as Judge Bingham has served America, and in doing so wins the esteem of the authorities and the people to whom he is accredited, he has achieved the highest success in diplomacy.

Mr. Yoshida, the Japanese Minister, arose and asked leave to add his high appreciation of Mr. Bingham, and the value which had been placed on his friendship to Japan by the government. He was proud to bear public tribute to Mr. Bingham's sincerity and friendliness, and to join in drinking his health.

Judge Bingham, in response to the sentiments of personal regard offered by Mr. Yoshida, acknowledged the courtesy to himself, and said that he had come hither to join the official representatives of His Majesty the Emperor, and also the people of Nagasaki in fitting testimonials of respect to General Grant, the friend of the United States of America, and the friend of Japan. He had come to Japan as Minister, bearing the commission issued by the distinguished guest of the evening. It had been his endeavor to faithfully discharge his duties, and in such manner as would strengthen the friendship between the two countries, and promote the commercial interests of both. He knew that in so acting he reflected the wishes of the illustrious man who is the guest of the Empire, and the wishes also of the President and people of the United States. "The Government of my country," said Mr. Bingham, "has, by a recent treaty with Japan, manifested its desire that justice may be done, by according to Japan her right to regulate her own commercial affairs, and to do justice is the highest duty, as it is the highest interest, of civil government."

On June 24, General Grant was banqueted by the citizens in the style of the daimios, the feudal lords of Japan. The place selected was the old temple in the heart of the city. The party numbered about twenty, including General Grant and party, Consul Mangum and family, and Consul Denny and family. The Herald correspondent accompanying General Grant speaks of this dinner as follows:

"The dinner was served on small tables, each guest

having a table to himself. The merchants of the city waited on their guests, and with them a swarm of attendants wearing the costumes of Japan. The bill of fare was almost a volume, and embraced over fifty courses. The wine was served in unglazed porcelain wine cups, on white wooden stands. The appetite was pampered in the beginning with dried fish, edible seaweeds and isinglass, in something of the Scandinavian style, except that the attempt did not take the form of brandy and raw fish. The first serious dish was composed of crane, seaweed, moss, rice bread and potatoes, which we picked over in a curious way, as though we were at an auction sale of remnants, anxious to rummage out a bargain. The soup, when it first came — for it came many times — was an honest soup of fish, like a delicate fish chowder. Then came strange dishes, as ragout and as soup, in bewildering confusion. The first was called namasu, and embodied fish, clams, chestnuts, rock mushrooms and ginger. Then, in various combinations, the following: duck, truffles, turnips, dried bonito, melons, pressed salt, aromatic shrubs, snipe, egg plant, jelly, boiled rice, snapper, shrimp, potatos, mushroom, cabbage, lassfish, orange flowers, powdered fish, flavored with plum juice and walnuts, raw carp sliced, mashed fish, baked fish, isinglass, fish boiled with pickled beans, wine, and rice again. This all came in the first course, and as a finale to the course there was a sweetmeat composed of white and red bean jelly cake, and boiled black mushroom. With this came powdered tea, which had a green, monitory look, and suggested your earliest experience in medicine. When the first pause came in the dinner, two of the merchant hosts advanced toward General Grant and read the following address: —

"'GENERAL U. S. GRANT: In the name of the citizens of Nagasaki we offer you a sincere welcome to this small town. We feel greatly honored by your visit to Nagasaki, and still more so by your becoming our guest this evening. Any outward signs of respect and hospitality we offer you are but a fraction of our kindly feelings toward you, and are quite inadequate to express the great admiration we have for you. On your return to your own great country, after having visited this Eastern Empire, we trust you will carry with you pleasant reminiscences and friendly feelings toward our country and people. We wish you a successful career and a long life and health to enjoy the illustrious name and position you have made for yourself. The dinner at which you have honored us with your company is given in this country to convey from the hosts their well wishes and the friendship they feel toward their honorable guest; and in the hope that a long and sincere intimacy may be promoted between our guest and those we have the honor to represent to-night, we have offered you this poor entertainment.

"'We have the honor to be, with much respect, your most obedient servants,

"'Awoki Kinhichiro,
"'Matsuda Gongoro.

"'*June 24, 1879.*'

"'General Grant arose, and said:

"'Gentlemen: I am highly honored by your address, and also by this sumptuous entertainment. I have enjoyed exceedingly my visit to Japan, and appreciate more than I can say the kindness that has been shown me by all persons. But I have enjoyed nothing more than this, because it comes from the citizens of Nagasaki, and is entirely unofficial. That I take as an especial compliment, coming as it does from the people and not the government. For while I am deeply gratified for all that your government is doing to render my trip here agreeable and instructive, I have a peculiar pleasure in meeting those who are not in authority, who are the citizens of a country. I shall take away from Nagasaki the most grateful remembrances of your hospitality and the most pleasant recollections of the beauty of the place. Again accept my sincere thanks for your kindness.'

"When the second course was finished — the course that came to an end in powdered tea and sweetmeats, composed of white and red bean jelly cake and boiled black mushroom — there was an interval. All arose from the table and sauntered about on the graveled walk, and looked down upon the bay and the enfolding hills. One never tires of a scene like Nagasaki; everything is so ripe and rich and old. Time has done so much for the venerable town, the eddies of a new civilization are rushing in upon Nagasaki. The town has undergone vast changes since the day when Dutch merchants were kept in a reservation more secluded than we have ever kept our Indians; when Xavier and his disciples threaded those narrow streets preaching the salvation that comes through the blood of Jesus; when Christians were driven at the point of the spear to yon beetling cliff and tumbled into the sea. These are momentous events in the history of Japan. They were merely incidents in the history of Nagasaki. The ancient town has lived on sleepily, embodying and absorbing the features of Eastern civilization, unchanged and unchanging, its beauty expressive because it is a beauty of its own, untinted by Europeans. We have old towns in the European world. We even speak as if we had a past in fresh America. But what impresses you in these aspects of Eastern development is their antiquity, before which the most ancient of our towns are but as yesterday. The spirit of ages breathes over Nagasaki, and you cease to think of chronology and see only the deep, rich tones which time has given and which time alone can give.

"But while we could well spend our evening strolling over this graveled walk and leaning over the quaint brick

wall and studying the varied and ever changing scene that
sweeps beneath us, we must not forget our entertainment.
On returning to the dining-room, we find that the servants have brought in the candles. Before each table is a
pedestal, on which a candle burns, and the old temple lights
up with a new splendor. To add to this splendor the walls
have been draped with heavy silks, embroidered with gold
and silver, with quaint and curious legends in the history
of Japan. The merchants enter again, bearing meats.
Advancing to the centre of the room, and to the General, they kneel and press their foreheads to the floor.
With this demure courtesy the course begins. Other
attendants enter, and place on each table the lacquer bowls
and dishes. Instead of covering the tables with a variety
of food, and tempting you with auxiliary dishes of watermelon seeds and almond kernels, as in China, the Japanese
give you a small variety at a time. Our amiable friend,
the Japanese Minister, warned us in the beginning not to
be in a hurry, to restrain our curiosity, not to hurry our investigations into the science of a Japanese table, but to pick
and nibble and wait — that there were good things coming,
which we should not be beyond the condition of enjoying.
What a comfort, for instance, a roll of bread would be, and
a glass of dry champagne! But there is no bread and no
wine, and our only drink is the hot preparation from rice,
with its sherry flavor, which is poured out of a teapot into
shallow lacquer saucers, and which you sip, not without
relish, although it has no place in any beverage known to
your experience. We are dining, however, in strict Japanese fashion, just as the old daimios did, and our hosts are
too good artists to spoil a feast with champagne. Then it
has been going on for hours, and when you have reached
the fourth hour of a dinner, even a temperance dinner, with
nothing more serious than a hot, insipid, sherry-like rice
drink, you have passed beyond the critical and curious into

the resigned condition. If we had only been governed by the Minister, we might have enjoyed this soup, which comes first in the course, and, as you lift the lacquered top, you know to be hot and fragrant. It is a soup composed of carp and mushroom and aromatic shrub. Another dish is a prepared fish that looks like a confection of cocoanut, but which you see to be fish as you prod it with your chopsticks. This is composed of the red snapper fish, and is served in red and white alternate squares. It looks well, but you pass it by, as well as another dish that is more poetic, at least, for it is a preparation of the skylark, wheat-flour cake and gourd. We are not offended by the next soup, which comes hot and smoking, a soup of buckwheat and egg-plant. The egg-plant always seemed to be a vulgar, pretentious plant, that might do for the trough, but was never intended for the dignity of the table. But buckwheat in a soup is unfitting, and, allied with the egg plant, is a degradation, and no sense of curious inquiry of investigation can tolerate so grave a violation of the harmony of the table. You push your soup to the end of the table and nip off the end of a fresh cigar, and look out upon the town, over which the dominant universe has thrown the star-sprinkled mantle of night, and follow the lines of light that mark the welcome we are enjoying, and trace the ascending rockets as they shoot up from the hillside to break into masses of dazzling fire and illuminate the heavens for a moment in a rhapsody of blue and scarlet and green and silver and gold.

"If you have faith, you will enter bravely into the dish that your silk-draped attendant now places before you, and as he does bows to the level of the table and slides away. This is called oh-hira. The base of this dish is panyu. Panyu is a sea fish. The panyu in itself would be a dish, but in addition we have a fungus, the roots of the lily and the stems of the pumpkin.

"While our hosts are passing around the strange dishes a signal is made, and the musicians enter. They are maidens with fair, pale faces, and small, dark, serious eyes. You are pleased to see that their teeth have not been blackened, as was the custom in past days, and is even now almost a prevalent custom among the lower classes. We are told that the maidens who have come to grace our feast are not of the common singing class, but the daughters of the merchants and leading citizens of Nagasaki. The first group is composed of three. They enter, sit down on the floor, and bow their heads in salutation. One of the instruments is shaped like a guitar, another is something between a banjo and a drum. They wear the costume of the country, the costume that was known before the new days came upon Japan. They have blue silk gowns, white collars, and heavily brocaded pearl-colored sashes. The principal instrument was long and narrow, shaped like a coffin lid, and sounding like a harpsichord. After they had played an overture, another group entered, fourteen maidens similarly dressed, each carrying the small banjo-like instrument, and ranging themselves on a bench against the wall, the tapestry and silks suspended over them. Then the genius of the artist was apparent, and the rich depending tapestry, blended with the blue and white and pearl, and animated with the faces of the maidens, their music and their songs, made a picture of Japanese life which an artist might regard with envy. You see then the delicate features of Japanese decoration which have bewitched our artist friends, and which the most adroit fingers in vain try to copy. When the musicians enter, the song begins. It is an original composition. The theme is the glory of America and honor to General Grant. They sing of the joy that his coming has given to Japan; of the interest and the pride they take in his fame; of their friendship for their friends across the great sea. This is all sung in Japanese, and we follow the lines through the mediation of a Japanese friend who learned his English in America. This anthem was chanted in a low, almost monotonous key, one singer leading in a kind of solo, and the remainder coming in with a chorus. The song ended, twelve dancing maidens enter. They wore a crimson-like overgarment fashioned like pantaloons — a foot or so too long — so that when they walked it was with a dainty pace, lest they might trip and fall. The director of this group was constantly on his hands and knees, creeping around among the dancers, keeping their drapery in order, not allowing it to bundle up and vex the play. These maidens carried bouquets of pink blossoms, artificially made, examples of the flora of Japan. They stepped through the dance at as slow a measure as in a minuet of Louis XIV. The movement of the dance was simple, and the music a humming, thrumming, as though the performers were tuning their instruments. After passing through a few measures the dancers slowly filed out, and were followed by another group, who came wearing masks — the mask in the form of a large doll's face — and bearing children's rattles and fans. The peculiarity of this dance was that time was kept by the movement of the fan — a graceful, expressive movement, which only the Eastern people have learned to bestow on the fan. With them the fan becomes almost an organ of speech, and the eye is employed in its management at the expense of the admiration we are apt at home to bestow on other features of the amusement. The masks indicated that this was a humorous dance, and when it was over four special performers, who had unusual skill, came in with flowers, and danced a pantomime. Then came four others, with costumes different — blue robes, trimmed with gold — who carried long, thin wands, entwined in gold and red, from which dangled festoons of pink blossoms.

"All this time the music hummed and thrummed. To

vary the show, we had even a more grotesque amusement. First came eight children, who could scarcely do more than toddle. They were dressed in white, embroidered in green and red, wearing purple caps formed like the Phrygian liberty cap, and dangling on the shoulders. They came into the temple enclosure and danced on the graveled walk, while two, wearing an imitation of a dragon's skin, went through a dance and various contortions, supposed to be a dragon at play. This reminded us of the pantomime elephant, where one performer plays the front and another the hind legs. In the case of our Japanese dragon the legs were obvious, and the performers seemed indisposed even to respect the illusion. It was explained that it was an ancient village dance, one of the oldest in Japan, and that on festive occasions, when the harvests are ripe or when some legend or feat of heroism is to be commemorated, they assemble and dance it. It was a trifling, innocent dance, and you felt as you looked at it, and, indeed, at all the features of our most unique entertainment, that there was a good deal of nursery imagination in Japanese *fetes* and games. A more striking feature were the decorations which came with the second course of our feast. First came servants, bearing two trees, one of the pine the other of the plum. The plum tree was in full blossom. One of these was set on a small table in front of Mrs. Grant, the other in front of the General. Another decoration was a cherry tree, surmounting a large basin, in which were living carp fish. The carp has an important position in the legends of Japan. It is the emblem of ambition and resolution. This quality was shown in another decoration, representing a waterfall, with carp climbing against the stream. The tendency of the carp to dash against rocks and climb waterfalls, which should indicate a lower order of intellect and perverted judgment, is supposed to show the traits of the ambitious man.

"The soups disappear. You see we have only had seven

distinct soups served at intervals, and so cunningly prepared that you are convinced that in the ancient days of Japanese splendor soup had a dignity which it has lost.

"With the departure of the soups our dinner becomes fantastic. Perhaps the old daimios knew that by the time their guests had eaten of seven soups and twenty courses in addition, and drank of innumerable dishes of rice liquor, they were in a condition to require a daring flight of genius.

"The music is in full flow, and the lights of the town grow brighter with the shades of darkening night, and some of the company have long since taken refuge from the dinner in cigars, and over the low brick wall and in the recesses of the temple grounds crowds begin to cluster and form, and below, at the foot of the steps, the crowd grows larger and larger, and you hear the buzz of the throng and the clinking of the lanterns of the chair bearers, for the whole town was in festive mood, and high up in our open temple on the hillside we have become a show for the town. Well, that is only a small return for the measureless hospitality we have enjoyed, and, if we can gratify an innocent curiosity, let us think of so much pleasure given in our way through the world. It is such a relief to know that we have passed beyond any comprehension of our dinner, which we look at as so many conceptions and preparations — curious contrivances, which we study out as though they were riddles or problems adjusted for our entertainment. The dining quality vanished with that eccentric soup of lassfish and orange flowers. With the General it went much earlier. It must be said that for the General the table has few charms, and, long before we began on the skylarks and buckwheat degraded by the egg plant, he for whom this feast is given had taken refuge in a cigar, and contented himself with looking upon the beauty of the town and bay and cliff, allowing the dinner to flow along. You will observe, if you have followed the narrative of our feast, that meat plays a small and fish a large part in a daimios dinner — fish and the products of the forest and field. The red snapper has the place of honor, and, although we have had the snapper in five different shapes — as a soup, as a ragout flavored with cabbage, broiled with pickled beans, and hashed — here he comes again, baked, decorated with ribbons, with every scale in place, folded in a bamboo basket.

"As a final course, we had pears prepared with horse radish, a cake of wheat flour and powdered ice. The dinner came to a close after a struggle of six or seven hours, and as we drove home through the illuminated town, brilliant with lanterns and fireworks and arches and bonfires, it was felt that we had been honored by an entertainment such as we may never again expect to see."

After having spent several days in this old town and its vicinity, the General and party bid adieu to the many friends and acquaintances, and embarked for Yokohama, where he was received with great and enthusiastic demonstrations. After a short reception to the princes, Ministers and high officials of the Japanese government, the General and party were driven to the railroad station, and at two o'clock the train entered the station at Tokio. An immense crowd was in waiting. As the General descended from the train, a committee of citizens advanced and asked to read an address. The following was then read in Japanese, by Mr. Fukuchi, and in English by Dr. McCartee:

"SIR: On behalf of the people of Tokio, we beg to congratulate you on your safe arrival. How you crushed a rebellion, and afterward ruled a nation in peace and righteousness, is known over the whole world, and there is not a man in Japan who does not admire your high character and illustrious career. Although the great Pacific Ocean stretches for thousands of miles between your country and ours, your people are our next neighbors in the East, and, as it was chiefly through your initiative that we entered upon those relations and that commerce with foreigners which have now attained such a flourishing condition, our countrymen have always cherished a good feeling for your people, and look upon them more than on any other foreign nation as their true friends. Moreover, it was during the happy times of your Presidency that the two countries became more closely acquainted and connected, and almost every improvement that has been made in our country may be traced to the example and lessons received from yours. For years past, not only our Minister, but any one of our countrymen who went to your country, was received with hospitality and courtesy. It is, therefore, impossible that our countrymen should now forbear from giving expression to their gratification and gratitude.

"Your visit to our shores is one of those rare events that happen once in a thousand years. The citizens of Tokio consider it a great honor that they have been afforded the opportunity of receiving you as their guest, and they cherish the hope that this event will still more cement the friendship between the two nations in the future We now offer you a hearty and respectful welcome.

"THE TOKIO RECEPTION COMMITTEE.
"*The 3d July, 1879.*"

General Grant said:

"GENTLEMEN: I am very much obliged for this kind reception, and especially for your address. It affords me great pleasure to visit Tokio. I had been some days in Japan, having seen several points of interest in the interior and on the inland sea. I have been gratified to witness the prosperity and advancement of which I had heard so much, and in which my countrymen have taken so deep an interest. I am pleased to hear your kind expressions toward the United States. We have no sentiment there that is not friendly to Japan, that does not wish her prosperity and independence, and a continuance on her part of her noble policy. The knowledge that your country is prosperous and advancing is most gratifying to the people of the United States. It is my sincere wish that this friendship may never be broken. For this kind welcome to the capital of Japan I am again very much obliged."

General Grant's home in Tokio was at the palace of Enriokwan, only a few minutes' ride from the railroad station. This palace was one of the homes of the Tycoon; it now belongs to the Emperor. If one's ideas of palaces are European, or even American, he will be disappointed with Enriokwan. One somehow associates a palace with state, splendor, a profusion of color and decoration, with upholstery and marble. There was nothing of this in Enriokwan. The approach to the grounds was by a dusty road that ran by the side of a canal. The canal was sometimes in an oozing condition, and boats were held in the mud. There is a good deal of ceremony in Enriokwan, with the constant coming and going of great people, and no sound is more familiar than the sound of the bugle. Passing a guard house and going down a pebbled way to a low, one-story building with wings, the palace of Enriokwan is reached. Over the door is the chrysanthemum, the Emperor's special flower. The main building is a series of reception rooms, in various styles of decoration, notably Japanese. There are eight different rooms in all. General Grant used the small room to the left of the hall. On ceremonial occasions he used the main saloon, which extended one-half the length of the palace. Here a hundred people could be entertained with ease. This room was a beautiful specimen of Japanese decorative art, and the General never became so familiar with it that there were not constant surprises in the way of color or form or design. Each of these rooms was decorated differently from the others. The apartments of General Grant and party were in one wing, the dining-room, billiard room and apartments of the Japanese officials in attendance in another wing. Around the palace was a verandah, with growing flowers in profusion and swinging lanterns. The beauty of the palace was not in its architecture, which was plain and inexpressive, but in the taste which marked the most minute detail of decoration, and in the arrangement of the grounds.

Enriokwan is an island. On one side is a canal and embanked walls, on the other side the ocean. Although in an ancient and populous city, surrounded by a teeming, busy metropolis, one feels as he passes into Enriokwan that he is as secure as in a fortress and as secluded as in a forest. The grounds are large, and remarkable for the beauty and finish of the landscape gardening. In the art of gardening Japan excels the world, and the visitors had seen no more attractive specimen than the grounds of Enriokwan. Roads, flower beds, lakes, bridges, artificial mounds, creeks overhung with sedgy overgrowths, lawns, boats, bowers over which vines are trailing, summer houses, all combine to give comfort to Enriokwan. Sitting on this verandah, under the columns where the General sat every evening, he could look out upon a ripe and perfect landscape, dowered with green. If they walked into the grounds a few minutes they passed a gate — an inner gate, which was locked at night — and came to a lake, on the banks of which is a Japanese summer house. The lake is artificial, and fed from the sea. They crossed a bridge and came to another summer house. Here were two boats tied up, with the imperial chrysanthemum emblazoned on their bows. These are the private boats of the Emperor, and if they care for a pull they can row across and lose themselves in one of the creeks. They ascend a grassy mound, however, not more than forty feet high. Steps are cut in the side of the mound, and when they reach the summit they see beneath them the waves and before them the ocean. The sea at this point forms a bay. When the tides are down and the waves are calm, fishermen are seen wading about, seeking shells and shellfish. When the tides are up, the boats sail near the shore, and sometimes as one is strolling under the trees he can look up and see through the foliage a sail float past him, firm and steady and bending to the breeze.

The summer houses by the lake are worthy of study. Japan has taught the world the beauty of clean, fine grained natural wood, and the fallacy of glass and paint. Nothing could be more simple, at the same time more tasteful, than these summer houses. It is one room, with grooves for a partition if two rooms should be needed. The floor is covered with a fine, closely woven mat of bamboo strips. Over the mat is thrown a rug, in which black and brown predominate. The walls looking out to the lake are a series of frames that can be taken out — lattice work of small squares, covered with paper. The ceiling is plain, unvarnished wood. There are a few shelves, with vases, blue and white pottery, containing growing plants and flowers. There are two tables, and their only furniture a large box of gilded lacquer, for stationery, and a smaller one, containing cigars. These boxes are of exquisite workmanship, and the gold crysanthemum indicates the imperial ownership. This was a type of all the houses that were seen in the palace grounds, not only at Enriokwan, but elsewhere in Japan. It shows taste and economy. Everything about it was wholesome and clean, the workmanship true and minute, with no tawdry appliances to distract or offend the eye.

The General's life in Enriokwan was very quiet. The weather had been such that going out during the day was a discomfort. During the day there were ceremonies, calls from Japanese and foreign officials, papers to read, visits to make. If the evening was free, the General had a dinner party — sometimes small, sometimes large. One night it was the royal Princes, the next the Prime Ministers, on other evenings other Japanese of rank and station. Sometimes he had Admiral Patterson or officers from the fleet. Sometimes Mr. Bingham and his family. Governor Hennessy, the British Governor of Hong Kong, was there during a part of his stay. General Grant was the guest of the Governor during his residence in Hong Kong, and formed a high opinion of the Governor's genius and character. The Governor was a frequent visitor at Enriokwan, and no man was more welcome to the General. Prince Dati, Mr. Yoshida, and some other Japanese officials, live at Enriokwan, and formed a part of the General's family. They represented the Emperor, and remained with the General to serve him, and make his stay as pleasant as possible. Nothing could be more considerate or courteous or hospitable than the kindness of their Japanese friends. Sometimes they had merchants from the bazaars, with all kinds of curious and useful things to sell. But when Mr. Borie went home, the reputation of General Grant's party as purchasers of curious things fell. Sometimes a fancy for cuririosities took possession of some of the party, and the result was an afternoon's prowl about the shops in Tokio, and the purchase of a sword or a spear, or a bow and arrows. The bazaars of Tokio teemed with beautiful works of art, and the temptation to go back laden with achievements in porcelain and lacquer was too great to be resisted, unless their will was under the control of material influences too sordid to be dwelt upon.

On July 8, three Princes and Princesses called at the palace and escorted General and Mrs. Grant to one of the Ministers, where a native dance was performed for their amusement. In the evening the grand reception, for which great preparations had been made, came off at the College of Engineering. It was the first of three great entertainments intended to be given the General in Tokio, for which thirty thousand yen had been subscribed. The weather during the afternoon had been threatening, but, though a few drops of rain fell, there was not sufficient to interfere with the brilliant display of Japanese lamps with which the roadway from the Enriokwan to the college, and the compound of the college, was illuminated. In the compound there were six thousand lamps of variegated colors, the majority having the national flags of Japan and America painted on them. At the entrance to the main hall was an arch, composed entirely of lanterns, which was a magnificent spectacle. The letters " U. S. G.," in green foliage, were suspended in the centre, and the flags of Japan and America, joined together, reached from one side to the other. From the branches of every tree and shrub in the grounds hung lanterns, presenting a most unique and picturesque appearance. The hall in which the reception took place was a fine building, capable of holding a thousand or more people comfortably on the ground floor, while the extensive galleries would contain several hundred persons. A more appropriate building for the occasion could not have been found in Tokio. The waiting-room was commodious and well filled with excellent seats, but rather poorly lighted. It would have been a great improvement if some lamps had been fixed on the walls, and thus have enabled visitors to distinguish their friends easily. The supper room was some distance away from the reception hall, and in another building, and the committee had prudently provided against any inclemency on the part of the weather by erecting a temporary roof over the whole path-way leading to it. As to the supper itself, little may be said; there was plenty of everything and everything of the best. Shortly after 8 o'clock the Governor of the Tokio Fu arrived in his carriage, and on alighting courteously saluted every individual in the waiting-room. At 9 o'clock General Grant, Mrs. Grant, General T. B. Van Buren,

Admiral Patterson and several Japanese of distinction left the Enriokwan and arrived at the college in a quarter of an hour. The guest of the evening was conducted to a room up-stairs which had been prepared for him. By this time over a thousand guests had arrived, including princes of the blood, Ministers of the different departments, Japanese naval and military officers, the Foreign Ministers, officers from the Richmond, Monongahela and Ashuelot, and many distinguished foreigners and native citizens. Soon the secretary of the entertainment committee cleared the way, and soon afterward General Grant entered, leaning on the arm of a Japanese official. Mrs. Grant was under the care of another. The General, Mrs. Grant, Mrs. Hennessy and Japanese Princesses were conducted to the far end of the room, where seats were provided. On a dais at their backs, which was prettily ornamented with flowers and shrubs, were stationed Admiral Patterson, Captain Benham, General Van Buren and several other personages of note. The large hall was crowded with people of all nationalties, dressed in bright and picturesque costumes, making as brilliant a display as any of the kind that had ever taken place in Tokio.

For over half an hour General and Mrs. Grant stood on their feet to shake hands with and receive the greetings of the people of Tokio. It was warm work while it lasted. The General with one hand returned the grasp of each person as he or she passed by, and wiped the perspiration off his brow with the other. The reception being over, a move was made for the supper room, and, a short time afterward, General and Mrs. Grant returned to the Enriokwan. Many of the guests also returned to their homes about the same time, but others remained to enjoy themselves. The excellent imperial and military bands, which had been playing in the grounds all the evening, were brought inside and discoursed alternately. A faint attempt was made to get up a dance, but no spirit was displayed, and it was not persevered with. And so this entertainment came to an end.

On the 9th, the General was to be received in Yokohama. During the forenoon General and Colonel Grant visited the military college in Tokio, and were received by its president. Every branch of the college was carefully examined, and a drill by the cadets witnessed. There were also present a large number of ministers, generals, councillors of state, and other officials. Three members of the committee of entertainment of Yokohama visited the General at the Enriokwan, to conduct him to the evening train. Arriving at the station about nine o'clock, they were received by the committee and escorted to the town hall, where the reception was held. The principal streets were gaily decorated with lanterns bearing the American and Japanese flags, and along one side of the street leading to the depot were several large dashi, or festival cars, in which native music and pantomime were performed. The town hall was brilliantly illuminated, and the imperial naval band in attendance gave a fine selection of music. After arriving at the hall, General Grant held a reception, which was followed by exhibitions of native dancing and acting. A well-spread table supplied the inner wants of the guests. The party returned to Tokio by a special train.

On the 10th, General and Mrs. Grant visited the female normal school at Tokio, in company with the acting Minister of Education, Mr. Tanaka, Mrs. Tanaka, and several members of the foreign department. On arriving at the school, they were received by the director, Mr. Nakamura. who conducted his visitors to the room where the students were learning their lessons. The General and Mrs. Grant were much pleased with the arrangements, and, having been shown over the various apartments, took their leave and proceeded direct to the educational museum at Uyeno, where they were entertained at a banquet. On returning to the Enriokwan, the General walked through the Uyeno gardens.

In the afternoon, a number of the reception committee of Yokohama visited the Enriokwan, and were received in the drawing-room of the palace. Admiral Patterson and staff, in full uniform, were present also. After presenting the gentlemen of the committee, General Van Buren said:

"General Grant, the gentlemen who have just been presented to you are representatives of the foreign community of Yokohama, a community composed of all nationalities, and gathered from almost every clime. They have commissioned me to greet you in their name, and to bid you welcome to Yokohama whenever you are prepared to honor them with a visit. They are familiar with your history, and believe that the eminent services you have rendered your country have, in some sense, been rendered to the world at large, and are entitled to a world's recognition. Appreciating the kind and generous hospitality extended to you by the government and people of Japan, the foreign residents of Yokohama desire an opportunity to meet you in person and to express to you personally their admiration and regard. To this end they propose to have an entertainment in the form of a garden party at such time as may suit your convenience, and they will be pleased to receive your assent to the proposition and your acceptance of this most cordial invitation."

General Grant replied: "I thank the foreign residents of Yokohama most cordially for their kind invitation, which I accept with great pleasure; but it will be impossible for me at present to fix a positive date for the entertainment. On the 16th instant it is arranged that I go to the mountains, to be gone ten days or two weeks. I expect to be back in Tokio the later part of the month, after which, before I leave Japan, which I now think will be on the

27th of August, I am to go north to Hakodate and vicinity. I think it would be safe, therefore, to fix the first week in August, or such a day as you may prefer."

The committee, after taking refreshments, were conducted about the grounds, which were in excellent order.

The next day, the party at the palace remained quiet. On the 12th, Saturday, what may be styled the "Feast of Lanterns," took place on the Sumida river in Tokio, and was of unusual brilliancy.

Shortly before eight o'clock, General and Mrs. Grant and Mr. and Mrs. Yoshida in one carriage, Colonel Grant, General T. B. Van Buren, Lieutenant Belknap and Mr. Young in another carriage, left the Enriokwan for the scene of festivities. Mr. Hachiska's residence on the river had been fitted up for the reception of the illustrious guest, who was met by the Japanese princes, members of the ministry, Mr. Mori, Hon. John A. Bingham, Miss Bingham, Mr. and Mrs. Hennessy (the latter astonished the natives by appearing in Japanese costume, and, when asked why she was so dressed, replied that it was not only convenient to wear Japanese clothing in hot weather, but she also wore it out of respect to Japan), and several others who were invited. In the locality of the house were several foreigners who had not been fortunate enough to be among the invited, but who were glad to have the privilege of obtaining a good view without being crushed in the crowd.

The streets and the Riogoku-bashi were thronged with visitors, and it was a pretty sight when seen to advantage. The river was ablaze with red and white lanterns, which, together with an almost incessant display of fireworks, formed such a brilliant spectacle as beggars description on paper. General and Mrs. Grant were delighted. They had never seen anything of the kind before, and the General expressed his opinion that he never expected to see such an interesting and beautiful illumination again.

At ten o'clock Mr. Hachiska's guests partook of a sumptuous repast, which had been provided; shortly afterward a terrific shower, such as occasionally bursts over this part of Japan, almost totally extinguished the illumination. The rain poured down in torrents, so that even passengers by the train could not shut it out of the carriages. As for the immense congregation of people on the bridges and in the streets, they were drenched in a few seconds. A rush was made for shelter, but no shelter was to be found, and the crowd surged backward and forward in a bewildered state for the space of half an hour. The same state of confusion prevailed among the boats. The rain put nearly all lights out, boats collided one with the other, and the shouts of the sendoes only made "confusion worse confounded." When the rain ceased, the majority of speculators had had their ardor sufficiently dampened to induce them to make for their homes, as speedily as jinrikishas could take them, which was not very fast, certainly. Every now and then a whole streetful of these vehicles would be blocked up, unable to move for several minutes.

About eleven o'clock General Grant and his party returned to the Enriokwan.

On July 4 occurred the reception by the Emperor at his palace. The hour for the reception was two o'clock in the afternoon. General Grant invited several of his naval friends to accompany him. The palace of the Emperor was a long distance from the home of the General. Their drive led them through the damios quarter and through the gates of the city.

The impression a foreigner gets of Tokio is that it is a city of walls and canals. The walls are crude and solid, surrounded by moats. In the early days of pikemen and sword bearers, there could not have been a more effective defense. After crossing a dozen or more bridges in the course of the drive to the palace of the Emperor, they arrived at a modest arched gateway. Soldiers were drawn up, and the band played "Hail Columbia." The carriages drove on past one or two modest buildings, and drew up in front of another modest building, on the steps of which the Prime Minister, Iwakaura was standing. The General and party descended, and were cordially welcomed and escorted up a narrow stairway into an ante-room. The home of the Emperor was as simple as that of a country gentleman at home. There are many country gentlemen with felicitous investments in petroleum and silver who would disdain the home of a prince who claims direct descent from heaven, and whose line extends far beyond the Christian era. What marked the house was its simplicity and taste. One looks for splendor, for the grand — at least the grandoise — for some royal whim like the holy palace near the Escurial, which cost millions, or like Versailles, whose cost is among the eternal mysteries. Here we are in a suite of plain rooms, the ceilings of wood, the walls decorated with natural scenery, the furniture sufficient but not crowded, and exquisite in style and finish. There is no pretense of architectural emotion. The rooms are large, airy, with a sense of summer about them, which grows stronger as seen out of the window and down the avenues of trees. The General was told that the grounds are spacious and fine, even for Japan, and that his Majesty, who rarely goes outside of his palace grounds, takes what recreation he needs within the walls.

The palace is a low building, one or at most two stories in height. They do not build high walls in Japan, and especially in Tokio, where earthquakes are ordinary incidents, and the first question to consider in building up is how far you can fall. The party entered a room where all the ministers were assembled. The Japanese Cabinet is a famous body, and tested by laws of physiognomy would compare with that of any cabinet ever seen. The Prime Minister is a striking character. He is small, slender, with an almost girl-like figure, delicate, clean cut, winning features, a face that might be that of a boy of twenty or a man of fifty. The Prime Minister reminded the visitors of Alexander H. Stephens in his frail, slender frame, but it bloomed with health, and lacked the sad, pathetic lines which tell of the years of suffering which Stephens has endured. The other Ministers looked like strong, able men. Iwakura had a striking face, with lines showing firmness and decision, and they saw the scar which marked the attempt of the assassin to cut him down and slay him, as Okubo, the greatest of Japanese statesmen, was slain not many months ago. That assassination made as deep an impression in Japan as the killing of Lincoln did in America. The spot where the murder was done was seen on the way to the palace, and the Japanese friend who pointed it out spoke in low tones of sorrow and affection, and said the crime there committed had been an irreparable loss to Japan.

A lord in waiting, heavily braided, with a uniform that Louis XIV. would not have disliked in Versailles, came came softly in, and made a signal, leading the way. The General and Mrs. Grant, escorted by Mr. Bingham, and their retinue, followed. The General and the Minister were in evening dress. The naval officers were in full uniform, Colonel Grant wearing the uniform of Lieutenant-Colonel. They walked along a short passage and entered another room, at the farther end of which were standing the Emperor and Empress. Two ladies in waiting were near them in a sitting, what appeared to be a crouching, attitude. Two other princesses were standing. These appeared to be the only occupants of the room. The General and party slowly advanced, the Japanese making a profound obeisance, bending the head almost to a right angle with the body. The royal princes formed in line near the Emperor, along with the princesses. The Emperor stood quite motionless, apparently unobservant or unconscious of the homage that was paid him. He was a young man with a slender figure, taller than the average Japanese, and of about the middle height. He had a striking face, with a mouth and lips that reminded one somewhat of the traditional mouth of the Hapsburg family. The forehead was full and narrow, the hair and the light mustache and beard intensely black. The color of the hair darkened what otherwise might pass for a swarthy countenance at home. The face expressed no feeling whatever, and but for the dark, glowing eye, which was bent full upon the General, one might have taken the Imperial group for statues. The Empress, at his side, wore the Japanese costume, rich and plain. Her face was very white, and her form slender and almost childlike. Her hair was combed plainly and braided with a gold arrow. The Emperor and Empress had agreeable faces, the Emperor especially showing firmness and kindness. The solemn etiquette that pervaded the audience chamber was peculiar, and might appear strange to those familiar with the stately but cordial manners of a European court. But one must remember that the Emperor holds so high and so sacred a place in the traditions, the religion, and the political system of Japan, that even this ceremony is so far in advance of anything of the kind ever known in Japan that it might be called a revolution. The Emperor, for instance, as the group was formed, advanced and shook hands with the General. This seems a trivial thing, but such an incident was never known in the history of Japanese majesty. Many of these details may appear small, but our party were in the presence of an old and romantic civilization, slowly giving way to the fierce, feverish pressure of European ideas, and one can only note the change in those incidents which would be unnoticed in other lands. The incident of the Emperor of Japan advancing toward General Grant and shaking hands, becomes a historic event of consequence. The manner of the Emperor was constrained, almost awkward, the manner of a man doing a thing for the first time, and trying to do it as well as possible. After he had shaken hands with the General he returned to his place, and stood with his hand resting on his sword, looking on at the brilliant, embroidered, gilded company, as though unconscious of their presence. Mr. Bingham advanced and bowed, and received just the faintest nod in recognition. The other members of the party were each presented by the Minister, and each one, standing about a dozen feet from the Emperor, stood and bowed. Then the General and Mrs. Grant were presented to the princesses, each party bowing to the other in silence. The Emperor then made a signal to one of the noblemen, who advanced. The Emperor spoke to him a few moments in a low tone, the nobleman standing with bowed head. When the Emperor had finished, the nobleman advanced to the General, and said he was commanded by His Majesty to read him the following address:

"Your name has been known to us for a long time, and we are highly gratified to see you. While holding the high office of President of the United States you extended toward our countrymen especial kindness and courtesy. When our ambassador, Iwakura, visited the United States, he received the greatest kindness from you. The kindness thus shown by you has always been remembered by us. In your travels around the world you have reached this country, and our people of all classes feel gratified and happy to receive you. We trust that during your sojourn in our country you may find much to enjoy. It gives me sincere pleasure to receive you, and we are especially gratified that we have been able to do so on the anniversary of American independence. We congratulate you, also, on the occasion."

This address was read in English. At its close, General Grant said:

"Your Majesty: I am very grateful for the welcome you accord me here to-day, and for the great kindness with which I have been received, ever since I came to Japan, by your government and your people. I recognize in this a feeling of friendship toward my country. I can assure you that this feeling is reciprocated by the United States; that our people, without regard to party, take the deepest interest in all that concerns Japan, and have the warmest wishes for her welfare. I am happy to be able to express that sentiment. America is your next neighbor, and will always give Japan sympathy and support in her efforts to advance. I again thank Your Majesty for your hospitality, and wish you a long and happy reign, and for your people prosperity and independence."

At the conclusion of this address, which was extempore, the lord advanced and translated it to His Majesty. Then the Emperor made a sign, and said a few words to the nobleman. He came to the side of Mrs. Grant and said the Empress had commanded him to translate the following address:

"I congratulate you upon your safe arrival after your long journey. I presume you have seen very many interesting places. I fear you will find many things uncomfortable here, because the customs of the country are so different from other countries. I hope you will prolong your stay in Japan, and that the present warm days may occasion you no inconvenience."

Mrs. Grant, pausing a moment, said in a low, conversational tone of voice, with animation and feeling:

"I thank you very much. I have visited many countries, and have seen many beautiful places, but I have seen none so beautiful or so charming as Japan."

The reception ceremonies over, our party returned to their home at the palace Enriokwan.

All day during the Fourth, visitors poured in on the General. The reception of so many distinguished statesmen and officials reminded one of state occasions at the White House. Princes of the imperial family, princesses, the members of the Cabinet and citizens and high officials, naval officers, Ministers and Consuls, all came; and carriages were constantly coming and going. In the evening there was a party at one of the summer gardens, given by the American residents in honor of the Fourth of July. The General arrived at half-past eight and was presented to the American residents by Mr. Bingham, the Minister. At the close of the presentation, Mr. Bingham made a brief but singularly eloquent address. Standing in front of the General, and speaking in a low, measured tone of voice, scarcely above conversational pitch, the Minister, after words of welcome, said:

"In common with all Americans, we are not unmindful that in the supreme moment of our national trials, when our heavens were filled with darkness, and our habitations were filled with dead, you stood with our defenders in the forefront of the conflict, and with them amid the consuming fires of battle achieved the victory which brought deliverance to our imperiled country. To found a great commonwealth, or to save from overthrow a great commonwealth already founded, is considered to be the greatest of human achievements. If it was not your good fortune to aid Washington, the first of Americans and the foremost of men, and his peerless associates, in founding the Republic, it was given to you above all others to aid in the no less honorable work of saving the Republic from overthrow." Mr. Bingham continued his speech, saying:

"Now that the sickle has fallen from the pale hand of Death on the field of mortal combat, and the places which but yesterday were blackened and blasted by war have grown green and beautiful under the hand of peaceful toil; now that the Republic, one and undivided, is covered with the greatness of justice, protecting each by the combined power of all, men of every land, of every tongue; the world, appreciating the fact that your civic and military services largely contributed to these results, so essential not only to the interests of our own country but to the interests of the human race, have accorded to you such honors as never before within the range of authentic history have been given to a living, untitled and unofficial person. I may venture to say that this grateful recognition of your services will not be limited to the present generation or the present age, but will continue through all ages. In conclusion, I beg leave again to bid you welcome to Japan, and to express the wish that in health and prosperity you may return to your native land, the land which we all love so well."

In response, General Grant said:

"LADIES AND GENTLEMEN: I am unable to answer the eloquent speech of Judge Bingham, as it is in so many senses personal to myself. I can only thank him for his too flattering allusions to me personally and the duty devolving on me during the late war. We had a great war. We had a trial that summoned forth the energies and patriotism of all our people — in the army alone over a million. In awarding credit for the success that crowned those efforts, there is not one in that million, not one among the living or the dead, who did not do his share as I did mine, and who does not deserve as much credit. It fell to my lot to command the armies. There were many others who could have commanded the armies better. But I did my best, and we all did our best, and in the fact that it was a struggle on the part of the people for the Union, for the country, for a country for themselves and their children, we have the best assurances of peace, and the best reasons for gratification over the result. We are strong and free because the people made us so. I trust we may long continue so. I think we have no issues, no questions that need give us embarrassment. I look forward to peace, to generations of peace, and with peace prosperity. I never felt more confident of the future of our country. It is a great country — a great blessing to us — and we cannot be too proud of it, too zealous for its honor, too anxious to develop its resources, and make it not only a home for our children, but for the worthy people of other lands. I am glad to meet you here, and I trust that your labors will be prosperous, and that you will return home in health and happiness. I trust we may all meet again at home, and be able to celebrate our Fourth of July as pleasantly as we do tonight."

Dr. McCartee, who presided, made a short address, proposing as a toast, "The Day We Celebrate." To this General Van Buren made a patriotic and ringing response, making amusing references to Fourth of July celebrations at home, and paying a tribute to the character and military career of General Grant. General Van Buren's address was loudly applauded, as were also other speeches of a patriotic character. There were fireworks and feasting, and, after the General and Mrs. Grant retired, which they did at midnight, there was dancing. It was well on to the morning before the members of the American colony in Tokio grew weary of celebrating the anniversary of our Declaration of Independence.

On the morning of July 7, General Grant reviewed the army of Japan. Great preparations had been made to have it in readiness, and all Tokio was out to see the pageant. The review of the army by the Emperor in itself is an event that causes a sensation. But the review of the army by the Emperor and the General was an event which had no precedent in the Japanese history. The hour for the review was nine, and at half past eight the clatter of horsemen and the sound of bugles was heard in the palace grounds. In a few moments the Emperor's state carriage drove up, the drivers in scarlet livery, and the panels decorated with the imperial flower, the chrysanthemum. General Grant entered, accompanied by Prince Dati, and the cavalry formed a hollow square, and their procession moved on to the field at a slow pace. A drive of twenty minutes brought them to the parade ground, a large open plain, the soldiers in line, and behind the soldiers a dense mass of people — men, women and children. As the General's procession slowly turned into the parade ground, a group of Japanese officers rode up and saluted, the band played "Hail Columbia," and the soldiers presented arms. Two tents had been arranged for the receccception of the guests. In the larger of the two were assembled officers of state, representatives of foreign powers, Governor Hennessy, of Hong Kong, all in bright, glowing uniforms. The smaller tent was for the Emperor. When the General dismounted, he was met by the Minister of war and escorted into the smaller tent. In a few minutes the trumpets gave token that the Emperor was coming, and the band played the Japanese national air. His Majesty was in a state carriage, surrounded with horsemen and accompanied by one of his Cabinet. As the Emperor drove up to the tent, General Grant advanced to the carriage steps and shook hands with him, and they entered and remained a few minutes in conversation.

At the close of the review, General Grant and party drove off the ground in state, and were taken to the Shila palace. This palace is near the sea, and, as the grounds are beautiful and attractive, it was thought best that the breakfast to be given to General Grant by His Majesty should take place here. The Emperor received the General and party in a large, plainly furnished room, and led the way to another room, where the table was set. The decorations of the table were sumptuous and royal. General Grant sat on one side of the Emperor, whose place was in the centre. Opposite was Mrs. Grant, who sat next to Prince Arinagawa, the nearest relative to the Emperor, and the Commander-in-Chief of the army. The guests, in addition to the General's party, were as follows: Her Imperial Highness Princess Aimayaura, their Imperial Highnesses Prince and Princess Higashi Fushimi, Mr. Saujo, Prime Minister; Mr. Iwakura, Junior Prime Minister; Mr. Okunea, Finance Minister; Mr. Oki, Minister of Justice; Mr. Terasnima, Minister of Foreign Affairs; Mr. Ite, Home Minister; Lieutenant-General Yamagata, Lieutenant-General Kuroda, Minister of Colonization; Lieutenant-General Saigo, Minister of War; Vice-Admiral Kawamusa, Minister of Marine; Mr. Inonye, Minister of Public Works; Mr. Tokadaifi, Minister of the Imperial Household; Mr. Mori, Vice-Minister of Foreign Affairs; Mr. Yoshida, Envoy to the United States; Mr. Sagi, Vice-Minister of the Imperial Household; Mr. Yoshie, Chief Chamberlain; Mr. Bojo, Master of Ceremonies; Prince Hachisuka, Prince Dati, Mr. Insanmi Naboshima, Mr. Bingham, and Mrs. Bingham; Ho-a-Chang, the Chinese Minister; Mr. Mariano Alvaray, Spanish Charge d'Affaires; Baron Rozen, Russian Charge d'Affaires; M. de Balloy, French Charge d'Affaires; Governor Pope Hennessy, and Mrs. Hennessy.

The Emperor conversed a great deal with General Grant through Mr. Yoshida, and also Governor Hennessy. His Majesty expressed a desire to have a private and friendly conference with the General, which it was arranged should take place after the General's return from

Nikko. The feast lasted for a couple of hours, and the view from the table was charming. Beneath the window was a lake, and the banks were bordered with grass and trees. Cool winds came from the sea, and, although in the heart of a great capital, they were as secluded as in a forest. At the close of the breakfast, cigars were brought, and the company adjourned to another room. Mrs. Grant had a long conversation with the princesses, and was charmed with their grace, their accomplishments, their simplicity, and their quiet, refined Oriental beauty. At three o'clock the imperial party withdrew, and the guests drove home to their palace by the sea.

Entertainments in honor of General Grant were constantly occupying public attention. He visited the various colleges, and pronounced the cadets of the military school as promising a body as any seen by him in Europe. He witnessed the annual ceremony of the opening of the principal river of Tokio, which consisted of a brilliant night congregation of illuminated boats, and the most successful of all displays in his honor, a theatrical performance, especially prepared.

On July 17, General Grant and party went to the shrine of Iyeyasu, the founder of the great Tokugausa family, at Nikko, a famous and sacred resort one hundred miles in the interior. After spending nearly three weeks, enjoying a delightful time, the General returned to the capital, and started on a new excursion to Kamakara, the ancient seat of military government, and its neighborhood, and in the mountain range of Hakone.

General Grant returned to Tokio, August 19th. During his stay at Tokio he was visited by the Mikado, who consulted on many important points of international policy, and to some extent of domestic policy. The confidence and reliance manifested by the government and people were unprecedented.

General Grant found himself burdened with unexpected questions in relation to Eastern policy. During his visit to North China both Prince Kung and the Viceroy, L. Hung Chang, laid before him their side of the Loochoo controversy, asking him to use his influence with Japan to prevent a serious misunderstanding between the two Empires. The General is believed to have replied that the other side would doubtless express themselves as strongly from their standpoint when heard, and, though a rupture would be lamented by all observers, he did not see that he had any right to interfere. The Japanese authorities on hearing this took great pains to prepare a documentary vindication of their claims, which was submitted for the ex-President's inspection by the Cabinet. This appearance of over-anxiety does not commend itself strongly to spectators generally, Japan's supremacy over the Loochoo Islands being so plainly defined and thoroughly established as to need no superfluous demonstration. But the circumstances are interesting as showing the weight attached to General Grant's influence and the favorable view taken of that gentleman by both governments.

General Grant had now reached the end of his journey and stay in Japan. He had been nearly two months within her Empire; had witnessed the most enthusiastic and the most spontaneous demonstrations of his trip, from first to last; he had been accorded more privileges such as no other ruler or potentate had ever enjoyed.

After exchanging a series of formal visits, and a delightful round of dinners, receptions and entertainments, the General and party embarked from Yokohama on board the steamer Tokio, September 3, for the United States. There were men-of-war of various nations in the harbor, each of which manned their yards and fired salutes of farewell. For half an hour the bay rang with the roar of cannon, and was clouded with smoke. The scene was wonderfully grand — the roar of cannon, the clouds of smoke wandering off over the waters, the stately, noble vessels streaming with flags, the yards manned with seamen, the guards on deck, the officers in full uniform gathered on the quarter-deck to salute the General as he passed, the music and the cheers which came from the ships, the crowds that clustered upon the wharfs, all formed a sight that once seen can never be forgotten. To the General and party this enthusiastic demonstration will ever be recalled with grateful remembrance, and was a fitting climax of his now historical "tour around the world."

---

* Eighteen pages are here added to correct omission in paging the illustrations.

CHAPTER XIX.

GENERAL GRANT'S RETURN.

After an absence of over two years, General Grant is on his way back to the United States, having sailed from Tokio on September 3, 1879, and will reach San Francisco about the 21st. During this period he has visited almost every European capital, and has seen with his own eyes the people of every nation. Everywhere — in England, Ireland and Scotland, in France and Germany, Italy and Austria, in Switzerland, as in Sweden and Denmark, Russia and Egypt, as in India and Siam, China and Japan — he has been welcomed by rulers and people alike, in a manner and with a splendor and fervor of hospitality which have rightly been felt, by the mass of the American people, as not merely a compliment to the General and ex-President, but as a gratifying evidence of good will toward us as a people. It is not pleasant to reflect that, while he was thus received and honored abroad, here at home there have not been wanting carping critics who indulged in petty fault inding with his conduct, as though they were jealous of the honors paid him — fortunately for our credit as Americans, however, this carping spirit has not been general. The public sense of propriety has frowned it down. It would have been more gracious and more creditable to our people had there been no such criticism and fault finding. While General Grant was President, he was, as every man in public office is, the subject of comment; his acts were the proper objects of criticism. But when he laid down the presidential office and retired to private life — it has always been thought and held that he ceased to be, in any proper sense, a subject of adverse public comment. When he went abroad it was, as is well known, in pursuance of a design he had long entertained, and which he would earlier have accomplished had not public duties detained him at home. That he was received with extraordinary honors everywhere in Europe and Asia was due not only to the exalted positions he had filled, but to the world-wide appreciation of the fact that under his skillful and vigorous command the greatest war of modern times had been brought to a successful conclusion, and the security and integrity of the American Union assured. His reception by people and rulers abroad was thus a token of universal good will, not merely toward the General, but toward the nation of which he was one of the chief citizens, and it was not a gracious act in any American to raise his voice in criticism of General Grant or of the honors showered on him.

The friends of General Grant viewed with alarm and disgust certain officious preparations ostentatiously making here for his welcome home. The plan of a monster excursion under the auspices of notorious politicians, when they were to furnish tickets to the Pacific coast and return for twenty-five dollars — fully expecting that fifty thousand persons would embrace the opportunity to witness the General's reception — and the ill advised motions of other politicians, in the New York and Pennsylvania Legislatures, in the same direction, were in the worst possible taste; and it is believed that none of the real friends of General Grant took any part in them, but tried to discourage them in every way. It was as an American, and not as a Republican politician, that General Grant received his spontaneous, honorable and gratifying welcome in every foreign land that he visited; and it is as an American, and not as a Republican politician, that we are confident he desires to be welcomed home. Hence, as before written, the politicians ought to be made to keep their hands off. Their help and management are not needed to secure the General a rousing and real welcome from his countrymen. Their officious interference, which looked as though they feared that without their manipulations the General might not be well received, was an offense to him, and, if it had been persevered in, could not fail to place him in a painful and even ridiculous position. Commenting on this intended hippodrome performance, the Utica (N. Y.) *Herald* said:

"Manufactured enthusiasm is always ridiculous; and it will be easy to make the reception of General Grant ridiculous in the eyes of the American people. When the late Secretary Seward returned from a similar trip abroad, where he was greeted with honors hardly less generous than those extended to Grant, he had a welcome to his home in Auburn, which made a profound impression upon the country, for there was visible in it the sincere personal esteem of his friends and neighbors, and the suspicion of an ulterior purpose did not enter. Somewhat similar ought to be the welcome extended to the first public man of the United States who has made the tour of the world since William H. Seward returned. We believe that General Grant himself will be least pleased with a grand reception. He is singularly averse to the blare and glamour of carefully arranged demonstrations. Notwithstanding his remarkable public experiences, he has retained that simplicity of taste and habit which distinguished him in the days of his obscurity. He hates the formality of a demonstration. He has suffered more annoyance, we dare say, from the excessive formality under which he has been compelled to make his travels, than from any other cause. He hates speech making, for he has sense enough to know that he is not felicitous at it. It would not be surprising if the ex-President's antipathy to parade led him to positively interdict any such uproar over his return as has been outlined."

The Cincinnati *Star* said, speaking of the same subject: "There is not the least probability that General Grant will end his voyage around the world by allowing himself to be used as a side-show to a circus on wheels. The cheap excursion mania is very strong among the American people, whether it be to visit some famous natural scenery, to attend a horse race, or see a two-headed baby; and a band of speculators have lately learned how to make money out of this tendency, in the American beehive, to swarm during the hot months of summer. It is assumed as quite certain that General Grant will give the cold shoulder to any such ovation as this contemplated, and that he will have both sense and money enough to remain quietly in San Francisco until the locust-like storm shall blow over, and the tired and disgusted excursionists seek their homes."

There is not an admirer or friend of General Grant who wants to see the General's return made a sort of hippodrome performance, exactly the reverse of the compliments paid to him abroad. The object of foreign nations and governments in honoring him was to pay a compliment to the American people, whom he in a certain sense represented; but the object of this excursion, and of the more recent political movements in legislature, was only to glorify him as a party man, and a possible party candidate; and to place him under obligation beforehand to the polititians who would rush forward to capture him as he landed; and to exhibit him through the country as their prey, in a manner which would leave the managers open to ridicule and make a burlesque of his whole journey.

There was really no danger or fear that the General's real and respectable friends would allow him to become a victim of such people. That he will receive a warm and universal welcome from his countrymen there is no doubt, and he deserves it; but it will not be managed by self-seeking and designing politicians. It will be a spontaneous, hearty, unsolicited welcome from the American people. His friends would prefer to see him make the journey from the Pacific shores to his home in Philadelphia, as he will, doubtless, prefer himself, with entire avoidance of ostentation, like a great and eminent, but nevertheless a plain, citizen returning to his native land after a visit to foreign countries. It would be ungracious in him to deny his fellow-citizens a sight of him, and he has now come to that age where traveling by easy stages, instead of rushing through on lightning express, is for his comfort and that of Mrs. Grant. He will find in the principal Western cities many of his old, personal friends, who will desire to once more shake his hand. In a natural way — without the distasteful management of tricksters and politicians — the General can see and be seen by the greater part of the country, and he will receive everywhere the warmest welcome an admiring and hospitable people can give him. No sensible man doubts that General Grant's name and fame are dear to every true American, or that he ranks in all hearts as the foremost American citizen of the day. His great and long services to the Union have secured to him the lasting, and indeed the increasing, gratitude and admiration of the people. His sterling qualities of honesty and clear common sense; his patriotic love for his country's welfare, and desire for the success of our institutions; his severe and arduous, and often thankless public service; the pathetic manner in which, on several occasions, he has publicly confessed his mistakes while asserting his good intentions; — all these are known to and valued by the people, and it is a sure evidence that, though he was, while President, the subject of hostile and often acrimonious criticism, no sooner did he leave the (to him) unhappy politics, than all ill-will disappeared, and he resumed, as of right, his high place in the affectionate regards of his fellow-citizens, without regard to party. He returns home from a long journey in foreign parts, at every stage of which the honors which have been paid him by eminent persons of all classes have been watched with pleasure by the whole American people; but the most distinguished honors of his life remain, and will be found in the spontaneous welcome home of his fellow-citizens. To them, now, he occupies a quite peculiar position; for, whatever designing politicians may propose, to the people he is a citizen who has honorably and laboriously fulfilled his term of faithful public service, and whom, for the rest of his life, they will regard, not as a partisan, not as the candidate of or even a member of a party, but as one raised above party, and who, living in such privacy as such eminence as his can secure, will be, while he lives, the trusted adviser of all administrations. As a private citizen, the most illustrious and the most trusted of the Republic, he will rise constantly higher in the general esteem and affection, and it will be the delight of all Americans to guard and honor his declining years. But to re-enter now the arena of partisan politics would be to imperil his great reputation; to weaken the hold he has on the hearts of the people; to descend to the level of common men — a descent into the mire from an elevation rarely attained by any man in history. Those who would tempt him to his fall are not his friends, but his worst and most dangerous enemies.

The recent statement made by Rear Admiral Ammen in regard to General Grant's intentions for the future definitely removes the latter from the political field. Admiral Ammen's statement is entitled to much reliance for several reasons. The Admiral himself is a man of high character, who would not make so important an assertion without considering himself sure of the facts; he has been on terms of close personal intimacy with Grant during life; the circumstances related by the Admiral bear internal evidence of the correctness of his conclusion; and, finally, General Grant's disinclination to be a "third-term" candidate for the Presidency is confirmed by others in a position to know his sentiments. Among the evidences of this determination is General Grant's reply to Li Hung Chang, the Viceroy of Tientsin, when the latter expressed the hope that his visitor would again become President of the United States. Grant's words on that occasion were as follows:

"Your Excellency is very kind, but there could be no wish more distateful to me than what you express. I have held the office of President as long as it has ever been held by any man. There are others who have risen to great distinction at home, and who have earned the honor, who are worthy, and to them it belongs, and not to me. I have no claims to the office. It is a place distasteful to me, a place of hardship and responsibilities. When I was a younger man these hardships were severe and never agreeable. They would be worse now. No man who knows what the Presidency imposes would care to see a friend in the office. I have had my share of it,— have had all the honors that can be or should be given to any citizen, and there are many able and distinguished men who have earned the office. To one of them it should be given."

General Grant could not have chosen language more emphatically declaring his disinclination to be a candidate without being actually offensive to the American people, and there is no reason why his word should not be accepted as honestly conveying the meaning which they imply.

The Hon. E. B. Washburne has also contributed additional confirmation of Grant's purpose through a private letter from Grant, written still more recently, in which the latter declares that he cannot conceive any possible circumstances which could induce him to consent to be a candidate. Both General Grant's best friends and his most uncompromising opponents accept the declination as final; among the former may be classed Mr. George W. Childs, of Philadelphia, and among the latter Mr. Murat Halstead, of Cincinnati. Mr. Childs says that Grant's recent declarations comport with his private utterances several months ago, and he has no doubt that they express Grant's real sentiments. Mr. Halstead also reports Grant as talking in the same way when both were in Paris, and he believes the ex-President to be sincere. Indeed, there is no doubt that Grant has repeatedly given expression to his desire and purpose to retire from public life, and there is no good reason to discredit his sincerity. Admiral Ammen affirms positively that the General will take the Presidency of the American Nicaragua Inter-Ocean Canal Company, and devote his energy and ability to the construction of the highly important international work for which that company is to be organized.

The story of General Grant's active personal interest in the Nicaragua International Canal scheme may be briefly restated as follows:

He was educated at West Point as a military and civil engineer. When he became President, he set about to determine for himself the best route for a water connection between the Atlantic and Pacific, and to that end dispatched at different times several officers of the army and navy to examine the several proposed routes. His investigation led him to the conviction that the Nicaragua Ship Canal will be the most desirable for American interests. The San Juan River, connecting with the Nicaragua Lake, furnishes a natural water route most of the way across the isthmus, and there will be only a strip on the west side of some seven or eight miles wide to cut through. These conditions will render the work far cheaper than the proposed deep-cut canal upon a level with the sea across Panama. The Nicaragua route also saves some seven hundred or eight hundred miles of ocean travel as far as American ships are concerned — about three hundred miles on the Atlantic and four hundred or five hundred miles on the Pacific in going from an American Atlantic port to a Pacific port, or to China or Japan. The fact that the Nicaragua route will be longer than the Panama route is more than offset by the saving in time and cost by the reduced ocean voyage. General Grant's convictions in the matter were strengthened by the information he obtained during his European tour. At the conclusion of the Paris conference on the Isthmus Canal, Admiral Ammen wrote to General Grant a clear statement of the case, urging him to consent to serve as President of an American company for the Nicaragua route. In the same inclosure, Ammen sent Grant a letter he had received from an American politician, insisting that Grant must hold himself free to run as the Republican candidate for President, and also his (Ammen's) reply to that letter, in which the position was taken that Grant's services in the army and as President should exempt him from any further demands on the part of the public. About the time Grant had received these letters, he had the interview with the Viceroy of Tientsin, in which he stated emphatically that he would not again be a candidate for the Presidency of the United States, and shortly after he telegraphed Admiral Ammen the two words, " I approve." Admiral Ammen adds:

" These letters are of a private character, and I do not desire that they should go out to the public for the present. It is hardly necessary for me to assure you that the enterprise is in the hands of men whose reputation is unquestioned, and whose interest in promoting the work will be greatly increased now that they know that General Grant is committed to its success. You know my views on this subject. They were made public through my letter to the Secretary of State a month ago. It would not be proper for me to enter into details regarding the organization just at present. I may say, now that General Grant's wishes are known or will be known when the facts I have given you are made public, that a new company will be rapidly formed in this country which will include in its ranks the leading capitalists of our own and European nations, whose purpose will be to construct the inter-oceanic canal under the leadership of General Grant."

On the 8th of September, Admiral Ammen received a letter from General Grant in reply to his letter of July 2, in which the Admiral urged upon his friend the importance of allowing the use of his name as one of the corporators for an inter-oceanic canal company via Nicaragua, and, if elected by the corporators, to assent to the proposition to serve as president of the campany. Deeming it important to hear from General Grant at the earliest moment, he suggested that if the proposition met his approbation he should telegraph " I approve." General Grant acknowledges the receipt of the letter, and states that on August 7 he telegraphed as suggested, in order that it might be a sufficient basis for Admiral Ammen to take the preliminary steps for the beginning of a movement which would effect an organization for the building of a canal. He then adds that he has given the subject serious consideration, and after two days' deliberation he is fully convinced of the importance of acting in the matter promptly. He is of the opinion that great care should be exercised in the formation of the company, and, when properly organized, the necessary steps should be had to secure from the Nicaraguan Government such concessions as will make the undertaking a practical business scheme. When these are secured he would be glad of the opportunity to devote his attention to the work, and would accept the Presidency of the Company with the determination to accomplish the task, and to that end would exert himself to push the work as rapidly as the surveys and engineering skill of his assistants would permit. The letter merely repeats what the General has frequently said to Admiral Ammen upon the importance of obtaining the most favorable concessions from the Nicaraguan Government, in order that the enterprise might enlist capital and secure the protection of the United States. He makes no allusion to politics whatever in this letter.

He expects to reach San Francisco some time in September, and be in Philadelphia in November, when the business matter can be talked over leisurely, and definite arrangements made for inaugurating the company.

Exceptions have been taken to the statement made, that the quiet purpose General Grant had in view during his tour through Europe was to learn for himself what encouragement the construction of an inter-oceanic canal would receive from European capitalists, if the enterprise were in American hands. That statement was based upon the correspondence which General Grant had with a prominent officer of our army, and to whom he wrote fully from time to time during his stay in Europe as to what he heard and learned on the subject. In addition to this, just before he left the United States, he had a long interview with President Hayes, which was wholly devoted to this inter-oceanic canal project. He explained to his successor his personal interest in the scheme, and all he had done during his administration to forward the surveys. He regretted that he had not been able to accomplish more than to finish the numerous surveys, but thought that this perfect work was a great step in the direction of settling the route to be chosen, and that he was satisfied that the Nicaragua line was the feasible one upon which to build the canal. He commended Admiral Ammen's interest in the project, and told the President that he had recalled him from a foreign station and appointed him chief of the Bureau of Navigation in the navy department, that he might be in a position where he could give his zeal unlimited sway in furthering the ambition of both the Admiral and himself, which was to determine accurately and as speedily as possible the best route by which the two oceans could be connected for the purpose of commerce. He regretted that he had not been able to do more, but was glad that so much had been accomplished as would enable President Hayes to take up the subject in a manner that warranted the hope that, during his term of office, something would be done to practically utilize the labor of our surveying parties. He explained his reasons for wishing to impress upon President Hayes his great interest in the subject, and added that he should not lose sight of it during his travels in Europe. He was confident that his experience abroad would only confirm the belief that this great project should be distinctly American, and would have to be undertaken by American engineers. So favorably did the President receive the views of General Grant, that, when the news came of the decision of the Paris Congress, he was prepared to reiterate the idea of the General, that an inter-oceanic canal must be an American project and carried out by American enterprise, expanding the Monroe doctrine in a broader sense than had ever been thought of by President Monroe or John Quincy Adams, who is credited with having originated it.

In explanation of the apparent neglect of the matter, President Hayes said that he was expecting, from time to time, to hear of the results which General Grant would develop in his visit to Europe. One of the results undoubtedly was the necessity which the French engineers saw they were under to anticipate the American plan, by calling a congress, and determining before its meeting to select another route. Then came the invitations to our

Government to send delegates to the Paris Congress. The matter was officially considered by the Cabinet, and it was deemed advisable not to send delegates, but to have representatives, who should merely set forth the work already accomplished, and the conclusions formed by the Commission appointed during President Grant's administration upon the practicability of the Nicaragua route. It was argued that, if we sent delegates, our Government would be held by the decision of the Congress, which was to be avoided under all circumstances, and therefore they should not go in an official capacity. Time was consumed before the Congress met, and then followed Rear-Admiral Ammen's prompt action in acquainting General Grant with the exact situation of affairs, and the importance of securing his co-operation. "In other words," said President Hayes, "we have waited patiently for the time to come when General Grant would give shape to this project, and now we are prepared to do everything in our power to promote its success."

It is not surprising that General Grant has determined not to re-enter American political life. A man who has had so brilliant and successful a career as he has had must have an ambition to preserve it for history, and it would be a hazardous experiment to resume public responsibilities. Grant has the good judgment to understand this, and the poise and self-control to act upon it. He is now the "Great Undefeated"; a campaign for a third term might hand his name down to posterity as the "Great Defeated."

The Nicaragua International project opens to him a field worthy of his ability. His name and energy will enlist the necessary capital and influence to give the Americans the control of the inter-oceanic route, and the completion of such a scheme, shortening the route between the Atlantic and Pacific coasts, and between Europe and the Indies, by several thousand miles, will be an undertaking in which an ex-President of the United States may engage with credit to himself and honor to his country.

There is reason both to commend and to congratulate General Grant upon the stand he has taken. His fame is as radiant now as it ever can be, unless some new danger shall threaten the Republic during his life, and in that case the American people will turn to him with such unanimity and confidence that he will be in no doubt as to his duty.

The reception of General Grant upon his arrival on our shores promises to be a magnificent ovation, a spontaneous and enthusiastic reception by the people of California, without distinction of party. Our record would be incomplete without giving an account of the preparations in progress.

Mayor Bryant, of San Francisco, in compliance with the clearly expressed sentiment of the citizens of that city, has named a number of the prominent citizens to confer with the Board of Supervisors with a view of making preparations for a suitable reception to General Grant. The names chosen by the Mayor in this connection represent every shade of political opinion, as was fitting in arranging for a demonstration which is neither democratic nor republican in its character, but purely national and patriotic. The list embraces men of all parties — George C. Perkins, Samuel Wilson, W. H. L. Barnes, M. S. Latham, Horace Davis, Eugene Casserly and John H. Wise. Here we have republicans and democrats, men who stood up for the North during the civil war, and men who honestly sympathized with the Confederate cause. Yet now they are all willing to ignore political differences, and old party feuds, and to unite in doing honor to a distinguished American citizen, whose name is identified with the history of his country, and whose character and career are a part of her historical treasures. As is eminently fitting on such an occasion, all petty political animosities disappear for the time, and the most eminent citizens of San Francisco, without distinction of party, will unite in paying honor to their distinguished guest.

The watch for the steamer Tokio, at the Cliff House, will, upon sighting the masts of the steamer, flash the intelligence in every direction.

Gradually the demonstration undertaken by the citizens of San Francisco, in honor of General Grant, has swelled into proportions far beyond all original expectations. What was designed at the outset to be a welcome by the people of that city has developed into a grand ovation by the people of the State of California. Deputations from Oakland, Sacramento, San Jose, Vallejo, Petaluma, the far-off orange groves of Los Angeles, and a hundred other cities and towns all over the State, and even from some beyond the boundaries of California, will join in the demonstration.

The preparations for the event have been upon such a scale of magnificence as will throw all previous celebrations, not excepting that of the Centennial of American Independence, into the shade. The unanimity of feeling and sentiment that is manifested by all classes of the community, without regard to differences of political opinion or social condition, is something amazing, and altogether unprecedented. The soldiers who fought for the Union, and those who upheld the cause of the Confederacy, will march side by side in the procession in honor of the man of whom General Lee said: "I have no hesitation in declaring that, both as a gentleman and an organizer of victorious war, General Grant hath excelled all your most noted soldiers. He has exhibited more real greatness of mind, more consummate prudence from the outset, more heroic bravery, than anyone on your side."

A telegram from San Francisco, dated September 18, says:

"The preparations are now complete. All the necessary arrangements are perfected, and everything is ready for the reception of the illustrious guest."

The following is a summary of what may be expected upon the arrival of the Tokio, as telegraphed from San Francisco:

When the City of Tokio appears in the offing, she will first be signaled from Point Labos to the Merchant's Exchange, whence the news will be disseminated. The Bell Telephone Company and the American District Telegraph Company will be notified, and they will inform all their stations, and the individuals with whom they are connected, and the flag on the Exchange Building will be hoisted at once, and a line of flags stretched from the staff to the front and rear of the roof. The officer at Point Labos will hoist a designated signal, thereby informing the commander of Fort Point, and also communicate with the Merchants' Exchange, and Captain Low, who is in charge at the Fort, will hoist the American flag and also use signals. Alcatraz and Angel Island will be signaled from Fort Point, if necessary.

Signal guns will be fired from the Fort Alcatraz and Angel Island from the time of sighting the steamer, and national salutes when the Tokio passes from the upper and lower Casemate Batteries at the Fort Point, Alcatraz and Angel Island.

As soon as the news is received at the Merchants' Exchange, eleven taps will be given three times, with due intervals, from all the fire alarm bells in the city. Church bells will be rung, and there will be the blowing of steam whistles at discretion. As soon as the Tokio is sighted, the Committee of Reception, with Jesse Grant and Mr. Dent, will go on board the Millen Griffiths and meet her as far out as possible, to notify General Grant of the preparations being made to welcome him. If necessary, they will detain the Tokio until the marine procession can be duly formed. Two hours will be allowed after the first signal for the starting of the barge steamers of the escort.

The China will leave the Pacific Mail Steamship Company's dock, and returning, disembark her passengers there. The St. Paul and Ancon will leave from the foot of Broadway. Much criticism has been excited by the arrangement for towing the yachts, which, as they are the most picturesque craft on the bay, will scarcely be rigidly adhered to.

The Tokio will proceed to her anchorage just south of the usual line of the Bakland Ferry.

As soon as convenient after the first signal, the Executive Committee will meet Mayor Bryant in parlor 160, Palace Hotel, wearing red, white and blue rosettes, and in the dress already specified. From the hotel they will take carriages to the ferry steamer, City of Oakland, which will convey them to the Tokio as soon as sufficient time has elapsed for the St. Paul, China, Ancon and other steamers to have disembarked their passengers, who will take their proper places in the procession.

The Oakland will run alongside the Tokio, and General Grant and suite will be transferred to her. Mayor Bryant will deliver his brief speech of welcome. General Grant will reply. Introductions will be in order, and the guest and committee will land and take their places in carriages at the head of the procession.

Dennis Kearney, the "sand-lots" braggart, proposed, in one of his violent, intemperate speeches to the workingmen of San Francisco, to burn General Grant in effigy. Just why this agitator wished to burn the General in effigy is not plain. Referring to this subject, the Chicago *Inter Ocean* says:

"In 1861 General Grant was a workingman at Galena, in this State. He offered his services to the Governor of

Illinois in any capacity where he might be useful, and his offer was accepted. Through the long years that followed, the Galena workingman maintained a modest bearing, and never boasted of his deeds or selfishly obtruded himself upon the public. He became the foremost man of the age, the most remarkable soldier of modern times, the twice-chosen President of a great nation, and the honored guest of almost every government on earth; but still his modesty did not forsake him, and he never for a moment forgot that his country was a republic and that he was a citizen of that republic.

"He is now returning from his long absence abroad, and will soon land upon the shores of the country he did so much to save. The people with almost one accord desire to do him honor; but Dennis Kearney proposes to insult him and insult them by a public indignity at the place where General Grant disembarks, and on the day of his arrival.

"There are some things that try the patience of a law-abiding people very sorely, and this is one of them. We do not know where Mr. Kearney was during our long struggle for national life, or what his services were; but we take it for granted that they were hardly superior to those of General Grant, and that the people of San Francisco ought to be able to express their gratitude and admiration for a great soldier, a former comrade, and an ex-President of the republic, without meeting insult from Kearney or his followers. San Francisco but voices the feeling of the nation in extending its welcome to General Grant, and the insult which Dennis Kearney contemplates is an insult to the country which protects his own carcass from violence, which shields him in his freedom of speech and which makes it possible for him to threaten this indignity without being kicked into the Bay of San Francisco.

We hope Mr. Kearney will think better of his proposition, and abandon it. If he does not, the cause which he advocates will receive a blow in this country from which it will not soon recover. The workingmen of Chicago, who believe in the right of Americans to welcome a distinguished citizen without a public insult of this character, should meet and promptly denounce the proposed outrage."

It is not believed that this silly threat will be carried out, or that any one will dare attempt to carry it out. Even the most rash and infatuated of his deluded followers must realize by this time that Dennis perpetrated a monstrous blunder when he indulged in that outrageous and disgusting menace. There has never been in San Francisco a more unanimous and overwhelming manifestation of popular indignation than that which has been caused by Kearney's infamous threat. A New York *Herald* dispatch of September 14th, says:

"On the sand-lots, where Kearney belched forth the braggart threat that he would burn General Grant in effigy, Confederate and Federal will meet and salute the honored citizen, and in that number will be many workingmen themselves who have listened to Kearney for the last time. Numerous rumors are abroad about the workingmen's party demanding Kearney's abdication. To-day, Wallock, the former Vice-President of the party, tried to pass resolutions pledging the workingmen to unite with all loyal citizens in demonstrations to the honor of General Grant, but Kearney opposed them in a violent speech, still evincing his cowardice over the effigy business, yet without manliness enough to avow his folly. It has, however, been demonstrated at the sand-lots, to-day, that Kearney has given himself his death wound. San Francisco has wiped out the reproach of Kearneyism."

The wisest thing which the sand-lot agitator will do will be to get out of town and hide himself away in some rural seclusion, until the storm which he has evoked by his rashness and folly shall have passed over.

CHAPTER XX.

ARRIVAL OF GENERAL GRANT.

The steamer City of Tokio, in which General Grant embarked for his homeward voyage, arrived in the harbor of San Francisco on Saturday evening, September 20. The long-expectant people of San Francisco had been for some days prepared to give a suitable welcome to the illustrious soldier, statesman and traveler, who, though a simple citizen, occupies a larger space in the world's regard than the proudest contemporary heirs of ancient thrones. The General's arrival at San Francisco completes his journey "around the world." In San Francisco the excitement over his coming reached fever heat, and the reception given him was on a scale of magnificence never before seen in this country.

Every one, during the forenoon of Saturday, was on the tip-toe of expectation over his arrival. The city was densely crowded, especially the hotels. As the Tokio did not arrive early in the day, it was generally believed that the General would not arrive before Sunday. The Reception Committee were discussing the propriety of postponing the reception until Monday, when, at a signal given by the fire brigade that the City of Tokio was sighted, the fire bells rang, whistles sounded, and the thunder of cannon reverberated over the hills and harbor, and a general uproar was created.

Every kind of business was suspended, and people poured forth in such numbers that in a few minutes the

GENERAL ULYSSES S. GRANT.

FROM A PHOTOGRAPH TAKEN IN SAN FRANCISCO, IMMEDIATELY UPON HIS RETURN,
BY I. W. FABER.

streets were densely crowded with citizens flocking toward the ferry down Market street. The sun was shining brilliantly, and the effect upon the decorated buildings, arches and flags was very fine. The utmost good humor prevailed; and, as evening approached, the streets were lined with people, and business wholly suspended, and the city turned out.

Immediately on receipt of the intelligence that the steamer City of Tokio was nearing port, the Reception Committee, consisting of Frank M. Pixley, ex-Senator Cole, General Miller and R. B. Cornwall, repaired to the tug Millen Griffith, lying with steam up at the Pacific Mail dock, and at once started to meet the incoming steamer. The Millen Griffith stood well out to sea, and several miles outside the Heads met the City of Tokio coming in. The tug drew alongside, and the Executive Committee, quarantine officer and customs officials and a number of representatives of the press, boarded the steamer. No ceremony was observed, except a general shaking of hands, and after the committee had announced the object of their visit, and informed General Grant of the reception prepared for him, the conversation became general, as the City of Tokio continued on her course. Soon after the government steamer McPherson came alongside, and Major-General McDowell, commanding the Division of the Pacific, accompanied by his staff, boarded the Tokio and rejoined his old comrade in arms.

While this was transpiring the general Committee of Arrangements, with several thousand invited guests, assembled on board the large side-wheel Pacific Mail steamer China, and a number of smaller steamers, while tugs took squadrons of the San Francisco yacht clubs in tow and started down the channel.

In the meantime it seemed as though the whole population of the city — men, women and children — had sought positions from which a view of the naval pageant could be obtained. Every eminence commanding the channel was black with assembled thousands. Telegraph Hill was a living mass of human bodies, and the heights beyond Presidio, the Clay street hill, the sea wall at North Point, and every pier-head, were covered with spectators.

The sun was declining in the west as the steamers and yachts, gay with bunting, moved down the channel. Low clouds hung along the western horizon. Mount Tamaulipas and the distant mountains north of the bay were veiled in a mist, and Mission Hill and the seaward heights of the peninsula were shrouded in a fog, but the channel was unobstructed, and the bold outlines of the Golden Gate rose sharply against the sky, while the bay itself, with the islands and shores of Alameda and Contra Costa were bathed in sunlight. From every flagstaff in the city flags were flying, and the shipping along the city front was brilliantly decked with ensigns, festooned flags and streamers. The impatient crowds that covered the hilltops stood straining their eyes to catch the first glimpse of the Tokio. A hundred times the cry was raised, "There she comes," as chance arrivals came in view between the Heads.

It was half-past five o'clock when a puff of white smoke from seaward, from off the earth-works back of and above Fort Point, and the booming of a heavy gun, announced that the steamer was near at hand. Another and another followed in rapid succession. Fort Point next joined in the cannonade, firing with both casemate and barbette guns, and the battery at Lime Point added its thunders to the voice of welcome. In a few moments the entrance to the harbor was veiled in wreaths of smoke, and as the batteries of Angel Island, Black Point and Alcatraz opened fire in succession, the whole channel was soon shrouded in clouds from their rapid discharges. For some time the position of the approaching ship could not be discovered, but shortly before six o'clock the outlines of the huge hull of the City of Tokio loomed through the obscurity of smoke and rapidly approaching shades of evening, lit up by the flashes of guns, and in a few moments she glided into full view, surrounded by a fleet of steamers and tugs, gay with flags and crowded with guests, while the yacht squadron brought up the rear, festooned from deck to truck with brilliant bunting. Cheer after cheer burst from the assembled thousands as the vessels slowly rounded Telegraph Hill, and were taken up by the crowds on the wharves and rolled around the city front, hats and handkerchiefs being waived in the air. The United States steamer Monterey, lying in the stream, added the roar of her guns to the general welcome, and the screaming of hundreds of steam whistles announced that the City of Tokio had reached her anchorage.

The crowds that had assembled on the hills and along the city, now, with a common impulse, began to pour along toward the ferry landing at the foot of Market street, where General Grant was to land. The sidewalks were blocked with hurrying pedestrians, and the streets with carriages conveying the committees. The steamers and yachts made haste to land their passengers, and in a few minutes the vicinity of the ferry landing was literally jammed with people, extending for blocks along Market street and the water front just in front of the landing, the entrances to which were closed and guarded. A space was cleared by the police and marshals, into which hundreds of carriages for use of the guests were crowded, and outside of that space line after line of troops and civic organizations were ranged, while the outside constantly increasing throng surged and pressed, excited and enthusiastic, cheering at intervals, and waiting impatiently for a first glimpse at the city's honored guest. Within the gates of the ferry-house were assembled the gentlemen charged with the duty of the immediate reception of General Grant, the Board of Supervisors ranged on the left of the gangway, and Governor Irwin and staff, and the Executive Committee, consisting of Governor-elect Perkins, W. H. L. Barnes, Samuel Wilson, William T. Coleman, Tiburcio Parrott, J. P. Jackson, John McComb, John Rosenfeld, Claus Spreckels, John H. Wise, W. W. Montegu, occupied the right, Mayor Bryant taking his position about half way down the center of the gangway.

About seven o'clock General Grant landed from the ferryboat Oakland, according to arrangement. As soon as the General stepped from the ferry, leaning upon the arm of General John F. Miller, he was introduced to Mayor Bryant.

The Mayor, after acknowledging the introduction, addressed General Grant as follows:

"GENERAL GRANT: As Mayor of the city of San Francisco, I have the honor and pleasure to welcome you on your return to your native country. Some time has passed since you departed from the Atlantic shore to seek the relief which a long period in your country's service had made necessary, but during this absence the people of the United States have not forgotten you. They have read with intense interest the accounts of your voyage by sea and your travels by land around the world, and they have observed with great pleasure the honors you have received in the different countries which you have visited, and the universal recognition which your brilliant career as a soldier and American citizen has obtained. They have felt proud of you, and, at the same time, of their country, which you have so fully represented. And now, sir, you are again on your native soil, and the thousands who here greet you remember that your home was once in this city. This bay, these hills, the pleasant homes about us, are familiar to you. Great changes, it is true, have taken place. The young city is now the rival of cities which were old when its history began. But the men to whom this marvelous prosperity is due were in those early days your personal associates and friends, and many of them are here to-day, waiting anxiously to take you by the hand once more. It is a pleasing incident of your journey, that, leaving your country at the ancient city of Philadelphia, Mayor Stokely expressed the hope of that city for a safe journey and a happy return. It is now my privilege to express the joy of San Francisco that the hope of her elder sister has been realized. The city desires to receive you as an old and honored resident and friend returning after a long absence, and to extend to you such courtesies as may be agreeable to you; and, in obedience to such desire, which extends through all classes, I tender to you the freedom of the city and its hospitalities. In the short time allowed us we have arranged a reception in your honor, and ask that for an hour you will permit us to present our people to you, and we beg that, while you remain in the city, yourself and your family and your traveling companions will be its guests. Permit me, in conclusion, to express the wish of each and every one of us for the future happiness and prosperity of yourself and every member of your family."

General Grant replied as follows:

"MAYOR BRYANT: I thank you and the city of San Francisco for this cordial welcome, and I feel great pleasure in returning to California after a quarter of a century's absence. I shall be glad to participate in the procession."

General Grant was then escorted to the carriage in which he rode with the procession. Mrs. Grant occupied another carriage with Hon. Frank Pixley, and Jesse Grant and John Russell Young, of the party, occupied another carriage.

After a delay of over an hour at the landing, at 8 o'clock the Presidential party was turned over to the Executive

Committee having in charge the reception. Then the Grand Marshal gave out his orders, and the immense concourse of citizens, who were ready to take part in the procession, were summoned to their places, and formed in the following order:

Detachment of Police.
Grand Marshal—Major-General W. L. Elliott.
Chief of Staff—Col. A. W. Preston.
Chief Aids—S. M. Taylor, T. McGregor, G. W. Smiley, C. M. Leavy, W. Harney, Lieutenant Henry Hammond, Colonel F. O. Von Fritsch.
Aids to Grand Marshal—D. W. White, D. Roth, B. Seguine, W. G. Elliott, Thomas Magner, A. T. McGill, Dr. J. M. McNulty, T. H. Goodman, P. W. Ames, N. T. Messer, G. W. Wharton, J. H. Thompson, H. Beudel, W. H. Simond, E. Carlsen, Z. B. B. Adams, T. C. Otis, A. S. Hallidie, I. Simon, C. C. Bemis, G. A. Fisher, L. Wadham, P. J. White, A. Harlow, D. Bigley, J. Austin, George S. Ladd, A. Laver, J. P. Martin, W. B. Larzelere, M. Doane, General J. Harris, C. N. Ellenwood, C. H. Carter, M. Skelly, George A. Case, C. L. Tetream, Henry Devenve, C. Van Dyke Hubbard, Walter Turnbull, A. Wheeler.
Volunteer Officers, Soldiers and Sailors of the War of the Rebellion, including ex-Confederate Officers, Soldiers and Sailors.
Second Brigade, Brigadier-General John McComb.
Oakland Light Cavalry escort.
General Ulysses S. Grant and the Honorable A. J. Bryant, Mayor of San Francisco.
Veterans of the Mexican War, as Guard of Honor.
Board of Supervisors and Executive Committee.
Regular troops of the United States Army.
His Excellency, William Irwin, Governor of California, and Staff.
Major-General Irwin McDowell, commanding Military Division of the Pacific, and Staff.
Commodore E. R. Calhoun, United States Navy, and Staff.
Judges of the Supreme Court of the United States, United States Circuit Court, and District Judges of the Ninth Circuit.
Committee on Parade and Decoration.
United States Senators and Representatives to Congress.
Foreign Consuls, Officers of the United States Army and Navy, and Marine Corps.
Judges of the Supreme Court of California and the District Courts.
United States District Attorney and Assistants, Registrars in Bankruptcy.
United States Marshal and Deputies, Collector of Customs, Surveyor of the Port, Naval Officer, United States Treasurer and Surveyor-General, United States Collector of Internal Revenue, and Deputies, Post-Master and Deputies.
State Officers, City and County Officers.
Board of Trade.
Oakland City Authorities.
City Authorities of Stockton.
Board of Trustees of the City of Benicia.
Committee of Citizens of Sacramento.

University Battalion.
Garibaldi Guard, Italian Bersaglieri, Austrian Jaegers.
St. Patrick's Cadets, Italian Fishermen.
California Pioneers, Territorial Pioneers, Patriotic Sons of America.
Delegation of the Fire Department.
American District Telegraph Messenger Boys.
Union League, McClellan Legion, Occidental Club.
Second Ward Republican Club, Eureka Club, Mutual Benevolent Society, West Indian Benevolent Association.
Oakland Literary and Historical Society.
School Children.
Handel and Haydn Society.
Grant Invincibles.
Nelly Grant Blues.
Organizations Not Yet Reported.
Steam Calliope and Bells.

The line of march decided upon was from the Market Street wharf, up Market Street to Montgomery, thence to Montgomery Avenue over Kearney Street, back to Market again, up the north side of Market Street, countermarching down Market Street, south side, passing in review at New Montgomery Street. On reaching Sansome Street, the procession was instructed to disperse. Probably no city on this globe ever beheld a grander sight than was the procession of Saturday night.

The streets were made as bright as day by the electric lights, and the decorations, fantastic and beautiful as they were under the glare of the sun, looked still more pleasing, rich and elegant under the soft and mellow light of the great lanterns which the greatest of modern inventors has given us. In the line of march a thousand banners flapped in the evening breeze. The starry flag of our country was of course the most prominent among them, but every nation on earth was represented by her colors, and the flag of the "lost cause," side by side with the flag of the Union, was not the least conspicuous.

The Grand Marshal and his aids were mounted upon the best horses that this State could produce — charging steeds, with all the pride and spirit of the thoroughbred flowing through their veins. The average Californian is large, well-formed, and handsome. There was not an ill-looking man among the fifty who marched at the head of the procession. The volunteer officers and soldiers and sailors of the war of the rebellion, including those who had fought with and against the great commander, made a magnificent display, and were cheered along the entire line of march. The band played "Battle Cry of Freedom," and an occasional war-whoop, such as has not been heard since Lee surrendered, resounded through the streets of the city. The Second Brigade, N. G. C., commanded by General McComb, the editor of the *Alta*, who was one of the Argonaut's of '49, followed. Then came a light cavalry escort from the beautiful and prosperous city of Oakland, across the bay. Then came the hero, himself, at the side of whom sat the Mayor of San Francisco, the Hon. A. J. Bryant.

As the General passed, the crowds along the street fairly shook the buildings with their cheers. The heart of General Grant must have been more gratified than at any time since his name became a distinguished one in the history of his country. He has met with enthusiastic receptions and cheers before, but it was when his services to the country were fresher in the minds of the people, and at a time when the soul of the nation was full of gratitude to all her defenders. But that feeling, were it but temporary, as is too often the case, has had time to die out.

Fourteen years of peace has many a time before buried the hero of a war. The commander of the Northern armies in the great rebellion must have felt, after he had accomplished all that the country could ask for, that his memory would soon pale, too. For, had he not been taught from childhood that republics were ungrateful? If he ever feared a change in the sentiment of his fellow countrymen, that fear must have disappeared that night. He could not feel but that the heart of the nation was unchanged; that it would never cease to honor him, that it would never become ungenerous, cold or distant to the man of its choice, as two hundred thousand men, women and children cheered him until their throats were sore. He must have felt that this republic, at least, was not ungrateful to him. He bowed his head, a trifle grayer than it was when he left the country two years ago, and waved his hat left and right to the surging, crazy populace. Never for a moment from the time the procession left the landing until he was taken into the Palace Hotel did his interest in the festivities slacken, or his wonderful presence of mind desert him. He was at once a smiling, courteous, jolly-looking American citizen, and a distinguished, dignified and honored American statesman and soldier. His bearing pleased the multitude, and it cheered again.

The great throng of people assembled in the vicinity of the hotel remained unbroken for nearly two hours after the passage of the General under the triumphal arch. The cheering was continuous on the outside, and the cries for a speech could be heard in the room where the General was receiving a select number of gentlemen. The cries for a speech became so loud that one of the members of the Executive Committee finally suggested to the General that he show himself to the populace, at least, and he consented.

What the General said when he appeared will never be known, for no human voice could be distinguished where fifty thousand throats were being tested, and a mighty swell of sounds drowned everything save the sounds themselves. The General appreciated the situation, saw that he was "bottled up," so to speak, and retired from the fight a defeated and defended man. He was kept out of his bed by visitors as long as decency would allow, and, after the excitement had subsided a little, was allowed to resume control of his own actions again. Although he must have been greatly fatigued, he did not show the slightest impatience during the trying ordeal of hand-shaking which he passed through.

There was not a prouder city in America that night than San Francisco. She felt that she had distinguished herself by honoring General Grant. She had not had the experience of eastern cities, but she had done fully as well as any of them could do. The General might meet with receptions grander than they had given him as he journeys toward the Atlantic, but he could not meet with a heartier one.

At 11 o'clock a chorus of about two hundred voices sang an anthem of welcome at the Palace Hotel. It was in the nature of a serenade, and was well rendered and received.

During Sunday General Grant made no public appearance other than to take a ride in the Golden Gate Park with Mayor Bryant. In the evening a crowd was drawn to the corridors of the Palace Hotel, but the General did not show himself.

The future movements of General Grant and party embrace a grand entertainment at the California Theatre on Monday, September 22. On Tuesday evening he will attend a reception given by Mayor Bryant. On Wednesday or Thursday night the grand banquet at Bellmont will be given. The following is one of the poems to be read at this banquet. It is, in its way, a novelty, and was written by the famous poet-scout, John Wallace Crawford. It will be read with a number of others.

>   Dear Gineral, I ain't no great scollar,
>   An' I never done nothin' to brag,
>   'Cept this: I wor one of the outfit
>   As fought for our star-spangled flag.
>
>   An' to-day, while yer toasted by scholars,
>   An' by big bugs as made a great noise,
>   Why, I thought it the squar' thing to write yer,
>   An' chip in a word for yer boys.

'Cos, yer see, we ain't got the colatral
  Nor the larnin' to dish it up right;
But ye'll find, should there be any trouble,
  Our boys are still ready ter fight.

As for you, if they didn't correll yer,
  You'd shake comrades' hands that yer seed,
An' that's why I wanted ter tell yer
  We'll just take the will for the deed.

But ye're back, an' the men of all nations
  Were proud to do honor ter yer;
An' I reckon, Ulysses, yer told 'em
  Ye were proud of yer comrades in blue.

For you, we are sure, of all others,
  Remembered our boys in the ranks
Who foliered yer inter the battle,
  An' gallantly guarded the flanks.

So, welcome! a thousand times welcome!
  Our land is ablaze with delight;
Our people give thanks for yer safety;
  Yer comrades are happy to-night.

We know yer are wearied an' tuckered,
  But, seein' as ye're a new comer,
Ye'll Grant us one glance on this line, if
  In reading it takes yer all summer.

The banquet at which this poem will be read promises to be one of the most brilliant affairs of the kind that California has ever had. The millionaires, the beauty and the talent of the Golden State, will be represented. It is said that at one table in the Bellmont mansion, the old home of Ralston, men will sit down whose aggregate fortunes will foot up nearly $200,000,000. Among them will be John W. Mackey, the bonanza king, and Messrs. Jones, Sharon, Flood, Fair, and other men of vast wealth who reside in that city. But the entertainment will not be confined to representatives of wealth alone, for every branch of the arts, sciences and industries of the Pacific States will be ably represented at the supper.

On the 30th he will go to the Yosemite Valley, remaining there about ten days. Then he will return to San Francisco and leave for Oregon. After visiting Portland, the Dalles, and other places, he will pay a visit to the Bonanza mines at Virginia City, where he will be the guest of his friend, John W. Mackey, the millionaire. After this he will go straight to Chicago, where he will attend the Army and Navy Re-union, November 5, then to St. Louis, and then to his old home at Galena.

Dispatches from Oregon, Nevada, Yosemite Valley and other parts of the country show that the grand welcome extended to the General at San Francisco will be but the forerunner of those yet grander that await him. His coming recalls the splendor of his military achievements. The popular heart quickens to welcome the hero of the war, who out of disaster organized victory.

The Romans were accustomed to give their generals a triumphal march on their return from successful campaigns of conquest by the sword. The whole world has united in making General Grant's trip around the world a triumphal march, and that, too, in honor at once of military and pacific records. The foremost soldier of this generation, to say the least, he was a promoter of good will among the nations, and especially of the policy of arbitration in international disputes. These two contrasting, yet not inconsistent, records, conspired to make him honored, and we might almost say revered, from Liverpool to Yokohama.

The journey, which is now over so far as concerns the outside world, was absolutely unique. History furnishes no parallel to it. It can hardly be possible for him to reach his final destination without being the recipient of most flattering ovations. There was nothing partisan about the reception at San Francisco. There were no distinctions of republican and democrat. Even the Confederate soldiers on the coast joined cordially in the honors, and well they might. Never did the victor show such magnanimity as Grant at Appomattox. When General Lee directed the horses in his command turned over, General Grant interrupted: "No, no; no horses, General Lee. Your people will need them all for plowing." That little incident, told by General Lee himself, fairly illustrates the policy he pursued then and ever afterward toward the South. The people of the United States might well join as one man in expression of affectionate respect for "the wanderer returned."

As General Grant's tour around the world is unprecedented in the annals of history, so his deportment appears to have been unexampled in its freedom from the least alloy of vanity. Surprised by the magnificent ovation in San Francisco, he embraced his old classmate and fellow soldier, General McDowell, in the presence of the eager multitude, with the warmth and abandon of a boy. A hundred ovations from the rulers and peoples of the Old World seem not to have lifted him a hair's-breadth in his own estimation. It seems to be as impossible to "turn his head" as it was during the Rebellion to turn the flank of one of his armies. The attentions showered upon him abroad have been gratefully received and acknowledged as marks of honor to his country, but personally regarded only as pleasing incidents of a journey undertaken with a purpose — the purpose of seeing the Old World and studying mankind, their habits, social customs and political institutions. From this purpose he was no more to be swerved by the blandishments of power than by the dictates of a false generosity before Fort Donaldson, when, to General Buckner's request for a commission to arrange terms of capitulation, he wrote: "*No terms other than an unconditional and immediate surrender can be accepted. I propose to move immediately upon your works.*"

Obstinacy and modesty are not often combined in the same character. With obstinacy there is usually much self-assertion, as in the case of Andrew Jackson. It is also true that the armor of an obstinate character is not infrequently successfully assailed by flattery. But General Grant is as impervious to flattery as he is free from the vice of self-assertion. The career of General Grant is scarcely less marvelous and far more illustrious than that of Napoleon I. But, while with Napoleon it was, "I am the State," with Grant it is, "I was an humble instrument in the hands of the people." Napoleon's confidence in himself bordered closely on belief in his own infallibility; but General Grant, in his letter accepting a second nomination to the Presidency, said, humbly: "Experience may guide me in avoiding mistakes inevitable with novices in all professions and in all occupations." Such a confession is rare in a state paper, and it shows the courage of an integrity fearless of results. To an unconspicuous friend General Grant once sent this message: "I am now convinced that I did you injustice. I regret it, and, if I ever have an opportunity, I will recompensate you." In this characteristic of daring to confess an error, whether in a state paper or in a communication to an humble friend, General Grant resembles Lincoln. The martyr President had no pride of opinion where public interest or private right was concerned; neither has General Grant. This quality is by no means peculiar to all great men. It is found only in characters which, intrinsically grand, are rendered almost sublime by their simplicity. Writing of General Grant in 1865, the New York *World* made this estimate of his character as a military man:

"When the mass of men look upon such a character, they may learn a truer respect for themselves and each other; they are taught by it that *high qualities and great abilities* are consistent with the simplicity of taste, contempt for parade, and plainness of manners with which direct and earnest men have a strong and natural sympathy. * * * Grant stands *pre-eminent* among all the generals who have served in this war in the completeness of his final results. * * * If anybody is so obtuse or wrong-headed as to see nothing great in General Grant beyond his marvelous tenacity of will, let that doubter explain, if he can, how it has happened that, since Grant rose to high command, this quality has always been exerted in conspicuous energy precisely at the point on which everything in his whole sphere of operations hinged. There has been no display of great qualities on small occasions; no expenditure of herculean effort to accomplish objects not of the first magnitude. It is only a very *clear-sighted and a very comprehensive mind* that could always thus have laid the whole emphasis of an indomitable soul so precisely on the emphatic place."

General Grant's series of receptions beyond the oceans was the logical result of this excellent estimate of his character as developed chiefly in his military career. Let it be admitted that General Grant's remarkable journey is merely evidence of the hero-worship to which mankind is so strongly addicted. Still it must be conceded that all the world does not unite to crown a man a hero without good cause. Napoleon ended his brilliant career miserably, a prisoner at St. Helena, held there by the fears and hates of all Europe.

General Grant, having enjoyed the highest honor the nation can bestow, returns from his triumphal tour around the world, to be made the recipient of a welcome as hearty, fraternal and tender as the subdued cry of joy with which the father embraces his first-born child returning from a long absence.

In the presence of this grand demonstration, this spontaneous outpouring of patriotism and affection, partisanship is hushed, and the American people, as a unit, receive back to their bosom and confidence the beloved General who beat back the waves of rebellion and saved the nation.

The welcome extended to him comes up from the hearts

of the people. It is expressive of the gratitude of the
nation — of the popular confidence in the tried captain in
war and leader in times of perilous civil commotion. It is
not confined to the Pacific slope. It is not confined to this
day or generation. The place which he to-day holds in the
hearts of the people is that which he will hold in the hearts
of the American people while the nation exists.

Perhaps nothing will better illustrate the high pitch of
public enthusiasm in San Francisco so much as the following extracts from the three leading newspapers there. The
Chronicle had a column leader headed, "Hail to the Chief,"
from which the following is selected:

"The jubilant peal of bells throughout the city, the shrill
scream of a hundred steam whistles, and the reverberated
thunders of artillery from the batteries of the fortresses that
guard our harbor and the Golden Gate, have announced the
arrival of San Francisco's expected guest. He returns to
this country after receiving the homage of the civilized
world, crowned with such honors as have never before been
bestowed by foreign nations upon any citizen of the United
States. Regarded everywhere as a great representative
American, the testimony of admiration and respect paid him
at every stage of his journey redound to the honor of his
country, with which, throughout the world, his name and
fame and illustrious deeds are identified. Thus the nation
itself derives fresh prestige from the renown and achievements of its most distinguished living citizen, who, without
official position, occupying a private station, with no favors
to bestow and no patronage to dispense, will be welcomed
home by his grateful countrymen with such tokens of confidence and enthusiastic affection as have never been exhibited by Americans to any citizen, or any illustrious visitor
from abroad, since the days of Washington and Lafayette;
and it is fitting that this should be so, for, assuredly, when
this generation shall have passed away, when the fierce pas-

sions engendered by a bitter strife shall have been tranquilized, the voices of prejudice and calumny that have been so loud against his great name will be hushed forever, and the verdict of impartial history will be that, since the foundation of our government, no American, however bright the halo that time has cast around his memory, has deserved better of his country than Ulysses S. Grant."

The *Call*, after reviewing the glorious war record of the General, and quoting his modest, magnanimous language to General Sherman, when the rank of General of the Army was conferred upon him, goes on to say:

"What picture of grandeur and simplicity of character is presented in this career; what magnanimity, what patriotism, what cool judgment, what clear-sighted sagacity, what singleness of purpose, what subordination of all egotistical and selfish considerations to duty and the public good! Here was a man who sought no personal ends, who had none of the airs of little greatness, who abhorred fuss and feathers, who never attitudinized before the public, or courted popularity by melodramatic vices; a man such as Tennyson has described the 'Iron Duke' to be — moderate, resolute, our greatest, yet with least picture foremost, captain of his time, rich in saving common-sense, and, as the greatest only are, in his simplicity sublime."

The *Alta Californian*, General McComb's paper, had a double-leaded editorial, as follows:

"The Tokio has come, and so has Grant, at present the foremost man of the nation, and whom San Francisco and California are pleased and happy to honor. He left this State more than a quarter of a century ago, when it was but a crude country, known chiefly for its gold and climate, and for the inrushing hosts of 'fresh-lipped men,' seeking gold, and anticipating a speedy return to the old homesteads. He left us and went to the East. Since then the scarcely more than a territory with a population of miners has become almost an Empire State, summing her population by the million, and boasting of her prolific soil, richer in its productions of breadstuffs than it had formerly been in its crop of gold; and General Grant cannot but be surprised, if not astonished, as he sees the evidences here of that intelligence, industry and confidence which have changed a sand bank into a city of a third of a million people. We noticed him as he rode through the streets last night over solid pavements, which he left as little better than sand and mud, as his eyes were seeking some well known and remembered shanty or abode of an ancient construction. But instead they followed up the facades of palace-like structures, their windows brilliant with illuminations of gaslight, electricity, and ladies' eyes from the Orient isles, just awakened from their dreams of centuries, and rushing forward in the race of a new civilization with the vim and vigor of a new-born people. He comes back to the scenes of his young manhood, to a people who have already built up here a State and city and civilization which will compare with any he has visited while girding the world about; and this people have shown their delight at his presence by a welcome which comes from the heart, as a tribute to the foremost man of the nation. And so say we all."

Sixteen pages are here added to correct omission in paging the illustrations.

THE PROCESSION OF MILITIA AND CITIZENS PASSING UP MONTGOMERY STREET TO WASHINGTON STREET, SAN FRANCISCO.

APPENDIX.

On the morning of September 23d the Methodist Conference, which had been in session for several days, called in a body on General and Mrs. Grant. Bishop Haven made an address of welcome, and a formal presentation to the General and Mrs. Grant followed. An hour was taken up before the presentation was concluded. The preparations made around the new city hall for the formal presentation of General and Mrs. Grant to the citizens of San Francisco were of an elaborate character. The Mayor's office, which was used as a reception room, was handsomely draped with flags. At half-past twelve o'clock a crowd began to assemble in front of the McAllister street entrance, and shortly after the passage, steps and every point of advantage were thronged with people. At the Market street side of the building there was also a large crowd awaiting the arrival of the veterans to fire salutes from the sand lots. As the hour for the reception approached, the crowd grew denser, filling up the corridors and entrances of the building. A squad of thirty policemen was detailed to keep the passages open. At a quarter to one the veterans — Federal and Confederate — arrived upon the "sand lots," taking up a position near Market street. The first gun was fired at ten minutes to one, the other thirty-seven guns succeeding each other at intervals of one minute. The people massed along the line of Market street. After the salute the veterans fell into line, entered the corridor, and marching down its length countermarched and took up a position awaiting the arrival of the General. A few minutes later the ex-President and party arrived at the McAllister street entrance and were greeted with cheers. The windows of the houses opposite and the housetops were crowded with people who waved handkerchiefs and sent up cheer after cheer as the party alighted. As the General proceeded along the pavement, escorted by the Mayor, the enthusiasm broke out afresh along the corridor. Running from the lower entrance to the Mayor's office were ranged the veterans, posted in two lines. Their commander, Colonel Lyons, stepped forward as General Grant and the Mayor reached the corridor, and said: "Now, boys, three cheers for your old commander!" The veterans responded with enthusiastic hurrahs. The party then proceeded to the Mayor's office, where a committee of ladies were waiting to receive Mrs. Grant and assist her. Mrs. Grant did not arrive until some time after the General, who took up his position in the centre of the room. The southeast corner of the room was assigned to the ladies.

Directions were then issued to admit the multitude. After a few of the invited guests had been presented to the General the crowd filed in, shook hands with the city's guests, and passed out at the Market street entrance after presentation to Mrs. Grant. All the afternoon a constant stream of visitors poured through the apartments, and all were greeted with a hearty shake of the hand, the General not adopting the suggestion of the Mayor that hand shaking might be dispensed with on account of the great rush, and expressing his opinion that he could "fight it out on that line all summer."

Previous to the salute on the "sand lots," the General reviewed the veterans at their rendezvous in Mechanics' Pavilion.

On the morning of the 24th General Grant visited the Produce Exchange, and witnessed a grand display of cereals of the Pacific coast, which no city in the world could probably excel. He was much gratified at the exhibition, and expressed in a few words his congratulations. After that, accompanied by General McDowell, a government tug conveyed him to all the forts in the bay, where he was received with military honors. Upon landing at Black Point, General McDowell's headquarters, the party was greeted by a salute, and the troops were drawn up in line to receive General Grant. At General McDowell's residence a collation was prepared, and a formal reception tendered to the distinguished guest. Among the prominent citizens present were Governor Irwin and Governor-elect Perkins, ex-Governor Stanford, ex-Governor Low, Senator Booth, Senator Sharon, ex-Senator Stewart, Justice S. J. Field, Judge Ogden Hoffman, D. O. Mills, and other distinguished citizens, generally accompanied by their ladies.

Before the reception began, the General was visited by the chief representatives of the Chinese community, headed by their Consul and the Chinese Vice-Consul, who read the following congratulatory welcome:

"GENERAL—We feel deeply gratified that we were permitted to meet you face to face, and express to you how sincerely we appreciate the fact that you have visited our country, and consulted with its rulers, and become familiar with the important features of both government and people. It gives unbounded pleasure to learn that you received a warm welcome, commensurate with the high esteem your noble deeds fully entitled you to at the hands of the Chinese authorities and people. Let us hope that your visit will have a tendency to bring the people of the oldest and youngest nations in still closer friendly and commercial relations. The Chinese of California join with your countrymen in the acclaim, 'Welcome home,' and add the sentiments that you may live long, and, like the great

Washington, be first in war, first in peace, and first in the hearts of your countrymen."

To this was added by the dignitaries:

"To GENERAL GRANT—We join our voices to prolong the pean which has girdled the earth, wafted o'er seas and continents. Praises to the warrior and statesman most graciously presented by the Chinese of California."

The General replied:

"GENTLEMEN—I am very glad to meet the representatives of the Chinese community, and receive this address. I have, as you say, just returned from a visit to your country. It was a most interesting visit—one that I shall always remember, and especially because of the kindness and hospitality shown me by the people and the authorities of China. For that I am grateful, and glad of an opportunity of expressing that gratitude so soon after my arrival at home. I hope that the remark you make about China breaking down the seclusion in which she has been shrouded for ages will prove true in all senses, and that China will continue to draw near to her the sympathy and the trade of the civilized world. The future of China will largely depend upon her policy in this respect. A liberal policy will enlarge your commerce, and confer great commercial advantages upon the outside world. I hope that America will have a large share in this. Again I thank you."

After presenting the address Colonel Be— said that Mrs. Grant had done more to break down the spirit of domestic exclusiveness that reigned in China than the warrior had done, by the honors shown her in Tientsin. He begged that she would accept a small casket of ivory as a memento of the occasion. The reception lasted till 6 o'clock; the party returned to the city, and in the evening attended Baldwin's theater.

The announcement that General Grant would visit the Baldwin theater sufficed to pack the building to its utmost capacity. The proscenium box designed for the occupancy of the General and his party, was handsomely decorated with flowers and national colors. The programme for the evening comprised the "balcony" and other scenes from "Romeo and Juliet," and "Diplomacy." General Grant and party arrived shortly before 9 o'clock, between the acts. A great crowd gathered at the entrance, cheering vociferously as he alighted. On making his appearance in the box the audience rose to their feet and cheered and applauded for several minutes, while the orchestra struck up "See, the Conquering Hero Comes," followed by a medley of national airs, accented by discharges of musketry from behind the scenes.

On the 25th General Grant visited Oakland, the residence of thousands of San Francisco merchants, and the second largest city on the Pacific Coast. The General was received with a salute of thirty-eight guns, the fire whistles, profusion of bunting, masses of people, and display of flowers of all descriptions at once announced that an ovation was in store for him. Mayor Andrus, of Oakland, who was formerly a carpenter, received General Grant with the following words:

"GENERAL GRANT: Your merited ovations have encircled the world; they have been as grand and varied as the nations that have offered them; and yet, along them all there has been no more earnest, sincere, and cordial welcome than the city of Oakland now extends to you—this pre-eminently city of homes and of families, of husbands and wives, of parents and children, of churches and schools. There is no tie more sacred and lasting than that of the family. At the family altar the fires of liberty are first kindled, and there patriotism is born. Love of home, of kindred, and of country is the source and foundation of our welcome to you—defender of our firesides and families."

The procession then formed and moved along Broadway. The enthusiasm of the populace was unbounded.

At the entrance of Clay and Fourteenth street 5,000 school children greeted General Grant, who alighted from the carriage, passing down one row of children and up another, while the little ones literally bestrewed his path with flowers, the High School singers chanting a glee, and Grant's Des Moines words, "The free schools are the promoters of that intelligence which is to produce us a free nation," hanging high above his head. All the girls wore white dresses, tastefully trimmed, and, as the General re-entered his carriage they cast showers of floral tributes at his feet. General Grant was visibly affected, and every now and then would stretch forth his hands to embrace some very small child who would approach timidly with her bouquet. Not alone the schools of Oakland, but those of Haywards, San Leandro, Alameda, and other suburban points were represented. A prettier display could not have been made. Garlands of red, white and blue streamers stretched across the street, while the national colors floated high above all on the city hall.

As the procession passed on again along Broadway and Twelfth streets, the words, "Welcome and Honor the Brave," in red geraniums and white candy tufts, were visible at more than a dozen houses. Soon after 1 o'clock the pavilion was reached, and General Grant, with the Mayor, took seats in a canopied dias in the center of the building, which was tastefully decorated with festoons, bouquets, wreaths and plumes of Pampas grass. On the wall facing the General were the words, "Honor to Grant," and over them the coat of arms of Illinois, surrounded by a wreath, while beneath and around were shields representing the other thirty-seven states. The First Regiment band played "Hail Columbia," and the Oakland Cavalry, Mexican War Veterans, and National Guard Infantry, together with representatives of Oakland's renowned Fire Department, marched in and around the halls.

About two o'clock the procession moved on to Tubb's Hotel, where an excellent lunch was spread. The arrangements were admirable. Every person entering the lunch-room had a ticket, and thus all confusion was avoided. At a quarter to four o'clock Mayor Andrus rose and proposed General Grant's health, after which, all speeches being taken as read or spoken, the party adjourned. The General entered a carriage with six horses, and was taken round the Fruitvale Road, toward the Mills seminary, the young ladies from which had come out in full force. Returning at 4:15 to the hotel, the carriages proceeded to Badger's Park, where an old sailors' and soldiers' camp-fire took place. Ex-President Grant was escorted to a platform, on which were ranged tables with pork and beans, coffee in camp-kettles, tin cups, platters and spoons, iron table-knives, tobacco and clay pipes, the camp-fire lights being visible from the platform. The Federal and Confederate veterans had here united to do him honor, and many were those who stepped up to the General, and reminded him of "Auld Lang Syne." About five o'clock Major L. B. Edwards silenced the cheering crowd, and said: "Veterans, allow me to introduce General Grant." The hero of Appomattox then stepped forward, and, amid breathless silence, spoke as follows:

GENTLEMEN OF THE TWO ARMIES AND NAVIES: I am very proud of the welcome you have given me. I am particularly happy to see the good-will and cordiality existing between the soldiers of the two armies, and I have an enduring faith that it will always be so. I hope we shall never have a foreign war; but, if we do, I doubt not you and your children will be found fighting on the same side, and against a common enemy. I hope the day will never come when it will be necessary for us to take up arms again. I am perfectly satisfied, from travel around the world, that no foreign power desires to come in conflict with us, should any difficulty unfortunately arise, that they will always be willing to submit to friendly arbitration, and that being all that we can desire, I feel confident America has a long career of peace and prosperity before her.

The enthusiasm created by this speech was indescribable. One veteran shouted, "That's the longest speech Grant ever made." A brief walk through the park terminated the proceedings, and at 5:40 General Grant took the train at Clinton station and returned to the city, thanking Mayor Andrus and W. W. Crane, of the arrangements committee, for their admirably organized reception.

The Mayor had previously handed General Grant a richly-mounted morocco case containing the freedom of the city, embossed on parchment; and armed with this, and both hands full of bouquets presented by children, the General returned at seven o'clock, with Shipping Commisioner Stephenson and United States District Judge Hoffman, to the Palace hotel. He made a brief appearance at the press banquet, then being given to John Russell Young, of the New York *Herald*.

In reply to a toast, General Grant responded, briefly expressing his gratification at the welcome awarded him in California, concluding with "The good opinion of my countrymen is dearer to me than the praise of all the world beside."

After attending the press banquet, the General and party went to the carnival at Mechanics' Pavilion, where more than ten thousand persons were assembled. Colonel Andrews, of the diamond palace, who organized this ball, signalized the occasion by presenting Mrs. Grant with a bouquet composed of the flowers indigenous to the various countries she passed through in her tour around the world. These flowers were placed in regular order, start-

GRAND ARCH ERECTED ON NEW MONTGOMERY STREET, SAN FRANCISCO.

ing from Philadelphia and ending with San Francisco. The bouquet-holder, five inches long, was of pure California gold, and inlaid with quartz, and a collection of other metals found on this coast. It was a costly present, and will undoubtedly be esteemed as a precious memento of the visit to California. Mechanics' Pavilion was superbly decorated with several hundred large stars, the fountains playing in the center space, opposite the box reserved for the Grant party. This box was magnificently arranged with flowers and flags, satin programmes being provided for the honored guests. Seven different committees, each composed of nine persons, were to decide upon the best-dressed lady, the best-dressed gentleman, and the most original character, lady and gentleman; the best sustained character, the best-formed lady, the handsomest blonde, the handsomest brunette, the best waltzer, the tallest lady, the shortest lady, the fattest lady, the leanest lady, the handsomest lady, the homeliest gentleman, the best-dressed girl, the best-dressed boy, and the best-sustained character, boy and girl. The prizes were seventy-nine in number. The only ladies' committee was that selected to decide on the children's prizes. At 9 o'clock commenced the grand march around the pavilion, a miniature mardi gras. Subsequent arrangements comprised a prize waltz at 11, at which only the competitors were allowed on the floor, forty soldiers of the First Regiment drilling shortly afterwards in the General's presence, and Haverly's Minstrels playing before him half an hour later. Midnight was fixed for the announcement and distribution of prizes. The supper arrangements were in the hands of the Baldwin and Palace hotel chiefs. Forty ushers officiated, and the whole thing was conducted on a scale of completeness rare even in older communities than San Francisco.

On the 26th General Grant and party left on a special

train for San Jose. As it passed San Mateo, the cadets of St. Matthew's academy were drawn up on a platform at "present arms." The whole population of the village behind them greeted the train with cheers. Flags were flying all over the town. The train arrived at San Jose at 11:30 A. M. There was an immense crowd at the depot, and the train was met by Mayor Archer and the committee. Upon stepping from the train, the Mayor, in a brief address, welcomed General Grant, who, in response, said:

MR. MAYOR AND LADIES AND GENTLEMEN — I am glad to see you all, and thank you for this kind reception. You speak of my reception by the sovereigns and princes of the world. I am prouder of this than all — this kindness from the sovereign people of my own country. Ladies and gentlemen, I thank you.

General Grant then, accompanied by Mayor Archer, entered a barouche drawn by four magnificent horses. The other guests followed, and the procession proceeded through the principal streets of the city, halting at the court-house, where one thousand school children stood, and bedecked the General's carriage with flowers, shortly afterwards uniting in singing "America." San Jose was festooned and decorated as befitted a rural country seat, the emblems being appropriate and handsome.

At 1 o'clock the Fair Grounds were reached, and an exhibition of fine stock was paraded before the party. A magnificent Australian horse was among the animals exhibited. The Mexican veterans were then introduced to Grant, and it was remarked, "You see, General, these veterans still live." "Yes," replied Grant: "most of those now living are older than I am but, when the last of them has dropped off, then I must be thinking of departing."

At precisely 2 o'clock began the trotting match between

Gov. Leland Stanford's Occident and Daniel Cook's horse Graves — the latter horse winning in three straight heats, time 2:20, 2:20, 2:23.

Shortly after 4 o'clock the party re-entered the carriages and drove to Santa Clara, passing the old Jesuit Seminary, built in 1773, and inspecting the splendid grounds of J. P. Pierce, formerly owned by Gen. William Lent, of Bodie Bonanza fame. While the carriages were passing through Santa Clara on the way back, a number of tanners in everyday working-clothes turned out and greeted their ex-fellow-craftsman.

San Jose, where all business was suspended, was again reached at 5 o'clock, and here the illustrious guests were vouchsafed a season of rest. As the evening drew on, ex-President Grant received a number of citizens at the Auzerias house, and at 8 o'clock took place the grand banquet, 100 gentlemen dining with Gen. Grant, and twenty ladies with Mrs. Grant. The party returned to San Francisco after 10 o'clock. The whole affair, under the auspices of Mayor Archer, Gov. Woods, T. O. Houghton, and G. F. Baker, was a grand success, and San Jose will undoubtedly remain enshrined in the General's memory in connection with his reception.

On the 27th the General visited the San Francisco Stock and Exchange Board. Pine street between Sansome and Montgomery was thronged with people in anticipation of his visit. The hall and lobby were densely crowded, a lane for entrance being kept open by the police. The Board-room which is a work of art in itself, was tastefully decorated with flowers, ferns and smilax. Business opened at the usual hour and soon afterwards the ex-President and his party arrived. President Peckham led his guests to the centre of the arena, those sacred precincts usually reserved exclusively for the brokers, and there, in an excellently worded speech, introduced the General to his fellow-brokers. The bulls and bears cheered, and shouted in unison for once in their lives, and then Mr. Peckham conducted the visitors to a dias canopied with rich flags of California silk, sprigs of evergreens, ferns and verdure in general. This dias, a little to the callers' right, commanded a full view of the proceedings, which thereupon re-commenced in good earnest. There was the ordinary hustling and jostling of the apparently infuriated maniacs, as they strove to obtain their number of shares, at five or ten cents below the market rates. Gen. Grant was much amused as he beheld them swaying to and fro. Sellers in pursuit of buyers, and *vice versa*. The General remained until the close of the Comstock call and then departed, escorted to the door by President Peckham, and Vice-President Lissak. The passage and steps were lined with ladies and gentlemen, forming an improvised guard of honor, till the General reached his carriage.

On leaving the Stock Board, Gen. Grant visited the Anglo-California bank, and subsequently the California market.

About 3 o'clock he accompanied Mrs. Grant to the California theatre to witness the last acts of the "Color Guard," and at night they were again at the same theater, with General and Mrs. McDowell and Mayor and Mrs. Bryant. The performance consisted of an opera "never," or, perhaps more correctly, "hardly ever," played in the East, in which Emelie Melville played "Josephine," and Frank Unger played the "Admiral's" part. After "Sir Joseph" had vocally narrated a wholly unfamiliar story, he was so loudly applauded that, removing his hat and turning to the mezzanino box to his left, he sang:

> "And now, as the ruler of the Queen's navee,
> I am pleased our honored guest to see,
> Who has sailed the briny ocean o'er,
> But has never seen the good ship "Pinafore."

He's the only man in the world, do you see,
That has never met the ruler of the Queen's navee."

Whereat the audience applauded enthusiastically, and Mrs. Grant smiled. As there were no physicians about, it is impossible to give a diagnosis of Grant's symptoms after seeing " Pinafore." Suffice it to say he is still an American, and " its greatly to his credit."

At 10 o'clock the General visited the camp-fires of the Federal and Confederate soldiers and sailors, at Mechanics' Pavilion. Only ex-soldiers were admitted to the floor, and it was estimated there were five thousand of these present, while the galleries were crowded with spectators. Not only coffee and hard-tack, but beer, cheese, crackers and plug tobacco formed prominent features of the entertainment. There seemed to be a lack of organization at this camp-fire. Invitations were issued by thousands in excess of the capacity of the building. The great idea of the managers seemed to have been a big demonstration, and to that end tickets were distributed right and left, admitting "bearer and ladies." The doors appear to have been placed in charge of irresponsible youngsters, who received those best qualified to enter, with fixed bayonets. Occasionally a squad of men would enliven the scene by charging the surging crowd, and those without tickets seemed, on the whole, to stand a better chance of getting in than those with tickets.

Crowds forced their way into the place until the floor must have contained from 7,000 to 8,000 persons. They climbed on chairs, on tables, and many were the breakdowns and numerous the screams. Meanwhile the sentinel barred the doors, and thus excluded men like Gen. McComb and Marcus Boruck. The veterans outside were indignant at being left out, grew uproarious, and some got step-ladders and scaled the walls, entering by the windows. Then sentinels from within battened down the windows, while policemen withdrew the ladders. Fortunately no one was injured, but a very bad feeling prevailed. On the estrade beneath which General Grant was seated were tents, cannon, and masses of bunting. General Grant, in reply to his health, expressed his pleasure at being among the veterans. All the orators who followed bellowed forth their remarks, and a lady orator, reciting some heroic verses, pitched her voice at about sixty-horse power. Ladies and invited guests fared no better than any one else. It was a scene notably never to be forgotten by those present.

General Grant's reception of public school children, at Woodward's Gardens, on the 29th, was the most enthusiastic ovation he had yet received. Before eleven o'clock not less than twenty thousand youngsters swarmed the Gardens, while the street cars were jammed, and thousands making their way to the rendezvous on foot. At 11:30 the General's arrival was heralded by a discharge of cannon, and the vociferous cheers of Lincoln school boys, who were drawn up at the entrance as a guard of honor. Escorted by the Board of Education, he walked between the files of children, crowded in every avenue, to the pavillion, where a stage had been arranged for the reception of the party. Ten thousand boys and girls were crowded in the building, and as the General made his appearance, the cheers, stamping, whistling and "cat calling" were deafening, while from every part of the building bouquets rained upon the stage and the occupants. After a few minutes the enthusiastic youngsters were reduced to comparative quiet, when Mr. Heister, President of the Board of Education, addressed General Grant as follows:

"GENERAL GRANT: Your loyalty to the public school system of the United States has impelled the school children of San Francisco to extend this special greeting. The children, their parents, and the Board of

Education, recognize in you a true and fearless friend of popular education, and are proud to look you in the face and take you by the hand. Allow me, sir, to present you to the children and teachers connected with the public schools of San Francisco. These happy faces will tell their own story."

Another uproarious outbreak of applause followed, after which the General addressed his audience to the following effect:

"It is a gratifying sight to witness this evidence of educational privileges afforded by this young city. The crowds gathered inside and outside this building indicate that every child of an age fit for school is provided for. When education is universally diffused we may feel assured of the permanency and perpetuity of our institutions. The greatest danger to our people grows out of ignorance, and this evidence of universality of education is the best guarantee of your loyalty to American principles."

More appropriate remarks could not have been made, and they deserve to be treasured up by the people as the embodiment of a great and incalculably important truth. No tampering with popular education should be tolerated in any part of the country. In the large cities the danger of this is very considerable.

At the conclusion of his remarks, Gen. Grant and the Board of Education made their way out of the building, and, following the winding avenues of the gardens, proceeded to the great amphitheatre on the other side of the grounds. Children by thousands lined the walks, and pelted the party with bouquets, while shrill cheers and the continual rattle of drums with which each class was provided, created a bedlam of noise. On reaching the amphitheatre, where at least 20,000 boys and girls were massed, the storm of floral missiles became heavier, and, on gaining the stand near the exit, the party proceeded, thoroughly dilapidated and crushed in appearance.

The General took a seat at the front of the platform, and the assembled throngs then marched by to enable each one to obtain a good look at him. As the enthusiastic throng surged by, hundreds of hands were thrust out for a passing shake, and the demand for autographs was altogether beyond the General's ability to supply. The shower of flowers was kept up, despite the efforts of teachers and members of the Board to stay it, and the party was almost overwhelmed with these tributes. At least 20,000 children were present, and, though the teachers were able to maintain reasonably good order, it was impossible to restrain the holiday spirits of the mass within the bounds of decorum.

At 1 o'clock the young legions were still marching past in review with drums, banners, mottoes, and flags, while the General maintained his position and faced the constant fire of bouquets with his accustomed tenacity and pluck.

At 2 o'clock the General returned to the Palace hotel and wrote some private letters. At 4 o'clock he, with his family, drove down to Milbrae, where he dined with a small party at D. O. Mills' house, returning late in the evening to the Palace hotel.

Gen. Grant and party left Oakland wharf for the Yosemite Valley at 8:30 A. M., Sept. 30th. The wharf was covered with a dense mass of people. As the train moved off three cheers were given. The General occupied a special drawing-room car, and accompanying him were Mrs. Grant, U. S. Grant, Jr., G. W. Dent, Gen. John F. Miller wife, and daughter; Miss Flora Sharon, Miss Jennie Flood, and John Russell Young. Throngs of people were gathered at various way stations. At Martinez, a salute was

VIEW OF THE PARLOR AND DINING ROOM OCCUPIED BY GENERAL GRANT AT THE PALACE HOTEL.

fired, and near the depot the houses were decorated with the National colors. At Antioch, school children were drawn up in line upon the depot platform, and waved their handkerchiefs as the train moved past. At Stockton, the General was welcomed by Mayor Hyat and escorted along a line composed of military companies, the Stockton fire department, Union veterans, and veterans of the Mexican war, to a carriage drawn by four white horses. The procession then formed and traversed the principal streets until the court house was reached, where there was a concourse of several thousand school girls dressed in white, who saluted the visitors by waving 'kerchiefs and clapping their hands. After passing the procession in review the General was driven to the Yosemite house, where he received the prominent citizens.

At the conclusion of the reception at the Yosemite house, the General retired to his apartments. At 4 o'clock the distinguished guest and his party entered the dining-room to partake of a collation offered by the leading citizens. After viands had been discussed, Gen. Grant, in reply to an address of welcome by Mayor Hyat, said:

"GENTLEMEN: I am very much pleased to be back in your city once more, which I have not seen in twenty-five years. I am very much obliged for the hearty reception at your hands, and will say that, though I have been here several times, I have never stayed so long before. When I was on the Coast before I visited Stockton six times, but this is the first time a roof ever sheltered me in your city. Among many gentlemen I met to-day was one who was sure he knew me at Knight's Ferry in 1849. While I would not dispute the gentleman's word, I was never on this side of the Rockies previous to 1852. I was only three times at Knight's Ferry in 1852 and 1854, and think some one must have been personating me there.

[Loud laughter.] However, I am glad to meet you to-day, and can never henceforth deny being in Stockton in 1879."

Dr. G. A. Shurtleff and State Senator Hudson, spoke briefly, after which the company broke up. The General and party left at 7:20 for the Yosemite, via Madeira, which point they reached after midnight, and remaining in the sleeping-car during the night, started by stage directly after breakfast.

Previous to his departure from Madeira, the General had a brief reception with citizens and residents of Fresno City, and among the number who congratulated him upon his return to his native land were several Union and Confederate veterans. At Fresno Flat he received further congratulatory calls from Fresno County veterans. The coach which conveyed the party was handsomely decorated. Thirty-six horses were used in the trip, six changes being made. Upon the arrival of the distinguished party at Clarke's Station they were met at the stage and welcomed by J. B. Bruce and S. Washburn, and escorted to the parlor of the hotel. The Mariposa brass band had crossed the mountains, a distance of thirty-six miles, to join in the ceremonies, playing "Hail to the Chief." Dinner followed, after which an informal reception was held in the hotel parlors. The General was serenaded, and retired at an early hour.

On the morning of October 3d the General and party entered the Yosemite Valley from Clark's Station, the General and Mrs. Grant occupying the front seat of the "coach and six," with the driver, fully determined to view the delightful scenery, which the visitors said surpassed anything they had observed on the Rhine or in Switzerland. Mrs. Grant was even more pleased than the ex-President, Monroe, the driver, stating to a bystander, " I never hauled a lady over these roads who was so enthusiastic."

At Lookout Point, whence there is a view of the distant San Joaquin Valley and the hazy Coast Range, the stage stopped awhile. At Inspiration Point, whence a sight is had of the whole valley, the point of view in some of Hill's pictures, the stage again stopped, and every one alighted. The General mounted the top of the stage, and sat for some time viewing the splendid prospect, and evidently appreciated fully its grandeur and beauty. When all were satisfied, the stage drove down the winding road and on to Bernard's seven miles distant. While going through the valley, the General allowed no object of interest to escape him. He noted all the domes, roads and peaks, and asked Monroe about hights and distances. The rest were equally delighted. At the lower bridge over the Merced, a dozen blasts had been set, which were fired in succession as the stage was passing, unrolling terrific echoes. Nearly all the population of the valley, including the tourists, were on horseback, skurrying all the roads, at the windows, or on the porches of the hotels, which were hung with flags and liberally adorned with boughs of evergreen. As the stage approached Leidig's, the proprietor of the hotel came out and tendered the hospitalities of his place to the party. At Black's the guests were on the front porch. The stage dashed on up to Bernard's, which had been trimmed with evergreens and flags, and in many ways given a gala appearance, though Mr. Bernard had but a few hours' notice of the honor intended him. As the vehicle neared the steps, the Mariposa band, brought here for the purpose, woke the echoes of the surrounding cliffs with "Hail to the Chief." Some cheering followed, and there was a general rush from the neighboring buildings toward the hotel. The party were hardly recognizable for dust. There were few greetings; all were at once shown to their rooms.

The following days were spent in exploring and visiting principal points of interest — Glacier Point, Sentinel

Dome, El Capitan, the Three Graces, the Three Brothers, Half Dome, North Dome and Yosemite Rock. After spending a few as delightful days as the General had yet seen, he, with his party returned to San Francisco, via of the Big Trees and Mariposa and Merced. Arriving by special train on the morning of the 7th, after spending a few hours in the city, the General and party left early in the afternoon, with Senator Sharon, for Belmont, where, on the following evening, a grand reception was tendered him by Senator Sharon. This fete at Belmont was the most brilliant gathering that had ever taken place on the Pacific Coast. The richness of ladies' costumes, the magnificence of internal decorations, and the brilliancy of the superb grounds, illuminated by thousands of Chinese lanterns, render the scene one of unsurpassed splendor. The preparations were worthy of Senator Sharon's reputation. Nothing had been omitted to give enjoyment to the guests, and lend eclat to the occasion. The picture gallery of the museum had been transformed into a vast banqueting-room, where, among other preparations for the visitors, figured one hundred baskets of champagne and fifteen thousand Eastern oysters. Three trains took the city guests down. The first, advertised to start at 7:30, left fifteen minutes earlier, owing to the number of persons waiting on the platform. Some of these had arrived at the depot as early as six o'clock.

Belmont was reached in about an hour, and there abundance of vehicles had been provided to convey the party to the mansion about a mile distant. Considering that each train consisted of ten cars, it will be understood this was no slight task. Numbers of ladies carried their toilets in baskets with them, so that the uninitiated might have thought them bent on a picnic excursion.

Nearly 2,500 guests were present. Dancing and banqueting were the order of the evening.

At 11 o'clock the following morning, Gen. Grant returned to the city, and at 12 o'clock was received by the Chamber of Commerce and Board of Trade at the Merchants' Exchange Building, in a manner exhibiting the greatest respect and admiration for the illustrious man. The two mercantile societies attended in full force. The rooms of the Chamber of Commerce were decorated in a gorgeous style for the occasion. Gen. Grant was escorted to the platform from the Chairman's desk by the Hon. J. P. Jones, and was met there by Governor-elect Perkins, the President of the Chamber of Commerce, and Jacob T. Taber, President of the Board of Trade. Mr. Jones introduced the General with these words:

"Presidents and Members of the Chamber of Commerce and Board of Trade: I have the honor of introducing a most distinguished citizen of the United States, honored at home and abroad, Gen. Ulysses S. Grant."

After enthusiastic cheers, Gov. Perkins made the following address of welcome.

"General Grant: The merchants of San Francisco, represented by the Chamber of Commerce and Board of Trade, have the honor to pay you their respects, desiring, as merchants, to express their appreciation of your services to our common country, recognizing the fact that universal prosperity is best promoted by domestic and national intercourse, and that through commerce and trade the nations of the world are brought in most intimate relations, to which great end peace is absolutely essential. They regard you as the great chieftain whose military genius restored domestic peace and civil law throughout our country. In the hour of triumph your magnanimity did not allow you to forget that the good-will of all our countrymen was as necessary as the success of the armies under your command. When intrusted with the highest office in the gift of the people you proved to the world how war could be avoided and peace secured by friendly arbitration. We regard you as an honorable representative of our Republican citizenship, more especially to be so esteemed because, although successful in our war you have so fully appreciated the advantages of peace, while the honors bestowed upon you by foreign potentates have never caused you to swerve from the path of Republican simplicity and true American citizenship. The merchants of San Francisco welcome you to your native land, wishing you a happy return to your home, many years of happiness, and an old age which shall command the continued honor and the reverence of your countrymen."

General Grant replied as follows:

"GENTLEMEN OF THE CHAMBER OF COMMERCE AND BOARD OF TRADE OF SAN FRANCISCO: I hardly know how to express my gratification at the kind and cordial reception you, and not only you, but the people in every place in the State and city that I have visited have given me. There is no question but that the prosperity of the country depends upon the class of people you gentlemen represent. It requires just such people as we see here to make it profitable for a man to labor with his hands; also, to make profits for the whole nation. Anybody who has been over the world as I have, has seen the degradation to which laborers have fallen without some head to guide them into the right course. In other countries the laborer is sunk far below the poorest and most abject citizen of this country. We have not a healthy person in America who is willing to work, who is not better off than the best laborers in any other country. We need not be envious or jealous of any country in the world."

Applause and hand shaking followed.

A scroll on which the address of the two associations was engrossed in a handsome manner, signed by the presidents and secretaries, was presented to the General, enclosed in a beautiful cylindrical case of Russia leather, with this inscription embossed in gold letters:

"To General U. S. Grant, from the Chamber of Commerce and Board of Trade of San Francisco."

After leaving the Merchants' Exchange the General drove to the Palace Hotel, and thence to Front street wharf, where a vast crowd had gathered to see him depart on the steamer St. Paul for Oregon.

The steamer and all other shipping in the vicinity were gayly decorated. As General Grant went aboard a beautiful American flag was run up to the masthead. There was no cheering among the people, who seemed sorry to have him go. Many distinguished people went on board to bid him good-by. The party from the tug, besides the General and his wife, included, among others, U. S. Grant, Jr., Miss Jennie Flood, ex-Governor Low, wife and daughter, Senators J. P. Jones and A. A. Sargent, Lieutenant Otis, John Russell Young, Louis Sloss, Captain Niebaum, Martin Bulger, Fred. Kabe, C. F. Crocker and Mrs. McDowell and daughter.

At 2:15 the St. Paul swung gracefully out from the wharf, amid waving of handkerchiefs, quiet farewells, and admiring remarks of the people.

The steamer St. Paul, with General Grant and party on board, arrived at Portland, Oregon, on the 14th, the citizens' committee and members of the press, having joined the General at Vancouver. Just before leaving the wharf at the latter place for Portland, the Honorable H. W. Corbitt, chairman of the committee of reception, made the following address of welcome:

GENERAL GRANT: I take pleasure in introducing to you this committee, and these distinguished officers and gentlemen. We come to welcome you, and tender you the hospitalities of the citizens of Portland; also to the friends that accompany you. We evidently do not now welcome the Lieutenant that left us twenty-six years ago; neither can we receive you as a Lieutenant-General, or as a General of the once great army of the Republic, nor as President of these once more united States; but we do receive you as a pre-eminently distinguished citizen, who has enjoyed all these honors, who has won so many laurels, and who has worn them with so much modesty and grace. It will be the pleasing duty of another to express more fully our sentiments, at the general reception tendered you Wednesday evening at our new pavilion, where we shall have the pleasure of presenting to you friends and citizens from all parts of the State and the adjoining territory, who desire personally to testify their appreciation of you and your valuable services to the nation. You are welcome, thrice welcome, to Oregon. It will give us pleasure to escort you to our city at your earliest convenience, where we hope to make your stay pleasant and agreeable.

General Grant replied in a few words, simply expressing his thanks.

At least twenty thousand persons had assembled in the vicinity of the dock, awaiting the arrival of the distinguished guest, amid the thunders of artillery, the clangor of bells and the screaming of whistles, the St. Paul came alongside her dock.

General Grant was met at the wharf by Mayor Thompson, who said: "General Grant, as Mayor of the city of Portland, on behalf of the citizens of this city, we extend to you welcome, and tender you the hospitalities of Portland."

General Grant simply replied: "Mayor Thompson, I thank you."

The party were then escorted to carriages in waiting. The procession, under charge of Grand Marshal Colonel

POPULAR OVATION TO THE EX-PRESIDENT WHILE PASSING BALDWIN'S HOTEL, SAN FRANCISCO.

McCracken, at once formed in the following order: Grand Marshal and aides, Twenty-first Regimental band, carriage containing General Grant, Mayor D. P. Thompson, Governor W. W. Thayer, and General O. O. Howard. The first division consisted of forty carriages containing prominent visitors and officials, Federal, State and military. Following these came carriages containing officers of the Municipal Government of Portland and East Portland, members of the Washington Territorial Legislature, and many other invited guests from abroad. The second division comprised various military companies, United States troops, and four militia companies of this city. The third division consisted of the entire Fire Department of Portland, five companies with their steam engines gayly trimmed and decked with flags and ribbons. The fourth division was composed of members of the Grand Army, civic societies and citizens.

The procession arriving opposite the Central school building, were met by two thousand or more school children, who were ranged along the sidewalk, dressed in gay holiday attire. When the carriage containing General Grant came opposite the centre column, the pupils' procession halted. Four little girls, each bearing in her hand a large and elegant bouquet, stepped forward from the front line and advanced to the carriage in which General Grant sat, and presented him with the floral offerings. He took the tributes and bowed his thanks. When the quartet withdrew and resumed their places in line, two thousand childish voices immediately struck up the National anthem "America." At the close of the singing, the Twenty-first Regiment band responded, and rendered an appropriate air.

The procession then resumed its line of march. These exercises were witnessed by many thousands, and constituted one of the most pleasing and attractive episodes of the day's demonstration. Continuing the line line of march, the procession moved down Morrison to Front, and down that street to the Clarendon hotel, where General Grant and party stopped. The city was attired in gay holiday trappings. Front and First streets presented to the eye a perfect wilderness of flags and bunting for nearly a mile. Shipping in the port displayed a profusion of flags and streamers on every hand. Enthusiasm assumed a form quite extravagant. For hours before the procession moved, and during the time it was in motion, the streets were jammed for many blocks by eager and enthusiastic thousands. At times the streets were so crowded that the procession moved with difficulty.

In the evening the General visited the Mechanics' Pavillion, and attended a ball, at which one thousand persons were present. Here he met many old comrades in arms.

Late in the afternoon of the 15th, General Grant visited, by special invitation, several public schools in the city in company with Mayor Thompson. Short addresses were made by the children, to which the General responded. On taking his leave Grant was heartily cheered by the children.

In the evening he was honored with a reception at the Cascades, which was an enthusiastic and fitting tribute. Eight thousand persons were present. Ex-Senator Corbitt welcomed the distinguished party, and was followed by Judge Strong in a most hearty manner. General Grant responded at some length, alluding to his early residence and acquaintance on the Pacific Coast. He concluded:

"In your remarks you have alluded to the struggles of the past. I am glad that they are at an end. It never was a pleasure to me that they had a beginning. The result has left us a nation to be proud of, strong at home, and respected abroad. Our reputation has extended beyond the civilized nations; it has penetrated even in the less civilized parts of the earth. In my travels I have noticed that foreign nations appear to respect us more than we respect ourselves. I have noticed the grandeur at which we have been estimated by other powers, and their judgments should give us a higher estimate of our own greatness. They recognize that poverty, as they understand it, is not known with us. And the man of comparative affluence, with them, is sometimes no better clad or fed than our pauper. Nowhere are there better elements of success than on the Pacific Coast. Here those who fought on opposite sides during the war are now peacefully associated together in a country of which they all have the same right to be proud. I thank the people again, through you, Judge Strong, for this reception."

At the conclusion of the response, General Grant was presented to the citizens. He remained at the Pavillion about an hour, during which time thousands came forward and shook hands with the guest. On leaving the Pavillion the party proceeded to the Newmarket theatre to witness a rendition of the military drama, " Ours."

On the 16th, the General and party visited Salem. They were met at the depot by a large crowd of citizens. Members of the Common Council acted as a committee of reception, and were in waiting at the depot. Mayor G. W. Gray met the Ex-President at the platform, and delivered a brief address of welcome, to which a very short response was made. The entire party then entered carriages and proceeded to the hotel. As the procession filed past the court house, General Grant was saluted by pupils with hearty cheers. The procession marched on to the hotel, and reaching which, the party alighted from the carriages and were conducted into the parlor. An address of welcome was delivered by S. C. Adams, to which the Ex-President responded in brief and fitting terms. The doors of the parlor of the hotel were thrown open, and a general public reception followed. The reception lasted about an hour, during which time over one thousand persons passed through the room and were presented to General Grant and the other members of the party. At two o'clock the reception ended, and the guests were escorted to the dining room, where a collation was spread; about one hundred and fifty persons sat down to the lunch. Among the party were Governor Thayer, R. P. Earhart, Secretary of State, and other State officials. Lunch being over, the party took carriages, and, preceded by bands, marched to the depot, and took a special train for Portland at four o'clock. Salem was handsomely decorated in honor of the event, and great enthusiasm was manifested. General Grant stated that it was the first time he had ever visited the city, and expressed himself as being gratified with its handsome, thrifty appearance, and the hearty welcome accorded him.

At Gervais the citizens assembled at the depot, and gave General Grant a hearty welcome. Flags were displayed from many buildings. The train stopped for only a few minutes. At Aurora a like enthusiastic welcome was given. At Oregon City over one thousand persons had gathered at the depot, and received him with deafening cheers and strains of music. Mayor Randall appeared on the platform, and in a few appropriate words welcomed the General, who responded by thanking him. The train stopped but a few moments, but hundreds improved the opportunity to shake hands with him.

In the evening he attended a grand sacred concert at Turn Halle, given by the Handel and Hayden Society, and the following day the entire party sailed on the steamer St. Paul for San Francisco.

On the morning of October 21, the steamer St. Paul, with General Grant and party on board, arrived at San Francisco, and the same evening they attended a reception at the residence of Charles Crocker. The house was elegantly decorated for the occasion, and a brilliant company numbering nearly eight hundred were present.

On the 22d, the General and party visited Vallejo, inspected the Mare Island works, and then boarded the train for Sacramento, arriving there at one o'clock, P. M. All along the route they were heartily greeted at stations, and a large concourse of people was at the depot when the train arrived at Sacramento. A procession was formed which competely filled the neighboring streets. Gov. Irwin and Mayor Turner escorted their distinguished visitor to a carriage; after marching through the principal streets, the procession halted at the Capitol, where the Hon. Henry Edgerton delivered an address of welcome.

General Grant responded, thanking the people of the city and State for their warm reception, which was alike at every place on the coast which he had visited. He said: "Of all the hospitality bestowed, all the honor conferred, there has been nothing so grateful to my heart as the receptions I have received at the hands of the people here. I would not say what has been done abroad. It has been all that could be done for mortal, but it has not been done for me. It has been done for the people whom I see before me, — for the people of a great country that is recognized abroad as one of the greatest countries of the world. If we all — every one of us — could see other countries, as I have seen them, we would all make better citizens, or, at least, the average of our citizens would be better."

In the evening, General Grant received in the Assembly room, and Mrs. Grant in the Senate Chamber. Twenty thousand people were in and about the building, which, with the grounds, was brilliantly illuminated with calcium lights, while fireworks were generally displayed during the passage of the party to and from the Capitol. Nine thousand people shook hands with the General.

At ten o'clock the following morning, General Grant and invited guests visited the Grammar school to meet the veteran soldiers and sailors and their families. He was introduced, and informally passed around the room, shaking hands with them. The children filed in and sang "America."

After lunch, the party proceeded to Pioneer Hall, where General Grant was presented with a certificate of membership in the Sacramento Society of Pioneers. The General returned thanks for the honor conferred, stating that he supposed his early participation in the struggles which made California a State had made him eligible as a Pioneer. He paid a warm compliment to California and her people.

Members of the society and their families were then presented.

The next place visited was Agricultural Park, where a grand military review and sham battle took place. General Grant there, as elsewhere during the day, entered with zest and spirit into the entertainment.

General and Mrs. Grant returned to San Francisco on the 24th. At 2 P. M., the General visited the hall of the California Pioneers, and was made a member; thence to the Mexican War Veteran's headquarters, and dined with Mayor Bryant. In the evening he attended the Pioneers' banquet at the Lick House.

Notwithstanding the lengthy stay of General Grant on the Pacific coast, the excitement continued as intense as when he arrived five weeks before. Every thing possible was done to show him personal respect; and even more than this was done to express to the distinguished guest a national appreciation of his past services to his country. People of all classes and political parties vied with each other in their attentions showered upon him. At the residences of Senator Sharon, Charles Crocker, Mayor Bryant and at the Palace Hotel, elegant entertainments were given him, and everywhere even more than imperial honors were paid him. He was made an honorary member of the California Pioneers, of the St. Andrews, Caledonian, Army and Navy Clubs, and, in fact, of every organization of note on the coast. Wherever he appeared he was greeted by an ovation. Fifty thousand people attended his public reception at the City Hall, while at Sacramento and Oakland the citizens turned out en masse on the occasion of his visit to those cities. Elegant, costly testimonials of regard were presented to the General and Mrs. Grant from admiring friends.

In the afternoon of the 25th, the General and party, with Mayor Bryant, Senator Sharon, and Charles Crocker attended an exhibition trot at Oakland, where a large crowd greeted the ex-President with cheers. The first trot was a field of eight trotters; between the heats St. Julian was brought out to beat the best time made by Rarus. At the word he passed under the wire at a square trot, and for the entire mile made not a slip, finishing in the unprecedented time of 2:12¾. The result was received with prolonged cheering, the General joining with the rest.

In the evening, before his departure for Nevada, a banquet, more elegant, more numerously attended than any ever before given in that city, was tendered him at the Palace Hotel. Invitations were issued to the representative men of the coast, and the result was that the banqueting hall was a perfect congress of learned and honored men. The banquet was held in the magnificent dining rooms of the hotel. These were gorgeously decorated for the occasion. Rare exotics and flowering plants were there in full bloom, the odor from which permeated the air. Mayor Bryant presided, and toasted the guest of the evening in an appropriate speech, to which the General responded as follows:

GENTLEMEN OF SAN FRANCISCO: The unbounded hospitality and cordiality with which I have been received since I first put my foot on the soil of California has taken deep root in my heart. It was more than I could have expected; and, while it entailed some little fatigue at times, I assure you I have been grateful for it. I have previously been in California and on the Pacific coast, but have been away a quarter of a century, and when I landed here the last time, I found that none of the pioneers had grown old, but if I should remain away another quarter of a century, I might be compelled to confess that some of you had grown old; and I want to see you again in your prime and youth.

Gentlemen, in taking my departure, I want to thank you all for the farewell reception given me this evening, and to express the hope that whether or not I am to have the happiness ever to visit your city again, I shall, at least, meet one and all of you elsewhere, and if it should not be in this life, that it may be in a better country.

At half past eleven o'clock at night, the General's party bade good-bye. The company took a special train for Nevada, being accompanied to the depot by many citizens.

General Grant's party arrived at Truckee station at about noon the following day. From this point they visited Lake Tahoe — one of the most beautiful places on the Pacific coast.

On arrival at the lake, the party was met by a number of ladies and gentlemen from Carson. General Edwards made a brief speech of welcome, after which the party took passage on a small steamer, and in an hour were landed at Glenbrook, where an open train, with two engines richly decorated, climbed up the mountain side, giving the guests a most magnificent view of the forest lake.

At Summit, only three miles distant from the lake, as the bird flies, but nine by rail, carriages were in waiting, and Hank Monk, of Horace Greeley notoriety, with four prancing greys, drove the General to the capitol of Nevada. On arrival there, the city seemed in a blaze. On the principal streets were bonfires twenty feet apart, which gave pleasant warmth to the welcome.

On the 27th, the General visited Virginia City. As the train approached the city, they were greeted with a chorus of whistles, salutes, firing, anvils and shouts. There was a terrific jam at the depot. Mayor Young delivered an address of welcome, extending the warm hospitality of a mining town, the hearts of whose people would on acquaintance prove, like the mines, to be warmer as they are explored. General Grant replied with a bow and word of acknowledgment. He was escorted to a carriage, the military forming a hollow square about him; the procession moving through the principal streets, they were joined by a large delegation from Carson. At the Savage office he reviewed the people, of whom there was an immense concourse in line. In response to persistent calls, the ex-President spoke briefly, thanking the citizens for the reception.

A sumptous lunch was served at 4 o'clock, after which the Mexican, Union, and Confederate veterans were received.

In the evening a general reception was given and largely attended, followed by a grand banquet.

On the 28th the General and party, as the guest of Mr. Mackey, visited the famous Consolidated Virginia Mine. After donning miners' costumes they entered the three-decked cage; the ladies of the party taking the middle deck. The cage was lowered very slowly to the 1750 feet level. After inspecting the drifts, the ladies of the party returned to the surface, while the rest of the party went down to the 2150 feet station, and thence to the 2340 feet station. After thoroughly exploring the different drifts, they returned to the surface. General Grant expressed himself as highly pleased with his visit.

While passing through the Assay Office a solid brick o gold and silver, four inches long and two and a half wide was presented to Mrs. Grant, with the following engraved inscription:

Souvenir of the Consolidated Virginia Mine to
Mrs. General U. S. GRANT.
Virginia City, Nev., Oct. 27, 1879.

Colonel Fair presented to Mrs. Grant a small phial with the inscription:

One-half of my first day's work in California,
1849.

Its value in dust did not probably exceed $40, but as a souvenir it was beyond price. Before changing their miners' dresses a splendid photograph was taken of the party. After bathing and dressing they were driven to the stamp and pan mills, where they finished a most instructive day's work. In the evening the General visited the hall of the Pacific Coast Pioneers, where he was made an honorary member. A badge of office and the credentials of the society were given him. He was introduced by Dr. Harris. Colonel Robert Taylor delivered the address, to which the General responded as follows:

MR. PRESIDENT, LADIES AND GENTLEMEN, MEMBERS OF THE SOCIETY OF PACIFIC COAST PIONEERS: Your President has already said what I feel in appreciation of my reception here. Nothing which I received abroad was such a source of pleasure to me. I do not mean by that to disparage my greeting abroad. It was honest and hearty, and showed the high esteem felt for our country by foreign nations. It would have been quite different a quarter of a

century ago. Now we are regarded as the most powerful nation on the earth. We have much which European nations have not—that is, we have a population which as yet does not threaten to crowd any inhabited district or exhaust the productiveness of the soil. We have an extensive soil and immense undeveloped resources to exhaust before our population will become so dense as to make the raising of sufficient to live on a serious problem. In this respect we have great promise for the future. The fact of the matter is, we are more thought of abroad than we think of ourselves. Yet, at the same time, we think considerably of ourselves, and we are a little conceited over our advantages. Newspapers and politicians, however, think there are a good many bad people in the world, and that things are on the verge of ruin, but I guess we are all right. Still, we can be improved. If I was not an American, I would not dare to talk like this for fear of being mobbed. I thank you all for this kindly expression of your esteem.

The following day General Grant, accompanied by Governor Kingkead, of Nevada, Colonel James G. Fair, U. S. Grant, Jr., Philip Deidenheimer, and a dozen invited guests, visited the Sutro Tunnel. Upon arriving at the town of Sutro his welcome was emphasized by the ringing of bells and blowing of whistles at the company's workshops, and by a heavy discharge of giant powder from the mountain tops overlooking the town.

The party were received at the Sutro mansion by Mrs. Adolphe Sutro, Superintendent H. H. Sheldon, and the officers of the company. After an examination of the works of the company at the mouth of the tunnel, and the reception of the citizens of the town and vicinity, a sumptuous breakfast was served.

The visitors went to the tunnel under the guidance of Superintendent Sheldon, Secretary Young, and Foreman

Bluett. The party were placed aboard the cars, and amid the cheers of the assembled citizens, disappeared in the darkness. Quick time was made underground. Shaft No. 1, one mile from the entrance, was reached in eight minutes; shaft No. 2, two miles from the entrance, in seventeen minutes; and the station of the north lateral tunnel, in thirty-five minutes. Here the party left the cars and walked to the north header, the better to examine the underground workings, and witness the performances of the powerful drilling appliances required in driving a work of this character. The covered boxes, which convey the steaming hot water from the Comstock mines, were also an object of considerable interest.

Returning to the cars the trip was continued to the face of the south lateral tunnel, after which the party were escorted to the 1640 foot station at the "Savage Incline," where they were given in charge of the officers of the Savage Company, and were hoisted to the surface at Virginia City.

Throughout the entire trip the General evinced great interest in what he saw. He considered the tunnel one of the greatest works of the age.

Leaving Virginia City on the 29th the General arrived at Ogden, Utah, on the 30th. Governor Emery and General Nathan Kimball welcomed him in addresses, to which he responded pleasantly. The special train left after half an hour's wait.

At Laramie 2000 persons had assembled, the train stopping for breakfast.

At Cheyenne, Gov. Hoyt and Gov. Pitkin, with their staffs, and prominent citizens of the State, received the General, and were joined by several hundred members of the G. A. R. from Nebraska and other States. There were no speeches at Sidney, where a large crowd had collected.

The General was introduced, but excused himself from making a speech. One old fellow in the crowd called out: "Old man, you can jest set it down that you've got jest as many friends in this Western country as anywhere else," to which General Grant good-humoredly replied that he was glad to hear that. The crowd gave him three cheers. It was then that the most curious incident of the reception occurred. One of the bumpkins, who must have been slightly muddled, sang out: "General, I'm from Connecticut, and when you go back there, tell 'em you saw out West a ——— from the old Nutmeg State." Grant, with great dignity, simply replied, "You should never swear. It has been a principle of mine never to swear at any time in my life." The reprimand was an effective one, and the fellow slunk away abashed.

At Central City, Clark, Silver Creek, Jackson and Columbus he found a hearty welcome. At Schuyler, State Senator Clarkson, brother of Bishop Clarkson, presented an address of welcome. The General replied:

SENATOR: I am very much obliged for the kind words which you have said on behalf of your people of this prairie town, and I only express the gratification I have felt at all other points in your State through which we have passed, when I say that apparently you have all been out. I am glad to see this prairie State growing as it appears to be, the ground being dotted all over with farms and prosperous villages, and I hope that you may realize your expectations after the census af 1880, in having at least three Representatives in the Lower House of Congress. I thank you, gentlemen, for your attendance and your kindness.

At North Bend, Millard's, a like cordial reception was given. As the train approached Omaha a salute of artillery announced the General's arrival. At the Union depot an immense crowd had assembled. The Grand Army, the

Ninth U. S. Infantry, headed by their regimental band, formed the escort. Gov. Nance, Mayor Chase, and General Crook riding with the General.

The order of the procession was as follows:

FIRST DIVISION.
Platoon of Police.
Battalion Ninth Infantry and Ninth Infantry Band.
Section of Battery.
Company G Second Regiment, N. S. M.

SECOND DIVISION.
Union Pacific Band.
Fire Department.

THIRD DIVISION.
Brandt's Band.
Leyran Singing Society.
Union Pacific Shopmen.
Civic Societies.
Mannerchor.

FOURTH DIVISION.
University Cadets with their Band.
Grand Army of the Republic.
Carriages containing Gen. Grant, party, escort and prominent citizens.

FIFTH DIVISION.
City Band.
Company H, Second Regiment, N. S. M.
Trade representatives.

The line of march was through the principal streets. Crowds from Lincoln, York, Nebraska City, Fremont and adjacent towns, made up the enthusiastic throng. The decorations on the line of the route were generous in numbers and attractive in display.

At Capitol Hill an address of welcome by Gov. Nance, was brief and eloquent.

GENERAL: On behalf of the State of Nebraska I extend to you a cordial greeting to Omaha, that vigorous young metropolis of the West. Nebraska is pre-eminently a patriotic State. A vast majority of our pioneers were with you during your marches, and helped achieve your victories at Donaldson and Shiloh, and the Wilderness, and finally at the surrender of Lee at Appomattox. Doubtless every regiment in every corps has its representative on Nebraska soil. As their confidence in you never wavered in the dark and troubled hours of the Nation's peril, I bid a double welcome to Nebraska to-day.

Mayor Chase in behalf of the city, said:

GENERAL GRANT: A very agreeable duty has devolved upon me upon this occasion, that of giving you welcome to our city. Since you were here four years ago, on this very spot where we stand, and addressed the school children, we are aware that you have traveled in foreign lands, that you have traveled at home, and made yourself as familiar with other countries as you were already with this, and we know full well the result of your travels. We are aware that the comity and amity of foreign nations has been greatly increased, and that their relations to this country have been favored by the fact that you have socially and freely had intercourse with those peoples abroad, and we are aware too, that our people throughout the United States have watched your progress wherever you have gone, from place to place, and from port to port, with the deepest interest, and you know full well, sir, with what gratitude American hearts have beat from the fact that you have been everywhere welcomed, not only as an American citizen, but as a representative of this Republic, both for your personal merits and virtues.

And now, General, permit me to say that, while this little city of 30,000 people is not capable of presenting to you such external decorations as you have witnessed in your travels you have nowhere been where warmer hearts beat for your welfare, and where more grateful greetings were extended to you. With gratitude to the kind Providence that has watched over you and yours in your travels, we remember with the greatest pleasure that you have returned to us to greet us once more. And now, sir, on behalf of this young city, I bid you again and again welcome, welcome, welcome.

Turning to the audience the Mayor presented General Grant to their view, and the air resounded with cheers for several minutes. As it ceased General Grant said:

LADIES AND GENTLEMEN OF NEBRASKA AND OF OMAHA: It would be impossible for me to make any number of you hear a word if I had anything very special to say. It is cold and windy, and there are multitudes waiting, and I will only say a few words, and that to express the gratification I feel at meeting you all here to-day. I state to you in addition how glad I am to get back again once more upon American soil. Wherever I have been in all my travels in the last two and a half years I have found our country most highly spoken of, and I have been, as a sort of representative of the country, most elegantly entertained. For the many kindnesses that I have received at the hands of foreign nations and Princes I feel gratified myself and I know that all of you do. The welcome given to me there has been a welcome to this grand Republic, of which you are all equal representatives with myself. As I have had occasion to say several times before since my arrival in San Francisco, we stand well abroad, infinitely better than we did twenty years ago, as a nation and as a people; and as a result of that to-day the credit of the United States in the European market is higher than that of any other country in the world. We are there more highly appreciated than we appreciate ourselves as a whole, and I can and will say that as individuals we do not think well enough of ourselves. Gentlemen, I say again that I am highly gratified at meeting you here to-day, and thank you.

The welcome was most cordial and enthusiastic. A public reception at the Custom House followed. In the evening a banquet at the Withnell House, at which 60 or more prominent citizens participated, this wound up the day and the General left immediately afterwards for Fort Omaha as the guest of General Crook.

On Sunday, Nov. 2, General Grant, General Crook, and escort, attended the First Methodist Church, where services were held. The church was filled to overflowing by regular worshipers and those drawn together out of curiosity to see the distinguished guest and visitor. The edifice was profusely decorated with banners, flags, evergreens, festoons and autumn leaves, and a small banner bearing the legend "Welcome" in bright gilt letters.

General Grant and escort were given a reserved seat well in front.

The opening prayer was made by Rev. James Haynes. In the closing invocation he referred to the more than ordinary character of the occasion, rendered extraordinary, in fact, by the presence of a distinguished fellow-citizen, who had been feted and honored all around the world; who was now returning in safety, and whose pleasure it was to worship with God's people to-day. They were thankful he was able to be with them, and the reverend gentleman prayed that he might always be on the side of virtue and religion; that his influence might always be on the side of right and justice, and that God's special blessing might rest on him and those who worshiped with him.

The sermon was delivered by Rev. J. B. Maynard, pastor of the church, and was an able discourse on the origin of the Christian Church, and an interposition of Divine Providence in the affairs of men. His illustrations on the latter head were singularly striking. "It wasn't the people," he said, "who selected Mr. Lincoln to guide the

Nation in the hour of its peril. He was brought forward and placed at the head of the Government by One who knew the coming evils, and who selected him to guide the Nation through the impending storm. The same is true," continued the reverend gentleman, "in regard to leading minds in and out of Congress, and eminently so in regard to the commanders of our army and navy. How blind most of their appointments, and how uncertain in consequence were our battles and campaigns! But at the right time, how strongly did an unseen power bring forward the men, and especially the *one great commander* to lead our armies through carnage and strife to final triumph of liberty! How clearly are God's acts vindicated! No matter how obscure and unpretending, God chose him, and we at once saw in him the man for the emergency. Thus did Omnipotent wisdom adjust the conditions of our final success."

The allusion was, of course, clear to everybody, including General Grant himself, though his immobile features would never have revealed it.

At the conclusion of the service the General and escort passed out first, and the pious and curious ones vied with each other to shake the hero's hand.

General Grant's eastern journey was resumed on the 3d. General and Mrs. Grant, Col. and Mrs. Fred Grant, and daughter left Fort Omaha about 8 o'clock, under the escort of the officers of the garrison, Companies G and H, Ninth Infantry, and the Ninth Infantry Band. The party and escort were met at the Withnel House by the Nebraska Grand Army of the Republic boys and the Citizens' Reception Committee. General Grant, Mayor Chase, and C. W. Mead, of the Union Pacific, rode together in a carriage to the depot, where a large crowd had collected to see the party off. The train was standing inside the Union depot, and its particularly handsome appearance made it the cynosure of all eyes. D. W. Hitchcock, General Western Passenger Agent of the Chicago, Burlington & Quincy, had laid himself out as he never did before to do something that would be memorable, and would redound to the credit of the road he represents.

Very little time was lost after the party reached the depot. The troops were drawn up on the right of the train, forming a passage through which the escort led General Grant and private party. The crowd cheered itself hoarse. The engine-bell rang, the band played "Marching Through Georgia," and at 9:55, amidst all the display of enthusiasm, the train moved out of the depot, and was soon on its way over the big bridge, out of Nebraska, and nearing Iowa. When it reached the middle of the bridge, General Manderson, who, with a number of the Nebraska Grand Army boys, had remained on board, formally transferred the party to the care of the Iowa Grand Army boys, who were represented by Major A. A. Perkins, of Burlington, Post Department Commander of Iowa. General Manderson was in his usually happy vein, and his speech was as follows:

COMRADE PERKINS: At their eastern terminus of the Union Pacific Railroad and the Eastern boundary of the State of Nebraska and in the middle of that classic stream, the Big Muddy, I have the pleasant duty to perform, of turning over to you the duty of escorting comrade Grant through the State of Iowa. I hope your journey will be as pleasant as ours was through the State of Nebraska, and wish you and your comrades good luck and continued prosperity.

Major Perkins, in a brief reply, accepted the trust.

As the train drew up at Council Bluffs, a large crowd welcomed it with cheers upon cheers. They were here joined by Gov. Gear and Col. Griswold, Department Commander G. A. R., where formal speeches where made. Col Griswold welcomed the General in the following address:

GENERAL GRANT: Knowing you would pass through our Department on your way home from your trip around the world, the Grand Army of the Republic, at our last semi-annual meeting, resolved to welcome you at our borders and escort you through the lines. We are here to perform that pleasant duty. I have the pleasure of introducing to you as such escort the officers and comrades of the Posts of the Department and the Chief Executive of our Commonwealth.

General Gear welcomed the General as follows:

GENERAL GRANT: On behalf of our people, I bid you welcome to the Commonwealth of Iowa, a welcome not alone to the soldier, who in the Nation's hour of supreme peril carried its flag to victory, nor yet to the public servant who in a critical period of this country's history, occupied the highest office, but also the illustrious citizen who, after many years of continuous and arduous labor in his country's service, has been enjoying a well-earned rest in visiting the people of the Old World, in seeing new phases of human life, and in returning home bringing an increase of honors to his country in the attention he has received at the hands of rulers and the people of other lands. To me, sir, is also allotted the pleasant duty of extending to you a hearty welcome in behalf of the Grand Army of the Republic of the Department of Iowa, whose membership is composed of your old comrades in arms, most of whom have followed you in many a perilous campaign, and shared with you the triumphs of many well-fought battle fields. From all parts of this Commonwealth they went forth to swell the ranks of the historic Army of the Tennessee, whose fame is so imperishably bound up with yours, and so inseparably a part of the Nation's brilliant military record. The men of that army, and many others of many remote regions here to-day, and all over our State, feel themselves to have been honored in your person in all parts of the world, and your brave comrades rejoice at the safe return of their renowned leader to his native land, a joy in which all of our people participate. We welcome, then with a glad welcome, you to our State, in the affection of whose people you have ever held a distinguished place. A hearty welcome to the soldier, statesman and citizen.

General Grant replied:

GOV. GEAR, AND GENTLEMEN OF THE GRAND ARMY OF THE REPUBLIC: I am very glad to meet you here, and I accept the escort which you have tendered me with great pleasure, having had your escort on former occasions when your protection was highly necessary. On this occasion I hope it will be a more joyous one than on previous occasions referred to. I believe that we might go through this State even without an escort, and with an escort without arms we are perfectly secure. Governor, it's not necessary for me to say more on this occasion than to thank you and the citizens of Iowa, not only for their escort, but for their good will, as expressed by you.

At Red Oak, Villasco, and Creston the General was received with enthusiastic and hearty ovations from the whole populace. At the latter place, in response to the address of the Mayor, he said:

CITIZENS OF CRESTON: I am very glad to meet the people of this State in your city. I looks very much as though a great many people had settled here within a very few years. My recollection is that the last time I crossed this part of the state, the praries had very little upon them except grass and prairie chickens. Now you have got people enough to stamp out the prairie chickens and to produce from the soil millions of bushels of grain to support and sustain human life, and make America prosperous. I am very glad to see all these citizens assembled, and glad to be among you."

Brief stops were made at Murray and Osceola. At Chariton he was received by all the school teachers and school children in the place. Col. Duncan welcomed the General. At its close, a novel portion of the reception awaited him. A precocious little girl of six years, Mary Cushman by name, who was held in her teacher's arms, presented Grant with a boquet, and in an innocent, childish verse, made him a little speech, which closed with a wish that he would "always love and remember his country." Grant kissed the little thing, who appeared to realize that it was the proudest moment of her young life.

At Albia, Chillicothe, Ottumwa and Mount Pleasant, vast crowds had collected. It was dark, and huge bonfires were sending out weird glare; the decorations and crowds surging to and fro showed off well in the light of the bonfires.

At Burlington the reception was one of the noisiest, liveliest and most brilliant on the route.

As the train entered the city they were received by long and piercing blasts from all the locomotives in the city, church and fire bells, salutes, and the display of fire-works, numerous bonfires and illuminations of nearly all the house windows, the great cheering crowds—all added to the noise and fury, and proclaimed a joyous welcome. The General was met by the mayor, who addressed his guest as follows:

GENERAL GRANT: Burlington bids you welcome. The formal words of greeting fall from my lips, but they find a sympathetic response in every heart in this great assemblage. If all these spoke, one word would rise and fill the autumn air with its glad chorus, until the rocks and cliffs of old Flint Hills would send back the cordial, hearty tones in re-echoing refrain the one word, "welcome." We have been deeply interested in the magnificent ovations and receptions that have been tendered you in the many lands that you have visited. They have been given you as a plain American citizen without rank, position or credentials. Your fame, however, as a warrior and a statesman preceded you, and each nation was proud to render you the homage due to one who had occupied and discharged the highest trusts in the Government of the United States with honesty and fidelity. The tones of welcome do not weaken as you journey towards your old home, but every city, town and hamlet on your route, from West to East, vie with each other in making the welkin ring with their shouts of welcome to our distinguished fellow-citizen."

General Grant replied:

"LADIES AND GENTLEMEN: The welcome I have received since coming into Iowa is exceedingly gratifying. I have seen a population in crossing your State, on a single line of railroad greater than that of the State a quarter of a century ago. This is remarkable, and shows a growth and enterprise in this great State that is most gratifying. The impossibility of making one hear all my remarks will force me to do as I have seen them do in Washington. I will ask permission to have my speech printed."

The speech was received with cheers and laughter by the crowd. The ex-President and escort were invited to carriages, and line of march taken up to the Mayor's house. The decorations encountered on every hand excited universal admiration. The party proceeded with its escort through the principal streets to Mayor Adams' residence, where, as soon as possible thereafter, its members retired to rest.

The following morning General Grant, Governor Gear and Mayor Adams drove round Burlington's numerous hills. At noon a reception was given to Iowa journalists at the *Hawkeye* office; here the General was presented with a copy of the *Hawkeye* printed on silk; this was followed at 1:30 P. M. by an elegant repast at the Mayor's residence, and later, by a public reception at the Barrett House, Mrs. Grant holding a reception at the Mayor's house, where were assembled the beauty and elite of the city to do her honor. The reception at the Barrett House over, the General and escort visited the High School building, where 6,000 school children of all ages, their teachers and members of the school board had collected. C. B. Parsons, president of the school board, extended a formal welcome, to which General Grant replied:

"MEMBERS OF THE SCHOOL BOARD, AND SCHOLARS OF THE CITY OF BURLINGTON, IOWA: It does me great pleasure to meet and see 5,000 or more of the school children of the city of Burlington. I think that if ever there is another war in this country it will be one of ignorance versus intelligence, and in that battle the State of Iowa will achieve a grand victory. Furthermore, I think that that war will be one of ignorance and superstition combined against education and intelligence, and I am satisfied that the children here will enroll in the army of intelligence and wipe out the common enemy, ignorance. I thank you for your kind attention."

A vast chorus of young, fresh voices then sang "America" The General was apparently much taken with the undisguised heartiness and earnestness of the reception he met. After a long season of hand-shaking, at 4 o'clock the ex-President returned to the Mayor's residence, where final preparations were made to resume the journey. A large crowd had collected at the depot, and cheered him as he ascended the steps. While the bands played and cheers of the people the train moved off.

At Monmouth a large crowd had assembled at the depot, and a dozen bonfires illuminated the scene. Capt. Walker introduced General Grant, who said:

"GENTLEMEN: I am very glad to get back to Illinois again, and very glad to see you all, but I have a great deal of sympathy with these press-men who are along with us, and who take down every word I say. I am a man of economy, I believe in economy, and they telegraph every word I say, and I want to save them expenses."

At Galesburg the biggest kind of a reception awaited the party. Mayor Greenleaf introduced the General to the crowd, numbering at least 5,000 people. General Grant responded as follows:

"LADIES AND GENTLEMEN: It would be impossible for me to make myself heard by all of you or a large fraction of you, even if I was in the habit of public speaking. I will do no more, therefore, than thank you for turning out at this time of night to welcome me on my way home, and I will say to you that in the two and a half years that I have been away from you I have had a very pleasant time. I have seen a great many pleasant people, and I have been very well received at every place I have been as a mark of respect and honor to the great country which you help to make up. But, as I have had frequent occasion to say since my return to my own country, I appreciate the welcome which I received from the sovereigns of my own country above all other receptions that they gave us elsewhere. I have had the pleasure of seeing the people of Galesburg out on one other occasion. I passed through in 1868, when I thought all the people in the city were about this spot. I am very glad to see you all again to-night."

The speech was received with cheers, but it was only

heard by those standing very near one side of the platform, and, when the General stepped to the other side of the platform, the crowd on that side cried out, "Speech!" "Speech!" "General, only a few words."

General Grant said:

"My Friends: I have only been in Illinois one hour, and during that time I have already made two speeches, and feel talked out."

A voice in the crowd—"We didn't hear the one you made here, General."

General Grant—"Well some one," (indicating a reporter back of him), "will be pretty sure to print what I said. You can buy a copy of the morning paper and find it all."

There were loud cries for Mrs. Grant, who appeared on the platform. She simply bowed, and soon retired; the train then again started, and a final three cheers were given as they moved on.

A short stop was made at Yates City, where the General was enthusiastically received by those in waiting.

Owing to the lateness of the hour the train was run down to Lombardville, some twenty-five miles off the main line, and run on to a side track until the following morning; the distinguished party having a two-fold object, to get the election returns unmolested by a large crowd of people, a skillful operator having been taken aboard at Galesburg, and a good night's rest. Early the following morning the train was run back upon the main line of the Chicago, Burlington and Quincy, arriving at Mendota at 9:20 A. M. Mr. Potter, Captain Walker and General Hitchcock, of the Chicago, Burlington and Quincy, turned the General and his party over to the Illinois Central Railroad. These gentlemen, who had been tireless in energy, lavish in expenditure, and delicate in their attentions to their distinguished guest, received the warmest thanks.

At Mendota vast crowds swarmed about the depot, whose cheers, united to the thunder peals of ordinance, conspired to make the noisiest and heartiest kind of welcome. A local reception committee were on hand, while Company F, Twelfth Battalion National Guards, under command of Capt. Ingalls, was drawn up on the platform. A line was formed, and General Grant passed through it, escorted by Gov. Gear, Collector Crocker, Mayor Hastings, Mr. Ruggles, and took seats in the first carriage. The procession formed with two bands at its head, followed by one platoon of militia in advance and one in the rear of the first carriage. The other carriages, containing the balance of the party and citizens followed, and the procession wound its way along the finely decorated streets to the First Baptist Church, where it halted. Arches had been erected over its front doors, under which the General passed, being made of flags and evergreens, bearing in large letters the word "Welcome." General Grant and escort passed up the church-aisle to the pulpit, which had been enlarged and handsomely decorated with flowers, flags and evergreens. An arch over its edge bore simply the word "Grant." The church was filled to overflowing with citizens generally, and a large delegation of school-children. Mayor Hastings and General Grant rose from the sofa where they had sat down, and Mendota's Executive delivered the following address of welcome:

"GENERAL GRANT: In behalf of the citizens of Mendota and vicinity, independent of party, I congratulate you upon your safe return to the State of Illinois and the near arrival to your home. We have read with the greatest interest of the honorable manner in which you have been received by the governments that you have visited, and are happy to realize that your distinguished services to your country were as fully appreciated abroad as they are at home. In your reception this morning the citizens of this city and vicinity have turned out en masse to greet you, manifesting the same enthusiasm, in the appreciation of your distinguished services in the field and as President of this great republic, as had greeted you from San Francisco to this point. We sincerely hope that your life may be long protracted, and that you may always realize the deep affection of a grateful public for the services you have rendered your country."

General Grant responded as follows:

"CITIZENS OF MENDOTA: The receptions which I have received on my return to my own country, upon my first arrival at San Francisco up to Mendota, have been to me gratifying. The receptions referred to abroad have been a mark of respect that foreign nations feel for the United States as a country, and for its citizens as energetic, progressive and independent people. The honor has been yours, and not mine. In getting back now, to my own home, I feel especially gratified to meet the citizens of my own state, and to be welcomed by them. I am sure I shouldn't want to stay long in Illinois if I didn't feel that I could have had a good feeling and a reception of the people of this State. In conclusion, ladies and gentlemen, I thank you for what I see here, before me, this morning, and for the words which have just been heard."

Hand shaking to an almost unlimited extent closed the reception at the church, after which the General was escorted back to the depot. Here the guests were joined by a large party of friends from Chicago, who had come down by special train to meet him and attend the reception at Galena, also by Gov. Cullom, who was greeted warmly by the General. Gov. Cullom after silencing the noisy crowd addressed General Grant in the following speech of welcome.

"GENERAL GRANT: On behalf of your old friends who are here present, and in the name of the people of the State of Illinois, I extend to you and to your family a sincere and heartfelt welcome home. This great central valley is proud to acknowledge you as the most honored and best-beloved of all her living sons. Eighteen years ago you left us in the service of our common country, at the head of the Twenty-first brave regiment of Illinois Volunteers. I need not recite to those present who join in the greeting, the well-known story of your progress. We have followed you every step, through all the dark days, which ended in the glorious success of the army of the Union, and which gave to you that which you so richly deserved—the position of General of the Army. Later, you were twice called to the highest civil office of the nation. Illinois at each time gave to you her voice in no uncertain tones. When you laid aside the cares and toils of office, and sought in foreign travels the rest and recreation which you so much needed, your fellow-citizens from your own State, have thrilled with pride and pleasure when they saw the recognition of your services to civilization and the age, of your abilities as a chieftain and a ruler, and of your virtues as a man by all the great and good of the entire world. Our pleasure and pride in following you from shore to shore, when nation vied with nation and princes with princes to do you honor, have not been lessened by any fear that all this adulation would in any way hurt you. We had an abiding confidence that the time would come when you would return among us, that same quiet, modest man whom we had last known, to assume your position and take your place as a private citizen. And in that place I want to remind you that one of your chief duties is to hold yourself in readiness when your country calls for your exertions either in the Cabinet of the nation or in the field. Again, in behalf of your old friends present, and in the name of the whole people of the great Republic, I welcome you home.

General Grant's reply was a practical verification of Governor Cullom's remark, that adulation could not hurt him. Without apparently noticing the Governor's allusion to what the future might bring forth, he responded:

"GOVERNOR: I thank the citizens of the State of Illinois, and I thank you, for the welcome you have extended to me. I shall make no further remarks now. Having been received in one of the churches of this city by the population of Mendota, and having already had an opportunity of taking, I think, nearly everybody by the hand, I will therefore reserve any thing further that I have to say for another occasion."

Gov. Cullom proposed three cheers for General Grant, which were given with a yell and hurrah that must, indeed, have assured the General of his welcome, if anything more were necessary.

The train moved off amid the cheers and hurrahs of thousands of people. The first stop was at Amboy, where a great crowd had assembled; a brief stop was made at Dixon, where the General spoke briefly. On the arrival of the train at Polo it was boarded by a reception committee appointed by the citizens of Galena. At Forreston, Freeport and Warren, large and enthusiastic crowds had collected. The approach to Galena for miles swarmed with people, who cheered and waved their handkerchiefs as the train flew by. Galena, the General's old home, was reached at 3:20 P. M., and the trip overland came to a temporary stop.

A salvo of artillery greeted General Grant as he entered his old home, and 10,000 citizens gathered at the depot and on the streets adjoining to give a royal welcome to

WELCOME AT GALENA.

America's most distinguished living citizen. The crowd pressed back and forth, and there was some trouble about the landing; but in a few minutes this was adjusted, and way was made for General Grant to his carriage. The depot of the Illinois Central is located in East Galena, while the city proper is on the other side of the river. When the General had reached his carriage, a procession was formed. The hour was late, and there was no time to lose if the business of the day was to be finished before nightfall. The procession was formed as follows:

<blockquote>
Veterans bearing colors of the old Forty-fifth Illinois Volunteer Infantry, better known as the Washburne Lead Mine Regiment.

Gen. W. R. Rowley, the only living member of General Grant's Individual Staff, and Chief Marshal of the Day.

Gen. John C. Smith, State Treasurer, commanding the Militia, and Capt. J W Luke, Aid and Assistant Marshal.

Two Companies of the Third Illinois Militia.

An Iowa Militia Company with Band, etc.

The Soldiers' and Sailors' Veteran Association of Jo Daviess County.

The Veteran Corps of Dubuque, Iowa.

The Dyersville, Iowa, Veteran Club.

Crippled Veterans of the War, in carriages.

Knights of Pythias from Dubuque and Galena.

Liberty and Neptune Fire Companies.

The carriage, drawn by four grey horses, which bore General Grant, Gov. Cullom, Senator McClellan, and Mayor Hunkins.

Distinguished visitors and well-known citizens in carriages.

A thousand citizens, many being old veterans.
</blockquote>

The procession moved rapidly through the principal streets to the corner of Main and Green streets, where a grand stand had been erected. Stretching across the street from the De Soto House to the stand was an arch, embowered in green. On one side it bore the mottoes, "From Galena to Appomattox Court House." "From Galena to the White House." "From Galena Around the World;" and also the words, "Welcome to Your Home, General." On the other side was the motto, "Loved at Home and Honored Abroad," and the names of "Grant," "Sherman," "Sheridan," "Rawlins." The whole was surmounted by a carved eagle, formerly the property of the Grey Eagle fire company. It was about 4:15 when the head of the procession halted in front of the grand stand, and the vast crowd there assembled set up a welcoming cheer. At last every thing was in readiness for the oratorical features of the reception. After an address of welcome from the Mayor, State Senator McClellan addressed General Grant, as follows:

"GENERAL: The Mayor and your fellow-citizens of Galena have assigned to me the pleasing duty of tendering you, in their name and on their behalf, a hearty welcome home again. Without distinction of party, sect, or nationality, all your neighbors and townsmen give you cordial salutation, and hail your return to your old home with joy and profound satisfaction. They are deeply sensible of the honor you do them in continuing to make this city your residence, and they will be only too happy to contribute so far as they may be able to render your stay here profitable and agreeable. You, sir, have been the recipient of many ovations, remarkable alike for their spontaneous heartiness and their almost imperial magnificence. Your journey from the Golden Gate to this place has been one continual triumphal progress, marked everywhere by demonstrations of honor, respect, admiration, and homage, never heretofore accorded to a private citizen in this country. We in Galena cannot vie with those splendid displays. We are too poor, and too few for that. In our little city we cannot give you the plaudits of hundreds of thousands of people: we cannot erect triumphal arches emblazoned with gold and silver; we are not able to provide royal banquets with princely service, but we are able and glad to give you the homage of honest, loving and loyal hearts.

"We can and do give you and your family a supremely, sincere and heartfelt welcome. Other cities may make grander and more imposing demonstrations, but be assured, sir, that no people in all this broad land are so glad to see you as are your fellow-citizens of Galena. None greet you with a warmer affection, none can be more proud of you, your achievements and your fame, and we come to-day in our own humble fashion, with none of that pomp and pageantry to which you are accustomed on like occasions, to give expression, as best we may, to the delight and satisfaction we feel in seeing you once more among us; to testify the love and respect we have for you as a man and a fellow-citizen, and the honor and esteem we entertain for you as a soldier and a statesman.

"In the dark days of 1861 you left us to fight the battles of your country. Your career since then has become a large part of that country's most interesting and eventful history. The nation's integrity vindicated and the Union restored, the highest military honors a grateful people could bestow were lavished upon you. Twice have the suffrages of a free people placed you in the highest civil position in their gift, a position more honorable than that of a King or Emperor, inasmuch as it is not determined by the accident of birth, but given as the reward of genius and ability, patriotism, and public service. As a private citizen you have just made the circuit of the globe. Nothing could equal the courtesies and distinctions you received from the powers of the old world, save the modesty, good sense, and democratic simplicity which characterized your reception of them. Imperial splendors, the glitter and glare of royalty, never for a moment dazzled your republican vision. The guest of kings and prime ministers of extended empires, you bore yourself with the quiet dignity of an American citizen. The just compliments of the titled and great to your illustrious services and personal worth you modestly disclaimed, and credited them all to your country. In the presence of sovereigns you never forgot that you were yourself a sovereign—one of a nation of forty million sovereigns—and it is most gratifying, sir, to your own countrymen to learn from a speech made by yourself, that you return to your native land a more ardent admirer of republican institutions than ever before, and that your love for your country has been increased and your faith in the progress, future greatness, and grand destiny of this nation has been strengthened by your observations and experiences abroad. In all your foreign travels you could doubtless say of your country with the poet:

> Where'er I roam, whatever realms I see,
> My heart, untraveled, fondly turns to thee.

"Again, in the name of this great congregation of patriotic, admiring, enthusiastic people, I bid you thrice welcome to this little town—a town of small importance, indeed, of itself, but made famous and heroic by the deeds of yourself, and those of many other distinguished men who have gone forth from us to do service to the State. Some of these, with their martial robes about them, sleep on battlefields, some are still with the army guarding the frontier, and some, illustrious in their several spheres as jurists, foreign ambassadors, and successful men of affairs, we have the pleasure of seeing before us on this occasion. They have come back to this, their former home, to unite their acclaim with ours in your honor to-day.

GENERAL GRANT'S RESIDENCE, GALENA, ILL.

"In conclusion, sir, permit me to express the wish that your future may be as serene and happy as your past has been eventful and glorious; and as you pass into the 'sere and yellow leaf' of life's autumn, may all that which should accompany old age, as honor, love, obedience, troops of friends be yours."

In response to this cordial greeting, General Grant spoke as follows:

"LADIES AND GENTLEMEN, AND CITIZENS OF GALENA: It is with some embarrassment that I reply. Your welcome is exceedingly gratifying to me, but it is difficult for me to reply to what I have just heard, and to what I have seen. Since I first left here, eighteen years ago, it has always been the greatest pleasure for me to return to Galena, and now, after an absence of two and a half years from your city, during which time I have visited almost every country in the world, it is a pleasure to be greeted in this manner by you. During my travels I received princely honors, but they were all due to this country, and to you as citizens and as sovereigns of so great a country. When I saw during my absence, especially in the far East, how hard the inhabitants had to toil even for a maintenance, I realized more than ever the greatness of our country, where want is scarcely ever known, and where the question of sustenance is not daily considered. I will only add, that I thank you again for your reception."

Brief but feeling remarks were made by Gov. Cullom, of Illinois; Gov. Gear, of Iowa; Gov. Smith, of Wisconsin; General Logan, Senator Allison, of Iowa; Hon. E. B. Washburne and Major Hawkes.

The open air ceremonies concluded with the presentation of Mrs. Grant to the people. Then three times three cheers were given to General Grant, and the out-door welcome home terminated.

*Sixteen pages are here added to correct omission in paging the illustrations.

General Grant repaired to the DeSoto House, where he received his friends. The parlors of the hotel were overflowing for fully an hour, and the hand-shaking was almost endless. The General submitted with good grace to it all, and occasionally, when he met an old acquaintance, the greeting was very cordial. Behind him stood the color bearers of the Forty-fifth Illinois Volunteers, with their battered ensigns.

In the evening the city was brilliantly illuminated, and there was a fine display of fire-works. During this display the triumphal arch, which was well stored with rockets, Roman candles, etc., became ignited, and an explosion followed that shook the windows of the buildings in the vicinity. Postmaster Huntington was injured in the fire. General and Mrs. Grant entertained a few friends at their residence; there were none but guests present from abroad, as the General will entertain his Galena friends later. And so ended the great reception, which was so general and generous on the part of Galena.

After a few days rest, General Grant left Galena at 5 o'clock Wednesday morning, November 12th, for Chicago. At nearly all of the stations on the route large and enthusiastic crowds collected, the train generally stopping a few moments to allow the General to satisfy their curiosity, and the General was often compelled to go through the ordeal of the pump, shaking hands with all who requested it. At one o'clock the train reached Park Row, and was received by General B. R. Raum, General Theodore Jones, Major A. Fitch, Colonel W. S. Oliver, General E. H. Murray, and Major H. C. McArthur, who escorted the distinguished guest to a carriage drawn by six horses. Then followed Mayor Harrison and Governor Cullom, who took a seat in the ex-President's carriage, and the cavalcade started. A body guard, consisting of officers Schumacher, Fife, Lueders, Soergel, Rierdon and Bruton, surrounded the carriage. At this moment a drenching rain set in, and the multitude that but a minute before was a packed, solid mass, began to move, at first slowly, and then quicker and quicker, until it almost reached a trot. Park Row and the lake front was transformed into a surging, seething mass of human beings and umbrellas, moving northward on Michigan avenue. It was a strange sight. In spite of the rain, patriotic throats would cheer, and resounding artillery would roar; in spite of the mud the crowd dashed on, cheering lustily, and in spite of all the elements combined, General Grant's advent into Chicago was signalized by a display of the most unbounded enthusiasm.

The procession having formed, the command to march was given about 1.30 o'clock, by Lieutenant General Phil. Sheridan, Grand Marshal, and the column moved in the following order:

FIRST DIVISION.
Detachment of mounted police, under command of Major George Heinzman.
Jefferson Barracks Band.
General Sheridan and staff.
General J. T. Torrence and staff.
First Regiment of Cavalry, Major Welter.
Second Regiment Infantry, Colonel Quirk.
Sixth Battallion Infantry, Colonel W. H. Thompson.
Sixteenth Battalion Infantry, Colonel Scott.
Battery D, Major Tobey.
Battalion of miscellaneous companies, Major De Young.
First Regiment of Infantry, Colonel Knox.
First Regiment Cadet Corps.
Lackey Zouaves.
Janesville Guards.

SECOND DIVISION.
Loesch's Military Band.
Captain Neely and Staff of aids.
GENERAL GRANT,
accompanied by Mayor Harrison and the Hon. Thomas Hoyne, in a carriage drawn by six caparisoned horses and escorted by the Society of the Army of the Tennessee.
Platoon of police, commanded by Acting Chief O'Donnell and associates.
Carriages containing Governor Shelby M. Cullom and General W. T. Sherman.
Carriages containing the Citizens' Reception Committee of 500.

Carriages containing distinguished maimed and crippled soldiers.
Lubbig's Milwaukee Band.
Society of the Army of the Cumberland, General Whipple.
Northwestern Band.
Society of the Army of the Potomac, General White.
Nevans' Military Band.
Union War Veterans.
Union Democratic War Veterans.
Veteran organizations in general Colonel Scribner.
Clarinda, Iowa, Cornet Band.
Mexican War Veterans.
Fort Wayne Band.
Grand Army of the Republic, Colonel Swain.
Grand Army Fife and Drum Corps Band.

THIRD DIVISION.
Columbus Barracks Band.
General Wallace and Staff.
Old Settlers, as invited participants, in carriages.
Judges of the Federal and State Courts, carriages.
The Chicago Common Council, carriages.
The Board of Cook County Commissioners.
Division composed of the County Clerk's and Sheriff's Deputies.
The City Clerk's and City and County Treasurer's Deputies.
Hyde Park authorities and South Park Commissioners.
First Regiment Trumpeters.
The Fire Patrol.
Illinois Skirmishers' Battalion.
Brothers of Union.
United Fellows.
Downer's Grove Band.
The Union Labor League.
Mail Carriers, detachment of 30.
The Danish War Veterans.
First Norwegian Total Abstinence Society.
Jacksonville Drum Corps.
Chicago Labor Union.
Stock Yards Troopers.
Langan's Band.
Chicago Turngemeinde.

FOURTH DIVISION.
Elgin Military Band.
General Sherer and staff.
Detachment of 14 engines and 4 trucks of the Chicago Fire Department.
Jackson, Mich., Band.
Division of 350 decorated wagons, escorted by the West, South, and North Park Police, mounted.

The commanders of the various divisions, who were seen after the march was over, stated that there were at

the smallest estimate 10,000 or 12,000 participants in the procession.

There were over 3,000, perhaps 3,500, in the First Division, over 2,500 in the Second, about the same in the Third, and nearly 1,500 in the Fourth. The route of march was about 4 miles long, and the rear of the column had not yet formed on Michigan avenue when the head had arrived at the Palmer House. The procession occupied about three hours in passing a given point.

From a balcony erected at the N. E. end of Palmer House General Grant reviewed the first and second Divisions, when the General descended and proceeded to the platform erected in the rotunda of the hotel, and on behalf of the citizens of Chicago was formally welcomed to the city by Mayor Harrison (a Democrat), who spoke as follows:

"GENERAL GRANT: The people of Chicago recognize in you the most renowned of America's citizens. They have watched you for several months journeying around the world. They have seen you the recipient of honors heretofore conferred only upon those of exalted rank; and yet, sir, you had no other passport than that you were an American citizen.

"Princes, rulers, and their people delighted to honor you, and in honoring you they lavished honor upon your country. This people, sir, now that you are returning home, are desirous of tendering you a befitting reception. With this end they have appointed a committee of five hundred gentlemen to receive you here in the heart of the city and to welcome you to the homes of our people and to the hearts of the people.

"Upon me as chairman of that committee, devolves the pleasing duty of clothing in words what their hearts would warmly express. Sir, for many long years you have been constantly before the eyes of this people."

"Eighteen years and two months ago a neighboring state had adopted the rule of neutrality in the dread internecine war then commencing. Our statesmen were deeply troubled and knew not how to solve the problem. You, Sir, like the Macedonian conqueror, with your sword cut the Gordian knot, and the first born daughter of the Constitution no longer wavered in her devotion to the Union and to the Union's flag. Two months after we saw you writing your name in blood at fiercely contested Belmont. Before the frosts of winter had thawed, you threw your regiments around Donelson. Its commander, feeling the death-grip upon him, asked for terms of capitulation. That laconic reply, "Unconditional surrender; I propose immediately to move upon your works," enriched the page of military literature, and 15,000 of Confederate prisoners came here to Chicago, living witnesses of your great victory. Ere the buds of spring had burst into the summer's flower, Corinth, and Pittsburg Landing were your trophies. And the waters of the Cumberland and Tennessee rivers flowed freely, bearing the stars and stripes through the Ohio, through on the Mississippi to Memphis and below; but the mighty river refused to carry you on to the gulf. Vicksburg, deemed impregnable, frowned upon its turbulent waters, demanding a toll of death. You resolved that Vicksburg should fall, and for you to resolve, has seemed in the past for you to do. After months of strategic movement, long marches, and many battles, you lay your army in front of the Gibraltar of the South. But Vicksburg was vulnerable only from the rear. Desirous of saving your army, you endeavored to make a new channel for the mighty stream. But the father of waters, despising your human efforts, rolled on majestically—on beneath the enemy's guns. Sir, unable to bridle the monster, you mounted his foaming back, rode through the storm of fire and hail of shot. Vicksburg fell, and Chicago shouted: "The backbone of the Confederacy is broken." Chattanooga, Lookout Mountian, and Missionary Ridge were then flowers in the chaplet encircling your brow. We then saw you at the nation's Capital commanding your country's armies. But your own special duty was to reach Richmond, which had in the past seemed a *noli me tangere*. You chose the line of the Wilderness, and to the immortal Lincoln you declared that you would 'fight it out on that line if it took you all summer,' thus giving evidence of the tenacity of your own will, rousing the wavering and lifting up the downhearted. You did, sir, 'fight it out on that line,' and Richmond was ours.

"We next saw you, sir, at Appomattox Court House, receiving the sword of the brave, but mistaken Lee. You handed it back to him. 'Keep it,' said you; 'a braver man never wore a sword.' You bade him keep his horses, for his folks would need them at the plow. You bade his armies return to their homes, to rebuild their broken firesides, and to re-establish their shattered fortunes. Sir, Chicago and the world then applauded the clement conqueror, as before they had admired the dauntless soldier. The bloody war over, you said, 'Let us have peace,' and a grateful nation lifted you to the highest position in its gift; aye, the highest in the world. Eight years you were President. Then, wearied with sixteen years of service to your country, you sought rest in travel, turning your eyes to the East. Moving off toward the cradle of the sun, you were greeted in all lands, and received every greeting in the name of your country.

"Sir, you have served your country nobly; your country has honored you grandly. Like the immortal Washington, you rose from the lowly walks of life, passed through all military grades until you commanded its victorious armies. Like him, you filled the office of President two long terms. He, when his two terms were over, was offered a crown; but, preferring the immortality of fame to temporary power, he retired to private life, lives in the hearts of his people, and all time will call him his country's father. You, too, sir, when your two terms were over, obeying that part of your country's Constitution in its unwritten traditions, hallowed by the example of the immortal Washington—you, too, retired, and you, too, sir, live and will live forever in your countrymen's hearts.

"Sir, in the name of Chicago and its people, I prophesy that when time shall have grown old; when the page of history shall have become dim by the side of the great quartet who have gone before you, your name, your statue, will be placed, and by the side of Washington, of Jefferson, of Jackson, and of the immortal Lincoln, will live the name of Grant.

"Sir, again allow me to tender to you a hearty welcome to the homes, to the fire-sides, and to the hearts of all the people of Chicago, regardless of creed or of party."

At the conclusion of the Mayor's remarks, General Grant bowed slightly, and responded as follows:

"MR. MAYOR, GENTLEMEN OF THE COMMITTEE OF RECEPTION, GENTLEMEN OF CHICAGO AND OF ILLINOIS: I feel very much honored by the welcome which I am receiving at your hands to-day. I feel highly honored by the speech of welcome which has just been uttered by your worthy Mayor. It is something that is so personal to myself that it would hardly be in good taste for me to respond to the language of it, and it leaves nothing, therefore, for me to do than to repeat my thanks to this committee and to the citizens of your city for the hearty reception which they have given me.

"In regard to one allusion, to my receptions abroad, I will say that in every case I felt it was a tribute to my own country. I will add, further, that our country stands differently abroad in the estimation of the Europeans and Eastern nations from what it did a quarter of a century ago. An American citizen is regarded in a different light from the American citizen of a quarter of a century ago. At that time it was believed that we had not a nation; that it was merely a confederation of states tied together by a rope of sand, that would give way upon the slightest friction. They have found out their grand mistake. They know that we have now a government, that we are a Nation, and that we are a strong, intelligent, and brave people, capable of judging and knowing our rights, and determined on all occasions to maintain them against either domestic or foreign foes. And that is the explanation of the receptions which you have received through me while I was abroad. Gentlemen, I thank you."

As General Grant concluded his remarks, the Mayor invited the crowd to come forward in twos and shake hands with the General, stating that the General had seen a great deal and was very hungry. Many of the old comrades came forward and reminded him pleasantly in passing of the last time they met.

The pressure of the crowd became so great that Mayor Harrison was compelled to ask them to desist, and at 4 o'clock the Mayor and Colonel George R. Davis took him in charge, and conducted him to his private parlor, where a small company was assembled, consisting of Mrs. General Grant, Mrs. Sheridan, the Hon. Thomas Hoyne, and others. After a few complimentary remarks, he was conducted to his carriage by General Chetlain and the Hon. Thomas Hoyne, and departed to take dinner at his son's house.

Speaking of the decorations, the *Inter-Ocean* of the 13th says: "The appearance of the city was a surprise to the people of Chicago themselves. The gay attire which they had been planning for weeks being richer and more complete than had been pictured in anticipation. There were a number of establishments that might be named which spent over a thousand dollars in each adornment; but when thousands worked with willing hands and loving hearts, if with a smaller expenditure of money, to swell the general welcome of the city to her guest, it would be perhaps unfair, as it is unnecessary, to mention the few who, in this respect, were able to surpass the rest."

"The grand arch, upon which the General first looked as he stepped from the cars, spanned his path, with the words, 'Chicago's Welcome,' and as he rode over the four miles of the route Chicago's welcomes were spoken "all along the line" in bowers of living green; in arches bright with the colors of gay bunting; in lovely festoons of flowers which drooped to the very ground from the highest tops of the brown-stone fronts of Michigan avenue; in rich canopies which carried their tributes out to the very steps of his carriage; in the magnificent trappings and beautiful hangings on marble fronts; in floating pendants and waving banners; in the millions of flags which covered the city almost as a great mantle of patriotism and loyalty, and finally in portraits on every side of Grant himself, and in matters which repeated again his own terse and patriotic utterances that have become the dearly-prized household words of the people.

"From out such wondrous profusion in decorations and such bewildering beauties of embellishment along four miles of thoroughfare, it is a manifest impossibility to describe the appearance of each building, or even any considerable number of the most prominent."

The St. Louis *Globe Democrat*, in speaking of the C cago reception on the 12th said, "Chicago was gloriously decorated. * * * The scenes along the route of the procession were almost beyond description, * * * the four hundred thousand people who lined the streets were wildly, madly enthusiastic." St. Louis *Republican* (Dem.): "The whole central part of the city was a gorgeous scene of patriotism, embodied in bunting and flowing out in colors such as would make the rainbow hide its head." It seems as if the whole Northwest had poured out its population to the citizen thus auspiciously returning to his home."

The Cincinnati *Commercial* said: "A noticeable feature of the decorations was that not only were buildings owned by Republicans replete with ornaments, but those of prominent Democrats were among the most brilliant in their display of colors and evergreens. Messrs. Field & Leiter, both outspoken Democrats, made a lavish display. The Democratic Palmer House, besides having made itself his headquarters during his stay, presented adornments in profusion, which were of the most patriotic character. McVicker, who is a life-long Democrat, enveloped his theatre from top to bottom with red, white, and blue, with flags at every available point, and allegorical paintings fifty-two feet long and fifteen feet high, representing General Grant as a tanner at Galena, as the victorious soldier at Appomattox, and as the inaugurated President of the nation.

The Cincinnatti *Gazette* said: "The military display was fine. * * * The reception in the evening was an indescribable ovation."

The Cincinnati *Enquirer* (Dem.) said: "This was Grant's day, The Soldiers of the State of Illinois, of the State of Indiana, of Michigan, and of Wisconsin gave him such a demonstration as was never before seen in this city, or indeed any Western city. There was no concealing or denying it because the enthusiasm was so unusual that everybody had to acknowledge the fact."

The Louisville *Courier-Journal* (Dem.) said: "General Grant and party appeared at the head of the second division, and the enthusiam was indescribable. He appeared tired, wearied, and exhausted, but as cheer on cheer arose he lifted his hat wearily and smiled. A description of the entire progress of the procession might be summed in the words, no living or dead man ever received such an outburst of enthusiam. Ten minutes after the procession started, the sun burst through the clouds, adding fresh zeal to the excitement. No such a rain storm has occurred this year; no such a depth of mud was ever known; so grand a street pageant was never seen, and no such wild and unbridled excitement was ever experienced, is the verdict."

The Indianopolis *Journal* said: "Chicago to-day gave Grant a heroic reception, a cosmopolitan welcome, and to her hundreds upon thousands of population there were added a hundred thousand visitors. Never has this city been so densely packed, and never was an American citizen accorded such a hearty greeting as has been given this man. Chicago is celebrated for great deeds, but this event will pass to record as the grandest and the greatest and there is no event in the prophesy of man that can call out a more brilliant one."

The Detroit *Post* said: "Chicago has never seen anything like this day in all its history, or rather, it has seen several occasions bearing some analogy to it, but none to equal it in magnitude. Never before has the city presented such a festive appearance. Millions of flags and banners were floating to the breeze, and every building on the South Side and thousands of private residences everywhere were covered with the decorations."

The formal reception by the society of the Army of the Tennessee, at Haverly's theatre, in the evening, fitly closed the extraordinary record of the day. The stage had been transformed into a picturesque war scene, the hills in the vicinity of Vicksburg rising in the distance, and nearer, the fortifications of the Union troops. Field pieces were in place pointing outward through the embrasures, and on them and about them were grouped artillery men in regulation dress. The grouping had a tableaux effect that brought into clear relief the gathering of distinguished gentlemen in front. The theatre was beautifully and elaborately decorated in flowers and evergreens.

In the parquette, dress circle, balcony and gallery was a select audience, taking in the members of the different army societies and many of Chicago's leading citizens. As many of the veterans wore uniforms, and as many of the ladies, even in the gallery were in full dress, the assemblage was a brilliant one, even for that city.

Prayer was offered by Rev. Dr. H. W. Thomas.

The first address of the evening was by the Hon. E. B. Washburne, who spoke a general welcome to the society and to General Grant. Mr. Washburne was at his best, and his courtly manner and well chosen words gave to his speech of welcome a special charm. A warm tribute to McPherson, and a graceful mention of Grant, called out responsive bursts of applause.

He was followed by Governor Cullom, who spoke the welcome of the state. His unusually clear cut tones, his dignified deliberation, and his special emphasis were hints to those who knew him that his speech was not to be an ordinary one, and it was not. His first reference to national sentiment and nationality was the signal for a hearty round of enthusiasm, and the plain talk that followed was applauded to the echo. He made a dramatic mention of

Grant that brought that gentleman to his feet in response to continued calls from the audience. A reference to the incomparable Sherman and the chivalric Logan compelled each of those gentlemen to follow the example of Grant, and rise in answer to the calls from the people in front.

Mayor Harrison spoke the welcome of the city, speaking in his usual style, and saying many good things, whenever he dropped an incidental remark about the distinguished ex-President, the audience stopped Mr. Harrison with cheers, and kept up the noise until General Grant arose and acknowledged the compliment with a bow.

General Sherman responded briefly and pointedly, his first remark, to the effect that Chicago was ready and willing, for a consideration, to feed the world, calling out a double round of applause.

The annual address, by General Gresham, was read in a smooth, lawyer-like manner, and, coming after the impromptu speeches, seemed at first as not likely to claim the close attention of those outside of army circles. But soon the people awoke to the realization that a scholarly gentleman was discussing vital questions of general interest, and the speaker not only had the closest attention of all, but the heartiest commendation.

After the presentation of a banner to the Society by General Logan in a graceful speech, and a response, half playful, half earnest, by General Sherman, it was announced that there would be a song. This was met by a determined call for General Grant, and he arose as if to excuse himself, saying he would fill the regular order on the programme. The audience, quick to see the drift of this remark, informed him that he was not on the programme, and insisted that he should go on. As he took from his pocket a few pages of manuscript, the crowd cheered, and the officers on the stage turned toward him with new interest on their faces.

The General stepped forward and said:

COMRADES OF THE SOCIETY OF THE ARMY OF THE TENNESSEE: After an absence of several years from the gatherings of the society of the Army of the Tennessee, it affords me heart-felt pleasure to again be with you, my earliest comrades in arms in the great conflict for nationality and union of all the states under our free and always-to-be maintained government. In my long absence from the country I have had the most favorable opportunity for seeing and comparing, in my own mind, our institutions with all European countries, and most of those of Asia—comparing our resources, developed and dormant, the capacity and energy of our people for upholding and developing its resources, with most of the civilized people of the world. Everywhere, from England to Japan, from Russia to Spain and Portugal, we are understood, our resources highly appreciated, and the skill, energy, and intelligence of the citizens recognized. My receptions have been everywhere kind, and an acknowledgement that the United States is a Nation, a strong, independent, and free Nation, composed of strong, brave, and intelligent people, capable of judging of their rights, and ready to maintain them at all hazards. This is a non-partisan association, but composed of men who are united in the determination that no foe, domestic or foreign, shall interpose between us and the maintenance of our grand, free, and enlightened institutions, and unity of all the States. The area of our country, its fertility, the energy and resources of our people, with a sparsity of population compared to area, postpones the day for generations to come when our descendants will have to consider the question of how the soil is to support them, how the most can be produced to sustain human life, without reference to the taste or desires of the people, and when but few can exercise the privilege of the plain luxury of selecting the articles of food they will eat, the quantity and quality of clothing they wear, but will remain the abundant home of all who possess the energy and strength, and make good use of them, if we remain true to ourselves. Such a country is one to be proud of. I am proud of it—proud that I am an American citizen. Every citizen, North, South, East, and West, enjoys a common heritage, and should feel an equal pride in it.

"I am glad these society meetings keep up their interest so long after the events which, in a sense, they commemorate, have passed away. They do not serve to keep up sectional feeling or bitterness toward our late foe; but they do keep up the feeling that we are a nation, and that it must be preserved, one and indivisible. We feel and maintain that those who fought, and fought bravely, on the other side from us, have equal claims with ourselves in all the blessings of our great and common country. We claim for them the right to travel all over this broad land and select where they please, the right to settle, become citizens, and enjoy their political and religious convictions, free from molestation or ostracism either on account of them or their connection with the past. We ask nothing more for ourselves, and would rejoice to see them become powerful rivals in the development of our great resources, sn the acquisition of all that shall be desirable in this life, and in patriotism and love of country."

The little speech was extremely well received, and as the General folded his paper and put it in his vest pocket, there was a round of applause, interrupted by a vigorous call for General Sheridan, which soon brought him to the front to make a happy little two-minute speech. Then, at the order of the now determined audience, came Pope, Oglesby, Schofield, and Mark Twain, each to speak briefly.

Frank Lumbard's quartet did fine service.

The tattoo was then given, and the president announced the society adjourned till the following morning.

The *Inter-Ocean* in summing up the welcome given General Grant, said:

Chicago has spoken her welcome. With what warmth and demonstrativeness is best shown in our reports giving particulars of the great display. If the warmth and earnestness of the great display are to be judged by the magnitude of the parade, by the numbers and enthusiasm of the people, by the presence in the procession of representatives of every department of government, every branch of business, every industrial interest, and every class of citizens, then Chicago has spoken as has no other community. The commanders and soldiers of the old armies, the commanders of the present army, the military authorities and military forces of the state, the different departments of the city government, the manufacturing and commercial interests of the state and city, were never before combined to speak so grand a welcome. Chicago has spoken as only Chicago can speak. And she means it.

The following day the General attended a reception given by the Union Veteran Club, given at McVicker's theatre, at 10:30 A. M. The speech making was preceded by an allegorical tableau.

The tableau presented a semicircle of young girls, with a throne in the middle of the are bearing the presiding genius. This central figure was a representative of Columbia, who excited unanimous approval. She was seated on a dais, and above her gleaming helmet she bore a standard —that of the Twenty-first Illinois Infantry—which was a mere tatter. The bare arms were bound at wrist and upper arm with broad gold bracelets. The pure white of the waist was relieved by a silken flag draped as the skirt. The lady, Miss Adeila Barker, by her many charms, presided a worthy Queen over the goddesses. On her broad shield she bore the salutation to General Grant, "In the name of the United States you saved, I welcome you."

The young and charming representatives of the states who supported them, were dressed in pure white, with strands of flowers caught in their skirts and clusters of flowers on the breast and in the hair. They wore graceful crowns of blue, edged with crimson and ornamented, each with three silver stars. Flowing down from the crowns, the luxuriant hair, in almost every instance blonde, reached to the waist. In her right hand each goddess held a blue shield bearing the name of a state and the words after it, "Welcome you." In the other hand she flourished a small flag.

Six little goddesses, representing the Territories, stood a little in advance of the main line, directly in front of Columbia, and bloomed all over with gay flowers.

A noticeable representative of a State was the tall brunette, bearing on her shield the legend, "Michigan welcomes you." Her raven hair sweeping down her shoulders was matched by a broad, black scarf, in memory of Chandler.

General Chetlain, President of the Union Veterans, made an address of welcome. An eloquent address by Gen. Hogan received hearty and enthusiastic notice; he was followed by General Grant, who said:

"COMRADES AND VETERANS OF THE LATE WAR: I was entirely unaware of the object of my coming here this morning. I thought it was to be the place where we were to meet this evening, or some other place. I was not aware that I was going to meet so many of my old comrades. I assure you it affords me great pleasure to meet you here, and to meet you everywhere.

"Veterans of the old war, and my former companions in

GENERAL GRANT ON THE LAKE SHORE DRIVE, LINCOLN PARK, CHICAGO.

all my travels, I have not been in a country, in hardly a town, and in hardly a place, in the two and a-half years that I have been away from my own country where I have not met some of your number. As we heard last night, wars, while not desirable, still are not always unattended with good. We believe sincerely that the war which we waged was attended with great good to our country. We believe that our victory redounded to the benefit of the vanquished, as well as to ourselves. We believe that they to-day would have been in a very much worse condition had their cause succeeded, and we certainly would have been infinitely worse off. Wars render another benefit. People who grow up in time of profound peace are very apt to vegetate and live along in the place, or near the place, of their birth, but having been torn away from their homes, as you all were, and having passed through the struggles and privations of the war, you were the more content to return to your homes, or to go to the best places for the development of your intelligence and your talents. The veterans of the war are now scattered over this broad land, are now developing our Territories, opening new mines, clearing new farms, and in every way adding to the greatness and prosperity of our nation. They are making our country felt, known, and appreciated wherever a flag can wave.

"Now, gentlemen, I have said a great deal more than I had any idea I could say when I got up. But, as Mark Twain very aptly remarked last evening, I could make a very much better extemporaneous speech if I had a couple of hours to prepare it."

The General's address aroused the wildest enthusiasm, the audience springing to its feet and giving round after round of applause. Hon. Emory A. Storrs delivered the address of the day, and was accorded a flattering reception. In response to repeated calls from the audience, Gen. Fuller, ex-Gov. Oglesby, Gen. Woodford, of N. Y., made brief but eloquent addresses. "Taps" ended the programme,

At 12 o'clock, General Grant lunched at the residence of Hon. E. B. Washburne. The affair was private and unostentatious. At 2:30 o'clock he attended the reception of the society of the Army of the Tennessee. Mrs. Grant received with the General. Receiving with her were Mrs. Gen. Logan, Mrs. W. Q. Gresham, Mrs. P. H. Sheridan, Mrs. A. L. Chetlain, and Mrs. Fred Grant. The ladies who received with the General, were in full dress.

Gen. Chetlain and Gen. Logan presented each of the long line, announcing their names and passing them on. The General stood the ordeal with grim silence, occasionally muttering a word with old acquaintances. Each comer was presented to Mrs. Grant, and the receiving ladies as far as possible, but the encounter with the General and his wife was generally sufficient for all who passed.

To carry out the programme of the day, at 3:30 the General was compelled to leave, and attend the reception of the Union Veteran Club, where the wildest enthusiasm was manifested. Shortly after 4 o'clock, he withdrew to his private parlors to seek the needed rest and prepare himself for the evening's business.

In the evening the General attended the grand banquet at the Palmer House, given by the members of the Army of the Tennessee. No handsomer sight was ever seen in Chicago than that afforded, when the 460 banqueters had all found seats at eighteen tables, which had been prepared for their reception. The hall was handsomely draped with flags and embellished with evergreens and flowers. Gen. W. T. Sherman presided. **The supper itself was a success.** We give the menu:

THIRTEENTH ANNUAL BANQUET
OF THE
SOCIETY OF THE ARMY OF THE TENNESSEE.

MENU.

Blue Point Oysters on the Shell.   Sauterne.
Green Turtle Soup.   Sherry.
Boiled California Salmon.   Holland Sauce.   **Claret.**
Parisienne Potatoes.
Roast Fillet of Beef, Larded with Mushrooms.
Champagne.
Croquets of Potatoes.
Cutlets of Minced Game.
Sweet-breads with Spinach.
Croquets of Chicken.
Roman Punch.
Roast Saddle of Venison.
Roast Prairie Chicken.
Buffalo Steaks.   Truffle Sauce.
Breasts of Ducks, Larded, Currant **Jelly.**
Fillet of Wild Turkey.   Cranberry **Sauce.**
Chicken Salad.
Shrimp Salad.
Celery Salad.
Neapolitan Ice Cream.
Ices.
Cakes, assorted.
Wine Jellies.
Charlotte Russe.
Meringes, assorted.
Fruits.
Hard Tack.
Roquefort and English **Cheese.**
Celery.
Coffee.
Cognac.
Cigars.

PALMER HOUSE, Nov. 13, 1879.

At 10:45 General Sherman arose and quieted the tumult and proceeded to say:

"GENTLEMEN: We have a long list before us, and one of the richest I have ever had spread before me. And I am extremely anxious that this evening shall be a bright one in our future memories. We can only accomplish this result by almost absolute silence; and I beg, almost implore of you, every man, to be just as quiet as possible, because sounds added together reverberate in this hall, and will spoil the best speech that can possibly be made."

He then complimented the musicians upon the excellence of their efforts thus far; and suggested that where the programme called for music, they simply give a soft strain and not a whole tune. "Make it, as it were, a loop between the speeches. With a few admonitions of this kind, I am sure we will have an evening, a night, if you please, of cheering entertainment.

"I do not pretend to say any thing myself; but will call the toasts in the order in which they are recorded on the programme, simply introducing each speaker. There happen to be three speakers absent, but their places have been filled by the Committee, and I have recorded their names, so that the speeches will follow each other in quick succession. Each speaker is requested to speak as long as he holds his audience. As to applause, gentlemen, recollect that that takes a good deal of time. A good, hearty laugh and marked applause are all right, but don't drawl it out into a long giggle, or into a noise. Let the applause be short and emphatic.

"Now, gentlemen, we will proceed at once to the regular order of the evening. And I am pleased to see everybody smiling and pleasant. Some of the speakers who are in your midst will speak from their present position, either by getting on a chair or standing as they please. But, wherever they are, I beg the audience to give them a respectful hearing."

"The first toast of the evening," said Gen. Sherman, "is Our Country—Her Place Among Nations, "and will be responded to by Gen. U. S. Grant."

As General Grant arose he was received with tumultuous applause and cheers, which lasted several minutes, the greeting being extremely cordial. When silence was restored he said:

"Mr. President and Gentlemen of the Society of the Army of the Tennessee, and Guests: Notice was sent to me some days ago that I was to respond to a toast here, but I paid no attention to it at the time, and had no idea, until I got here, of the toast I was to reply to. I had relied upon it that there would be half a dozen or more speakers before I would be called upon, and that, during that time, there would be a man out in the hall I would want to see, or thought I would exert some other flank movement by which I would get out of it. Finding, however, after my arrival here, that I was to be the first one called upon, and hardly feeling it would be proper to look for that man so early in the evening, I put in a substitute, but the President of your Society has not called upon the man. I know if he h d called the name on his paper you would have heard much more said about the position of our country among the nations of the earth than I can say to you. I can feel what the Mayor would probably have said if the President had called upon him. But, as I have to say a word, I shall rely now upon your signifying, in a very few moments, your disapprobation of what I am saying, so as to let me off. The President has given notice that we are not to speak any longer than we can hold the audience. Our Nation we have been in the habit ourselves of looking upon as being one of the first nations of the earth.

"For a long period back the Yankee has had not only a very respectable opinion of himself individually, but of his country as a whole. It has been our own opinion that we had nothing to fear in a contest with any other Power. I am pleased to say, that from the observations that I have been able to make in the last two and a half years, we are beginning to be regarded a little by other Powers as we in our vanity have heretofore regarded ourselves. We do, among other nations, I think, to-day, not only in our own conceit, but in the acknowledgment of other nations, occupy the position of one of the first Powers in all that goes to make up a great nationality. We have the strength, we have the individual self-assertion, independence; and we have to a greater degree than almost any other nation the power of colonizing, of settling up new country, opening it and developing it. We have also the very great advantage of being without neighbors to molest or make us afraid. It is true we have a northern frontier, and we have a southern frontier, but we get along with a very small army. We keep no standing army. What little we do keep, as some one remarked the other day, is a standing army because it has no time to sit down. Mr. President [who was seated], I find you filling the position with a good deal of ability. I don't know of anything I can specially add to what I have said, except in the way of advice; and that is, let us be true to ourselves; avoid all bitterness and ill-feeling, either on the part of sections or parties, toward each other, avoid quarreling among ourselves, and we need have no fears for the future of maintaining the stand that we have taken among nations, so far as opposition from foreign nations goes. Gentlemen, I am much obliged for your attention."

The "President and Congress" was responded to by General Logan, in an eloquent address, which was received with rapturous applause. "The Army of the Tennessee" was responded to by General Hurlburt, and was a glorious tribute to its two commanders, Grant and Sherman. The speaker took his seat amid great enthusiasm and cheers. The toast, "Our First Commander, Gen. U. S. Grant," was responded to by Col. Vilas, of Madison, Wis.,—a War-Democrat—as follows:

"Your call invites me, sir, I am conscious, to give expression to the profound feeling with which every heart of our assembled companions respond to the stirring sentiment. But how shall I attempt to choose, in the brief compass the occasion allows, from the multitudinous thoughts that crowd the mind? Our first commander, the illustrious General, whose fame has grown to fill the world! Nay, more! Our old Band of the Tennessee was his first army! What honorable memories of old association you, companions, may now recall! How splendid was your entrance on the scene of arms! The anxious eye of the North had long been fixed on the Eastern theatre, almost unconscious of the new-formed Army of the Tennessee and its unknown General. Suddenly there fell on the startled ear the roar of your fight at Donelson and your chieftain's victorious cry,—which waked the country's heart to ecstasy, and rung, like a prophetic knell, the doom our Army of Salvation bore to Rebels,—'Nothing, but unconditional surrender.'

"Then, but a few days later, there burst, at Shiloh, upon this Army of the Tennessee, the flame and fury of 'the first great field-fight of the war.' In desperate doubt the night-fall of the bloody day closed on the unequal struggle. Higher, then, rose the iron resolution of that great commander. Urged by cautious counsel to prepare the way for retreat, with trust in your valor, he gave the characteristic answer, 'I have not despaired of whipping them yet.' And loyally, on the morrow, was he vindicated in that reliance, as he rode before his soldiery, driving the enemy over the victorious fields. How darkly comes back in recollection the long and dismal toil in the pestilential swamps before impregnable Vicksburg. The sky was overhung in gloom, and the soaked earth sunk under the foot. Unlit by the flash of powder, unheralded by the noise of arms, in miserable darkness, the last enemy irresistibly plied his fatal work, changing the river levees—where only was solid ground for burial—into tombs for our trebly-decimated ranks. Then, again, new light broke from his troubled genius on the scene, and displayed the possible path of valor. Breaking past the rebel battlements and across the great river, he flung our army into the midst of the hostile host, like a mighty gladiator surrounded by his foes, choosing no escape but in victory. There, with fiery zest, in fierce rapidity, he smote the foe the crushing strokes for Fort Gibson, Raymond, Jackson, Champion Hills, and Black River, and seized the doomed city with the unrelenting grasp of his Army of the Tennessee.

"And when, on the new birthday of the Republic, her flag shook out its beautiful folds above the ramparts of that boasted citadel, the territory of revolt was finally split in twain,—the backbone of the Rebellion was broken.

"Such, in a glance, your splendid story, companions, under our first commander. He and his army of the Tennessee entered on the page of history together. Together they achieved the first great prophetic triumphs for the Union; together they followed and fought her enemies from field to field, pushing our advancing arms in steady career towards the Gulf; nor were their efforts for our country disunited until, having dismembered the vast Rebellion, the beginning of its utter downfall had been seen.

"Guided by his genius, your army had learned to fight only to conquer. Parted from him, it forgot not the teaching. Its march and war struck every revolted State save two, but never General anywhere lamented over its retreat from the field of arms. Joyfully may we point to that exalted fame which, rising like a pinnacle of the Alps, breaks through the firmament above to carry up the name of the unconquered Grant; for it is our felicity that, on the solid base from which it lifts, history has written the proud legend of the Army of the Tennessee, which never shunned and never lost, a battle with its foes.

Joined to it by such a story, and especially when so assembled, his old associates and soldiers in war, we may rightfully without censure and without adulation, claim and speak the just measure of his merit and renown. Nor shall his presence deny that satisfaction to us. His reputation is not his, nor even his country's alone. It is, in part, our peculiar possession. We, who fought to aid its rising, may well rejoice in its meridian splendor.

The foundations of his title are deep laid and safe. There was reaction in the minds of our people after the intense strain of war, and many distracting subjects for attention. But, with regained composure and reflection, his reputation augments, and its foundations appear more and more immovably fixed for lasting duration. They spring not from merely having enjoyed possession of the honors of place and power which his countrymen have bestowed; others have had them too. They lie not specially on his shining courage and personal conduct before the enemy, who was never outdone in calm intrepidity, nor in the splendid daring with which he ever urged the battle he immediately ordered; though long these will live in song and story. Beyond the warrior's distinction, which was his earlier glory, his is the true genius of the General. The strategic learning of the military art was to him a simple implement, like colors and brush to a Raphael, not fetters to the mind. How like a weapon in a giant's hand did he wield the vast aggregation of soldiery whose immensity oppressed so many minds! How easily moved his divisions, yet how firm the place of all! How every soldier came to feel his participation a direct contribution to the general success. And when, at length, his merit won the government of the entire military power of the North, how perfect became, without noise or friction, the co-operation of every army, of every strength, throughout the wide territory of war towards the common end! Subordinate every will and jealous soul, the profound military wisdom of the capital even, to the clear purpose and comprehensive grasp of the one commanding mind. Then how rapidly crumbled on every side the crushed revolt! When shall we find in past records the tale of such a struggle so enormous in extent, so nearly matched at the outset, so desperately contested, so effectively decided? Through what a course of uninterrupted victory did he proceed from the earliest engagements to a complete dominion of the vast catastrophe! Nor should it be forgotten, he fought no barbarians, ill-equipped, undisciplined, not commanded by educated skill; but against soldiers of the finest spirit, armed with the best weapons, standing on their own familiar ground, and led by veteran Generals of well-trained science, one of whom, at least, was never overmatched on his chosen field before.

"Spare, in pity, the poor brain which cannot see, in this career, more than a dogged pertinacity! Out upon the unjust prejudice which will consciously disparage the true meed of genius! Leave it where his reliant silence leaves it; leave it to history! leave it to the world.

"But in the great cause, so well understood, and the great results to men, so well accomplished, the basis of his renown is justly broadened. For the salvation of this Government of freedom for mankind we took up arms. When liberty was safe they were laid down again. Risen to the highest seat of power, he has descended as a citizen of equal rank with all. This goes to the soul of American liberty, ennobling individual citizenship above all servants in office. His is indeed the noblest grandeur of mankind who can rise from the grasp of overtopping power above the ambition of self to exalt the ambition of humanity, denying the spoils of the brief time to the lasting guerdon of immortal honor. The judgment of immediate contemporaries has been apt to rise too high or fall too low. But let not detraction or calumny mislead. They have ever been the temporal accompaniments of human greatness. That glory cannot rise beyond the clouds, which passes not through the clouds. We may confidently accept the judgment of the world. It has been unmistakably delivered. But lately, as he had pressed his wandering course about the round earth, mankind have everywhere bowed in homage at his coming, as the ancient devotees of the East fell before the sun at rising. These honors were not paid to his person, which was unknown; they were not paid to his country, for which he went on no errand, and whose representative never had the like before; they were not paid to him as to some potentate of a people, for he journeyed not as a man in power. They have been the willing prostration of mortality before a glory imperishable.

"His memory shall, indeed, be in the line of the heroes of war, but distinctive and apart from the greater number. Not with the kind of Alexander, who ravaged the earth to add to mere dominion; nor of Belisarius, who but fed the greedy craving of an imperial beast of prey; not with Marlborough, Eugene, Wellington, who played the parts set them by the craft of diplomacy; not with the Napoleons, who chose "to wade through slaughter to the throne, and shut the gates of mercy on mankind;" not with Cæsar, who would have put the ambitious hand of arms on the delicate fabric of constitutional freedom; America holds a higher place in the congregation of glory for her heroes of Liberty, where sits in expectation, her majestic Washington. In nobler ambition than the gaining of empire, they have borne their puissant arms for the kingdom of man, where Liberty reigneth forever. From the blood poured out in their warfare, sweet incense rose to Heaven; and angels soothed, with honorable pride, the tears which sorrow started for the dead.

"Home again now, our first commander, after the journey of the world! Here, here again, we greet him, at our social board, where with recurring years, we regale on the deeper-ripening memories of our soldiership for Freedom. Partakers of the labors, the perils, the triumphs, which were the beginnings of his glory, we join now, with exultation, in the welcoming honors by which his grateful countrymen tell their foreknowledge of the immortality of his renown. Long and many be the years, illustrious leader before your hour of departure come! Green and vigorous be your age, undecayed every faculty of mind and sense, in full fruition of the well-earned joys of life; happy in the welfare of your native land, the love of your countrymen, the admiration of the world!"

The vast assembly rose to its feet as the eloquent Colonel concluded his response and sat down. The hall resounded with applause and cheers, and everybody waved a napkin or a handkerchief in the air to show appreciation of what must be considered as the most dignified and scholarly response, made all the more enjoyable by the Colonel's eloquence, of the entire evening. Colonel Vilas was obliged to respond to all this enthusiasm by remounting his chair and receiving three rousing cheers as he did so.

The "Officers and Soldiers of the Mexican War," responded to by General Woodford. "The Army of the Potomac," responded to by Leonard Swett. "The Army of the Cumberland—its leaders." Response by General Wilson. "The other Armies." Response by General Pope. "The Volunteer Soldiers," by Colonel Robert G. Ingersoll. "The Patriotic People," Emory A. Storrs. "Woman," General Fletcher. The last regular toast of the evening was, "The Babies; as they comfort us in our sorrows, let us not forget them in our festivities," responded to by Mark Twain. He said:

"I like that. We have not all had the good fortune to be ladies. We have not all been generals, or poets, or statesmen, but when the toast works down to the babies we stand on common ground, for we have all been babies. It is a shame that, for a thousand years, the world's banquets have utterly ignored the baby, as if he didn't amount to anything. If you will stop and think a minute,—if you will go back fifty or a hundred years to your early married life, and recontemplate your first baby,—you will remember that he amounted to a good deal, and even something over. You soldiers all know that when that little fellow arrived at family headquarters you had to hand in your resignation. He took entire command. You became his lackey—his mere body-servant, and you had to stand around, too. He was not a commander who made allowances for time, distance, weather, or any thing else. You had to execute his order whether it was possible or not. And there was only one form of machinery in his manual of tactics, and that was the double-quick. He treated you with every sort of insolence and disrespect, and the bravest of you didn't dare to say a word. You could face the death storm of Donelson and Vicksburg, and give back blow for blow, but when he clawed your whiskers, and pulled your hair, and twisted your nose, you had to take it. When the thunders of war were sounding in your ears, you set your faces toward the batteries, and advanced with steady tread, but when he turned on the terrors of his war-whoop, you advanced in the other direction, and mighty glad of the chance, too. When he called for soothing-syrup, did you venture to throw out any side remarks about certain services being unbecoming an officer and a gentleman? No. You got up and got it. When he ordered his pap bottle, and it was not warm did you talk back? Not you. You went to work and warmed it. You even descended so far in your menial office as to take a suck at that warm, insipid stuff, just to see if it was right,—three parts water to one of milk,—a touch of sugar to modify the colic, and a drop of peppermint to kill those immortal hiccoughs. I can taste that stuff. And how many things you learned as you went along! Sentimental young folks still take stock in that beautiful old saying, that when the baby smiles it is because the angels are whispering to him. Very pretty, but too thin—simply wind on the stomach, my friends. If the baby proposed to take a walk at his usual hour, 2 o'clock in the morning, didn't you rise up promptly and remark, with a mental addition which would not improve a Sunday-school book much, that that was the very thing you were about to propose yourself? Oh! you were under good discipline, and, as you went faltering up and down the room in your undress uniform, you not only prattled undignified baby-talk, but even tuned up your martial voices and tried to sing "Rock-a-by baby in the tree top," for instance. What a spectacle for an Army of the Tennessee! And what an affliction for the neighbors, too, for it is not everybody within a mile around that likes military music at three in the morning. And when you had been keeping this sort of thing up two or three hours, and your little velvet-head intimated that nothing suited him like exercise and noise, what did you do? You simply went on until you dropped in the last ditch. The idea that a baby doesn't amount to anything! Why, one baby is just a house and a front yard full by itself. One baby can furnish more business than you and your whole Interior Department can attend to. He is enterprising, irrepressible, brimful of lawless activities. Do what you please, you can't make him stay on the reservation. Sufficient unto the day is one baby. As long as you are in your right mind don't you ever pray for twins. Twins amount to a permanent riot. And there ain't any real difference between triplets and an insurrection.

"Yes, it was high time for a toast to the masses to recognize the importance of the babies. Think what is in store for the present crop! Fifty years from now we shall all be dead, I trust, and then this flag, if it still survive (and let us hope it may), will be floating over a republic numbering 200,000,000 souls, according to the settled laws of our increase. Our present schooner of state will have grown into a political leviathan—a Great Eastern. The cradled babies of to-day will be on deck. Let them be well trained, for we are going to leave a big contract on their hands. Among the three or four million cradles now rocking in the land are some which this nation would preserve for ages as sacred things, if we could know which ones they are. In one of these cradles, the unconscious Farragut of the future is at this moment teething; think of it, and putting in a word of dead earnest, inarticulated, but perfectly justifiable profanity over it, too. In another the future renowned astronomer is blinking at the shining milky way with but a liquid interest, poor little chap! and wondering what has become of that other one they call the wet nurse. In another the future great historian is lying, and doubtless will continue to lie until his earthly mission is ended. In another the future President is busying himself with no profounder problem of state than what the mischief has become of his hair so early, and in a mighty array of other cradles there are now some 60,000 future office-seekers, getting ready to furnish him occasion to grapple with that same old problem a second time. And in still one more cradle, somewhere under the flag, the future illustrious commander-in-chief of the American armies is so little burdened with his approaching grandeurs and responsibilities as to be giving his whole strategic mind at this moment to trying to find out some way to get his big toe into his mouth—an achievement which, meaning no disrespect, the illustrious guest of this evening turned his attention to some fifty-six years ago; and if the child is but a prophecy of the man, there are mighty few who will doubt that he succeeded."

Letters of regret were read from President Hayes, members of the cabinet, governors of states, judges of the Supreme Court, civil, military and naval officers. The *Chicago Tribune*, speaking of speeches at this banquet, said:

' These were specimens of oratory, for the most part, that every American may be proud of; one or two of the addresses were so brilliant that, like Ingersoll's eulogy on Blaine in the Cincinnati Convention, they are likely to find their way into the prints of all countries; one or two others were strikingly characteristic of the humor and sentiment of the American people. In an oratorical tournament General Grant is, of course, better as a listener than as a talker; he is a man of deeds rather than words. The same might be said of General Sherman, though, as presiding officer and toast-master of the occasion, his impromptu remarks were always pertinent and keen."

Col. Bob. Ingersoll succeeded in retaining the laurels which was so long since placed upon his brow, though when Col. Vilas, of Madison, sat down, it was thought that even Ingersoll's powers of oratory would be severely taxed to arouse equal enthusiasm. Ingersoll's theme —"The volunteer soldiers"— was one that drew from his warm heart the most earnest outpourings of gratitude and eulogy. He had an opportunity to pay a tribute to the men whom he most loves and respects in all the world, because they fought freely and heroically in the cause of the nation and universal humanity. His speech glittered with hyperbole, rendered more brilliant by the orator's earnest delivery, and nearly every word seemed like a beautiful picture to the delighted senses of his hearers. What more bountiful imagery could have been presented than when he spoke of the volunteer soldiers as "the defenders of humanity, the destroyers of prejudice, the breakers of chains," or, again, as "the saviors of the Republic and the liberators of men!" How striking the figure that Lincoln, in his Emancipation Proclamation, "copied with the pen what the grand hands of brave comrades had written with their swords!" How picturesque the greeting to Grant as, "the great leader who, having put a shining band of friendship—a girdle of clasped and loving hands around the globe, came home to find that every promise made in war has now the ring and gleam of gold!" How appropriate and stirring was his final apostrophe, ending: "Let us drink to all the living and all the dead—to Sherman, and to Sheridan, and to Grant, the laureled soldiers of this world, and last to Lincoln, whose loving life, like a bow of peace, spans and arches all the clouds of war!" There is little wonder that Ingersoll was interrupted at every sentence with loud and ringing applause, though the night was far spent and the assembled hundreds weary."

The speech of Col. Vilas, who responded to the toast, "Our First Commander—U. S. Grant," was a genuine surprise. Even those who had reason to expect something brilliant from him must have been astonished at the rich garnishment of language which this Wisconsin orator brought to Grant's glory. The latter-day prejudice against what is known as "fine writing" was dissipated by the sonorous and well rounded periods which he turned off so magically, and which took the multitude off their feet. This tribute to Grant's renown was the more effective because it came from an old Democrat, and there was something very like a pointed rebuke to many members of his own party when Col. Vilas exclaimed: "Spare, in pity, the poor brain which cannot see in this career more than a dogged pertinacity! Out upon the unjust prejudice which will consciously disparage the true meed of genius! Leave it where his reliant silence leaves it,—leave it to history, leave it to the world." The sketch of Grant's military achievements was rapid, impetuous, and vivid, but the most eloquent part of the speech was that contrasting America's military heroes with those of other nations, illustrating their worthier motives, and ending: "In nobler ambition than the gaining of empire, they have borne their puissant arms for the Kingdom of Man, where Liberty reigneth forever; from the blood poured out in their warfare sweet incense rose to Heaven, and angels soothed with honorable pride the tears which sorrow started for the dead."

There were other speeches at the Palmer House banquet which, if not so spirited as the two from which we have quoted, were still specimens of oratory of which all Americans will be proud. Notable among these were the address of Gen. Woodford who spoke for the Army of the Potomac, and that of Mr. Storrs, who paid tribute to the patriotism of those who fed and clothed our armies. Mark Twain's speech was a characteristic specimen of that peculiar American humor that perplexes the people of other lands and other manners, and its success is best attested by the roars and convulsions of laughter with which it was received at an hour when people ordinarily find it difficult to hold up their heads and keep their eyes open. His sketch of the immature heroes of the future was made up of genuine wit, and, altogether, he was delivered of one of the happiest efforts of his life.

The eloquence of the Palmer House banquet will be felt throughout the length and breadth of the land, and will be memorable in the annals of the Army of the Tennessee till the last survivor of that Association shall pass away.

On the 14th, Col. and Mrs. Fred Grant gave a reception at their home from 12 to 4 o'clock, and was one of the most pleasant gatherings given the honored guest, and was attended by the elite of the city. Everything was elegant and in perfect order. A profusion of rich and elaborate reception toilets were displayed by the ladies present, and the tasteful blending of colors served to lend an additional beauty to the already brilliant picture.

Mrs. Grant was richly attired in a princess dress of heavy royal purple velvet, with front of fringe and purple beads; corsage square, and filled in with point lace; heavy wrought gold bracelets; diamond cross and earrings; hair in coil, fastened with tortoise comb.

Mrs. Fred Grant wore a rich dress of white striped grenadine, embroidered with white silk, with clusters of pinks and white roses; diamond jewelry; hair dressed high, with gold band and bangles, and gold ornaments.

In the evening a reception by the Chicago Club at their club house, was second only, perhaps, in importance in the series of receptions given General Grant, to that of the banquet by the Army of the Tennessee; 1,200 were present. Mr. and Mrs. Grant and the reception party arrived early, and took their places in the card room—which is the largest apartment in the building—promptly at 8 o'clock, in the following order: Mr. Grant, with Mrs. Grant immediately on his right. Next came Mrs. Gen. Sheridan, then Mrs. Fred Grant, then Mrs. Rebert Lincoln and Mrs. Wirt Dexter. Immediately on the left of General Grant stood Mr. J. M. Walker and E. B. McCagg, who acted as an introductory committee.

At about 10 o'clock supper was announced.

At about 10:45 o'clock the guests began to call for their carriages and take their departure for their homes. From this time forth the rooms rapidly thinned out, for at a little after 11 o'clock the reception closed, and Mr. and Mrs. U. S. Grant, accompanied by their son, Col. Fred Grant, and his wife, were driven away to the home of the latter.

Everybody seemed to be well pleased with the entertainment, and from beginning to end it was a stupendous success. The Chicago Club established its reputation for giving receptions at the entertainment given in honor of President and Mrs. Hayes a year ago, but last night's effort capped the climax. Not a break or a hitch was perceptible throughout, and every person must have felt that special arrangements had been made for his or her entertainment. A more thoroughly enjoyable occasion is not on record in Chicago.

On the Saturday morning the Mexican veterans called upon the General in a body, and were received with great warmth and cordiality. Speeches were made by Leonard Swett, Col. Buell, of California, Hon. A. L. Morrison and others. The speakers were rewarded by prolonged applause. At two o'clock a general reception was given at the Grand Pacific Hotel, and was very generally participated in by the people. The reception closed promptly at five o'clock.

In the evening Potter Palmer entertained the distinguished guests, and was fully up to the high order of entertainments which had been given to the General since he first planted foot in Chicago. It being Saturday, the reception was not intended to be prolonged until a late hour. At eleven o'clock, the guests were greatly diminished in numbers, and General and Mrs. Grant took their leave of Mr. and Mrs. Palmer, and drove to their son's residence with the latter and his wife.

The display of elaborate and costly toilets outshone any previous display of the week, and each lady seemed to vie with the other in the elegance of her costume.

Mrs. General U. S. Grant wore an elaborate toilet of white satin, with white duchess lace front and shirred bottom, black drapery of lace and trimming of rich embroidery and pearls, very low corsage and short sleeves; heavy wrought gold bracelets, and diamond and pearl ornaments.

Mrs. Potter Palmer was richly dressed in a white satin plaited skirt, trimmed with wine and gold brocade; superb diamond ornaments.

Mrs. Col. Fred. Grant wore a rich robe of white satin, covered with Spanish lace; gold coronet and diamonds.

Mrs. General Sheridan was tastefully attired in a plain black cashmere dress, cut low, and trimmed with duchess lace; jet ornaments.

On Sunday morning, the General attended the Centenary Methodist Church, H. W. Thomas, D. D., pastor, being "at home" during the rest of the day only to his most intimate friends.

The visit of the school children to General Grant at the Exposition building on Monday was one of the most notable features of his sojourn. The huge building swarmed with the little people, forty or fifty thousand in number, all of whom had an opportunity to see the hero of the war of the rebellion, and many of them a chance to shake hands and speak with him.

The Calumet club entertained the General and Mrs. Grant, in the evening at their club house. The guests were not so numerous as at the Chicago club reception on Friday evening. There was a decided effort made to eclipse the other affair by making the list smaller and more select. There was a greater display of dress and fashion also. The people present numbered about five hundred, and besides being representative of the first society of Chicago, comprised also a fair proportion of distinguished persons from abroad who were in the city.

The toilets were generally of the most fashionable make, and of extremely rich materials. Experienced society people expressed astonishment at the beauty of many of the costumes worn and at the brilliancy of the display of jewelry —diamonds especially seemed to be as fashionable as ever, and imported laces for neck wear and trimming were almost the rule.

Mrs. General Grant was attired in an elegantly made white silk, watered, in combination with garnet brocaded silk, with rich fringe of the same; elegant oriental fan, bouquet, tortoise-shell comb in hair, which was dressed high; elegant diamond brooch, and solitaire pendants.

Mrs. Colonel Grant wore a combination cream-colored and wine-colored brocaded silk; point lace and diamonds.

The menu was of the most artistic pieces of culinary art seen in Chicago for many a day, and will doubtless become one of the models of the season. It was as follows:

CALUMET CLUB.
Reception to
GENERAL AND MRS. GRANT.

MENU.

Escalloped Oysters.
Oyster Patties a la Bachamel.

Gelatine of Turkey with Truffles, en Belle Vue.
Boned Partridge with Jelly, en Voliere,
Boned Quail with Truffles, a la Regence.
Sliced Buffalo Tongue, a la St. Hubert.
Breast of Chicken, with Mayonaise, a la Parisenne.
Gulf Shrimp Salad, Wine Jelly.
Fillet of Salmon with Mayonaise.

Rolled Sandwiches.   Vienna Cream Rolls.

Ornamental Confectionery.

Assorted Creams and Ices.
Pudding Glace.   Bisque Glace.
Pudding, a la Viesselrode.
Charlotte Russe, Wine Jelly.
Assorted Cake.

Fruit.   Coffee.

November 17, 1879.

    The last day of General Grant's stay in Chicago was crowded full of incidents of interest. In the forenoon occurred a visit to the Chicago Commandery of the Order of the Loyal Legion of the United States, where General Grant was formally received and decorated as a member of the Order. Then followed a call from the only four surviving veterans of the war of 1812 residing in Chicago, all of them octogenarians, and proud of the privilege of greeting a military hero who was born ten years after their services ended. General Grant's visit to the Protestant Orphan Asylum, the first charitable association organized in Chicago, was an important episode in the history of that worthy institution, and a memorable experience for its inmates. In the evening the General shed the lustre of his presence upon the performance at McVicker's Theatre, as the guest of the Second Regiment, and thus ended the public portion of his sojourn in Chicago.

    The General and Mrs. Grant left Chicago Wednesday morning for their home at Galena, where they arrived safely the same day.

    The *Inter-Ocean*, in summing up the week's series of entertainment, said:

    "The demonstration last night at McVicker's closed the

week in Chicago devoted to the reception of General Grant. The week has been a memorable one, and Chicago may well be proud of the record she has made. There has been, from the time of the great demonstration on Wednesday, scarcely a break in the line of receptions and entertainments. On Wednesday there were over one hundred thousand strangers in Chicago, and these, with the citizens who took part in the parade, or who turned out to witness it, swelled the crowd on the streets to over three hundred thousand. Although people were wild with enthusiasm and greatly excited, not a single serious accident occurred that day or during the week. The railroads centering in Chicago brought the great crowd of visitors to the city within the space of twenty-four hours, and although scores of extra trains came in such a way as to bewilder through passengers and suburban residents, there was little confusion, no disarrangement of time tables, and no accidents.

"Chicago has succeeded in speaking vociferously a most hearty welcome to General Grant, and in prolonging the festivities and formalities incident to so great an occasion without having the record marred by any public or private calamity."

In all these gatherings Grant has been the central figure. The people have employed every possible means to express their enthusiam and good feeling. The numerous receptions, banquets, and informal meetings were but the outgrowth of this sentiment. Not content with a general shout of acclamation, or with one great outburst of enthusiasm, finding expression in swelling cheers and elaborate decorations, the people of Chicago have sought to testify their appreciation of the work and character of General Grant in ways that seemed to them most fitting and most expressive. They had only a week in which to speak volumes, and they have made good use of the time.

The series of receptions has been in effect a continuous ovation, and when the people say good-bye to General Grant, on his departure for Galena to-day, they will feel that, after all that has been said and done during this week, so remarkable for its demonstrations, Chicago has not spoken half as earnestly as she feels. Through all this experience General Grant has conducted himself in such a way as to make old friends still more devoted, and to make new ones quite as enthusiastic as the old ones.

CHRONOLOGICAL.

AROUND THE WORLD CONDENSED.

The following chronological statement marks the leading incidents of General Grant's round the world tour:

MAY, 1877

Departure from Philadelphia	17
Arrival at Queenstown	27
Arrival at Liverpool	28
Arrival at Manchester	30

JUNE.

Arrival at London	1
Banqueted by Duke of Wellington at Apsley House	2
Reception at Minister Pierrepont's	5
Presented with the freedom of the City of London	15
Dinner with the Marquis of Lorne and Princess Louise	16
Breakfast with London literati	18
Dined with the Reform Club	18
Dinner with the Prince of Wales	19
Banqueted by the Trinity House, the Prince of Wales presiding	24
Visit to Queen Victoria at Windsor Castle	26–27
Banqueted by Liverpool citizens	28
Dinner with London Journalists	30

JULY.

Address by deputation of British workingmen	3
Banqueted by the United Service Club, Duke of Cambridge presiding	3
Reception at the American Legation	4
Departure for the Continent	5
Arrival at Brussels	6
Dinner with the King of Belgium	8
Banqueted at Frankfort	12
Laid corner-stone of new American Protestant Church at Geneva	27

AUG.

Visit to Lake Maggiore	5
Visit to Copenhagen	18
Returned to England	25
Presented with the freedom of Edinburg and banqueted	31

SEPT.

Presented with the freedom of Glasgow and banqueted	13
Monster labor demonstration in the General's honor at Newcastle-on-Tyne	22
Visit to Sheffield	26
Visited Shakspeare's tomb	28

CHRONOLOGICAL.

	OCT.
Visit to Sartoris family at Southampton	2–15
Banqueted at Birmingham	16
Departure for Paris	24
Arrival at Paris	25
Call upon President MacMahon	26
Visited by the Count de Paris and the Duchess of Magenta	27
Grand Banquet at Minister Noyes'	29
	NOV.
Dined by President MacMahon	1
Banqueted by American residents in Paris	6
Feted by Mrs. "Bonanza" Mackay	21
	DEC.
Visit to Lyons, France	2
Visit to Marseilles	3
Visit to Genoa	15
Visit to Naples	17
Meeting with Prince Alfred, the Duke of Edinburg, at Malta	28
	JAN., 1878.
Arrival at Alexandria, Egypt	5
Arrival at Cairo	7
Visited by the Khedive of Egypt	8
Departure for trip up the Nile	16
	FEB
The Holy Land reached at Jaffa	10
Reception at Jerusalem	13
	MARCH.
Arrival at Constantinople	3
Banqueted by the British Minister to Turkey	4
Banqueted by the King of Greece	13
	APRIL.
State dinner by King Humbert of Italy at Rome	15
Florence visited	20
Venice reached	23
	MAY.
Arrival at Turin	5
Visited Paris Exposition	10
Visited by President MacMahon and the Duchess of Magenta, Prince Hassan of Egypt, Prince Albert and Prince Frederic of Austria, Prince and Princess of Denmark	14
	JUNE.
Dined by Prince Orloff, Russian Minister to Paris	3
Dejeuner at the Hague with H. R. H. Prince Frederick, uncle of King of Holland	6
Dined by the Burgomasters of Rotterdam	8
Grand banquet at Amsterdam	12

CHRONOLOGICAL.

Arrival at Berlin	26
Interview with Prince Bismarck	27
Special audience with the Crown-Prince of Germany	27

JULY.

Reception by King Oscar of Norway and Sweden at Christiana	13
Banquet at Stockholm	24
Arrival at St. Petersburg	30
Visited by Prince Gortschakoff	31

AUG.

Audience with the Czar	1
Formal interview with the Czar	4
Dinner with Prince Dogaroff at Moscow	10
Audience with the Emperor of Austria	19
Dinner with the Austrian Imperial family	21
Dined by the citizens of Zurich, Switzerland	23

OCT.

Dined by Minister Noyes at Paris	3
Interview with ex-President Castelar of Spain at San Sebastian	9
Interview with King Alfonso	13
Arrival at Madrid	16

NOV.

Dinner with King Louis of Portugal	1
Breakfast with the Duc de Montpensier at Madrid	9
Dinner with Lord Napier of Magdala, at Gibraltar	18

JAN., 1879.

Arrival at Dublin, Ireland, and presented with freedom of the city	3
Feted at Londonderry	6
Reception at Belfast	9
State dinner and reception by President MacMahon at Paris	14
Arrived at Marseilles	21
Sailed for India	22

FEB.

Arrival at Bombay	13
State dinner and reception by the acting Governor at Bombay	17
Visit to the Maharajah of Jaypore	20
Visit to the Maharajah of Burtpoor	24
Visit to Delhi	26
Arrival at Calcutta, and banquet by Lord Lytton, Viceroy of India	28

MARCH.

Visit to British Burmah	23

APRIL.

Visit to Singapore	1

CHRONOLOGICAL. 487

Entertained by the King of Siam	14
Arrival at Saigon, Cochin China	25
Arrival at Hong Kong	30
MAY.	
State dinner at the Government House	3
Arrival at Hong Kong and entertained by the Viceroy	6
Reception of a deputation of Chinese	7
Arrival at Shanghai	19
Interview with the Viceroy, Li-Hung Chang, at Tientsin	24
JUNE.	
Arrival at Pekin	3
Interview with Prince Kung, Regent of China	5
Arrival at Nagasaki, Japan	21
State dinner by Governor of the Province	23
Banqueted by Nagasaki citizens	24
JULY.	
Tokio visited	3
Grand Reception by the Emperor of Japan	4
Banquet by the Emperor of Japan	7
Visit to Yokohama	9
Visit to Shrine of Iyeyasu	17
AUG.	
Private conversation with the Emperor of Japan	10
SEPT.	
Departure from Yokohama	3
Arrival at San Francisco	20
NOV.	
Arrival at Galena	5
Arrival at Chicago	12

Catalogue of Our Publications.

Subscription and Trade Books.

General U. S. Grant's Tour Around the World.
Edited by *L. T. Remlap, (Palmer.)*

Contains a full and accurate description of General Grant's Tour; the receptions, both public and private, tendered him; addresses of welcome—his responses; his conversations with public men, and a full description of entertainments, gossip, etc.; also receptions on the Pacific Coast, and the unprecedented series of receptions at Chicago, November 12th to 20th, inclusive. Elegantly illustrated. One large quarto volume, 500 pages. Fifteenth thousand ready November 20, 1879. The only book on the General's Tour printed in ENGLISH and GERMAN.

Cloth, Back and Side in Black and Gold................................. $2 00
" Gilt Edges, Back and Side in Black and Gold................ 2 50
Popular edition. Paper cover... 1 25

Leaders of Our Church Universal,
From the successors of the Apostles to the Generation just departed. A "Book of Saints," from the Evangelical stand point. Comprising EARLIER leaders, LATER leaders in Europe, America, Asia, Africa and Oceanica, by Dr. Ferdinand Piper, of Germany; and Dr. Henry McCracken, of America. The reader is carried along with glowing interest through the five successive periods.— "The Church's Spread in the South," "in the North;" "The Church's Centralization;" "The Church's Reformation," and "The Church's Reformed Progress."

The names of the European writers are of the most eminent: Tholuck, Krummacher, Neander, Hagenbach, Van Oosterzee (of Holland), Lechler, Lorimer (England), MacCrie (England), Monod (Paris), with more than a score of others hardly behind these in eminence and world-wide reputation.

The following is the complete roll of American writers: Dr. H. C. Alexander, Dr. Robert Beard, Dr. C. W. Bennett, Dr.

W. M. Blackburn, Dr. S. L. Caldwell, Dr. Rufus W. Clark, Mrs. Helen Finney Cox, Dr. Timothy Dwight, Dr. J. H. Goode, Dr. Lewis Grout, Dr. Arch. A. Hodge, Dr. Samuel Hopkins, Dr. Z. H. Humphrey, Dr. J. B. Jeter, Dr. Herrick Johnson, Mrs. Helen Kendrick, Dr. D. R. Kerr, Dr. Heman Lincoln, Dr. Henry MacCracken, Dr. J. M. Pendleton, D. W. K. Pendleton, Prof. B. F. Prince, Bp. W. Bacon Stevens, Mrs. Harriet B. Stowe, Dr. Thomas O. Summers, Bp. J. Weaver, Dr. A. Webster, Dr. Thomas Webster, S. Wells Williams, LL. D., Bp. R. Yeakel, representing the fourteen denominations.

Four appendices are added. Appendix III. is a "Table of Statistics of our Church Universal by Denominations and Countries." Appendix IV. is an "Index of One Thousand Biographical illustrations contained in the Lives, for the use of the Preacher and of the Teacher in the Sabbath-school." This will prove exceedingly valuable.

The books elegantly prepared with cut-in notes, elegantly illustrated, over 1,000 Royal Octavo pages

Cloth, Back and Side in Black and Gold............................. 4 00
Arabasque Morocco.. 5 50
Half Turkey Morocco, Library Style.................................. 6 50

The True Life; or, Highway to Fortune, Happiness and Heaven. Bp *J. P. Bates, A. M.*

The design of this work is a harmonious combination of subjects and themes never before embraced in a single volume. Fortune, Happiness and Heaven constitute the three principle objects of Life. It is adapted to all classes of people, of every age, avocation or condition: the wide range and fundamental nature of topics treated and immense territory of thought, feeling, sentiment and doctrine traversed, will insure for the work an immense sale. One large Quarto volume of over 700 pages, elegantly illustrated. Printed on heavy super-calendered paper, and bound in

Cloth. Back and Sides in Black and Gold......................... 3 50
" Gilt Edge, Back and Sides in Black and Gold........... 4 00
Heavy Morocco, Library Style... 5 50

The Masque Torn Off. By *T. DeWitt Talmage, D. D.*,

author of "Crumbs Swept Up," "Around the Tea Table," "Abominations of Modern Society," "Sports that Kill," etc., etc.

One large Octavo Volume, of 526 pages, elegantly illustrated with 14 full-page Engravings. Contains the discourses as lately delivered in the Brooklyn Tabernacle—giving Dr. Talmage's experiences and observations as lately seen by him, in company with two elders of his church and three high police officials, during their midnight explorations in the haunts of vice of New York City. They have been *revised by him for this work*, and are written in his strongest descriptive powers—sparkling with graceful images and illustrative anecdotes, terrible in their earnestness, uncompromising in his denunciation of sin and wickedness wherever found, sparing neither friend nor foe, rich nor poor. Every page of intense interest. No one can read this work without taking new interest in the subjects treated. The work contains nearly FORTY CHAPTERS—on as many subjects—and are Dr. Talmage's best efforts in his earnest, aggressive warfare upon the foes of society, and the exposure of the traps and pitfalls that beset the youth of our land in every city. He sounds a *note of warning*, and points out the ONLY WAY to escape these pits of darkness and social and moral ruin.

Cloth.. 2 00
" Gilt.. 2 50
Half Morocco 3 50

Festival of Song.

A Library of the Choicest Selections from the Greatest Poets of the English Language, with an admirable and interesting Commentary on the qualities and circumstances of the Poems and their Writers by the Compiler, Frederick Saunders, author of "Salad for the Solitary and the Social," "Evenings With the Sacred Poets," etc. In one superb Royal Octavo volume of over four hundred large pages, printed on tinted paper of the finest quality, bound in elegant and Durable Bindings, and Illustrated by Seventy-three Exquisite Engravings, by Members of the National Academy of Design, of New York, with numerous Magnificent Full-page Portraits of the Poets, and Autograph Stanzas in Fac-simile.

Finest English Cloth, thick Beveled Boards, in Black and Gold. 3 75
Finest English Cloth, thick Beveled Boards........................... 4 50
Half Russia Leather, Full Gilt Back (Library style)............... 5 50
Full Turkey Antique, Sides and Back Richly Stamped, Gilt Edges (superb)... 8 00

The Gospel Awakening. Edited by *L. T. Remlap.*

Comprising 150 Sermons and Addresses, Prayer Meeting Talks, Bible Reading and Prayers of the Great Revival Meeting, conducted by Moody and Sankey in Philadelphia, New York, Chicago, and Boston, as well as in Great Britain, with the Proceedings of the Christian Conventions of Ministers and Laymen, from verbatim reports by our own Phonographer and those of the N. Y. Tribune, Chicago Inter-Ocean, and Boston Globe. Also, the Lives of D. L. Moody, I. D. Sankey, P. P. Bliss, Maj. D. W. Whittle, Rev. Joseph Cook, Rev. George F. Pentecost, and Miss Frances E. Willard. Also, Sermons, Bible Readings, and lectures by Joseph Cook, George F. Pentecost, D. W. Whittle, and Miss Frances E. Willard. The work forms a large Crown Octavo Volume of 861 closely printed pages. Sent by mail, postage paid, on receipt of the price. This book is equal to 1,800 pages of any $2.00 Moody book published. 13 Illustrations.

Cloth.. 2 50
" Gilt.. 3 00
Sheep.. 3 25

The True Path; or, Gospel Temperance.

Giving the Life, Work, and Speeches of Francis Murphy, Dr. Henry A. Reynolds, and their co-laborers. Embracing also a history of the Woman's Christian Temperance Union. *No book published possesses the interest this does.* It is just what the people want, and not loaded down with stuff that has been published a hundred times and was out of date years ago. The work is written in a fresh, racy style, and just meets the popular demand. In purchasing a history of the Temperance movement, see that your book is entitled "The True Path." It contains 700 large 12mo. pages, with 12 fine Engravings.

Extra Cloth, Ink and Gold, price................................ 2 00
Extra Cloth, Ink and Gold, Full Gilt................................ 2 50

The Great Redemption, or Gospel Light,

under the labors of Moody and Sankey, at the Cleveland Tabernacle, containing the Sermons and Addresses, Bible Readings, Prayer Meeting Talks and Prayers of the Great Revival Meetings held in Cleveland, October and November, 1879. The sermons in this volume are all new and contained in no other volume published, also containing full report of the proceedings of the Christian Convention of Ministers and Laymen. From the stenographic reports taken *verbatim* for *The Cleveland Leader*, carefully revised and corrected; also, the lives of Dwight L. Moody and Ira D. Sankey, with their portraits. One large volume of 500 pages.

Cloth, Back and Side in Black and Gold........................ 2 00
Sheep, Library Style... 2 50

Abbott's Illustrated New Testament,

with explanatory notes. By *John S. C.* and *Jacob Abbott, D. D., LLD.*

Embracing also a brief Biography of Our Savior, the Christ, Biographies of the Writers, as well as of the Prominent Men and Women of the New Testament; An Analysis of the Gospels, showing their Mutual Relations; A History of the English Translation of the Bible; A Complete Harmony of the Gospels, Illustrative Tables Relating Chiefly to the New Testament, viz: The Miracles of Christ, Parables of Jesus, The Discourses of Jesus, etc., etc., with Fifty full-page Maps and Engravings, Twelve of which Illustrate the Parables. One Crown Octavo volume of 650 pages.

Cloth, imitation Morocco.. 2 00
American Morocco, Marble Edges................................ 2 50

The Home Guide,

An Encyclopædia of All Things of Every Day Life.

As an Encyclopædia of domestic science, we know of no book that approximates to it in the fullness of its information.—*Chicago Post.*

Its practical, economical and hygenic features will be recognized by every one who examines its pages.—*N. W. Lumberman, Chicago.*

No home can afford to be without this book.—*New Covenant, Chicago.*

For a generation to come it will be ranked with the few books which are a blessing to the home.—*Journal, Chicago.*

Especial value to those upon whom devolve the responsibilities of household management.—*Tribune, Chicago.*

Elegantly Illustrated. 522 Octavo pages, 68 illustrations.
Price 2 00
Cloth, gilt 2 50

One Fold and One Shepherd.—A new book on Visible Church Unity. By *Rev. John Scotford.*

Author of "The Judd Family," or "An Evening Visit and what came of it." With an introduction by Rev. W. C. McCune. Elegantly Illustrated. The object of this book is to show that this unity can be secured without the surrender of any truth vital to Christian character, or any view of duty that individual Christians may cherish. It therefore offers a basis upon which all the disciples of Christ can unite. In doing so it discusses the various hindrances to union and removes them out of the way. One volume, 8 illustrations, 420 pages, price, cloth............ 1 50

Times of Refreshing.—A History of American Revivals.

Containing a full description of the Great Revivals of the past One Hundred and Forty Years—Personal Sketches of Eminent Revivalists—Narratives and incidents connected with their work, with a thorough discussion of their Philosophy and criticism of Methods. Illustrated with fine life-like Portraits of Messrs. Whitefield, Nettleton, Baker, Finney, Moody, Sankey, Maj. Whittle, P. P. Bliss, Hammond, Francis Murphy, Pentecost and Miss Frances E. Willard. By Charles L. Thompson, D. D., late Editor of the *Interior*, Chicago, now of Pittsburg. 480 pages, 12 illustrations.

Price 2 00
Cloth, gilt 2 50

light Sides of City Life. *T. De Witt Talmage.*
Large 12mo. 160 pages. Paper... 50

Glowing with impassioned fervor, he wages deadly war against the vices of the day in their most enticing form.—*N. Y. Tribune.*

Traps for Men. *T. De Witt Talmage.*
12mo. 180 pages.. 50

Nothing but the breaking down of the press can prevent his discourses having an immense sale.—*Reading* (Pa.) *Times.*

Foes of Society. *T. De Witt Talmage.*
12mo. 170 pages. Illustrated.. 50

He does not know how to soften a denunciation, or kid-glove a lie, cheat, or a sham.—*Providence* (R. I.) *Press.*

Hand Book of Bible Readings.—Edited by H. B. Chamberlin, with an introduction by D. W. Whittle on *Bible Readings*, how to prepare and how to use them; a chapter by Joseph Cook on "*Bible Reading* and *Bible Marking*" and 500 Bible Readings and Studies by D. L. Moody, Henry Moorhouse, D. W. Whittle, George Muller, Rev. W. S. Rainsford, B. A.; Rev. J. H. Vincent, D. D.; Rev. W. F. Crafts, B. F. Jacobs, Rev. George F. Pentecost, Rev. H. M. Parsons, Rev. J. H. Brooks, D. D.; Rev. George A. Hall, R. H. McBurney, L. W. Munhall, J. W Dean, George C. Needham, Rev. C. M. Whittlesey, Rev. John Gordon, Rev. T. B. Stevenson, and many others.

176 pages, 16mo. paper covers.................................... 50.
Cloth... 75

The Bible and Sunday-School.—Edited by Rev. W. F. Crafts. It contains Outline Lectures, "Bible Readings," and Addresses by Lyman Abbott, D. D.; Rev. Henry Ward Beecher, Richard Newton, D. D.; Rev. W. F. Crafts, Mrs. W. F. Crafts, C. H. Payne, D. D.; H. W. Warren, D. D.; P. P. Bliss, Miss Jennie B. Merrill, Rev. J. L. Hurlbut, Rev. H. M. Parsons, Miss Frances E. Willard, Miss M. E. Winslow, M. C. Hazard, Esq.; A. O. Van Lennep, Charles M. Morton, D. L. Moody, Ralph Wells, E. O. Haven, D. D.; J. H. Vincent, D. D.; and others.

These Outline Lectures are arranged in a form suitable for a Regular Course of Normal Class Study, or for personal study. The divisions are as follows:

1—THE BIBLE, THE WORD OF GOD.
2—THE BIBLE AND ITS STUDENTS.
3—THE BIBLE AND ITS TEACHINGS.
4—THE BIBLE AND CHILDHOOD.
5—THE BIBLE AND APPLIANCES.
6—THE BIBLE AND THE WORLD.

171 pages, 16mo. paper cover.................................... 50
Cloth... 75

The Coming Man is the Present Child; or, Childhood the Text-Book of the Age.
By *Rev. W. F. Crafts.*

The following points about the book make it specially attractive:

1. It has *a Score of Beautiful Engravings* of child life, most of them copied from famous sculpture and paintings in great galleries of Europe, collected especially for this book. These pictures will greatly interest *Parents, Artists,* and *Teachers.*

2. The book has short, characteristic events from the *childhood of fifty great men*, with pictures accompanying, which will also attract the interest not only of *Parents* and *Teachers*, but also of the *Boys* themselves.

3. The book has *numerous incidents of child life*, short, bright, amusing things. This feature will greatly *interest all educators*, while it amuses the general reader. A "**Childhood'**ary," containing 100 cute definitions from
is a point of interest in the book.

4. The theoretical portion of the book (12 chapters) discuss the *relations of Childhood to the age, to science, to temperance, to education, to religion, etc.*, each chapter commending itself to pastors, parents, teachers, and all lovers of childhood.

Paper covers, 156 pages, 16 Illustrations, price.   60

Instincts and Incidents of Childhood.
By *Rev. W. F. Crafts.*

This little volume gives in a scientific "Cabinet" four hundred "specimens" of the sayings and doings of children, arranged as if upon "Shelves" and in "Cases" under the seven instincts of childhood as discovered by Froebel, and made familiar through the Kindergarten System. The incidents will be found not only instructive to students of human nature, but highly amusing and interesting to all classes of readers.

115 pages, 5 Illustrations. Paper covers.................................. 40

Lessons for Little Folks. For Home and Sunday-School.
Including Songs and Recitations, also Thoughts for Older Folks. By *Mrs. V. J. Kent.*

This book contains attractive material for use in Primary Classes, and is suitable as a help for Teachers, and also as a gift for children. 174 pages. Paper................................ 50
Cloth.. 75

Nail Heads, or Helps for Primary Teachers.

By *Mrs. George Partridge*, with an introduction by J. Bennet Tyler.

Commendation from a S. S. worker. "Let me speak a word to the Primary Teachers about that excellent book, 'Nail Heads,' by Mrs. George Partridge. It is a little book, not expensive, and contains, in my opinion, the best help, outside of the Bible, that a primary teacher can find. I have used it in my class with great satisfaction. The books are so few that really aid in the work, that I hasten to give my testimony in regard to this, and hope that you will each secure a copy. One needs only to examine it to see that it was prepared by a WORKER, and contains only that will HELP. Its simplicity and directness are very marked. MRS. G. R. ALDEN ('Pansy'),
"New Hartford, N. Y."

Cloth, limp.. 35
Handsomely bound, tinted paper.. 50

From Earth to Heaven. By *A. P. Graves, D. D.*

Mr. Graves has made this book to enlarge his Evangelistic usefulness. It contains a sketch of his life, a fine steel-plate engraving of himself, many of his most valuable revival sermons and Bible Readings, and several important reform papers. In its size, nearly 350 pages, it is worth $1 50, but to put it in the reach of all the people, the price is put down to.............. 1 00

Down Grade. A book to save tempted young men. *A. P. Graves, D. D.* 5th thousand now ready.
  Cloth.. 60

Twenty-five Letters to a Young Lady. Just published. *A. P. Graves, D. D.*
  Cloth.. 60

Sermons for Boys and Girls. *Rev. J. G. Merrill.* (*Just published.*)
  160 pages. Cloth.. 75

Hints on Bible Marking. By *Mrs. Stephen Menzes*, with preface by D. L. Moody.
  32 pages, sq. 18mo. Paper.. 15
  Paper, per dozen.. 1 25

How to Study the Bible. By *D. L. Moody.*
  A valuable little work, which should be carefully read and studied by all who desire to enjoy the study of the WORD.
  Paper cover.. 15
  "   "   per dozen.. 1 25

A Dictionary of Scripture Proper Names. With their pronunciation and explanation.
  Cloth.. 25

Froggy's Little Brother. By *Brenda.*
  A Temperance Tale for Children, handsomely Illustrated, 294 pages.. 1 25

The Little Captain.—A Temperance Tale.—By *Lynde Palmer.*
  Illustrated, 131 pages.. 50

25 Sermons to Children.—By *Rev. J. G. Merrill.*
  70 pages, paper cover.. 25

Our Christmas Gift.—By *Mrs. V. J. Kent.*
  Handsomely printed in Blue and Red, tied together with Blue Ribbons... 25

THE STYLOGRAPHIC PEN.
A Neat, Clean, Air-tight, Fountain Pen,

Can be carried in the Pocket with perfect safety. Holds sufficient ink for Twenty-four Hours Continuous Writing.

A. T. Cross' Patents.

October 6, 1868; April 10, 1877; May 1, 1877; June 12, 1877; January, 20, 1878.

The Pen is very simple in its construction, and is easily understood and managed, and if thoroughly understood requires but little attention or care. Never allow any one to meddle with your Pen who does not understand it.

N. B.—Should the needle become *bent* by accident so as to prevent its working freely, it can be straightened by rolling it between two flat smooth surfaces with slight pressure. If you fail to put it in order, return the Pen to the address below. If you should break the filler, ask your druggist for a medicine dropper. If any part of your pen is lost or injured at any time, send it to us by registered parcel, in a small paste-board box, with your name and address plainly written across one end of the wrapper, enclosing twelve cents to pay return postage and registration fees, and we will return it in good order at as slight cost as possible.

PRICE LIST.

The numbers indicate the Style of the Stylographic Pen as follows:

NET.

No. 1, Gold Mounted, 6 inches long, Solid Iridium (Diamond) Point							$5 00
No. 2, "	"	4½	"	"	"	"	4 50
No. 3, Chased,	6		"	"	"	"	4 50
No. 4,	"	4½	"	"	"	"	4 00
No. 5, Gold Mounted, 6			"	Iridium Alloy,		"	4 00
No. 6, "	"	4½	"	"	"	"	3 50
No. 7, Chased,	6		"	"	"	"	3 50
No. 8,	"	4½	"	"	"	"	3 00

N. B.—Positively the Gold used in mounting the Stylographic Pens is 18 carats fine. Pure native Iridium is absolutely indestructible, and each solid Iridium (Diamond) point, is hereby warranted for the term of three years.

J. FAIRBANKS & CO.

Lightning Source UK Ltd.
Milton Keynes UK
UKHW040929180920
370091UK00001BA/64